Walter A. Maier (1893-1950), professor of semitic languages and Old Testament at Concordia Seminary for twenty-eight years, held a Ph.D. degree from Harvard University. He achieved fame as the first speaker on the Lutheran Hour, a radio broadcast which began in 1930. At the time of Maier's death, the Lutheran Hour was heard over nearly 1200 stations in 52 nations, in 36 languages. *The Book of Nahum*, his only commentary, was first published in 1959.

The Book of
Nahum

A Commentary

Walter A. Maier

Baker Book House
Grand Rapids, Michigan

PHOTOLITHOPRINTED BY CUSHING - MALLOY, INC.
ANN ARBOR, MICHIGAN, UNITED STATES OF AMERICA

Foreword

For approximately a decade prior to his death in 1950 Dr. Walter A. Maier, during the leisure time which the busy Lutheran Hour speaker found at his disposal, carried on an extensive exegetical study of the Book of Nahum. The results of this favorite project of his are embodied in this volume.

It was the author's ardent wish to see his work through the press, but the Lord willed otherwise. This task remained for others who were in sympathy with Dr. Maier's theological views. In dealing with the voluminous materials left by the author it was the constant aim to preserve the text of Dr. Maier's manuscript verbatim as much as possible, but to abridge, and occasionally to condense, where this seemed desirable without impairing the original. In no instance were the author's conclusions modified or altered.

Thought was given to the possibility of bringing the work up to date so far as references to the literature of the past decade are concerned. But since this would have introduced matter into the book which was not available to the author, the idea was abandoned. Nor did this entail any great loss, inasmuch as the critical attitude toward the text of Nahum and its interpretation has undergone little change in principle during the last ten years, so that the author's criticisms of unwarranted text emendations and interpretations still hold good.

The book reflects the convictions which the author championed throughout his preaching and teaching ministry. To Dr. Maier the prophet's message is the Word of the living God, who is not unconcerned when a nation abuses its power in the interest of selfish aims to oppress and despoil weaker nations. The consistent disregard of justice in international relations will in the end bring on terrible retribution by the hand of the agents whom God appoints for this purpose. Of this, Nineveh's downfall is an awful example in the world's history.

In regard to the Hebrew text of Nahum, Dr. Maier maintains the conservative view that in general it is intact in the form handed down through the centuries. Consequently the interpretation of Nahum's message must be based on this received text without resorting to subjective emendations and arbitrary conclusions about what the prophet intended to convey. The author believes that the text as presently constituted makes sense and that it is the exegete's business to determine the meaning of the prophet's message accordingly.

Finally, in contrast, Dr. Maier goes to considerable length to point out the inadequacy of the generally adopted modern higher critical approach to the Book of Nahum by showing how scholar is pitted against scholar in emending and rearranging the text, and on this basis subjectively interpreting the prophet without being able to reach any unanimous conclusion.

It may be taken for granted that in liberal circles Dr. Maier's book will meet with little appreciation. However, among those who still find in the Old Testament Scriptures the Word of God "profitable for doctrine, for reproof, for correction, for instruction in righteousness," Dr. Maier's interpretation of the Book of Nahum should prove a source of enlightenment and of comfort as they view the situation in the world today. And may God grant His blessing to this end.

GEORGE V. SCHICK

Contents

KEY TO ABBREVIATIONS

The following abbreviations appear in the commentary:

1) For the names of authors: Arn.: Arnold; Bev.: Bevenot; Bi.: Bickell; Bu. Budde; Dav.-Lan.: Davidson-Lanchester; Del.: Delitzsch; Dr.: Driver; Du.: Duhm; Ehr.: Ehrlich; Ew.: Ewald; Grz.: Graetz; Gun.: Gunkel; Hal.: Halevy; Hap.: Happel; Hpt.: Haupt; Hen.: Henderson; Hngs.: Hengstenberg; Htz.: Hitzig; v.Ho.: van Hoonacker; Hst.: Horst; Hum.: Humbert; Jnk.: Junker; K.-G.: Kautzsch-Guthe; Kl.: Kleinert; Kue.: Kuenen; Lu.: Luther; Mrt.: Marti; New.: Newcome; No.: Nowack; Oo.: Oort; Or.: Orelli; Ri.: Richter; Ries.: Riessler; Ru.: Ruben; Sel.: Sellin; G.A.Sm.: G. A. Smith; J.M.P.Sm.: J. M. P. Smith; Stk.: Staerk; Stnh.: Stonehouse; Umb.: Umbreit; Wllh.: Wellhausen.

2) For the ancient versions: Aq.: Aquila; Ⓖ: Septuagint; Θ: Theodotion; Ⓛ: Old Latin; Ⓜ: Masoretic Text; Ⓢ: Syriac; Σ: Symmachus; Ⓣ: Targum; Ⓥ: Vulgate.

3) For grammars and lexicons: Ges.: Gesenius; Gra.: grammar; Hwb.: Handwörterbuch.

For the full titles see the Bibliography.

Translation of
THE BOOK OF NAHUM

The Book of Nahum

Chapter 1

1 The Burden of Nineveh
  The Book of the Vision of Nahum, the Elkoshite

2 A zealous God and an Avenger [is] Yahweh.
  An Avenger [is] Yahweh, and wrath [is] His.
  An Avenger [is] Yahweh for His adversaries,
  And He [is] a Reserver [of wrath] for His foes.

3 Yahweh [is] long-suffering, but great in power,
  And will assuredly not leave [the guilty] unpunished.
  Yahweh — in whirlwind and in tempest [is] His way;
  And clouds [are] the dust of His feet.

4 He rebuketh the sea, and He drieth it up.
  And all the rivers He maketh dry.
  Bashan droopeth and Carmel,
  And the bloom of Lebanon droopeth.

5 Mountains quake on account of Him,
  And the hills melt;
  And the earth heaves before Him;
  Yes, the world and all who dwell in it.

6 Before His anger, who can stand?
  And who can maintain himself in the burning ire of
      His fury?
  His wrath is poured out like fire,
  And the rocks are torn down by Him.

7   Yahweh [is] good
As a Stronghold in a day of affliction,
And He knoweth those who trust in Him.

8   But with an overrunning flood
He will make an end [to] its place,
And His enemies He will pursue with darkness.

*   *   *

9   Why do ye meditate concerning Yahweh?
He Himself is making an end.
Oppression will not rise up a second time.

10   For [they shall be] like thorns entangled
And drunken when they carouse.
They shall be consumed
As stubble fully dry.

11   From thee went out
One who plotteth evil against Yahweh,
A counselor of Belial.

12   Thus saith Yahweh: Even if [they were] complete and
so numerous
And so protected, yet did they pass away.
I afflicted thee;
Not will I afflict thee again.

13   And now
I will break his rod from off thee,
And thy bonds I will tear apart.

14   And Yahweh hath ordained concerning thee:
No more of thy name will be sown.
From the house of thy gods I will cut off graven image
and molten image.
I will make thy grave, for thou art despised.

Chapter 2 *

1   Behold! On the mountains feet of a herald proclaiming
        peace!
    Celebrate thy festivals, O Judah! Pay thy vows!
    For Belial will not again pass through thee. He is
        altogether destroyed.

            *   *   *

2   A disperser is come up before thee. Guard [the]
        fortress!
    Watch [the] way! Strengthen [the] loins!
    Make [thy] strength mighty to the utmost!

3   Because Yahweh hath cut off the pride of Jacob,
    As the pride of Israel;
    Because plunderers have plundered them
    And spoiled their vine branches.

4   The shield of His mighty ones is reddened. Men of
        might are in scarlet.
    Chariots [are] in fiery steel on the day of His preparing,
    And the cypress spears are swinging.

5   Chariots career madly in the streets.
    They overrun one another in the squares.
    Their appearance [is] like torches.
    As flashes of lightning they speed to and fro.

6   He remembereth His mighty [ones].
    They stumble [over themselves] in their advancing.
    They hasten to her wall,
    And the protection is set up.

7   The gates of the rivers are opened,
    And the palace sways.

* In the King James Version this is 1:15.

8   And Huzzab is stripped. She is brought up,
And her handmaidens are moaning, as [with] a sound
    of doves.
[They are] taboring upon their breasts.

9   And [thus] Nineveh is like a pool of water from [the]
    days of lamentation;
And they are in flight.
"Stand, stand" [they cry], but no one turneth around.

10   Seize booty of silver! Seize booty of gold!
For there is no end to the store,
And abundance of all desirable articles.

11   Desolation and devastation and dilapidation
And melting heart and smiting together of knees and
    writhing in all loins!
And the faces of all them gather redness!

12   Where [is] a dwelling place of lions
And fodder for the cubs
Which a lion went to bring?
There a lion's brood [lived],
With no one to terrify [it].

13   A lion, tearing prey for the need of his cubs
And strangling for his lionesses;
And he filleth his caves with prey
And his lairs with ripped carcasses.

14   Behold, I [am] against thee,
The oracle of Yahweh of Hosts.
And I will burn her chariots in the smoke,
And a sword shall devour thy young lions.
And I will cut off thy prey from the earth,
And the voice of thy messengers shall not be heard
    again.

Chapter 3

1   Woe to a bloody city!
    All of it [is] falsehood. [It is] full of robbery.
    Prey doth not depart.

2   Crack of whip
    And rumble of wheels!
    And galloping horse
    And jolting chariot!

3   Rearing rider and flaming sword and flashing spear
    And host of slain and multitude of dead bodies!
    And no end of the corpses;
    They stumble over their corpses,

4   Because of the many harlotries
    Of the harlot fair in grace, the mistress of witchcrafts,
    Who selleth nations through her harlotries
    And peoples through her witchcrafts.

5   Behold, I am against thee — the oracle of Yahweh
        of Hosts.
    And I will uncover thy skirts upon thy face,
    And I will show nations thy nakedness
    And kingdoms thy shame.

6   And I will cast abominations on thee, and I will make
        thee vile,
    And I will place thee as a gazingstock.

7   And it will come to pass that everyone who sees thee
        will flee from thee
    And will say: "Nineveh is laid waste.
    Who will mourn for her?"
    Whence can I seek comforters for thee?

8   Art thou better than No of Amon
     That [was] situated on the rivers?
     Water [was] round about her
     So that a sea [was] a rampart;
     Her wall [was] from the sea.

9   Ethiopia [was] her strength, and Egypt; and there was
          no end [to it].
     Put and Libyans
     Were among thy help.

10   Even she went into exile in captivity.
     Even her babies were dashed to pieces at the head of
          all streets.
     And for her nobles they cast a lot,
     And all her mighty ones were bound in chains.

11   Thou, too, wilt be drunken;
     Thou wilt be hidden.
     Thou, too, wilt seek a stronghold against enemies.

12   All thy fortresses
     [Are] fig trees with first-ripe fruits.
     When they are shaken,
     They fall into [the] eater's mouth.

13   Behold, thy people in thy midst [are] women!
     For thine enemies the gates of thy land are open wide;
     Fire has consumed thy bars.

14   Draw thyself water for a siege!
     Strengthen thy fortifications!
     Go into the soil! Knead the clay! Grasp a brick mold!

15   Then fire will devour thee.
     A sword will cut thee off.
     It will devour thee as the young locust,
     [Though] thou multiply thyself as the young locust
     And increase thyself as the locust.

16 Thou hast made thy merchants
    More than the stars of the heaven,
    [Yet] the young locust strippeth and flieth away.

17 Thy guards [are] as the locust,
    And thy scribes as a swarm of grasshoppers
    Which alight on the wall on a cold day.
    And the sun riseth, and they flee,
    And their place is not known. Where are they?

18 Thy shepherds slumber, O King of Assyria;
    Thy mighty ones rest [in death].
    Thy people are scattered on the mountains, and there
        is no one to gather [them].

19 There is no healing for thine injury.
    Thy wound [is] grievous.
    All who hear the message concerning thee will clap
        [their] hand over thee.
    For upon whom hath thine evil not passed over
        continually?

Introduction to
THE BOOK OF NAHUM

I. The Message of the Prophet

A single theme pervades Nahum's prophecies: Nineveh, the haughty capital of the Assyrian Empire, will be destroyed. An "end" (1:8) is to be made of this boasting, pagan citadel, an "end," Nahum repeats (1:9), in which the cruel community "shall be consumed as stubble fully dry" (1:10). Yahweh will dig a grave, a final resting place, for the devastated metropolis (1:14). Anxious eyes, peering along frontier mountain ridges, are urged to behold the messenger with the good tidings that Belial-Nineveh "is altogether destroyed" (2:1). She is devastated, desolated, dilapidated (2:11). The "dwelling place of the lions" is gone (2:12). "There is no healing" for her mortal injury. (3:19)

As the fatal factors contributing to this downfall of the world metropolis, Nahum envisions Assyrian pride, which plotted "evil against Yahweh" (1:11), the flagrant idolatry which worshiped graven and molten images in the houses of its gods (1:14). Because the Almighty has denounced Nineveh with the sentence "I am against thee" (3:5), her doom is sealed, since He, who controls the forces of nature, takes vengeance on His adversaries, is "great in power," and will "not leave [the guilty] unpunished." (1:2-6)

From rebellion against the Lord flow Nineveh's consequent wickedness and inhumanity, since crimes against God always bring in their wake crimes against men. In a long catalog of Assyrian social transgressions the prophet indicts Nineveh for its drunkenness (1:10), bloody cruelty, lies, robbery, continued rapaciousness (3:1), crafty schemes, witchcraft, international treachery. (3:4)

Above the destruction, which the prophet envisions with remarkable clarity and in striking agreement with historical fulfillment, rings a note of comfort for God's people. The rod of Assyrian oppression will be broken (1:13); Judah can celebrate her solemn feasts, perform her sacred vows; for the wicked one shall no longer pass through her (2:1). From the guarantee of deliverance, Nahum's countrymen are to draw this encouraging lesson: "Yahweh is good as a Stronghold in the day of affliction, and He knoweth those who trust in Him." (1:7)

Although the book shows no sharp divisions, the following is a convenient outline:

1. *The Title* (1:1)

2. *The Introductory Ode* (1:2-8). Nahum describes God's strength, His wrath toward His enemies, His patience, His power, His irresistible destruction, His goodness and protection for those who seek refuge in Him. The prophet announces the divine resolve to destroy Nineveh utterly, "with an overrunning flood." (1:8)

3. *The Prediction of Nineveh's End* (1:9—2:1). The prophet proclaims the city's doom (1:9, 10). The reason for its devastation lies in the fact that the Assyrians planned evil against Yahweh (1:11). They worshiped idols (1:14) and cruelly used the rod on Israel (1:13). Therefore, though the Ninevites be powerful and well armed, their defeat is inevitable. They will pass away (1:12). Their rod will be removed (1:13). Judah and Jerusalem will not be afflicted a second time by the Assyrians (1:12). All this is positively assured; therefore Judah is directed

to behold a messenger of peace bringing the news of Nineveh's extirpation, to observe joyous festivals, to pay vows; for the tyrannical city will be wiped out. (2:1)

4. *The Dire Picture of Nineveh's End* (2:2-14). The doomed city is now directed to defend itself (2:2) when Yahweh comes to take revenge for His oppressed nation (2:3). The weapons, chariots, and soldiers of the advancing enemy are described (2:4,5). Nineveh's mighty men are pictured hastening to the walls in the defense of the capital (2:6). But the river gates are opened; the city, flooded, is as a pool (2:7). Women are led away captive (2:8); others take to flight (2:9). The plunder is endless (2:10). Terrifying fear overcomes the inhabitants (2:11). Nineveh, the lions' den, filled with prey, is captured. (2:12-14)

5. *The Prophetic Denunciation of Nineveh* (3:1-19). The murderous city, filled with lies and robbery (3:1), will be captured after great slaughter by powerful enemies (3:2,3). Since Nineveh lured nations by harlotlike treachery, she will receive harlotlike treatment and parade naked in her disgrace. An object of universal reproach, she will have no sympathizers or comforters (3:4-7). She will fare no better than Thebes in Egypt, which was strong, well situated, and supported by powerful alliances, yet went down in bloody defeat. How, then, can Nineveh hope to escape (3:8-10)? Her effeminate inhabitants, assailed while drunken (3:11,13), will vainly seek to make a defense. Her suburbs and fortresses will easily and quickly fall to the invader (3:12). The gates of the city will be opened to the enemy (3:13). Fire will sweep throughout the streets (3:13,15). Even new defenses, hurriedly thrown up, will be taken (3:14). Though Nineveh's merchants and leaders be as many as the swarming locusts, they will all desert the doomed capital (3:16,17). Its inhabitants will be scattered in the mountains, never

to be gathered again (3:18). Amid universal applause Nineveh
will disappear forever. (3:19)[1]

[1] This simple division of the book is not accepted by most modern critics
(although Junker essentially agrees with it). Instead, Horst, e. g., offers the following arrangement: 1:1: Title; 1:2-10: Song of Praise; 1:11, 14: Denunciation
of Nineveh; 1:12, 13; 2:1-3: Prophetic Liturgy; 2:2, 4-14: The Storming of
Nineveh; 3:1-7: The Disgrace of Nineveh; 3:8-17: Threatening Ode Against
Nineveh; 3:18, 19: Ironical Lament over Nineveh. — J. M. P. Smith divides the
book in this way: The Superscription, 1:1; The Avenging Wrath of Yahweh,
1:2-10; Words of Comfort to Judah, 1:12, 13; 2:1, 3; The Fall of Nineveh,
1:11, 14; 2:2, 4-14; The Imminent and Inevitable End, 3:1-19. — Such patterns
call for radical rearrangement of the text and for arbitrary omissions and alterations.
This partition of Nahum's oracles into artificially constructed questions and answers,
the interchange of human and divine voices, the alternating of individuals and
masses in statement and response, which allegedly makes the book a liturgy and
therefore implies that it is a chain of literary fragments, is biased, arbitrary,
and unfounded.

II. The Person of the Prophet

THE PROPHET'S NAME

The name Nahum probably means "full of comfort." [2] It does not occur elsewhere in the Old Testament, but it is probably related to Naham (1 Chron. 4:19), Nahamani (Neh. 7:7), Menahem (2 Kings 15:14), Tanhumeth (Jer. 40:8), and to Nehemiah ("Jehovah comforts"). The name seems to have been fairly common. Many potsherds found in southern Palestinian localities bear the inscription "of Nahum, son of Abdi," which perhaps indicates a hereditary family of potters.

The appropriateness of the prophet's name is evident, since Nahum brought full comfort for Israel in the dark days when the Assyrian rod cut hard into its shoulders. His assurance that Ninevite despotism would be broken; that the day would soon dawn when Judah could celebrate its happy festivals, knowing that no tyrant from the Tigris would ever overrun its lands again — this consolation made Nahum's name a symbol of his message, a token of the rich assurance which he, as God's servant, brought his downtrodden countrymen. However, this agreement of the prophet's name with his purpose does not justify the assertion that Nahum originally had a different name, which was replaced by an editor who felt that the consolatory character of

2 The formation of the name is similar to חַנּוּן, "full of grace," and רַחוּם, "full of compassion."

17

his message should re-echo in his name. There is no more reason for this assumption than there is for questioning the genuineness of "Isaiah" or "Jeremiah."

THE PROPHET'S CHARACTER

Nothing is known of the prophet except that he was "an Elkoshite," but his whole style, vocabulary, and presentation point to a cultured mind.

As usual, when the Scriptures are silent, criticism speaks, and sometimes with overassurance. Thus Nahum has been called a "provincial" prophet, marked by "rural blindness," "a rustic" from "the hinterland," filled with resentment against the sins "which provoke the peasant in any large city." It is also asserted that "Nahum's country origin is confirmed by the rural imagery which he uses," since "his pictures are drawn from the Bashan, the Carmel, and the flower of Lebanon (1:4), from the over-flowing stream (1:8), from the fig trees with first-ripe figs (3:12), from the cankerworm about to burst from its chrysalis (3:16), and the locusts and grasshoppers (3:17)."[3] Yet the prophet Isaiah, admittedly a man of the city, has proportionately many more references to country life and agriculture than Nahum. He mentions, e. g., the ox and the ass (1:3), the plow, the plowshare, and the pruning hook (2:4). With detail he discusses farm implements: the harrow (28:24); the "threshing instrument" (28:27); "cart wheel" (28:27); the threshing shovel (30:24); the threshing fan, or fork (30:24). He, too, although urban, discusses the grasshopper (40:22). If a single occurrence of Bashan indicates that Nahum was a rustic, what does the double mention in Is. 2:13 and 33:9 imply, not to adduce Isaiah's three passages on Bashan, Lebanon, and Carmel, 33:9; 35:2; 37:24? Again, Isaiah was not an agriculturalist, but he was acquainted with figs (38:21) and fig trees (34:4). As for the

---

[3] Louis Finkelstein, *The Pharisees* (1938), p. 306.

"overflowing stream," Isaiah has ten references to streams, and seven of his passages speak of overflowing waters. Similar vocabulary comparison with other prophets would likewise show that the isolated mention of trees, rivers, mountains, and insects does not necessarily imply rural origin.

Again, Nahum's alleged "lack of delicacy which would have astonished the better-bred urban writers and speakers" is assumed to indicate that he was born on the farm.[4] In support is quoted 3:5, addressed to Nineveh: "Behold, I am against thee; and I will uncover thy skirts upon thy face; and I will show nations thy nakedness and kingdoms thy shame." It is unwarranted, however, to accuse country folk, as contrasted with city dwellers, of obscenity. Moses, bred in the learning of the Egyptians, employs the same picture (Deut. 27:20), and Jeremiah, the prophet of Anathoth, likewise uses almost identical language in 13:22, 26.

Finally Nahum is branded "a village prophet" because he saw Assyria as "a hated and cruel foe, but not an imperialistic oppressor. He denounces her unsparingly and predicts destruction for her; but in all his vehement words not a syllable escapes him to reproach her with tyrannical rule of her subjects. . . . Assyria's treatment of her subject nations arouses in him as little comment as does the neighboring farmer's treatment of his wives, slaves, employees, and the smaller peasants."[5] Even a superficial reading of the text reveals that Nahum pointedly indicts Nineveh, "a bloody city" (3:1), for selling peoples (3:4), for filling herself with prey (2:13, 14). The very fact that in her destruction Nineveh is to be made a gazingstock for the nations (3:6) is an expression of divine retribution for her cruelty toward others. Besides, it is a mistake to believe that farmers at that time had no interest in the denunciation of international cruelty. Amos of Tekoa was a herdsman and a pincher of sycamore figs, but the

<hr>

[4] Loc. cit.   [5] Op. cit., p. 308.

Old Testament contains few more devastating indictments of inhumanity abroad as well as at home in Israel and Judah than his.

No unbiased reader can study Nahum's prophecies without concluding that the sacred writer, far from being an uncouth, semiobscene rustic, was, on the contrary, a man of outstanding qualities. His reverence for the Almighty, trust in divine justice and goodness, condemnation of national iniquity, positive conviction that God will keep His word — these are qualities of true greatness. Add to them Nahum's mighty intellect, his patriotism and courage, his rare, almost unequaled, gift of vivid presentation, and he indeed looms as one of those outstanding figures in human history who have appeared only at rare intervals. Because he, as the Almighty's spokesman, chosen to predict Nineveh's end, recorded his utterances by divine inspiration, all attempts at disparagement should stop, and Nahum should be recognized as a mighty prophet.

We know nothing of the seer's life or destiny. Like many of God's eminent agents, he lived and died without benefit of a biographer. Tradition concerning his career has no historical basis.

THE PROPHET'S HOME

Nahum is described as "the Elkoshite" (1:1), a term which some early commentators, as Jerome records, regarded as a reference to Nahum's father. No reliable information, however, corroborates the view that Elkosh is the personal name of the prophet's father. More frequently in such connections the Hebrew termination ־, corresponding to the English termination "ite," appears with the names of countries or cities to form ethnic or geographic designations. This meaning is suggested here by the analogous usage at the beginning of Micah (1:1), where the prophet is called "the Morasthite," designating him not as the son of Moresheth, but as a native or inhabitant of Moresheth. Similar forms are also "the Shilonite" (1 Kings 11:29), "the Tishbite" (1 Kings 17:1), and "the Anathothite." (Jer. 29:27)

The Location of Elkosh

Although the term "the Elkoshite" is generally accepted as designating "an inhabitant of Elkosh," the location of this place is uncertain, especially since it is not mentioned in any other Old Testament passage. Among the several attempts at identification we may note the following:

The Assyrian Location

On account of the consonantal similarity of the two names, the village of Al-Qûsh, two days' journey north of Nineveh (ca. 25 mi. north of present-day Mosul) and east of the Tigris, has been accepted by some as the prophet's home, but archaeological investigations have shown that consonantal echo is no conclusive proof of identity.

Local tradition favors this Assyrian site. Layard [6] describes Al-Qûsh as "a large Christian village," containing, "according to a very general tradition, the tomb of Nahum, the prophet," and the "place is held in great reverence by Mohammedans and 'Christians, but especially by Jews." This tradition has been discredited by the argument that "there is no evidence that Al-Qûsh . . . is older than the Arab period, while the tradition which locates the tomb there is not found before the sixteenth century." It is true that Layard reports that "there are no inscriptions, nor fragments of any antiquity about the place." At best, however, this is an argument from silence; and other popular identifications have been accepted with no more ancient authority and background.

This theory of the Assyrian location, however, is suspicious because of the characteristic facility with which native folklore has found the alleged tombs of Scripturally and historically important people. The reputed resting places of Jonah, Obadiah,

---

[6] Austen Henry Layard, *Popular Account of Discoveries at Nineveh* (1857), pp. 165, 166.

Jephthah, Cyrus, as well as a competitive tomb of Nahum which Benjamin of Tudela visited at Ain Japhata in southern Babylonia, are all based on late and unreliable legends.

It is further held that Elkosh must have been in Assyria because of the detailed acquaintance with Nineveh which the prophet's book exhibits. He is said to write with "the familiarity of an eyewitness." Friedrich Delitzsch [7] maintains that the prophet was a descendant of one of the captives exiled to Assyria by Sennacherib. Without positive historical basis for the contention that Sennacherib brought Hebrew prisoners to the vicinity of the Assyrian Al-Qûsh, Delitzsch constructs the theory that these exiled Hebrews, together with their predecessors, the Israelites taken at Samaria's destruction in 722 B. C. (who, however, were not settled in Assyria proper, 2 Kings 17:6; 18:11), helped to bring about the fall of Nineveh. — The prophet's presentation does reveal an Assyrian impress, faithful and accurate, but not so intricate that his home must be found in that country. Armies from the Tigris were no novelty for the Western countries, and many cultured Palestinians doubtless had a detailed knowledge of the Assyrian hosts. Habakkuk offers an intimate picture of the Babylonian cavalry; yet must we deduce from his graphic portrayal of "the Chaldeans, that bitter and hasty nation," that he lived in a Chaldean community or was a citizen of Babylon? The conclusion is never drawn that because Nahum describes the situation and depicts the destruction of No-Amon, he must have been a resident of Thebes. It should be conceded that even if he had been an eyewitness of the military operations near Nineveh, this fact alone would not necessarily involve the location of his birthplace or home.

Recourse has also been taken to the prophet's language in the attempt to show Nahum's Assyrian origin. Assyrian terms and Aramaisms in his book are considered to be decisive indi-

---

[7] Friedrich Delitzsch, *Die grosse Täuschung* (1926), II, 80.

cations of an Assyrian Elkosh. Neither *Huzzab* (2:8), sometimes regarded as the name of Nineveh's queen, nor *tiphsâr* (3:17 [from the Assyrian *dupsharru,* "scribe," "recorder"]), nor any of the miscalled Aramaisms (see below), shed light on the author's home. The purity of Nahum's language and style, which betray no sign of contact with the Aramaic dialect spoken by the Hebrew exiles, cannot be overlooked; for if, assuming an Assyrian homeland for the prophet, the announcement of doom had been written five hundred miles from Jerusalem, its Assyrian coloring would certainly bear testimony to its foreign origin.

Kirkpatrick [8] holds that Nahum wrote outside Judah, because in addition to the claims for the Assyrian origin of his oracles, just listed, "the absence of reproof and the idealization of Judah are most satisfactorily accounted for by the hypothesis that he wrote at a distance from Palestine." But the prophet by no means ignores Judah's sins. Nor is there any evidence whatever to indicate that he "idealizes" Judah. Kirkpatrick's statement: "He [Nahum] betrays no sign of a close acquaintance with Judah and Jerusalem," overlooks Nah. 1:12; 2:1; 2:3.

Discordant with this theory of an Assyrian location is the background of the book itself. We should expect that the irrepressible hope of return from exile would be unmistakably expressed in the outcries of an author banished from his homeland, as, e. g., in Ezekiel's book. There should be words of comfort to his fellow sufferers; yet of all this not a syllable in the entire prophecy!

Finally, an Assyrian community, such as Elkosh (which is not mentioned in extant cuneiform records), whether great or small, would require some geographical specification for the Hebrew readers, to whom otherwise the bare mention of this place would be unintelligible.

[8] A. F. Kirkpatrick, *The Doctrine of the Prophets* (1907), p. 250.

The Galilean Location

Chiefly because of Jerome's remark in his *Prologue to the Prophet Nahum:* "Helkesei is to the present day a little village in Galilee, small indeed and barely showing traces of the ruins of ancient buildings; but known to the Jews and pointed out to me also by the guide," a Galilean site has been sought for Elkosh. Jerome, however, does not define more closely the location in Galilee at which he saw the traditional place of the prophet's home. Purely because of consonantal similarity, Elcesi (or Elcesai) has been identified with the modern El Kauze near Rama in the territory of Naphtali, seven miles southwest of Tibnin.

Another Galilean location with which Elkosh has been identified is Capernaum, supposedly meaning "the village of Nahum." But neither Josephus nor Jerome found any connection between the Savior's "own" city and the proper noun "Nahum." Besides, all associations of "the village of Nahum" with the prophet are missing; for "Nahum" was a common designation among the Jews, and the city might have been named for anyone of several illustrious men who bore this name. No evidence has been produced to show that Capernaum ever was called Elkosh. In spite of the fact that a late Jewish tradition points to the reputed tomb of Nahum near one of the supposed sites of Capernaum, Tell-Hum, any Galilean location is open to the objection that in the prophet's days the ten tribes had been in exile for two generations and that the religious interests of the OT then centered about Judah and Jerusalem.

Thus the difficulty involved in all these suggestions for a Galilean location becomes apparent. Each lacks everything more than consonantal resemblance and vague patristic endorsement. This similarity and support are far outweighed by the inherent improbability that the Northern Kingdom, destroyed in 722 B. C., would be the birthplace and home of a prophet who

lived and worked three quarters of a century later. It is unlikely
that a prophet of God would dwell in this deserted territory among
its hybrid people. Practically all OT interest in Galilee ceases
after the fall of Samaria, and place names are given only in isolated
instances. His reference is to Sennacherib (Judah), not to Sargon,
Tiglathpileser, and others who overran Samaria. The additional
circumstance that Nahum's oracles contain no specific allusion
to the people of Galilee may be significant.

The Judean Location

A southern Elkosh in Judah is suggested by several patristic
writers. Cyril of Alexandria identifies Elkese as "without doubt
a village of the Jews." Only conflicting testimony exists regarding
a more definite location. Pseudo-Epiphanius places Elkese "beyond the Jordan toward Begabar of the tribe of Simeon," though
Begabar (near the ancient Eleutheropolis, the modern Beit-
Jibrin), far from being "beyond the Jordan," is about twenty-five
miles southwest of Jerusalem. Hesychius Presbyter writes of
Nahum: "He was from Elkese, beyond Tenbarein of the tribe
of Simeon." Besides these divergent statements, the OT Syriac
version by Paul of Tella, which inserts the textual notes of
Epiphanius and of Pseudo-Epiphanius, offers the reading: "Nahum
was of Elkosh beyond Bet Gabre of the tribe of Simeon." [9]

The recurrent emphasis on "the tribe of Simeon" has led
some modern commentators to look for Elkosh in southern Judah.
No contemporaneous site in that locality, however, corresponds
decisively to Elkosh. G. A. Smith suggests the possibility of equating Elkosh with Umm Lākis, "some six and a quarter miles east
from Beit-Jibrin at the upper end of the Wady es Sur," where
"there is an ancient well with the name Bir el Kūs." Others
have contented themselves with an undefined location near
Eleutheropolis.

[9] See G. A. Smith, *The Book of the Twelve Prophets* (1929), II, 78 ff.

No certainty thus exists as to the specific site of the prophet's native city. While the Judean location offers none of the objections involved in a Galilean or Assyrian Elkosh, it enjoys the support of several significant factors. It has the advantage of placing Nahum into the southern kingdom, where alone we should expect to find the prophet in the seventh century, long after the destruction of Samaria.

The evident interest of the book also centers in the South; for the appeal in 2:1 is specific: "Celebrate thy festivals, O Judah! Pay thy vows! For Belial will not again pass through thee. He is altogether destroyed." Whenever in Nahum's prophecies the oppressed victims of Nineveh's brutalities are addressed, they are, by direct inference of this passage, identified as the inhabitants of Judah. One of Assyria's heaviest sins is its wicked counseling against Yahweh (1:11). For the prophet's age this blasphemy could be directed only against the God worshiped in Judah and Jerusalem.

Objection to the assumption of a Judean home for Nahum has been raised by Duhm and others, who insist that the prophet must have lived beyond the confines of Judah because he allegedly overlooks the sins of his people and entirely disregards the increased danger which might arise for Judah after the destruction of Nineveh. But Nahum did not ignore Judah's sins. Besides, Ezekiel, who lived in Babylon, was not unmindful of the moral delinquencies of his fellow countrymen, so that foreign residence need bear no relation to the denunciation of Judah's sins or any implied silence concerning their iniquities. Nahum is the messenger of comfort and consolation; and while his appreciation of God's inexorable justice is as keen as any other prophet's (1:2, 3, 8), and while he has a clear understanding of the Almighty's universal judgment, which must include Judah, it is the purpose of his book to strengthen the faith of his fellow countrymen that "Yahweh is good as a Stronghold in the day of affliction, and He knoweth those who trust in Him." (1:7)

III. The Book of the Prophet

THE DATE OF NAHUM'S PROPHECIES

It has become a commonplace to date the Book of Nahum between the fall of Thebes and the fall of Nineveh. But a wide range of conflicting theories and of mutually exclusive dates has sought recognition within these limits.

Not Written Shortly Before the Fall of Nineveh. — One group of interpreters puts Nahum's prophecies as close as possible to the destruction of the city and finds the historical background of the book in the situation which prevailed a year or two before the capital fell. As long as 606 B. C. was accepted as the date of Nineveh's fall, the years 609 or 608 B. C. came into consideration.

Thus Sellin first placed the book at 609 B. C. and with considerable detail showed why we must accept "as late a date as possible." He asserted that the prophet's alleged silence concerning the sins of Jerusalem would be utterly unthinkable, for example, at the time of Manasseh (698—642 B. C.), whose royal crimes shrieked to heaven for vengeance, but quite concordant with the spiritual environment of Josiah's reform, "when the people had the sure conviction that now Jerusalem had again become Jahweh's city." On the other hand, Sellin declared, it is certain that Nahum's prophecy must be placed before Pharaoh Necho in 608 B. C., since it would be reasonable to conclude that the whole tone of the prophet would be fundamentally different if written later.

27

J. M. P. Smith tentatively selected 608—606 B. C. for another reason. He suggests: "The degree of animosity toward Nineveh accords better, perhaps, with the post-Deuteronomic date, 608—606 B. C., than with the pre-Deuteronomic period."

Another statement of his, however, is more specific and likewise holds that the book must be late because "the fall of Nineveh is thought of as imminent. . . . The invasion of Assyria has already begun." This imminence, however, is read into the text. Had the prophet predicted the city's destruction within a few years, he could have employed pointed Hebrew words, constructions, and indications to denote immediate futurity. To explain Nahum's vivid language as a description of almost contemporaneous events and to say that when he wrote, Nineveh "was threatened with *immediate* [our italics] destruction" or that "the enemy was *already* [our italics] in the land, and her downfall seemed certain," is to misinterpret the significance of the prophet's statements and syntax.

In addition to cuneiform documentary sources which automatically rule out any year after 612 B. C., one cogent reason against such late dating remains. From 626 to 609 B. C. Judah and Jerusalem were not troubled by Nineveh. Years before this time the Assyrian dominion had ended. Egypt was now the formidable foe, and under Psamtik I (663—609 B. C.) the armies from the Nile had swarmed to the frontiers of Palestine, after capturing Gerar, Ashkelon, Ashdod, and other cities near the border. His son Necho II (609—593 B. C.), in the second year of his reign, defeated Judah with his army of Egyptian soldiers and Greek mercenaries, killing King Josiah, 608 B. C. Jehoahaz, Josiah's second son, who reigned for only three months, was killed in Egypt. Then Josiah's oldest son, Crown Prince Eliakim, pro-Egyptian in his policy, was established king. Judah paid its overlords on the Nile one hundred talents of gold and exhausted its national treasury. Shortly before 606 B. C., therefore, no Assyrian dominion persisted to harass Judah, for the old rule of the Tigris country had been completely replaced by the Egyptian sovereignty. It is just as much out of place to picture Nahum directing his denunciations against Nineveh, the deceased overlord of Judah, in this period after 612 B. C., as it would be for a Northern poet, a few years subsequent to the defeat of the Southern States in the Civil War, to predict the collapse of the Confederacy. This contradiction cannot be explained away under the colorless assumption that "the news of the approaching end of a former taskmaster was a ray of light amid Egyptian darkness."

British Museum Tablet 21,901 has furnished 612 B. C. as the true date of Nineveh's collapse, but the general tendency among critical writers has been to repeat the previous principle of procedure and to date the prophecies very close to 612 B. C. W. O. E. Oesterley and Theodore H. Robinson declare: "The fact that the fall of the city was expected would tend to place Nahum's oracles . . . in or soon after 616 B. C." Otto Eissfeldt asserts that the prophecies are not to be dated too far before 612, because the effect among the nations would be greater, the closer the prophecy came to the destruction. J. M. P. Smith maintains: "Nahum spoke apparently just before the downfall of Nineveh in 612 B. C." Horst believes that almost all "pieces" of the prophecy were written "shortly before 612." Bevenot concludes: "By assuming that Nahum wrote between 620 and 614 . . . we can do full justice to all the internal evidence of his prophecy." Robert H. Pfeiffer reduces the span of years and lays down these limits: "The poem was undoubtedly written between 625 and 612, and probably between 614 and 612." [10]

Contrary to the proposition that "the prophecy of Nahum

---

[10] W. O. Oesterley and Theodore H. Robinson, *An Introduction to the Books of the Old Testament* (1934), p. 389. Otto Eissfeldt, *Einleitung in das Alte Testament* (1934), p. 462. J. M. P. Smith, *The Prophets and Their Times* (1925), p. 123. Robert H. Pfeiffer, *Introduction to the Old Testament* (1941), p. 596.

was probably delivered shortly before this event," as George Foot Moore summarizes,[11] the internal evidence of the book itself points to a much earlier date. The description of Nineveh is certainly not that of the degenerate nation after 626 B. C., the death of Ashurbanipal, not even the picture of the empire in its declining power. On the contrary, Assyrian might is unchecked (1:12); its prey "does not depart" (3:1); its merchants are multiplied "more than the stars of the heaven" (3:16); it still is the harlot who "selleth nations" (3:4). This is not the picture of Assyria in 616 B. C. or later, for after the end of Ashurbanipal's long reign evil days broke, with dissension from within and wars of freedom from without. Ashur-etil-ilani, who succeeded Ashurbanipal, his father, in 626 B. C., lived in a royal residence characterized by its meagerness.[12] Under his successor (622 B. C.) Sin-shar-ishkun, another son of Ashurbanipal, the Assyrian provinces began to slip away. Nabopolassar established complete, independent rule for Babylonia by 616 B. C. and began his wars of Mesopotamian conquest. After 626 B. C. Nineveh was not the powerful empire continually stalking its prey and ensnaring nations.

Another argument for a date at least several decades before 612 B. C. is the decisive fact that when the prophet pens his prediction, Judah is definitely under the Assyrian yoke, restrained by its bonds (1:13). Groaning under Ninevite tyranny, the Hebrews are in no mood to celebrate their festivals (2:1). Obviously Nahum must have written while Judah suffered the affliction of Assyrian rule. The entire purpose of the book demands this background, and its statements imply this dating. At what time, then, was Judah subjected to Assyrian exploitation? During the entire reign of Manasseh (698 to 642 B. C.) Judah was a vassal state. Both Esarhaddon (680 to 668 B. C.) and Ashurbanipal (668 to 626 B. C.) list Manasseh as among their

[11] G. F. Moore, *The Literature of the Old Testament* (1913), p. 292.

[12] Albert Ten Eyck Olmstead, *History of Assyria* (1923), pp. 627 f.

tributary vassals. It was not until 626 B. C., the year of Ashurbanipal's death, that any hope of freedom from Nineveh's yoke crystallized. At that time Josiah (639—608 B. C.), the grandson of Manasseh, found the Assyrian Empire so weakened that he could omit paying tribute; and the great reform in 621 B. C., which cleansed the temple in Jerusalem also of Assyrian idols, became a symbol of Judah's complete political independence. The Assyrian officers were so powerless that Josiah's men could invade the Samaritan territory and destroy the high places there.

We are entitled to conclude, therefore, that Nahum, chafing under the Assyrian oppression, must have penned his prophecies no later than the early years of Josiah, who began his reign in 639 B. C. To place the prophet after 626 B. C., and especially after 621 B. C., is to make his words an oracle against a nation which no longer harassed Judah and a people whose power had already been broken.

Not Written Shortly Before 626—625 B. C. — These considerations also help to set aside the opinion of those (e. g., Stonehouse) who have found the occasion for Nahum's prophecy in a supposed attack on Nineveh led by Cyaxares, the Median king, about 626—625 B. C. According to Herodotus, militant Cyaxares renewed the hostilities against the Assyrians after his father Phraortes, embattled against Nineveh, had perished. Soon after Cyaxares began the siege of Nineveh, a formidable army of Scythians under King Madyes marched against Media from the northern shores of the Black Sea, ca. 626—625 B. C. It is held that the prophet, beholding the turbulent conditions in the vicinity of Nineveh, believed that this was the beginning of the end and so shaped his prediction. More specific is the claim advanced by Stonehouse's elaborate presentation. He holds that the one who "planneth evil," mentioned in 1:11, is not Sennacherib, as generally supposed, but the Scythians, who threatened Israel in 626 B. C. The prophet, it is alleged, was so impressed with this incident that he wrote his book perhaps in the very next year.

However, the one who "planneth evil" specifically aimed his wickedness "against Yahweh," and it is difficult to see how the Scythians could be thus characterized. Nothing we know indicates that they directed their advances into Judah against God. The context, as well as the pointed force of the entire prophecy, indicates that Nineveh, or one of its leaders, must have been the deviser of evil. The explanation of 1:11 shows that the historical background of the verse is not the Scythian invasion.

Again, it is urged that Nahum must have prophesied at the time when he could bring this indictment against Nineveh: "Behold, I am against thee" (2:14; 3:5). Stonehouse concludes that the circumstances of the year 626—625 B. C. best meet this demand. He holds that it was only then that a prophet of God could predict Nineveh's fall, since previously "no indication of it had been discernible." In 626—625 B. C., however, the city's danger was evident, and therefore the prophet could safely foretell its imminent end. So clear were the indications of destruction, in Stonehouse's opinion, "that it would have been altogether remarkable had no prophet of Jehovah appeared at that moment." — This is an unwarranted stricture of divine prophecy. The messengers of God's will do not wait until destruction is evident before making their predictions.

Again, it is held that the prophet wrote in 626—625 B. C. because he makes no mention of Israel's sin and because in that year Israel was on the way to moral improvement. Here is the alleged situation as Stonehouse recreates it: "When he [Nahum] wrote, the internal condition of Judah was such that he had every hope of her ultimate reformation; for it is not necessary to infer that she was then actually a 'reformed' people; all that there is need to infer is that there were not wanting signs that she was responding to the teaching of her prophetic leaders. And this is what we believe was in reality happening in 625. We believe that largely owing to the strong protest of Zephaniah and Jeremiah and to the Scythian invasion, which brought about a wiser administration in the capital, movements for the better were already on foot which, inspired by the teaching of the prophets and gaining popularity from the course events were taking, were fast reaching that stage which would permit of a thorough reformation being carried out." All this is pure conjecture. We have no assurance that four years before Josiah's reign this remarkable change had already overtaken Judah. The real improvement came after the reform; nor is it necessary to look for a time when Judah's conduct was particularly God-pleasing. As has been shown elsewhere, the prophet implies his own people's sins; and the fact that he does not devote a large section of his small book to a denunciation of their ingratitude and wickedness may be explained by the assumption that his consuming purpose was to foretell the siege and destruction of Nineveh.

Above all, however, the entire assumption on which the 626—625 B.C. dating is based lacks conclusive evidence. No details of Cyaxares' assault have survived. Indeed, Herodotus is the only authority for this invasion, and it has been seriously questioned. No proof has been adduced to indicate that Cyaxares actually threatened Nineveh at that time or that the Scythians brought the city relief. Again, as has been shown, neither the Assyria nor the Judah of the period subsequent to Ashurbanipal's death corresponds with the two countries as delineated by Nahum. Besides, the deductions to be made from the mention of No-Amon (3:8) point to a date before 626—625 B.C. Finally, if the prophet thought that Nineveh would surrender to the attack of Cyaxares and gave his prophecies this direction, he would have been mistaken and discredited in the eyes of his countrymen; for the capital survived all assaults which Cyaxares at that time may have been able to direct against it.

Not Written Shortly Before 648 B. C. — Some commentators have sought to date Nahum's prophecies in connection with the civil war which began during the days of Shamash-shum-ukin, about 648 B. C. According to this opinion, as it has been more fully developed in the light of subsequent Assyrian discoveries, the prophet believed that at this time Nineveh's downfall was in the immediate offing and that Shamash-shum-ukin would lead his Babylonian troops into Assyria.[13] It is held that at this time Nahum could have anticipated the fall of Nineveh, because the vassal states were in rebellion against Ashurbanipal.

This dating cannot be accepted because it limits the power of prophecy and ascribes to Nahum only that faculty of anticipation which every keen-minded observer shares (and which in this instance proved utterly erroneous, since Ashurbanipal completely quelled the Babylonian revolt), and because the book does not picture Assyria as endeavoring to crush the uprising of rebellious lands in her extensive empire. On the contrary, according to Nahum, Nineveh's dominion is still widespread (3:4), and its dens are full of prey and rapine (2:12). Its merchants are more numerous than the stars in the heavens (3:16). Never in Shamash-shum-ukin's revolt was Nineveh even threatened, for the Babylonian rebel king's efforts were directed not toward the city's destruction but toward emancipation from the Assyrian yoke and the resultant freedom for the southland. How disastrous to incorporate into the OT prophetic writings a prediction which within a year or two would be proved fantastic by Shamash-shum-ukin's defeat and Babylon's devastation!

Written Before 654 B. C. — If the prophet's words be regarded as describing Nineveh at the zenith of its power and Judah groaning under Assyrian tyranny, how long before 648 B. C. (the destruction of Babylon) can the date of these oracles be placed? The earliest possible year is established by the book itself, in its reference to the capture of Thebes (3:8-10). Here-

[13] So, in general, Friedrich Eduard König, *Einleitung in das Alte Testament* (1893), p. 332.

tofore the accepted date of this event has been 664 or 662 B. C.,
Assyriologists endorsing the later year and Egyptologists the
earlier. The sources of this chronology are found in Ashurbanipal's records. Through the publication of all his available
historical prism fragments it is now possible to fix the time for
the razing of Thebes approximately four years earlier. The date
668—667 B. C. seems definitely assured by the statements in
Edition F, col. 1, 11. 35—38, which put the second Egyptian
campaign of Ashurbanipal's later prisms definitely into that
monarch's *"Rêsh Sharrûti,"* the beginning of his kingship. Ashurbanipal's so-called first campaign of the later editions was in
actuality appropriated from his father. It seems certain that both
the Egyptian campaign and the expedition against Ba'ali of Tyre
preceded the Kirbit campaign, so that the fall of Thebes also
for this reason may be placed at approximately 668—667 B. C.[14]

Again, it may be asked, How long after 668—667 B. C.
did Nahum pen his oracles? The reference to the capture of
"populous No" gains in effectiveness under the assumption of an
authorship dated soon after the event. Even critics have conceded
that Ashurbanipal's conquest of the Egyptian city must have
taken place only shortly before the book was written. Thus
Schrader[15] writes: "It is scarcely probable that a prophet, 'even
after several decades,' should have referred to this event as one
that was clear to all and stood vividly before the imagination . . .
if we have here a catastrophe befalling a foreign race and not
one that immediately concerned the people whom the prophet

[14] Several Assyrian records describing the fall of Thebes are preserved in
Ashurbanipal's inscription. The oldest and best of these is Edition E of the prism
accounts. The historical prism fragments of Ashurbanipal have been translated and
edited by Arthur Carl Piepkorn, who holds that "Edition E must be reckoned the
oldest historical account in Assyrian that has come down to us from the reign of
Ashurbanipal." At a date shortly after E (ca. 667 B. C.) are to be placed the
large cuneiform tablets (British Museum registration numbers K228 and K2675).
The best edition of K228 is still George Smith's *History of Assurbanipal* (1871),
pp. 39—43. See also Streck, II, 158 ff.

[15] Eberhard Schrader, *The Cuneiform Inscriptions and the Old Testament*
(1885—1888), II, 152.

was addressing." Wellhausen (*Die kleinen Propheten*) agrees that the capture of No-Amon cannot have occurred decades before the prophet's utterances. He writes: "The event to which 3:8 refers cannot be decades old but must lie close to the present time of the prophet." Wellhausen believes, however, that Nahum does not refer to the destruction of No-Amon under Ashurbanipal. He presupposes another subsequent destruction of Thebes, of which secular history knows nothing.

Besides, if Nahum had written after 648 B. C., he could have more graphically mentioned the devastation of other cities closer to his time than the sack of No-Amon. He could have featured the more startling catastrophe which occurred twenty years after Thebes' fall, the capture of Babylon in July of 648 B. C., one of the most horrifying massacres in all history.

Again, it must not be overlooked that although the Assyrian troops destroyed No-Amon, this metropolis did not drop out of existence. In 654 B. C., only thirteen years after the Assyrian sack of the city, Psamtik I captured Thebes. While his new government established itself at Sais, and Thebes no longer retained political leadership, No-Amon remained a center of importance. The rhetorical question in the prophet's argument: "Art thou better than No of Amon?" would lose force if Nahum wrote about 616 B. C., the year, in general, favored by present-day criticism. By that time No-Amon had thrown off the Assyrian yoke, had rebuilt itself, and could tauntingly proclaim that she, the ancient city on the Nile, had proved both her strength and Nineveh's weakness by casting off the Assyrian rule.

In summary, the Book of Nahum, implying the destruction of Thebes but not its restoration, was probably written shortly before 654 B. C., when Thebes began to rise from its ruins. This dating also harmonizes with the fact that the prophet nowhere mentions the Medes, the Scythians, or the Babylonians, whom we now know to have conquered Nineveh, as Assyria's enemies.

If the book was written before 648 B.C., the nonmention of the Medes is easily explainable, for their independent kingdom under Dioces began only in 645 B.C. The Scythians were not known to Judah at this time, and the Babylonians (who played a small part in crushing the city) were internationally insignificant. If the prophet wrote shortly before 612 B.C., however, it would be difficult to see why he would not mention the Medes, who by this time had developed formidable powers; the Scythians, whose devastating strength was clearly understood; and the Babylonians, who, politically renascent, were on the way to assume world dominion. The prophet who otherwise enumerates Ethiopia, Egypt, Pût, Lubim (3:9) by name, would not have passed by the opportunity of mentioning specifically the destroyers of Nineveh. Since he wrote before the Medes, Scythians, and Babylonians came into international power, he cryptically omitted the record of their names.

This date (ca. 654 B.C.) also harmonizes with the inferential picture of Judah which may be drawn from the prophet's statement — God's people are still under Nineveh's yoke (1:13). Their country is like a vine branch, ravaged and cut by spoilers (2:3). The followers of the Lord are not able to celebrate their joyful festivals, to pay their vows; but after the triumph which Nahum envisions would be realized, full religious exercises could be resumed (2:1). This is not a representation of Judah after the death of Ashurbanipal, in the reign of King Josiah, when the Assyrian pressure was removed, but the picture of Judah during the days of Manasseh (698—643 B.C.), who paid tribute to Esarhaddon and Ashurbanipal and who was taken captive to Babylon.

Not Written in the Exilic or Maccabean Ages. — Until recently only a few of the most radical commentators endorsed the opinion that the Book of Nahum was written after the momentous events which it predicts. Lately, however, the claim has gained support that the book is a *post eventum* description of Nineveh's downfall. Sellin and Humbert, both advocates of the theory which views the book as a liturgy, hold that the prophecy was written a few months after Nineveh's collapse. The former supports his thesis by his interpretation of 1:1b, 12; 2:1b; and 3:18 f. as references to the past, although each of these passages, as will be shown (see commentary), refers directly or indirectly to the future.

A later exilic date is assumed for the book by Riessler. While it is universally taken for granted that Nahum deals with Nineveh, the Assyrian capital, Riessler has developed the astonishingly fantastic theory that the threats voiced by this prophecy are not directed against Nineveh on the Tigris but against an otherwise unimportant city in northern Mesopotamia. Riessler's argument, concisely stated, holds that the description of Nahum's city agrees with that of Babylon as given by Isaiah and Jeremiah. This, however, is not the celebrated Babylon, world metropolis; it is rather to be identified with Sur (Tyre), again, not the well-known Tyre, but a vague Nineveh in Eden, or more specifically, the Bît Adini on the Euphrates, where the river, breaking through the Taurus Mountains, begins its western course. This, he believes, was a Neo-Babylonian commercial center which under King Amel-Marduk reached the importance of a residence city; and he insists that the prophets gave to this "Nineveh" on the upper Euphrates the name "Babylon." He thus concludes that Nahum's Nineveh, Isaiah's and Jeremiah's Babylon, Ezekiel's Tyre, are all the Neo-Babylonian city at Beth Eden and that the prophecies were written after the Babylonian exile, with the exception of the title, the "alphabetic psalm," and a half dozen other verses, written by an otherwise unidentified Nahum.

This process of presentation, according to which Riessler first states how much Nahum's city resembles Babylon and then how much it differs from it; also how similar it is to Tyre and yet how divergent, has found no significant support and indeed deserves none. His reasons for refusing to find the traditional Nineveh in Nahum are of no force. Thus he maintains that, according to the prophet, the city is surrounded by water; but the passages he adduces to show this to be a fact refer to Thebes. He arbitrarily declares that chapter 3:8 ff. deals with a Mesopotamian city and that the countries there mentioned are not the well-known Ethiopia, etc., but districts in Assyria. He likewise insists that the city which Nahum dooms lies on a high rock; yet the prophet nowhere makes this statement, directly or by implication.

Riessler's arguments are not only inconclusive but also are contradicted by the salient facts that Nineveh and Assyria are both addressed in the prophecy; that the localities featured in 3:8 ff. have a recognized place in Nineveh's history; that the fulfillment of Nahum's prophecies definitely points to Nineveh and to no other known city; and that the book was written more than a century before the end of the Babylonian Exile.

Haupt consigned large sections of the book to that convenient Maccabean period (ca. 175 B. C.) which, far from being the golden age of Hebrew literature which produced Nahum's classic style, has left no evidences of anything more than literary mediocrity. The arguments in behalf of this Maccabean dating are invalid. Haupt maintains that there is a "notable difference between Nahum and the pre-exilic prophets," but this is overdrawn and indecisive, since, for example, Hosea, Amos, Micah, and Isaiah, partially contemporaneous, also differ in many respects, being independent authors. Haupt's assertion that the allusion to No-Amon (3:8) is a disguised reference to the failure of Antiochus Epiphanes' efforts to take Alexandria patently contradicts basic facts, and his further assertion that the indictments of Nineveh on the charges of harlotry and witchcraft were in fact indictments of Antiochus for his religious intolerance and tyranny cannot be dignified with serious consideration. The specific reference to the Minor Prophets found in Ecclus. 49:12 shows that the work of the Twelve was definitely fixed long before the Maccabean period.

Similarly Happel assigns Nahum to the Maccabean age. He, too, holds that the Nineveh in Nahum is not the Assyrian capital but an eschatological type of God's enemies, the Seleucid kingdom, which, he maintains, is frequently found in later apocalyptical writings. According to his analysis, each of the three chapters was originally independent, written by three different authors, the first in 167 B. C. and the other two in 168 B. C. The first chapter, he maintains, alphabetic and produced by an unidentified Nahum, was worked over when joined to the two subsequent chapters in 165 B. C., with the result that the alphabetic sequence was destroyed. Happel's reconstruction not only is theoretical and destitute of factual support but also contradicts the plain statements of the book.

THE LITERARY ASPECTS OF NAHUM'S PROPHECIES

Style

With few exceptions, those competent to judge have acknowledged Nahum's literary excellence. Bewer[16] declares: "Nahum was a great prophet. His word pictures are superb, his rhetorical skill is beyond praise." From the days of Bishop Robert Lowth and his oft-quoted applause: "Of all the minor prophets none seems to equal the sublimity, the ardor, the daring spirit of Nahum," a long procession of commentators has paid tribute to his literary genius. Keil insists that in many details Nahum's language is not inferior to the classical style of Isaiah and Micah in power and originality as well as in clearness and purity. J. M. P. Smith agrees that the prophet's poetry in some respects is "unsurpassed in the OT." Nahum, he concludes, lifts "the narrative out of the commonplace into the majestic." Carl

[16] Julius A. Bewer, *The Literature of the Old Testament in Its Historical Development* (1922), p. 139.

Sumner Knopf calls Nahum "a master of poetic technique vying with Homer or Pindar."[17]

The analysis of his style reveals *originality and independence* as one of Nahum's literary pre-eminences. He borrows little from his predecessors. With the exception of the psalmlike introduction (1:2-7), which, because of its broad statements describing the Lord's power and its devastating effect on all opposing resistance, has parallels in previous books, Nahum seems to refer only once to an earlier prophet, when in 2:1 he mentions "feet of a herald proclaiming peace," an echo of Is. 52:7.

The number of words which Nahum alone, of all OT writers, employs emphasizes the literary originality of the prophet. Equally significant is his use of words in sense, form, or construction peculiarly his own.

Noteworthy, too, is Nahum's *purity* of presentation. His Hebrew is so evidently of classical vocabulary, grammar, and syntax that those who have sought to push the book wholly or partly into the Maccabean period are discredited merely on the evidence of language, just as those who advance the theory of an exilic or postexilic authorship cannot explain the vast difference between Nahum's style and the diction of Haggai or Zechariah.

With this independence of expression and this purity of diction Nahum combines his unsurpassed *power of description* and photographic depiction. For this swift, realistic presentation (he uses a minimum of words; note the asyndetic construction, e. g., in 2:2) he draws freely on the resources of Hebrew syntax. The rhetorical question (1:6,9; 2:12; 3:7,8,19), the elliptical sentence (3:2), the apostrophe (2:1 ff.), the metaphor and simile (Nineveh pictured as a harlot, 3:4; its dwelling place as the den of the lions and the feeding place of young lions, 2:12; its fortresses as ripe figs, 3:12; its leaders as locusts, 3:17; its people as folded thorns and dry stubble, 1:10), lend unusual vividness.

[17] Carl Sumner Knopf, *The Old Testament Speaks* (1933), p. 255.

With all these pictures, however, the prophet's certainty that Nineveh will surely be destroyed is absolute.

Assonance and alliteration are featured with unique emphasis, for example in 2:11: *bûqāh ûmᵉbhûqāh ûmᵉbhullāqāh*, which the English can imitate only in combinations like "desolation, devastation, dilapidation." The change of person and number is often abrupt and unheralded (1:9, 11, 12, 15; 2:2, 8, 9, 10, 13; 3:1, 5, 18). Despite his epic terseness, which sometimes complicates exact reproduction in translation, Nahum applies the power of repetition (1:2) and employs four synonyms for one word in a single verse. (1:6)

No New Year's Liturgy

Within recent decades it has been contended that the real purpose of Nahum's book has consistently been overlooked and misunderstood. Instead of regarding his oracles as a prophecy, this theory holds, they must be interpreted as a temple liturgy. So precisely has this hypothesis been developed that the date for the introduction of the liturgy is determined as the autumn of 612 B. C., the *Rôsh Hashshānāh* (New Year's) festival in Jerusalem. This opinion was first advanced by Humbert,[18] but has received strong support from Sellin[19] and partial endorsement by Horst and others.

In support of this revolutionary theory it is maintained that the vividness and accuracy of the prophecies suggest an origin after the event. But this is a circle argument; it denies the force of Biblical prophecy and its harmonious agreement with the facts of fulfillment.

[18] It was developed in his "Essai d'analyse de Nahoum 1, 2—2, 3," *Zeitschrift für die alttestamentliche Wissenschaft*, III (1926), 266—280; "Nahoum II, 9," *Revue des études juives* (1927), pp. 74—76; "La vision de Nahoum, II, 4-11," *Archiv für Orientforschung* V (1928), 14—19; "Le probleme de livre de Nahoum," *Revue d'Histoire et de Philosophie religieuses* (1932), pp. 1—15.

[19] In his *Einleitung in das Alte Testament*, p. 116, he agrees: "We have learned to know the Book of Nahum correctly only recently. It concerns a liturgy for the festival, which was celebrated in Jerusalem immediately after the fall of Nineveh in 612."

Then Humbert insists that if the book were a prophecy, it would be directed to the people of Jerusalem; but since, as he contends, it is not, and has no distinctive marks of prediction, it could well be a liturgy. He asks: "Would it not be strange, the case of this Israelite prophet who, without dedicating a single oracle to his own people, discharges this volley of invectives on the head of the distant Ninevites?" But Nahum does address his fellow countrymen. The warning and the comfort of the introduction (1:2-7) include his coreligionists first of all. The promise of 1:12b is addressed to Judah; and 2:1, appealing: "Celebrate thy festivals, O Judah! Pay thy vows," etc., besides specifically mentioning his country, is introduced with a reference taken from Judah's sacred Scripture.

Again, it is urged that the very form of the book, its syntactical abruptness, its questions, point to ritual form and usage. Humbert asks: "Further, the questions, the answers, the oracles, the lamentations, the dirges, the changes of individual and collective voices, of human and divine voices, the multiplicity of interlocutors . . . what is this, if not a liturgy?" He divides the book into sharply defined antiphonal sections containing the questions of the priest and the responsive answers of the people. His procedure is, however, without support in the text itself. The careful reader searches in vain for interlocutors, choir sections and solos, for the regular interchange of individual and collective voices, required by this theory. Questions and answers are not necessarily characteristic of liturgical or antiphonal arrangement. Some OT sections, for example, certain pilgrimage psalms (120 to 134), indeed seem to have been capable of adaptation for liturgical rendition; but the reading of Psalm 120 presents thought and language development entirely different from that offered by Nahum. Besides, the subject matter of these prophecies does not well lend itself for liturgical arrangement.

This chief argument for the late dating of Nahum derives from the literary analysis championed on OT study by Gunkel and applied to Nahum by Humbert. This analysis, it is alleged, reveals that the book is a chain of fragments of various literary classes and features questions and responses, passages by soloists or by choruses, individual pronouncements and collective utterances, the voice of the prophet and the voice of God, all of which form a liturgy commemorating Nineveh's destruction.

Exponents of this theory further maintain that the antiphonal and liturgical character of the book is indicated by the psalm with which it commences. But psalms are found in other OT passages, where no liturgical usage is indicated. See Hab. 3; Is. 25:1-5; 26:1-6.

Humbert likewise finds proof for the liturgical usage in 1:9a, which, under his interpretation, becomes a liturgical question with a response by the choir or congregation in 1:9b, 10. However, to secure a suitable antiphonal interchange, Humbert alters the text; and the weakness of his position is shown by the fact that his chief supporter, Sellin, does not agree with him in locating the antiphonal reply. While Humbert pictures the congregation or choir answering in vv. 9b and 10, Sellin (p. 362) tears 2b from its context and places it after 9b as the response.

Finally, Humbert further states that the Book of Nahum is actually the drama of the fall of Nineveh, just as "in the Roman Catholic worship the sacrifice of the Mass depicts the drama of Calvary," or exactly as in the old Egyptian records the dramatic fragments illustrate and represent the myths of Osiris, Seth, and Horus. This requires a dramatic partition, of which the text is innocent. The graphic description of Nineveh's end is plainly not antiphonal.

No decisive facts support this theory, whereas it is invalidated by several specific facts, other than the general objections indicated. It is built on a radical mutilation of the text. To secure address and reply, questions and answers, Nahum's words are arbitrarily altered to read as required.

Again, this theory would make Nahum a *post eventum* description of Nineveh's fall, while the book is clearly *prae eventu.* The whole presentation, the use of the imperfect and the prophetic perfect for future events, indicate that the book is a prediction (see 1:14; 3:5,7). The inferential description of Nineveh, as of Judah, is not that of 612 B. C., but of approximately a half century earlier. Not one statement can be labeled as subsequent to the fall. If the book were written after 612 B. C., we would expect precise mention of Nineveh's enemies, the Babylonians, the Medes, and the Scythians, as well as other specific references, in place of the more general anticipatory terms. Appeals like "celebrate thy festivals!" would be out of place in 612 B. C., because Judah had observed its holy days, especially under Josiah, before that time. The construction: "Behold, I am against thee" in 2:14; 3:5 is used in other parts of the OT to indicate future destruction. See Ezek. 5:8; 26:3.

Again, the weakness of the theory is demonstrated by the fact that exponents of this innovation discover three variously different backgrounds for the event allegedly commemorated: the New Year's festival, the Feast of Tabernacles, and a victory celebration. Humbert admits that his classification of Nahum as a ritual for the *Rôsh Hashshānāh* (New Year) liturgy is utterly conjectural. The whole idea of a New Year's service with such antiphonal readings is absolutely without foundation. We have no evidence whatever that a celebration of this kind was actually held in Jerusalem.

Again, a study of known Jewish liturgies for the Day of Atonement, Passover, Feast of Weeks, and Tabernacles reveals an entirely different literary presentation and a distinctly different subject matter. Such liturgies not only mention the historic event to be commemorated as an occurrence of the past, but they also feature a note of thanksgiving, which is clearly missing in Nahum. It is difficult to conceive of a New Year's, victory, or Tabernacles ritual without repeated voices raised in gratitude to God.

Likewise there is little probability that within a few months after the fall of Nineveh a temple ritual of this kind could be completed and accepted. No parallel instances indicate such rapid adoption.

Finally, the superscription to the prophecies, "The Burden of Nineveh — The Book of the Vision of Nahum," clearly shows that these chapters were not conceived and written as a liturgy. As "burden," "book," and "vision" they served the nonliturgical purposes for which also other OT sections designated by these three terms were written.

Poetry

The analysis of Nahum's style indicates that his presentation is by no means prosaic. He has a sublime subject, God's avenging, protecting righteousness. He employs poetical diction, with its choice words, idiomatic meanings, exceptional inflections, and peculiar syntax (the absence of articles, relatives, and particles). For these reasons and because of the well-developed, artistically balanced parallelism, his book, like other prophetic oracles, should be classified as poetry. To these two characteristics, poetic subject and poetic style, modern interpreters generally add a third mark of Nahum's book, poetic measure.

Commentators diverge widely, however, in their theories of the metrical patterns employed by Nahum. In harmony with the principles laid down by E. Sievers [20] the accents in each line

---

[20] The following explanation of Ges., Gra., 2 r, presents a basic outline of the present theory of Old Testament meter: "Hebrew poetry, as distinguished from the quantitative Classical and Arabic and syllabic Syriac verse, is *accentual*. The number of unstressed syllables between the beats (*ictus*) is, however, not arbitrary, but the scheme of the verse is based on an irregular anapaest which may undergo rhythmical modifications (e. g., resolving the *ictus* into two syllables or lengthening the arsis so as to give a double accent) and contraction, e. g., of the first two syllables. The foot always concludes with the *ictus*, so that toneless endings, due to change of pronunciation or corruption of the text, are to be disregarded, although as a rule the *ictus* coincides with the Hebrew word-accent. The metrical scheme consists of combinations of feet in *series* (of 2, 3, or 4), and of these again in periods — double threes, very frequently, double fours in narrative, fives in Lamentations . . . and very often elsewhere, and sevens."

have been counted and the various lines classified according to frequency. Thus J. M. P. Smith holds:

a. In the mutilated alphabetic acrostic, 1:2-10, "hexameter rhythm prevails throughout . . . with the caesura after the third beat, except in line one, where it follows the fourth beat."

b. The verses 1:12, 13; 2:1, 2, 3, now torn out of their order and context, form "a single eight-line strophe in almost perfect elegiac rhythm."

c. The section 1:11, 14; 2:1, 3-13 comprises five strophes, "the first four having six lines each and the fifth only three. The elegiac rhythm reveals itself in 1:11; 2:2, 7, 8, 9, 12, 13. . . . The variants from this are tetrameter and hexameter lines."

d. The section 3:1-19 embraces six strophes, "having 8. 6. 6. 6. 8. 4. lines each. . . . Elegiac rhythm occurs here in 3:4b, 5, 6, 8a, 11, 12, 14, 15, 18, 19; the remaining lines are chiefly tetrameters and hexameters."

No other interpreter agrees wholly with this specific division. Nor are the underlying principles on which this metrical scheme is based and the procedure by which its patterns are reached accepted in this commentary. The frequent occurrence of elegiac verse (the qînā rhythm or lamentation verse) is, of course, conceded. This dirge style is exemplified by a verse consisting of two members, the second of which is at least one accent shorter than the first. But that the remaining verses are chiefly tetrameters and hexameters and that those lines which do not have the four or six main accents are to be stretched or reduced by Procrustean practices are assumptions which involve many arbitrary factors; and so unsatisfactory is the final result that the whole procedure condemns itself.

In maintaining this hexameter-tetrameter pattern, Smith, as all metricists, feels under no restraint to adhere to the transmitted text. With explanations like: "It is an abnormally long line" an entire section of a verse is dropped (1:3a). With the statement that his procedure is motivated by "the need of another beat in the line" (1:7a), a new word, not found in the text at all, is gratuitously added. If instead of three beats before the caesura in a hexameter line Ⓜ offers only two, an added "Jehovah" is produced to supply this metrical deficit (1:7b); but if a line contains more than six beats, a "Jehovah" is discarded as metrical surplus (1:2a). Changes involve other changes; verses are transposed with nonchalance and finality; the sequence and divisions of verses are arbitrarily rearranged, and alterations, dictated only by the rigidity of an assumed pattern, present a radically mutilated version of the prophecies. For none of the changes, transpositions, omissions, or additions can decisive manuscript evidence be adduced.

When Nahum's prophecies, thus reconstructed, are studied, three questions suggest themselves: How is it possible, if Hebrew poetry is accentual, that the author's pattern of measured stress was frequently set aside, the whole book willfully deranged, and the text of most of its verses deliberately corrupted? No parallel for this procedure exists in any other literature. Hellenists, for example, never meet their hexameters in comparably degenerated, conflated, or apocopated form. No assumption of editorial stupidity or scribal forgetfulness can account for the disorganization metricists claim to find or justify the slashing to which they resort. — How, on the other hand, can Ⓜ, bristling, as it allegedly does, with metrical defects, offer a forceful and logical presentation, while the tendential rearrangement of these verses to suit metrical predilection involves a chain of difficulties? — When the reconstructing poetasters finish and the results of their efforts are surveyed, is the completed product a work of superior beauty, with its unsystematic sequence of elegiacs, tetrameters, hexameters, and other measure patterns, all in forty-seven short verses?

The complete subjectivity of this metrical analysis may be seen by comparing and contrasting Smith's alterations with the emendations proposed by others. Sellin, for example, makes fundamental changes in almost every line of section 1:2 to 1:10. But because he believes that each verse consists of a double trimeter rather than of hexameters, as Smith holds, his reconstruction (motivated by such phrases as "the meter confirms," "the meter demands," "it destroys the original meter") departs drastically from Smith's.

Attention will be called to other extremes voiced in the advocacy of meter patterns for the portions of the book after 1:10. But the procedure in the opening verses is typical and leads to the conclusion: Nahum's poetry is not metrical in the sense that it is built on rigid patterns of main accents to form trimeters, tetrameters, hexameters. With Smith arbitrarily multiplying his changes in the (M), Sellin introducing his conflicting alterations, the other exponents of counted accents presenting still further divergences, the various theories of metrical analysis patently offer no acceptable key to the poetical structure of Nahum.

Even the predominance of the qînā rhythm cannot be adduced to show exact metricism, as Sellin suggests when he posits a system of three beats for the first line and two for the second as the standard, prevalent qînā pattern. This $3+2$ system is not followed consistently in the book, even after the $3+3$ pattern of the miscalled "alphabetic psalm," and Sellin himself is forced to list a number of verses in which this sequence of beats is avoided.

While Nahum's prophecies thus reveal little of metrical system and strophic regularity, the parallelism, characteristic mark of Hebrew poetry, is varied and striking. In this development of balanced thought, clothed in the artistry of elevated language and exalted style, we are to find the marks that separate the poetry of Nahum from the prose of other Old Testament books. The prophet wrote his lines first of all for their message rather than for their form. The literary and poetic effect was secondary. As he transmitted his oracles, they were read or chanted without the regular accentual sequence required for classical poetry. Perhaps every reader could reproduce these verses, disregarding the unaccented syllables, according to his own feelings, much as ancient English ballads, devoid of metrical framework, could be variously rendered by individual bards and minstrels. The effect on the Hebrew ear could have been about as pleasing as the regular accentual sequence now is to us.

Unity

Nahum's three chapters, on manuscript authority and versional testimony, present a literary unit. They are, as title and linguistic evidence confirm, his authentic writings without the addition of multiplied glosses. In maintaining the unity of these prophecies, however, it is not necessary to assume that the whole book was written at one time and in a single flow. On the other hand, there is no justification for Horst's classification of the verses as oracles of threats, satires, visions, and promises of deliverance.

This view is opposed in principle and in detail by the literary analysis of modern criticism. Almost every one of the forty-seven verses has been said by one critic or another to contain a subsequent addition. Before Gunkel's attack no serious doubt had been expressed concerning the unity of the book. A few critics had challenged the appropriateness of the "double title," and Hitzig had questioned the authenticity of 3:8-10, but George Adam Smith well summarizes: " 'Nahum's prophecy,' said Kuenen in 1889, 'is a whole.' In 1891 Cornill affirmed that no question of authenticity arose in regard to the book; and in 1898 Wellhausen saw in chapter one an introduction leading 'in no awkward way to the proper subject of the prophecy.' "

The assertion that individual words or clauses are glosses will be treated in the exposition of the verses involved, but attention is here called to the larger and more important of the alleged additions. No consensus prevails among the literary analysts concerning the portions to be deleted as spurious. A section excised by one commentator may be retained by another.

1. *The Title, 1:1.* — The opinion is voiced that the present text offers a double title and that the words "The Burden of Nineveh, the Book of" must be ruled out as unauthentic.

The double nature of this superscription, however, is in itself no argument against its authenticity. The assertion that the titles of other prophetic books offer no parallel cases, even if it were true, should, of course, not be regarded as decisive.

The further point is urged that the two component parts of the superscription, "The Burden of Nineveh" and "The Book of Nahum," collide. But these phrases actually supplement each other, the first offering the subject and the second the author. Because the message is so pointed and specific, it is accorded the first position in the title. The prophecies of Micah (1:1) and of Amos (1:1), e. g., are superscribed by a verse which embraces both the author and the general subject of his message. Hosea (1:1, 2) begins with a double title. Isaiah (13:1) commences his series of predictions against foreign nations with a title very similar to Nahum's opening verse.

The third charge raised against the "Burden of Nineveh" brands this title as inappropriate, since much of the book, it is stated, does not concern Nineveh. Reference is made specifically to the general tenor of the verses with which the prophecy opens. This initial section, however, forms the majestic prelude which pictures Yahweh's power as it is applied in the case of Nineveh. The whole book, directly or indirectly, deals with the doomed city. Likewise the words of Amos, "which he saw concerning Israel," embrace much that does not directly concern Israel (e. g., 2:1 f.; 2:4 f.); yet these extra-Israelite references do not invalidate the general force of the title.

J. M. P. Smith further objects: "The order of the parts

['The Burden of Nineveh, the Book of the Vision of Nahum the Elkoshite'] would have been exactly the reverse had they both been due to the prophet." This is an unfounded criticism, for while in some instances the author may be named first and the other specifications follow, no literary canon imperatively demands a stereotyped sequence; and evidence for the inversion of the usual order is found in the reversal of the normal "A Psalm of David" into "David's Psalm." (Ps. 40:1)

However, not only do the suggestions advanced to eliminate "the Burden of Nineveh" lack cogency, but one factor, at least, makes the phrase an essential part of the text. The city of Nineveh is mentioned for the first time in 2:9. Without the title, then, all the previous second- or third-person pronominal suffixes referring to Nineveh would have no expressed antecedent, and the reader would be left in suspense as to the identity of the doomed city. Even notable critics have accepted the integrity of the title.[21]

2. *The Alleged Alphabetic Acrostic, 1:2-10.* — With few exceptions commentators within the last fifty years have regarded 1:2-10 as a later addition, many asserting that it is a postexilic psalm prefixed to the genuine Nahum. The reasons advanced for this late dating are, first of all, the insistence that this section (and some include the following two verses, others the following six) were originally "an alphabetic eschatological psalm" (Sellin), an acrostic in which each verse began with a successive letter of the Hebrew alphabet. This, it is alleged, points to the years after the exile. (J. M. P. Smith)

This question of acrostical arrangement has been the sub-

---

[21] For example, Hitzig, *Die zwölf kleinen Propheten* (1938), p. 215: "No satisfactory reason for denying that the prophet himself wrote it (the title)." Wellhausen, *Die kleinen Propheten*, etc. (1898), p. 155: "No objection can be raised against the age of the title." See also Alfred Jepsen, *Nabi, soziologische Studien zur alttestamentlichen Literatur und Religionsgeschichte* (1934), p. 50: "No valid argument can be advanced against the originality of the superscriptions in Nahum and Obadiah."

ject of long and protracted study, in which, unfortunately, too much controversy centered in the debate concerning the priority of its discovery. The facts in the history of this discussion are these: Pastor G. Frohnmeyer of Württemberg appears to have been the first to call attention to the initial letters in 1:3-7.[22] He apparently made no claim for any exact complete acrostical arrangement, but is quoted as granting "the sequence of the letters to have an influence upon the arrangement of the prophet's thought." No detailed development of this scheme was made until 1880, when Bickell declared that originally the successive letters of the alphabet must have followed regularly and at the beginning of each distich. He did not risk carrying this scheme beyond v. 7. Two years later Bickell discussed the acrostic again. In 1886 he considered the verses in 1:7-10. In 1893, before the meeting of the Vienna philologists, he carried the acrostic to 1:10, and in addition he professed to find in the *'Āleph* and the *Bêth* distichs another acrostic, a cryptic abbreviation for Nineveh.

In the same year Gunkel extended the plan of the acrostic through to the end of the Hebrew alphabet, including 2:1, 3 in the new arrangement, despite the fact that Wellhausen had labeled these verses as interpolation. This provoked another contribution by Bickell, in which he extended his acrostical discovery, like Gunkel, to embrace the entire alphabet, although in detail the two arrangements offer striking differences. In 1895 Gunkel restated his position with some modifications and additions. In 1898 Wellhausen asserted that the acrostic could not be proved beyond 1:2-8 and branded the reconstructions of Bickell and Gunkel as "total failures." In 1900 Otto Happel, Roman Catholic priest in Kitzingen, issued *Der Psalm Nahum*, contending that the alphabetic sequence was to be found in 1:2—1:15, in which, sometimes following Bickell or Gunkel

---

[22] See Franz Delitzsch, *Biblischer Kommentar über die Psalmen* (1894), p. 115.

and sometimes striking out for himself, he formed a new alphabetic sequence from 'Āleph to Têth. In 1901 Arnold, in *Zeitschrift für die alttestamentliche Wissenschaft,* criticized Bickell and his work as "fantastic" and indicted his "eccentricities" and his treatment of Gunkel's efforts. He placed the statements of the two scholars side by side to show their fundamental divergences, accused them of repeated violations of Hebrew idiom or poetry, and declared: "In their eagerness to add one more to the alphabetic poems of the later Judaism they [Bickell and Gunkel] . . . decapitated a masterpiece of Hebrew literature." He then proceeded to emend the text of 1:1—2:3, dividing it into eight sections, four of which are calmly labeled as "the contributions of a later redactor, of little intelligence, resourcefulness and taste." He discovered "the distorted fragments of an alphabetic poem" in 1:2-10 and 12b and suggested this as the process by which the alphabetic fragments came into their present condition: When the redactor had "written down the title [of the Book of Nahum] he bethought himself of a fine poem of his own day descriptive of Yahweh's great power and this inevitable destruction of His enemies. This, he thought, would make an excellent introduction. Had his work been clean-cut, we should have agreed with him. But unfortunately he was none too familiar with the poem. Not only did he not remember all of it; he had forgotten the original order of what he retained, and even the fact that the poem was alphabetic had slipped his memory. He got as far as the second line of 'Āleph when" the alleged difficulties described by Arnold began. Finally "by devious paths he had arrived at Sāmekh, which he wrote down, and then for the life of him he could think of no more. He gave it up, and turned to the legitimate business of transcribing Nahum." Similarly, in principle, Pfeiffer writes: "A redactor living about the year 300 B.C. prefaced Nahum's superb ode, dating from the years immediately preceding the fall of Nineveh in 612, with an alphabetic psalm of his own time. Of this psalm he vaguely remembered the first part, substituting for the rest remarks of his own, some of which were Biblical quotations quoted from memory. . . . It is clear that he did not copy the alphabetic psalm from a manuscript but wrote it down as best he could from memory. He had not only forgotten the second part of this poem, but, being unconscious of the alphabetic arrangement of the lines, he paraphrased certain lines, thereby obliterating the original acrostic structure."

Today critical consensus limits the alleged acrostic to 1:2-10. Cf. Marti, Haupt, Staerk, Duhm, J. M. P. Smith, Sellin, and others.

The evidence in behalf of an original acrostic form is summarized by J. M. P. Smith: "The acrostic structure of 1:2-10 is too clearly apparent to be a subject of reasonable doubt. Eight of the lines as they stand in Ⓜ offer the desired initial letter, while four or five more are easily recovered by slight emendations and transpositions, some of which are necessary apart from all requirements of the acrostic. This fact is recognized."

This summary, however, does not state the case. Ⓜ does not offer the desired initial letter in eight cases. The actual sequence of initials is the following: *'Āleph* (v. 2); *Yôd* (v. 3); *Gimel* (v. 4); *Hē* (v. 5); *Lāmed* (v. 6); *Têth* (v. 7); *Waw* (v. 8); *Mêm* (v. 9); *Kaph* (v. 10). These basic facts should be noted concerning the sequence of initials in the nine verses:

1. Only five verses start with a consonant of the group *'Āleph* to *Têth.*

2. Four consonants in the group *'Āleph* to *Têth* are missing, namely, *Bêth, Dāleth, Zayin, Hêth.*

3. Four consonants, not embraced in the group *'Āleph* to *Têth,* are added, namely, *Yôd, Lāmed, Mêm, Kaph.*

4. Not a single instance of the proper alphabetic sequence of even two letters occurs.

5. Only two of the nine consonants are in the position of alphabetic order, namely, *'Āleph* in v. 2 and *Gimel* in v. 4.

6. Nor is there a general alphabetic progress, for in four of the total of eight successions a consonant of later alphabetic order precedes a consonant of prior alphabetic appearance.

It ought to be evident, therefore, that the text, as it stands, offers no evidence of alphabetic arrangement. Nor do the processes by which the missing initials are supplied, unwanted consonants elided, and incompatible order brought into alphabetic sequence, gain our confidence. The attempts at emendation are sometimes so violent, the transpositions so arbitrary and involved, that they condemn themselves. To restore the acrostical pattern, J. M. P. Smith, for example, introduces these radical changes in 1:2-10:

V. 2: The entire second line is omitted and, because it starts with a *Nûn,* placed after v. 9, "where it belongs alphabetically."

V. 3: The first part of the verse is branded as a gloss because it departs "from the alphabetic order." This verse should start with a *Bêth,* and since the first *Bêth* in the line is found in *besûphāh,* everything preceding that word is elided, although the Masoretic punctuation and the balanced parallelism of the verse make this second part begin not with *besûphāh* but with "Yahweh."

V. 4: After the *Gimel* "the acrostic calls for an initial *Dāleth.*" So a *Dāleth* must be found. Admittedly "it is quite clear that the opening word of the line was *'umlal,*" but the groundless supposition is advanced that "if a scribe depended largely upon his memory, not slavishly eying his copy, the resemblance in both form and meaning between *'umlal* and *dālal* [a questionable term which the acrosticians have drafted] might easily have occasioned their interchange." By thus assuming slip-shod copying, poor text reading, and reliance on memory, a dubious word is foisted on a text which is perfectly clear and emphatic as it stands.

V. 6: This verse calls for a *Zayin* in place of its initial *Lāmed*. Smith dogmatizes: "The key word in the acrostic is *za"mô*. Hence *liphnêy* must be transposed," although this involves a syntactical difficulty.

V. 7: The second part of this verse is to furnish the initial *Yôd*. The *Waw* before the *Yôd* is declared objectionable; hence it must be dropped.

V. 8: In this verse the acrostic demands a *Kaph*. Therefore the first two words are transposed to the end of v. 7, although this involves a clash in syntax and connection.

V. 9: *Lāmed* is the desired consonant here. Only one initial *Lāmed* appears in the verse, at the beginning of 9c. So this clause is torn from the end of the verse and prefixed at the beginning, because "the exigencies of the acrostic structure require the placing of this line here rather than where it is in Ⓜ."

V. 10: The acrostic theory calls for an initial *Mêm*. Consequently 9a is severed from its true connection and transposed to v. 10.

This *tour de force* is so arbitrary and the procedures followed by other advocates of acrosticism so divergent that the claim for an original alphabetical arrangement should be completely rejected.

The acrostic theory also suffers on other counts. The question immediately suggests itself: "How could the acrostic be lost?" The answer cannot be given by pointing to Psalms 9 and 10 and stating that they were originally acrostic and alphabetic. If the acrostic existed in this clear and definite form, only the most stolid scribe could have neglected to guard and perpetuate the evidence of its presence. The copyist is, therefore, charged with having written from memory, having read incorrectly, having forgotten his lines. But why attribute scribal stupidity to the recorders of this assumed acrostic and stronger eyes to the copyists who reproduced Lamentations 1—4, Psalms 34, 37, 111, 112, 119, 145, and other alphabetic sequences?

The majority of critics are satisfied with assuming that originally the acrostic embraced only half of the alphabet. Immediately this question demands answer: "Why an incomplete acrostic?" One of the most plausible explanations for the motif behind the alphabetic arrangement is the idea of completeness. As the writer exhausted the letters of the alphabet, so he exhausted his subject. If, then, the alphabetic initials symbolize completeness, an acrostic from 'Āleph only to Lāmed or Mêm would defeat its very purpose. The case for original alphabetism would be stronger, were there proof of the familiar twenty-two-letter sequence. No one has ever satisfactorily shown this completion, and only few have asserted its original existence, Bickell, Gunkel, Happel, v. Hoonacker, and Horst excepted, who seek alphabetic order also in 9-14. Most scholars are ready to concede that no regular, consecutive order can be found for the letters in the second half of the alphabet; but few will swing to the alternative extreme suggested by Arnold, who pictures the scribe as recalling a fine poem, yet forgetting the obtrusive fact that it was alphabetic, forgetting even its lines and reproducing it freely from memory, until he arrived at the impasse where "for the life of him he could think of no more" and "gave it up." Few will likewise follow Eissfeldt,[23] who seriously suggests that perhaps there was so little room on the roll that the copyist could use only the first part of the alphabetic psalm. He also maintains that perhaps the Lāmed line (v. 9) or better the misplaced Nûn line in v. 2 offered a suitable contact with the Book of Nahum and that he therefore stopped the acrostic at this place.

[23] *Einleitung in das Alte Testament* (1934), p. 463: "Then the question also suggests itself, Why was only the first half of the alphabetic psalm placed into (the text)? Perhaps — this would be a purely mechanical explanation — there was so little empty space on the roll in question that it did not permit the acceptance of the whole psalm. Or it seemed to the redactor that the L line (v. 9b) or the N line (v. 2b) was a good contact with the Book of Nahum, and for this reason he accepted the psalm only up till this point. But we do not get beyond conjectures!"

Duhm offers a similar explanation. He holds that a late owner of Nahum's prophecies wanted to write a psalm at the beginning of the book, but overestimated the empty space at the beginning of the roll and therefore could not use all of his psalm. He did manage, however, by crowding and writing between the lines of the genuine Nahum, to squeeze in the material up till the letter "Āyin.

Wellhausen, less specifically, believes that some later student of the text started to rearrange Nahum alphabetically, but encountered so much difficulty that he stopped in the middle of the alphabet.

Loeher [24] has another theory. He holds that at some later date, after Nahum's oracles had been completed, they were prefixed with an introduction. An alphabetic poem was chosen for this purpose, but only the first half was used, since that part alone suited Nahum's message, and the second part, whatever it might have been, was not regarded as appropriate. These and similar opinions are purely conjectural and are contradicted not only by the known accuracy in the copying of the OT but especially also by the statements of Scripture concerning their origin, purity, and preservation.

Nor do we find any occasion for the alphabetic arrangement. When did the OT writers resort to this sequence? Driver answers: "When the subject was one of a general character, that did not lend itself readily to logical development." [25] And Keil asserts: "This alphabetical structure . . . has remained confined to didactic songs and poems, whose subject matter is expressed in separate sentences, such as do not admit of being rounded off and treated exhaustively by an internal development and an organically arranged distribution of the succession of ideas." [26] Yet this introduction to the prophecies of Nahum is not so general that

[24] *Theologische Literaturzeitung* (1901), Spalte 37.

[25] Samuel Rolles Driver, *Introduction to the Literature of the O.T.* (1914), p. 368.

[26] Johann Friedrich Karl Keil, *Introduction to the O.T.* (1867), I, 446.

it presents no logical development. V. 2 describes the avenging fury of God. Vv. 3, 4, and 5 show His sweeping power, which can paralyze and destroy even the forces of nature. Therefore v. 6 declares the futility of resisting Him, while v. 7 emphasizes the hopeful safety offered by trust in divine power. In vv. 8 and 9 these principles are applied to Nineveh and Israel. What have we here if not sound, logical development that requires no aid of alphabetic order?

In summary, no evidence of acrosticism has been advanced, while its claims are vitiated by several weighty considerations: no satisfactory explanation is given for the incredible circumstance that the Hebrew copyist did not recognize the alphabetism which modern interpreters easily discern; no justification has been offered for the incomplete arrangement, restricted, as it is usually admitted, to the first half of the alphabet; no satisfactory occasion proposed for recourse to acrosticism. Why, then, claim an original alphabetic sequence? Even critical writers have asked themselves this question and have either assumed noncommittal attitudes or adopted the position here taken that 1:2-9 is not derived from an original acrostic.

Even if it were assumed that at one time an original acrostic, psalmlike poem existed from which the verses of Nahum had been freely reproduced without retention of rigid sequence, this in itself would be no proof that these introductory verses were non-Nahumic, of later origin. Just as well as any hypothesized editor, Nahum himself could have written this free rendition of the original version. The appropriateness of these lines at the beginning of the predictions against Nineveh should not be questioned. They answer the three questions uppermost in the minds of those who are to read the announcement of the dire calamity: First: Why will God destroy Nineveh? Vv. 2 and 3 ascribe this to the inevitableness of divine, retributive justice. Second: Can God destroy powerful Nineveh? Vv. 4-6 declare the vast omnipotence of His divine power. Third: What will happen to God's children when this consuming wrath flares high? V. 7 answers in assurance that God will prove Himself a Stronghold to those who trust Him. With these promises, the transition, vv. 8 and 9, easily leads over to the prophet's specific theme.

Critics like Horst have conceded that a poet of Nahum's ability certainly could have written these introductory verses and that in all likelihood the prophet himself added this introduction under the impress of events in 612 B.C. It should be borne in mind that the use of an alphabetical arrangement, even if it were demonstrable in the case of Nahum, would not in itself demand a later date. The Lamentations of Jeremiah, which was written soon after the destruction of Jerusalem, in 586—587 B.C., only slightly more than a half century after the date we now ascribe to Nahum, features the alphabetic order, and there is no reason to assume that this usage originated in Lamentations.

However, the prevalent attitude will countenance no association of Nahum with these initial verses. Having decreed prior acrosticism, it proceeds to assert that "the artificial acrostic form is also out of keeping with the vigorous and vital style of Nahum." This contention, besides involving an erroneous assumption, is built on the additionally fallacious theory that Nahum would not have employed an acrostic or adapted a modified form. The history of literature is replete with examples showing that brilliant poets have adopted acrostical arrangements. Because of the psalm-like character of these first verses, parallels in hymnody are particularly appropriate. Hailed as the queen of Lutheran chorales, Philip Nicolai's "Wie schön leuchtet der Morgenstern" offers acrostic initials designating "*W*ilhelm *E*rnst, *G*raf *u*nd *H*err *z*u *W*aldec." One of the best-beloved hymns of comfort, translated into many languages, is "Befiehl du deine Wege." No hackneyed writer penned these lines. They are from the pen of Paul Gerhardt, acclaimed "the greatest hymn writer of Germany, if not indeed of Europe." Yet this sacred song features an acrostical arrangement.

Evidences of acrostical arrangement and inclination are found in the Hellenistic writings of the Alexandrian age and in the Latin writers from the early days of Ennius and Plautus. The Renaissance poets of Italy, the early German and Slavic writers, Elizabethan poets, and more modern writers, like Edgar Allan Poe, featured the acrostic. No literary critics have objected that this form is not compatible with the vigorous style of these writers; yet this fallacious contention denies that Nahum was the author of 1:2-9.

It is possible, however, to go a step further. Suppose that these verses were originally acrostic, and suppose that they do not have the vigor and vitality of those parts usually conceded to Nahum; even this difference of style would not be a decisive argument against Nahum's authorship, for secular writers have often developed several styles, with differences markedly greater than those allegedly existing between the introduction and the body of Nahum. Scott's *Life of Napoleon* and his *Lady of the Lake;* Milton's *Paradise Lost* and his *Areopagitica;* Luther's "A Mighty Fortress" and his *Exposition of the Book of Genesis* — these and many other authors have prose and poetry styles which exhibit greater variances than that which is said to mark this initial psalmody and Nahum's subsequent prophecy.

If, therefore, as has been shown, there is no real evidence for original acrosticism; if it is possible by altering the text and changing the verse order in other prophetic sections to make acrostics which likewise never existed; if, even conceding theoretically and *argumenti causa* that Nah. 1:2 ff. may have been alphabetic, there is still no reason for questioning the Nahumic authorship and giving this introduction a late, postexilic date, it should·be clear that the arguments raised against the authenticity of these verses must fall.

3. *The Alleged Interpolations.* — Again, the authenticity of this section is attacked under the charge that it contains "only theological abstractions," that "the language and ideas here are

not those of the prophets, but those of the postprophetic, eschatological psalmists." This is an unmitigated error. The language
and ideas of this introduction, quite to the contrary, are those
of the prophets. Even a superficial survey reveals, verse after
verse, thoughts — and frequently phrases — exactly parallel to
those of the great prophets.

It has also been asserted that this section must be placed
into the later postexilic period because its "language is general
and contains no specific allusion to Nineveh" (Stonehouse).
This charge of "general" language and absence of reference to
the Assyrian capital is, of course, contradicted by the fact that
Nineveh is mentioned in the title and alluded to in subsequent
pronominal suffixes. Statements like these from Stonehouse show
the presumptive, arbitrary nature of higher criticism. He says:
"The fact that the section clearly serves a didactic purpose, calling
attention to the teaching underlying the announcement of Nineveh's overthrow and Judah's consequent deliverance — namely,
that Jehovah has regard for those (i. e., Israel) who seek refuge
in Him, and is full of wrath toward those who (like the Assyrians)
oppose themselves to Him — betrays the age of reflection rather
than of active prophecy. What concerned Nahum was the announcement of Nineveh's fall, not the indication of the lesson
it might have for his people and later generations." On what
grounds can the premise be proved that Nahum was not concerned with the lesson that Nineveh's fall might have for
his people?

Likewise regarded as interpolations are vv. 12, 13 of the
first chapter and vv. 1, 3 of the second. The charge against these
verses is that they artificially balance "the foregoing judgment
upon the heathen with an announcement of deliverance for the
people of God" (Stonehouse). It is asserted that 1:12, 13,
together with 2:1, 3, "look back upon a long period of suffering
and forward to the dawn of a new era. They anticipate the
immediate cessation of Judah's afflictions with the concomitant

entrance of the Messianic era of peace and power. It is questionable whether any portion of the postexilic age was wholly devoid of such hopes. Suffering was the common lot of Israel all through this period. As the vassal of one or another of the great world powers, her pride [sic] was continually humbled and she was as continually looking and longing for deliverance. At times, the Messianic hope burned brightly, e. g., in the days of Zerubbabel. These verses probably reflect some such period as that when the world-power of the day seemed to be tottering to its fall and the hopes of faithful Israel were kindled to fresh vigour. The fall of Nineveh, to which Nahum confidently looked forward, can hardly have occasioned such vivid and · certain confidence of immediate relief for Israel as these verses reflect; for at that time Assyrian power in Syria had long come to an end and Judah was under the heel of Egypt." (Stonehouse)

In their context these verses in no way justify such inferences and conclusions. They simply say that the overthrow of Nineveh in the height of its power is to assure Judah that it will never again suffer affliction at the hands of this despot nation. Destruction is so positive that the prophet summons Judah to begin celebrating its festivals.

Nothing in these verses even remotely suggests an era of power or of political might such as was erroneously attributed to the Messianic reign. Not a line depicts Israel as continually humbled by one or another of the great world powers. Instead, Israel is portrayed as continually harassed by Nineveh. The objection that in Nahum's day "Assyrian power in Syria had long come to an end and Judah was under the heel of Egypt" is based on a patent misunderstanding of Nahum's date. If the book was written shortly before 606 B. C., as most radical critics held until 1923, it would be true that Israel was under Egyptian dominion. Now, however, with the time of the city's destruction definitely established as 612 B. C. and the inferential data pointing to a considerably earlier date for the authorship of the prophecy, we must place Nahum and his book in the years when Syria and Palestine were under Assyrian rule. That Judah was dominated and oppressed by Assyria during the reign of Esarhaddon (684—668 B. C.) and during the reign of Ashurbanipal (668 to 626 B. C.) is an uncontroverted historical fact. These verses, therefore, fit Nahum's situation admirably. Writing while Judah suffered under the Assyrians' oppression (1:13), when it had been afflicted by their tyranny (1:12), the prophet promises that the Ninevite Belial will be utterly cut off and that he shall no more pass through Judah. — How arbitrary is J. M. P. Smith's assertion that these verses "seem to presuppose the exile; and they concern themselves with the upbuilding of Zion, while Nahum's interest is in the fall of Nineveh!" We search the prophet in vain for any indication of a captivity or the longing for a return. Not a syllable shows any concern with the upbuilding of Zion, which is not even mentioned in the entire book!

Other arguments for the removal of 12b, 13, 15; 2:2 are furnished by Stonehouse. He holds that these verses are addressed, not to Assyria but to Judah. Thus "they break the original connection and are certainly an after-insertion." — Concerning the real address of the verses see the discussion in the subsequent commentary. Stonehouse declares that the phraseology (cf. Is. 52:7) and the announcement encouraging Judah to keep her feasts "almost certainly indicate that the historical background is that of the exile." But the Assyrian tyranny could be so strong that Israel could not celebrate its festivals and that it would welcome the news of deliverance which came when the messenger appeared on the mountains on the horizon.

If these verses are removed as later additions, where in the entire book is the element of comfort? It was Nahum's purpose in recording his prophecies to strengthen the hearts of God's children. Every prophet has this goal. Why rob Judah of the assurance that the Almighty will afflict them no more by means of the Assyrian scourge (v. 12)? Why take away the promise

that Judah's yoke and burden will be removed in the destruction
of Nineveh (v. 13), or deprive the nation of the pledge that
a messenger of peace and good tidings would bring assurance
that solemn festivals could be kept and sacred vows per-
formed? (2:1)

If this section were postexilic and spurious, it could be
reasonably expected that the language would be parallel to that
employed, for example, by Haggai, Zechariah, Malachi. A study
of these sections, however, reveals the complete absence of
Aramaisms.

Another difficulty arises when vv. 12, 13 and 2:1 are
eliminated. Since part of the title in v. 1 and most of vv. 2-10
have been removed by most critics as later and spurious, only
vv. 11 and 14 are retained from the body of the entire chapter.
These two verses, when thus isolated, form no acceptable beginning to the prophecy; they have no real connection; and they
lack all transition to the subsequent context.[27] Thus the willful
emendations of metricists and literary reconstructionists require
us to assume, without any cogent explanation, that some scribe
(or scribes) deliberately removed twelve and one half of the
fifteen verses now embraced in the first chapter and substituted
an incomplete and imperfect acrostic. Why or how OT scribes
removed these verses has never been answered acceptably. The
facts transmitted to us concerning the reproduction of the text
certainly offer no justification for procedures as radical and senseless as those demanded by these extreme excisions.

Verse 3 of chapter 2 has frequently been termed a later
postexilic addition. Moses Buttenwieser[28] declares: "Nahum 2:3,

[27] John Merlin Powis Smith, *The International Critical Commentary,
A Critical and Exegetical Commentary on Micah, Zephaniah, Nahum*, etc. (1911),
p. 269, tries to explain this fragmentary beginning in this way: "The genuine
Nahum first appears in 1, 11. 14; 2, 1. 3. This, however, is scarcely to be accepted
as the original opening of the prophecy. It is altogether too abrupt and broken.
The probability is that the acrostic has displaced some material which formed the
original beginning of the prophecy."

[28] Moses Buttenwieser, *The Psalms* (1938), p. 236.

'The Lord will surely restore the vine Jacob even as the vine Israel, for ravagers have ravaged them and destroyed the vines' . . . is an Exilic addition to the pre-Exilic prophecy of Nahum. From the fact that this verse of Nahum is modeled after Psalm 80 and that 'Behold, upon the mountains the feet of him that brings good tidings, that publishes peace!' of the preceding verse is copied from Is. 52:7, it may further be concluded that the addition dates from the closing year of the Exile, that either it was, like Isaiah, chapter 13, written when the news of Cyrus' invasion of Babylonia reached Palestine or, like Is. 21:1-10, when some short time later the news of the fall of Babylon arrived. Now the interpolator's declaration, 'The Lord will truly restore the vine Jacob [that is, Judah] even as the vine Israel,' shows that he understood Psalm 80, his model, as imploring God that He restore Judah together with the Joseph tribes." This is a glaring instance of highhanded procedure. Note the assumption involved in this position! First of all, the text is arbitrarily altered. In the second place, Buttenwieser asserts that Nah. 2:3 is based on Ps. 80. This again is pure assumption. Nahum may with equal propriety have secured his picture of the vine from Is. 5 or Jer. 12:10, or he may have used the picture without any borrowing. Likewise the dating of Ps. 80 as exilic is without decisive foundation. Even radical interpreters like Gunkel refuse to label the psalm as exilic. In the third place, the verse says nothing about the restoration of "Judah together with the Joseph tribes."

Verses 18 and 19 of chapter 3 are regarded as extraneous by Wellhausen and other interpreters.[29] The first count on which they are labeled as later additions is that they "seem to reflect the fall of Nineveh" (J. M. P. Smith). However, these verses cannot have been written after the city fell, for the verbs in the

29 Also by Eissfeldt, Sellin, Marti, and, in a somewhat hesitant manner, J. M. P. Smith. Partially also by Duhm and Stonehouse. Note, however, that Stonehouse says of this section: "There can be no question of the authenticity." The verses "bear throughout the stamp of originality, and in content correspond in every respect to what, according to the title, purports to be the message of Nahum."

perfect are simply prophetic, and the projection into the future is assured by the one imperfect. The use of the prophetic perfect is abundantly illustrated in previous verses (e. g., 2:14; 3:5, 6); and the interchange of this prophetic tense with the imperfect is, of course, a frequent syntactical device. See Ges., Gra., 106 n. Even J. M. P. Smith has to admit: "It cannot be said with certainty, of course, that Nahum is not here in imagination placing himself at some point in the future, whence he looks back upon Nineveh's ruin. This is a common enough method of procedure with the prophets. Hence, the question of the date of vv. 18, 19 must remain open."

The second charge on which the two closing verses are labeled as glosses alleges that they depart from "the strophic norm of their context." If every verse which refused to comply with the pattern demanded for Nahum by the metricists were elided, much of the book would be eliminated. It is scientifically presumptuous for J. M. P. Smith to say: "Strophic symmetry demands the closing of the poem with v. 17, where an eight-line strophe ends, thus balancing the eight-line strophe with which the poem began." This poem, ch. 3, does not begin with an eight-strophe line in the Ⓜ. It is octostrophic only after Smith cuts out the sections which to him are metrically difficult. Nor is the section which he suggests as the conclusion (vv. 14-17) made up of eight strophes. This pattern is secured only after lines are elided as marginal notes, dittography, etc. Besides, why must a poem that starts with a strophe of eight lines end similarly?

Again, vv. 18 and 19 have been set aside as spurious because they are regarded as a "gratuitous addition." Sellin declares that after the vivid description of Nineveh's demise these verses are not only superfluous but quite jejune. Such criticism is prompted only by bias, for the material in these verses is predominantly new. The address to Assyria's king is graphic. The clapping of hands at the news of Nineveh's finis is dramatic. The question with which the chapter and the book close is emphatic. These more elaborately constructed final verses may be compared with the conclusion found in some psalms (e. g., 2:12) as in some prophetic books (e. g., Amos 9:14, 15; Hos. 14:9); for any unusual length, repetition, or form in the last verses may be intentional, to help create an elaborate finale.

If vv. 18 and 19 be eliminated, the prophecies are deprived of certain remarkable statements. The book would close without saying anything about the final scattering of the Assyrian people in the mountains and about the joy with which the news of the city's end would be greeted.

If the prophecy were to close with v. 17, it would end with the relatively unimportant statement that the high Assyrian officials are like locusts, who flee when the sun rises, and "their place is not known. Where are they?" If it ends with v. 19, as it does, it concludes with the question: "Upon whom hath thine evil not passed over continually?" This is manifestly the more forceful conclusion, particularly also because it stresses the moral reason for Nineveh's fall — one of the paramount lessons of the entire book.

The authenticity of other sections has been similarly assailed. The only section in which drastic elimination of entire verses has not been demanded is 2:4-14. Even here, of course, expressions within the individual verses have been radically altered.[30]

In summary, it may be stated that every verse in the entire three chapters has been assailed by some important critical writer as non-Nahumic. Most modern interpreters remove at least one third of the verses as spurious glosses. In the sections regarded

[30] Sellin, *Das Zwölfprophetenbuch*, p. 373, denies the authenticity of the entire section 3:8-17. He insists: "True, one can hardly say with certainty that the whole makes an original unit." His objections to the Ⓜ are considered in the subsequent treatment of the individual verses. Eissfeldt, *Einleitung in das Alte Testament*, p. 461, extends the question of the authenticity to the entire third chapter and seems to assume three component parts for 3:1-19. He says: "With 3:1 a second 'Woe' commences, and it can hardly be ascertained whether chapter 3 is to be regarded as a unit, or rather whether it must be divided into three units."

as authentic every verse has been subjected to drastic alteration, emendation, addition, change of words or phrase order. In this way some recent exegetical works change at least two thirds of the entire prophecy. These extremes mark the fatal weakness of such radical exegesis, showing both the arbitrary nature of its *modus operandi* and the unsatisfactory force of its conclusions. No other literature on earth has suffered by such arbitrary excisions and additions. Significantly enough — and this is one of the strongest defenses for the position taken in this commentary — the Book of Nahum, when read as preserved in the Ⓜ, presents a poem, in the Hebrew sense, which for vividness of presentation, order of development, and force of prophetic forecast stands unexcelled in all literature.

THE DOCTRINES OF NAHUM'S PROPHECIES

The Indictment of Nahum's Doctrine

The prevailing critical attitude toward Nahum's message brands his prophecies as inferior or even insignificant. "He is the least attractive of the prophets; in the history of religion he holds an inferior place" (Bewer). He is "a representative of the old, narrow and shallow prophetism" (J. M. P. Smith). "Nahum is a worse prophet than Zephaniah, with less conscience and insight" (G. A. Smith). "In a religious and prophetic sense the contents of the book are not important" (Cornill). "There is nothing specifically religious in this exultant outburst of joy over the inevitable downfall of the Assyrian Empire" (Pfeiffer). The climax of protest is reached in "No right-minded person can approve of his sentiments" (Cadman).[31]

---

[31] See J. A. Bewer, *The Literature of the Old Testament in Its Historical Development*, p. 139. J. M. P. Smith, *The International Critical Commentary, A Critical and Exegetical Commentary on Micah, Zephaniah, Nahum*, etc., p. 281. G. A. Smith, *The Book of the Twelve Prophets* (1929), II, 89 f. Carl Heinrich Cornill, *The Prophets of Israel* (1904), p. 78. Robert H. Pfeiffer, *Introduction to the Old Testament* (1941), p. 595. Samuel Parkes Cadman, *The Prophets of Israel* (1933), pp. 101, 102.

The Charge that Nahum Ignores Israel's Sins

A frequently repeated indictment charges Nahum with ignoring the sins of Israel. Judah's sins are implied, however, in 1:12, where God comforts His people: "I have afflicted thee; not will I afflict thee again." If the interpretation suggested in the commentary for 2:3 be adopted and the translation accepted: "Yahweh hath cut off the pride of Jacob, as the pride of Israel," the indictment of Judah's sins is plain and unqualified, for this statement implies a past judgment executed on Judah (Jacob) because of its "pride," a visitation which recalled the punishment of arrogant Israel (the Northern Kingdom). This explanation, far from glossing over Judah's sins, places it on the same level with sin-destroyed Israel.

Besides, the introduction, 1:2-7, shows that God "will assuredly not leave the guilty unpunished," including, of course, the wicked in Judah and Israel. When the prophet asks: "Before His anger who can stand? And who can maintain himself in the burning fire of His fury?" (1:6), Israel is in no wise excluded. The mention of Yahweh's blasting, withering power in connection with Bashan, Carmel, and Lebanon (1:4), all Israelite locations, indicates the same universal code of ethics which marked particularly the eighth-century prophets.

The reason Israel's sins are not presented in the same scathing denunciation that characterized some of Nahum's predecessors is not that the book was allegedly written after 621 B. C. and the supposed discovery of Deuteronomy as a *pia fraus,* but simply that the prophet has one all-consuming theme, the destruction of Nineveh. We have seen that Nahum's prophecy was written long before Josiah's reform. If the recession of Israel's sins into the background is a mark of prophetic inferiority, oracles like those of Obadiah, Habakkuk, or Jonah, and on the same principle even New Testament books, Philippians, for example, must be similarly branded. The focused point of view maintained from the beginning to the end of Nahum's prediction is that

Nineveh has deserved her fate, that her collapse is the punishment for her grave moral lapses and not a mere triumph of Judah over heathendom.

Similarly, over against the parallel charge that the prophet does not make "the coming of deliverance dependent upon an improvement of the people" and that Nahum thus stands in opposition to his predecessors,[32] it must be kept in mind that Nahum's theme is the destruction of Nineveh, not the future of Israel. To demand that his presentation follow an outline current a century before his time for situations fundamentally different from the theme of his utterances is to place an unwarranted stricture on the prophet's freedom of expression.

The Charge that Nahum Shows Gloating Hatred and Malicious Joy

Another frequently repeated accusation charges Nahum with cruel gloating over the destruction of Nineveh and that the whole prophecy is the product of "hatred and malicious joy." [33]

However, many parallels in the Major and the Minor Prophets, before and after Nahum, exhibit rejoicing over the defeat of similar tyranny. The emotions of the ages are repeatedly mirrored in the OT when its writers, as the voices of oppressed humanity, exultantly greet the dawn of deliverance. The prophet says nothing more, and perhaps considerably less than, for example, Amos does in his denunciation of six foreign nations (1—2) or than Isaiah in his eleven chapters (13—23) devoted to the prophetic condemnation of heathen powers.

Withal we search in vain for the hatred of "malicious joy." Nahum was not moved solely by exultation over the prospect of Nineveh's defeat. On the contrary, a very definite moral basis for his indictment may be found in the fact that he specifically denounces bloodshed, plunder, and political tyranny. What exag-

---

[32] G. A. Smith, p. 280.

[33] Willy Otto Alexander Staerk, *Ausgewählte Poetische Texte*, etc. (1908), II, 170: *"Aus Hasz und wilder Schadenfreude ist die ganze Dichtung . . . geboren."*

geration and misrepresentation in Staerk's charge that "Nahum's fantasies revel in the atrocities of the destruction"![34] Have all these disparagers of the prophet overlooked the significant facts that the first person plural is never used in the entire book and that the first person singular is employed only of God, never of Nahum or Israel? The book is the most objective of all the prophets. It expresses not only Nahum's personal feelings but also the attitude of his people.

The Charge that Nahum Is the Prophet of Incipient Judaism

Bertholet,[35] followed wholly or in part by others, and qualifiedly by Sellin,[36] shows the extremes to which tendential interpretation may resort, particularly under the influence and dictates of *religionsgeschichtliche* reconstructions. He makes Nahum the prophet of incipient Judaism because his predictions allegedly betray a proud disdain of the heathen, represent Judah as righteous in a world of unrighteousness, and thus pave the way for a separation of Israelites from non-Israelites.

Only a misreading of Nahum's three chapters can lead to these inferences. The outlook of the prophet is international. Nineveh is doomed not only because she has oppressed Israel, but also because she has terrorized the world. Nahum, of course, writes for his countrymen and contemporaries, as every prophet does; yet his indictment of Nineveh for its persecution of Judah is subordinated to the charges that Nineveh has sold *"nations* through her harlotries and *peoples* through her witchcrafts" (3:4); that her wickedness has passed "continually" over all nations (3:19). While Nineveh's downfall ends oppression for

---

34 Op. cit., pp. 179, 180: "Nahum and his circles have learned nothing from God's revelation in history. . . . With evident delight his fantasy gloats over the scenes of horror to be enacted at the conquest of Nineveh, and he feasts his eyes on the pictures of human suffering."

35 Alfred Bertholet, *Die Stellung der Israeliten und der Juden zu den Fremden* (1896), pp. 105 ff.

36 Sellin, *Das Zwölfprophetenbuch*, p. 316.

Judah, it assures deliverance to the rest of the tyrannized lands; for Yahweh proclaims: "I will show *nations* thy nakedness and *kingdoms* thy shame" (3:5). The prolog (1:2-7) is the introductory evidence of the prophet's international outlook, and the following verses repeatedly show that Nahum is not a proto-Pharisee gloating in arrogant nationalism over the downfall of a Gentile nation; he is rather a seer of God who declares that the haughty city has decreed its own destruction because of its moral corruption, its oppression of Judah and other nations, its violence, bloodshed, lies, deceits, and, above all, its rejection of God. Alfred Jepsen writes: "It would certainly be too hasty to conclude that the 'Nabis' left the moral law out of consideration. No reason exists for this assumption. Rather do the reproaches with which Nahum and Habakkuk charge Nineveh and the Chaldaeans, show that they have a sharp feeling for the violation of the moral law. Robbery and murder, harlotry and ensnaring constitute Nineveh's wanton offense, in addition to the basic sin that she planned evil against Jahweh (2:13; 3:1, 4; 1:11). . . . Always, however, rebellion against Jahweh, rejection of His Word, is the real sin from which everything else follows." [37]

The Charge that Nahum Is a False Prophet

Some regard Nahum as a patriot rather than a prophet, thus identifying him with Hananiah (Jer. 28), the four hundred opponents of Micaiah ben-Imlah (1 Kings 22:6 ff.), and the so-called false prophets in general. Marti charges: "Nahum is a precursor of those 'false' patriotic prophets, against whom Jeremiah later battled so vehemently." [38] J. M. P. Smith arbitrarily groups Nahum with the false prophets, ascribes doctrinaire attitudes to him, and assumes: "For such prophets [as Nahum] the relation between Yahweh and His nation Israel was indissoluble.

---

[37] Alfred Jepsen, *Nabi, soziologische Studien zur alttestamentlichen Literatur und Religionsgeschichte* (1934), p. 206.

[38] Karl Marti, *Dodekapropheton,* in *Kurzer Handkommentar zum Alten Testament* (1903), p. 306.

Yahweh might become angered at His people and give them over temporarily into the power of the foe. But He could no more wholly abandon them than a mother could desert her child. The obligation upon Israel was to be loyal to Yahweh as He was loyal to her; to eschew all foreign cults; to perform the cultus of Yahweh with zealous adherence to all of its requirements; and to conform to the traditional customs and ethics of the community. The possibility that new occasions might teach new duties, that the advancing civilization with its more complex life might render the old usages and laws inadequate, and that Yahweh might care more for full justice and overflowing mercy than for the blood of bulls and goats had not been realized by them. The teaching that for a lack of fundamental, ethical qualities Yahweh was intending to bring destruction upon His nation was branded by them as treason both to Israel and to Yahweh. Patriotism and religion combined in requiring the belief that Yahweh was able and willing to deliver His people out of every danger. Never could He suffer the adherents of other gods to triumph permanently over His own people. Never could the land of Judah and the temple of Yahweh be desecrated by being abandoned to the possession of the heathen. Nor could insult and injury to Yahweh and His people be allowed by Him to go unavenged. To men of such a way of thinking, the prospect of the downfall of Nineveh would bring a joy without alloy. The prophecy of Nahum is a faithful transcript of the thoughts and feelings of a prophet with such a point of view." [39]

Every statement in this code of false-prophet principles which higher criticism has ascribed to Nahum is contradicted by the book itself. The prophet knows nothing of an indissoluble relation "between Yahweh and His nation Israel." He does not even mention this union, but he does say that while God is "a Stronghold in the day of affliction" (1:7), He is "a Reserver

[39] *The International Critical Commentary. A Critical and Exegetical Commentary on Micah, Zephaniah, Nahum,* etc. (1911), pp. 281 f.

of wrath for His adversaries" (1:2), including Israel. In not a single syllable does Nahum teach that God "could no more wholly abandon them [His people] than a mother could desert her child." The words of Nahum warn: "Yahweh . . . will assuredly not leave *the guilty* unpunished" (1:3), whoever they are. As God's messenger he knows nothing of conforming "to the traditional customs and ethics of the community." There is similarly not a syllable of foundation in the text for the objection that the prophet has not realized "that Yahweh might care more for full justice and overflowing mercy than for the blood of bulls and goats." The fact that Nahum does not pronounce his conviction on this score — as he does not voice his opinion on a hundred other subjects — is an argument from silence and could be employed repeatedly against portions of the New Testament with the same lack of force. Were the prophet guided by this "patriotism," we certainly should be able to find evidence of his obsession, references to the injustice his country had suffered. As a matter of record, however, Nahum mentions Judah only once by name, and he insists that Nineveh will be destroyed because of its rebellion against Yahweh, the social injustices, the inhumanities, and the repeated cruelties it has inflicted on other nations as well as Judah.

Similarly every reference in J. M. P. Smith's critical disparagement of this book springs from what the author does not say in the compass of three short chapters. What proof can be found in the book for this alleged teaching: "Never could the land of Judah and the temple of Yahweh be desecrated by being abandoned to the possession of the heathen"? what evidence that "Yahweh is willing and able to deliver His people out of every danger"?

The associating of Nahum with the "false prophets" is entirely spurious; for if he who predicted the doom of Nineveh is classified with those who falsely proclaimed security instead of downfall, then Isaiah and Jeremiah, Amos and Hosea, and others exhibit similar tendencies, for each of these proclaimed the collapse of world powers. Besides, nothing in Nahum's oracles would lull his own people into carnal security, a characteristic of the false prophets (Jer. 6:14; 8:11), nor confirm Israel in its sins, causing it to forget Yahweh's name (Is. 56:10; Jer. 23:27). The emphatic warnings in Nahum's oracles against evil (wherever or whenever it occurs and by whomever it may be committed) are the expressions of objective truth which never mark the pseudo prophets. Finally, unfailing evidence of the false seer is the professionalizing of his office, the desire for personal gain (Micah 3:11). He seeks to support the wicked and oppress the righteous (Ezek. 13:19-21). He practices gross sins. "They commit adultery and walk in lies. They strengthen also the hands of evildoers" (Jer. 23:14). "They have committed villainy in Israel and have committed adultery with their neighbors' wives and have spoken lying words in My name" (Jer. 29:23). These characteristics are foreign to Nahum.

Caustic criticism has forgotten that the forty-seven short verses of Nahum's prophecies are "the burden of Nineveh." The small book is treated as though it were a compendium of theology, and without any basis in the prophet's own utterances detailed theological opinion is ascribed to him on subjects on which he has not expressed himself.

The Charge that Nahum Is Opposed to Other Prophets

Another count on which Nahum's doctrinal content suffers indictment is the charge that his attitudes clash with the utterances of other prophets. His whole position, it is said, contradicts the position of Zephaniah, who also predicted the fall of Nineveh. The assertion is made that while Zephaniah unsparingly denounces the wickedness of the mistress city on the Tigris, he is also emphatic in raising his voice against Israel's sins, while Nahum completely ignores these. It has been shown, however, that Nahum in no way exempts Israel or condones its wickedness.

The emphasis on national delinquency which Zephaniah features is due to the fact that his oracles are not characterized by a specific focus on Nineveh. He indicts also Phoenicia, Philistia, Canaan, Moab, Ammon, Ethiopia, and Assyria; for Zephaniah's central theme is God's judgment on all nations, including Judah. That Nahum's message is essentially God's judgment on Nineveh does not put Zephaniah and Nahum in opposition. Two prophets may write on two different subjects, employ individual phraseology and personal point of focus; yet they may be thoroughly united in their basic convictions. Why must we demand that all sacred writers feature the same subject and treat it in the same way? Such strictures are placed on no other literature.

Nahum is also pitted against the prophet Jeremiah. Thus J. M. P. Smith writes: "The contrast between the messages of Nahum and that of Jeremiah, his contemporary, is striking. To the prophet of larger vision and deeper insight, the event which filled Nahum's entire range of vision, was of relatively slight importance. The passing of the Assyrian dominion is not even mentioned by Jeremiah, nor does the name of Nineveh appear once in his utterances. The two men belonged to different religious and political parties. If Nahum was not in active opposition to Jeremiah, he was at least indifferent to his efforts. Instead of grieving over the sin of Judah and striving with might and main to warn her of the error of her ways that she might turn and live, Nahum was apparently content to lead her in a jubilant celebration of the approaching death of Assyria. Jeremiah was too overwhelmed by sorrow and alarm for his own people to obtain any solace from the misfortunes of another, which could bring no relief for the desperate situation of Judah." [40] This

---

[40] John Merlin Powis Smith, *Prophecy and the Prophet in Ancient Israel* (1923), p. 114. For his restatement of the same point of view and for similarly unwarranted conclusions see his *The Prophets and Their Times* (1925), p. 125. But Sellin admits, *Zwölfprophetenbuch*, p. 358: "As certainly as there is a deep-rooted difference between Nahum and his contemporary [!] Jeremiah, it has been wrong to construct a direct contrast between him and all other genuine 'Yahweh-prophecy!'"

is a typical instance of misstatement and misdirected conclusion. Smith asserts that Jeremiah "had nothing to say upon the subject of Assyria's overthrow"; but he overlooks Jer. 50:18, where the prophet specifically refers to the overthrow of Assyria. Moreover, he predicts this destruction in much the same way as Nahum does, ascribing it to God's punitive justice, as a punishment for the cruelties inflicted on Israel. Since Jeremiah wrote much later than Nahum, his was not the burden of Nineveh, but the burden of Jerusalem and subsequently the burden of Babylon. The assertion that Nahum and Jeremiah were contemporaries and that the prophet of Nineveh was opposed or indifferent to the prophet of Jerusalem is higher critical fiction. It should also be borne in mind that Jeremiah's attitude toward Judah and its sins varied in the degree of its intensity. After the Josianic reform his remarks were tempered, and only when Jehoiakim discarded the reform was Jeremiah's denunciation sweeping and unsparing.

Marti issues this similar indictment: "Nahum speaks exclusively of Nineveh and the destruction of the Assyrian Empire. In no way does it enter his mind that Jahweh Himself stood behind the Assyrians, as Jeremiah and his predecessors believed. On the contrary, he finds the cause for the destruction of Nineveh in the disaster which the Assyrians secretly planned against Jerusalem. That the Assyrians administer Jahweh's punishment on the godless nation, Judah, is completely forgotten, just as not a single word points to the sins of the people of Judah. Not only the purpose of Nahum's prophecy is totally different, but also his whole attitude is unlike that of a Jeremiah or of his predecessors. This appears most clearly in the estimate of Jerusalem's value. According to Jeremiah Jerusalem deserved destruction. According to Nahum the outrage planned against Zion is an offense which precipitates Nineveh's fall." [41]

Each assertion in this indictment is either patently incorrect or misdirected. First of all, Nahum does not speak "exclusively

[41] Karl Marti, *Das Dodekapropheton* (1904), p. 305.

of Nineveh"; his oracles are directed in comfort also to Judah (1:9, 12b, 13; 2:1). In the second place, Marti's contention: "In no way does it enter his [Nahum's] mind that Jahweh Himself stood behind the Assyrians," is an unjustified overstatement. Even critics should hesitate to declare what can enter a prophet's mind. Nahum may have proclaimed much more to his people than the message contained in the short compass of these forty-seven verses. Besides 1:12 ("I afflicted thee; not will I afflict thee again"), which seems to refer to the suffering endured by Judah in Sennacherib's invasion, directly ascribes affliction to God. In the third place, Nahum, delineating Nineveh's end, need not picture the city as Yahweh's agent; for Nineveh served this purpose in the past, when it punished Israel and Judah. Now the Assyrian capital is to be destroyed because of its excessive cruelty, rapacity, and tyranny. For that punishment God has another agent, the assailants of the city. It is altogether unjustified to demand that every prophet who mentions Assyria — in whatever role it may be cast — must picture it as a divine agency. In the fourth place, Marti patently is wrong in stating that Jeremiah believed "Jahweh Himself stood behind the Assyrians." Jeremiah does not refer to Nineveh or Assyria in connection with Judah's suffering. In the fifth place, Marti is incorrect in maintaining that Nahum traces Nineveh's collapse exclusively to the evil "which the Assyrians secretly planned against Jerusalem." Nahum does not even mention Jerusalem; but he does show that the Assyrian metropolis is doomed because it planned evil against Yahweh (1:11), because it is a bloody city (3:1), and because it has enslaved God's people. (1:13)

Nahum is similarly placed in opposition to Isaiah by Duhm.[42] He maintains that whereas Isaiah recognizes Assyria as Yahweh's instrument, Nahum regards Ashur as the inveterate foe of Yahweh and His people. But Isaiah and Nahum view the Assyrian Empire at different times and therefore in different roles.

[42] Bernhard Laward Duhm, *Israels Propheten* (1916), p. 200.

Even Isaiah himself quotes God as declaring both: "O Assyrian, the rod of Mine anger, and the staff in their hand is Mine indignation" (Is. 10:5), and "through the voice of the Lord shall the Assyrian be beaten down" (Is. 30:31). Yahweh may indeed use an enemy of His people for divine purposes. — Moreover, a comparison of Nahum with Isaiah emphasizes parallel presentation and similarities of thought. Isaiah speaks of Assyrian pride and idolatry, predicting its defeat and pillage and employing the figures of thorns and fires, which vividly recall Nahum's predictions (Is. 10:5-19). Isaiah, like Nahum, foretells that the defeat of Assyria removes the yoke from God's people. (Is. 14:25)

In all these attempts to establish contradiction between Nahum and other prophets, the obvious fact is overlooked that the ancient seers, as modern writers do, may view the same theme or concept from different angles and that variety of presentation does not presuppose mutually exclusive theological principles. It is just as unwarranted to place Nahum's short, specifically directed prophecy denouncing Nineveh in opposition to Jeremiah's or Isaiah's large and comprehensive oracles with their varied purposes, as it would be to infer that one sermon on the Nativity and another on Christ's substitutionary death are inconsistent or to maintain that the short Letter to Philemon was written by an apostolic mind ignorant of the great issues in the Epistle to the Romans.

Much more stress must be laid on the unity and harmony which exist in all prophetic writings. The emphasis which Nahum places on the existence of God, His control of all human affairs, His worldwide influence, His power, His justice, His hatred of sin, His mercy; the sacred seer's reiteration of the close connection between national welfare and national morality — do not these themes pervade other books of Scripture? Not only does Nahum feature the same thoughts as the other prophets, but he employs the same themes, sometimes almost the same words, which they frequently used. Even critics have conceded that Nahum's doctrinal presentation agrees with that of his predecessors. Even Stonehouse comes to an essential agreement with our position in these words: "To sum up, then, we believe that a careful consideration of Nahum's prophecy will tend to show that he was an ethical prophet; that he was a prophet of Jehovah in the sense that Amos, Isaiah, and Jeremiah were; that there is no indication that he did not share their religious aspirations and beliefs; and that any attempt to bring him into essential opposition to Jeremiah cannot be successfully maintained."

The Charge that Nahum Reflects Pan-Babylonian Eschatology

Under the leadership of J. F. H. Gunkel a trend of interpretation developed which sought to connect certain utterances in Nahum's book with the Babylonian creation story, *Enûma ēlish.* In 1895 Gunkel published his *Schöpfung und Chaos in Urzeit und Endzeit,* containing a compendium of Old and New Testament passages, which allegedly reflect the primitive Babylonian cosmological representations of Enlil and Tiamat engaged in mortal combat. Even to the careful reader, a thoughtful study of Nahum's text fails to bring any indications of such primeval conflict, yet Gunkel and pan-Babylonianists generally find traces of Akkadian gigantomachy, e. g., in 1:4: "He rebuketh the sea, and He drieth it up."

First of all, Gunkel asks: "How is the mention of the sea to be explained?" He assumes that this cannot be classified with the so-called Sinai theophanies, but must be associated with an ancient legend in which "Yahweh certainly had something to do with the sea." We must go back, he insists, to an old storm manifestation in which Yahweh's anger burned against the ocean; and there is, he holds, only one ancient tradition in which this element is fundamental, the Babylonian creation myth.

Apart from radical, pan-Babylonian circles, however, Gunkel's injection of the Enlil(Marduk)-Tiamat struggles as the base and prototype of many Biblical records, including this verse of Nahum, has generally been rejected. Because of its groundlessness and of its extremes many critical writers have disavowed its implications. However, Sellin revives this opinion with his statement that the Book of Nahum is "a hymn to the divinely moral nemesis which, maintaining itself finally and inexorably throughout history, is represented in the colors of the primeval picture of the battle of the gods." [43] He finds specific parallels to the Babylonian creation story.

The case for the Babylonian origin of this section and for its influence on the prophet's conception of God must be dismissed, since it utterly lacks evidence. Sellin finds a duel ("Zweikampf") in 2:14 and 3:5, which contain the Almighty's utterances against Nineveh. In his commentary Sellin lists such passages as 1:4: "He rebuketh the sea, and He drieth it up." This he calls a reflex from the old myth of the battle between the light god and the chaos monster; 1:6: "His wrath is poured out like fire, and the rocks are torn down by Him." This is classified as an allusion to "the old myth of the fire-flood." In 2:1, "Belial" is described as "a very ancient word . . . a designation of the power of darkness in contrast to that of the light." In 2:2, "the scatterer" is termed "a motif word of the dragon conflict." In 2:4 the "red" of the verse is labeled another "motif of the dragon struggle." In 2:5 the lightning (used only as comparison) likewise is regarded as another element in the mythical conflict. All these passages, however, are fundamentally separated from every conception of a Marduk-Tiamat conflict. With the same principles and procedures we could conclude that every time God is quoted as pronouncing a sentence of doom on a sinful people we must go back to a Babylonian substratum.

Equally fantastic is Gunkel's overstressing of the sea in 1:4. To discern in this plain statement: "He rebuketh . . . the sea, and He drieth it up," a reminiscence of the myth prefigured in

43 *Einleitung in das Alte Testament* (1935), p. 117.

the struggle of *Enûma ēlish* is to give free reign to fancy. Yet on the basis of these references to the rebuking of the sea rests the hypothesized but nonexistent "Zweikampf" and the affirmation that the prophet borrowed his picture of rebuking the sea from cuneiform cosmogony!

Besides the decisive considerations that any theological dependence upon Mesopotamian mythology would vitiate the entire Biblical conception of the Old Testament Scriptures and that crass pan-Babylonianism (particularly in the fantastic extremes of the astral theories) has been properly rejected by later sober scholarship, this glaring contradiction remains: Why would Nahum, in his dire prophecies against Nineveh, use in reference to the God of his people a heathen motif which Assyrian kings, Israel's enemies, delighted to perpetuate in the burnished copper of their temple gates?

The Defense of Nahum's Doctrine, Its Profound Truth

Turning now to the positive consideration of Nahum's doctrines, one is impressed with his striking presentation of God and the divine attributes. With eloquent beauty the prophet pictures Yahweh in His *universality,* destroying Nineveh (1:12-14), cutting off its prey "from the earth" (2:14), showing the nations its nakedness (3:5). The Lord of Hosts is portrayed in His *justice,* punishing Nineveh, as an Avenger to His foes" (1:2), refusing to "leave *the guilty* unpunished" (1:3). He is presented in His *omnipotence,* rebuking the sea and drying up the rivers (1:4), making an utter end of Nineveh (1:9); in His *majesty,* since His way is "in whirlwind and in tempest, and clouds are the dust of His feet" (1:3), and even "mountains quake on account of Him . . . and the earth lifts itself before Him, yea, the world and all who dwell in it" (1:5). Yet He is also described in His *mercy,* since He is "long-suffering" (1:3), "good," and "a Stronghold in the day of affliction" (1:7), and though He has afflicted Judah, yet He will afflict her no more (1:12). Finally, God is delineated in His *faithfulness.* "He knoweth those who trust in Him." (1:7)

Nahum also offers a detailed and pragmatic presentation of God's government, the relation which exists between national prosperity on one hand and the recognition of the Lord and morality on the other. Nineveh is to fall, not because it is a large, non-Israelite, wealthy, commercial city, but because it is a godless and idolatrous city (1:11, 14); because it is a lustful, rapacious, crafty, violent city (3:1; 2:13, 14; 3:4). Its destiny is to illustrate the axiom that "righteousness exalteth a nation, but sin is a reproach to any people." (Prov. 14:34)

The book also abounds in stating and implying profound, practical lessons for our age. The warning against the pride of Assyrian haughtiness that insolently resists God (1:11) should be invoked to rebuke parallel tendencies in our times. The woe chanted against "the bloody city" (3:1) should be repeated in our day which, more than any other generation in modern history, has suffered from war's carnage. The destiny of Nineveh, the vampire queen of the nations, who had ruled with unchecked oppression, should deter those twentieth-century dictatorial empire builders who would stride ruthlessly over prostrate nations in adding conquest to conquest. The fortresses that fall like ripe figs, the hastily erected defenses, the fleeing armies, the heaped corpses — these symbols of a doomed, bloated militarism, bristling in its own might and then dying in its own blood, are replete with meaningful warnings for our world, which has seen the most widespread wars of aggression.

Nor is the comfort which the prophet's name implies restricted to his age. The prediction of complete annihilation for the world empire's metropolis, the sustaining pledge of God's power and justice which Nahum brought Judah, reach our generation when the might-makes-right philosophy seeks to guide international policies. Pointedly Luther summarizes: "He [Nahum] teaches us to trust God and to believe, especially when we despair of all human help, human powers, and counsel, that the Lord stands by those who are His, shields His own against all attacks of the enemy, be they ever so powerful." (St. Louis ed. XIV:1355)

We who are God's can keep our "festivals" and perform our vows in faith if we, too, behold on the mountains the feet of a herald proclaiming peace (2:1). Nahum probably borrows this assurance of comfort from the evangelist of the OT (Is. 52:7), and St. Paul (Rom. 10:15) applies these words to the promise that the good tidings contained in the Gospel of Christ's peace will be brought to the heathen world. Since the Isaianic passage is thus Messianic in its context and citation, and since Nahum uses almost identical language, the conclusion is close at hand that the prophet of comfort looked beyond the messengers announcing the destruction of Nineveh and the resultant peace to the divine Messenger who was to bring the good tidings of reconciliation and peace everlasting.

The pages of Nahum are of extraordinary value in underscoring the validity of OT prophecy and the divine nature of these Scriptures. No human document of such restricted size has ever attempted to foretell in detail the march of future events; and none ever could. Yet when Nineveh fell and in dramatic succession one prediction after another was literally fulfilled, a great calm must have dawned in the hearts of all who could measure history as it complemented prophecy. Today we need more of that unshaken faith in the power of God and in the prevalence of His Word which animated the prophet. Human promises and predictions have too regularly collapsed in these decades of delusion. We, too, must have an immovable, unshaken base on which we can build for the ominous future. In the eternal truths of this small but inspired book, and in the fulfillment of its prophecies, we, too, must find the Lord, who is "a Stronghold in the day of affliction," and conclude that if God kept His word in breaking the yoke of Nineveh's tyrannical power, He can assuredly solve the perplexities of our individual lives. The deserted mounds over Nineveh's ruins at Kouyunjik and Nebi Yunus are not only the perpetual warnings that the retribution of divine justice never misses its mark; they also write in universal language history's testimony to the power of God, which makes His pledges of grace the certain promise of deliverance.

In these oracles of Nahum, then, we have not a book which has "no traces of religious interest"; [44] not the product of a small prophetic mind who suffers in comparison with great prophetic geniuses, but a divine revelation which, with its warning and comfort, was never more applicable to any age than to ours. Nahum should be rescued from the obscurity into which it has fallen through misunderstanding, ignorance, malice, and indifference, and proclaimed as part of the church's vital message to our day.

THE BACKGROUND OF NAHUM'S PROPHECIES — NINEVEH

To understand the full import, scope, and precision of Nahum's forecasts, it is necessary to realize the dominant role played by Nineveh in the prophet's day, to learn some of the essentials of her topography, to consider the international policies and practices radiated from the residence city. Nahum's moral wrath, his profound trust in God, his assured confidence in the ultimate triumph of righteousness and the inevitable collapse of tyranny, cannot be visualized properly unless viewed against the macabre background of Nineveh's long and bloody domination. One reason this startling book has not been worthily evaluated even by many Bible readers, and has been almost completely neglected by others, is that the very vastness of the cataclysm it predicts has not been realized.

[44] Friedrich Delitzsch, *Die grosse Täuschung,* pp. 31, 32: *"Keine Spur von religiösem Interesse."*

Nineveh's History

In Nahum's day Nineveh (Assyrian *Nina* or *Ninua*) looked back on a long and varied history. Uncertainty reigns as to when the Assyrian city is first mentioned in cuneiform records. Hammurabi (ca. 2200 B. C.) definitely designates the Assyrian Nineveh when in his Code (IV, 60—62) he calls himself "the king who made the name of Nana (Ishtar) glorious in Emashmash [the temple of Ishtar], in Nineveh." However, for centuries after Hammurabi little of consequence is heard of Nineveh. Shamshi Adad I (ca. 1830 B. C.) rebuilt the temple of Ishtar at Nineveh, doubtless indicating that the North country was under the complete control of the South. For approximately 450 years the city is passed over in almost complete silence. About 1500 B. C. Napuli is listed as the Mitanni King Tushratta's governor at Nineveh, similarly indicating a Mitanni sovereignty. A century later a Mitanni king offers to send a statue of the Ninevite Ishtar to the Egyptian Pharaoh, indicating perhaps the city's cultic importance as well as its subjection to Egypt.[45] Shalmaneser I (ca. 1300 B. C.) rebuilt the Ishtar[46] temple erected by Shamshi Adad, an unidentified ancestor. Ashurnasirpal (883—859 B. C.) carried on a similar restoration. In the following centuries Nineveh does not play the outstanding role which its later supremacy might presuppose. It is mentioned relatively infrequently, never as the capital of the kingdom, but rather as the center of a province. Shalmaneser III (ca. 858—824 B. C.) appears to have made the city a base for military operations. Perhaps it was the neglect of his royal patronage that fomented Nineveh's revolt against him.

During Shalmaneser's reign Israel came into its first contact with Nineveh. A series of conquests and tribute exactments began, which was later to help destroy the Northern Kingdom and bring Judah into complete submission. Shalmaneser declares:

[45] See Tell el-Amarna Letter No. 19, in Joergen Alexander Knudtzon, *Die El-Amarna Tafeln in Umschrift und Übersetzung* (1915), I, 143.

[46] Leonard William King, *Records of Tukulti Ninib* (1904), I, 131.

"In the year of Dâian Assur I . . . departed from Nineveh,"[47] and he continues to record that he met "Ahab the Israelite" with 2,000 chariots and 10,000 soldiers. Thus from Nineveh came the first Mesopotamian to ravage Israel. In the account of his fourth campaign (842 B. C.), doubtless starting as usual from Nineveh, Shalmaneser states:[48] "At that time I received the tribute . . . of Jehu, son of Omri" (!). On his black basalt obelisk the picture of Jehu, on his knees before the Assyrian monarch, is accompanied by this legend: "Tribute of Iaua (Jehu), son of Omri (mâr *Humri*). Silver, gold, a golden bowl, a golden beaker, golden goblets, pitchers of gold, lead, staves for the hand of the king, javelins, I received from him."[49] Again the destroyer had come forth from Nineveh.

Adad-nirâri IV (805—782 B. C.) had this inscription carved into the wall of his royal abode: "Palace of Adad-nirâri, the great king, the mighty king, king of the universe, king of Assyria . . . Hatti [the Hittite country], Amurru [the Amorite land] in its totality, Tyre, Sidon, Humrî (Omriland, Israel), Edom, Palastu [Philistia] up to the great sea of the setting suns — I brought (these lands) in submission to my feet."[50] Israel is here called the land of "Omri" because of the importance that king had assumed. Tiglathpileser III (745—727 B. C.), however, extended the conquest south into Judah itself. He records what is apparently the defeat and tribute of Azariah of Judah.[51] Unquestioned, however, is his reference to Menahem (Menihimmu), 2 Kings 15:14-23, of Samerina [Samaria], whose tribute he received.[52] In his 733—732 B. C. campaign, the Assyrian king's inroads into Israel became stronger. Tiglathpileser boasts: "The land of Bît-Humria [the house of Omri] . . . all of its people, together with their goods, I carried off to Assyria. Pakaha

[47] 854 B. C. Daniel David Luckenbill, *Ancient Records of Assyria and Babylonia* (1926—27), I, 222 f.

[48] Ibid., p. 243.   [50] Ibid., p. 262.   [52] Ibid., p. 276.
[49] Ibid., p. 211.   [51] Ibid., p. 274.

(Pekah), their king, they deposed, and I placed Ausi (Hoshea) over them as king. 10 talents of gold . . . as their tribute I received from them." [53] In confirmation of 2 Kings 15:29, 30, Tiglathpileser, at the invitation of Ahaz, had come down to aid Judah and Jerusalem against Israel and Damascus in the Syro-Ephraemitic War. As Isaiah (7:16) had prophesied, he captured Damascus, defeated Israel, and deported many of its people to various parts of the empire. Judah was theoretically spared for the time, but actually it became a vassal state, for Tiglathpileser states (Nimrûd tablet): "Tribute of . . . Iauhazi (Jehoahaz), of Judah . . . (I received)." Jehoahaz is the Biblical Ahaz, who, this cuneiform record tells us, went to Damascus to pay Tiglathpileser homage and to show his loyalty in a practical way by bringing tribute.

Thus both Israel and Judah had now felt that Assyrian scourge; but this was only the beginning. In 722 B. C. Shalmaneser V, son of Tiglathpileser (727—722 B. C.), besieged Samaria. He died during these operations and was succeeded by Sargon II (721—705 B. C.), founder of a new dynasty. Before his first year was completed, Samaria fell into his hands, and his inscription recounts: "[At the beginning of my rule, in my first year of reign] . . . Samerinai (the people of Samaria) . . . [27,290 people, who lived therein] I carried away; 50 chariots for my royal equipment, I selected from [among them]. . . . People of the lands [my hand had conquered, I settled therein. My official I placed over them as governor]. Tribute, tax, I imposed upon them as upon the Assyrians." [54] Sargon also declared his intention in a broken passage "to (punish) Judah, Edom, Moab." The actual fulfillment of this threat against Judah is not definite.

Sargon's son, Sennacherib (705—681 B. C.), invaded Judah in full force. He recounts:

> As for Hezekiah, the Jew, who did not submit to my yoke, 46 of his strong, walled cities, as well as the small cities in their neigh-

[53] Ibid., p. 293.   [54] Luckenbill, op. cit., II, 2.

borhood, which were without number — by leveling with battering-rams (?) and by bringing up siege-engines (?), by attacking and storming on foot, by mines, tunnels, and breaches (?), I besieged and took (those cities). 200,150 people, great and small, male and female, horses, mules, asses, camels, cattle and sheep, without number, I brought away from them and counted as spoil. Himself, like a caged bird, I shut up in Jerusalem, his royal city. Earthworks I threw up against him — the one coming out of the citygate, I turned back to his misery. The cities of his, which I had despoiled, I cut off from his land to Mitinti, king of Ashdod, Padi, king of Ekron, the Silli-bêl, king of Gaza, I gave. And (thus) I diminished his land. I added to the former tribute, and laid upon him the giving (up) of their land, (as well as) imposts — gifts for my majesty. As for Hezekiah, the terrifying splendor of my majesty overcame him, and the Urbi (Arabs) and his mercenary (?) troops, which he had brought in to strengthen Jerusalem, his royal city, deserted him. In addition to the 30 talents of gold and 800 talents of silver, (there were) gems, antimony, jewels (?), large *sandu*-stones, couches of ivory, house-chairs of ivory, elephant hide, ivory, ebony (?), boxwood (?), all kinds of valuable (heavy) treasures, as well as his daughters, his harem, his male and female musicians, (which) he had (them) bring after me to Nineveh, my royal city. To pay tribute and to accept servitude, he dispatched his messengers.[55]

This is the cuneiform account of events set down in 2 Kings 18 and 19, as in the parallel Is. 36 and 37. The Bible states that although Jerusalem was besieged and the Assyrians were so confident of their victory that they boasted blasphemously, nevertheless "the angel of Yahweh went forth and smote in the camp of the Assyrians a hundred and fourscore and five thousand. And when they arose early in the morning, behold, they were all dead corpses" (Is. 37:36). It is not necessary here to consider the various explanations offered to bring the cuneiform record and the Biblical account into harmony. They are not mutually exclusive. Suffice it for our purposes to recall that Sennacherib, who came forth from Nineveh, his newly made capital, was the enemy

[55] Luckenbill, *The Annals of Sennacherib* (1924), pp. 32 ff.

of Judah, who captured more than 200,000 of its people, destroyed forty-six strongholds, and small cities "without number,' and received thirty talents of gold and 300 talents (800, according to the cuneiform record) of silver, besides other heavy booty.

Esarhaddon (681—668 B. C.) regarded Judah as a vassal kingdom, for he set forth in a building inscription: "I summoned the kings of the Hittite-land (Syria), and (those) across the sea, Ba'lu, king of Tyre, Manasseh, king of Judah." [56]

It should thus be borne in mind that one Assyrian king after another spoiled Israel and later Judah. Shalmaneser III, Adad-nirari IV, Tiglathpileser III, Sargon II, Sennacherib, Esarhaddon, all had laid bloody hands on God's people.

Significantly, the worst of these invasions came from Nineveh. Indeed, as Assyria hastened to its end, that city assumed increasing and almost exclusive importance. Prism B, recording the achievements of Ashurbanipal, who ruled at Nahum's time, mentions Nineveh as "the city of my lordship." The grand monarch repeatedly boasted that it was Nineveh to which he returned after his arduous campaigns. To Nineveh came the distant chieftains who kissed the royal feet, rebel leaders paraded in fetters, distant and deceitful kings tied with dog chains and made to live in kennels. To Nineveh were sent gifts of far-off tribute, heads of vanquished enemies, crown princes as hostages, beautiful princesses as concubines. In Nineveh rulers who experienced rare mercy carried brick and mortar for building operations. There recalcitrant captives were flayed, obstinate opponents crushed to death by their own sons. The Nineveh against which the prophet thunders divine denunciation had become the concentrated center of evil, the capital of crushing tyranny, the epitome of cruelest torture. Before the beginning of the seventh century and Sennacherib's reign other cities had been royal residences: Calah, Ashur, Dûr Sharrukin; but Sennacherib made

[56] See Luckenbill, *Ancient Records,* etc., II, 265.

Nineveh his capital, the world metropolis, the source of un-measured woe for Judah, as for other, far greater nations.

No reason is given for his choice of an ancient but other-wise none-too-prominent city, to which previous kings, with the exception of Shalmaneser III and Sargon, had paid relatively little attention. Pointedly Olmstead remarks: "There was no city of its size or sanctity in all Assyria which was so little associated with the fame of any previous monarch." [57] Yet Sennacherib selected well from the point of view of both military defense advantages and commercial location, as the persistence of Mosul may em-phasize.

In 702 B. C. Sargon began his magnificent public works and building operations at Nineveh. In eighty short years the place was to become the capital of the empire, the largest city in the world, and then — a widespread heap of ruins. No other city of comparable size has risen to parallel height in such a short time nor so rapidly dropped to equally abysmal depths.

It was Sennacherib, however, who gave Nineveh its prom-inence and brilliance after selecting its site for his capital. He undertook these measures by which the place was made a worthy residence for royalty:

1. *Enlargement and Reorganization of the City.* According to Sennacherib's figures, the boundaries of Nineveh totaled 9,300 cubits when he began his operations there.[58] Through his enlarge-ments 12,515 cubits were added, making the total perimeter 21,815 cubits. It has been pointed out that this figure corresponds to an area two thirds as great as that of the Rome enclosed

[57] Olmstead, *History of Assyria,* p. 318.

[58] R. Campbell Thompson and R. W. Hutchinson, *A Century of Explora-tion at Nineveh* (1929), p. 120, fn. 1, point out that this is slightly smaller than the perimeter of Kouyunjik. As indicated by its ruins, the dimensions of this mound aggregate over 11,100 cubits, enclosing an area of about 1,800 acres. It seems conclusive, therefore, that Sennacherib refers only to the royal section of the city. Significantly few private houses have been found in the Kouyunjik mound. While ordinary homes would disappear more quickly than imposing palaces, much of the area at Kouyunjik has been accounted for by royal structures, their courts, and adjacent lands.

within the Aurelian Wall. The population has been estimated at 300,000. Probably these dimensions and figures refer only to Nineveh proper and do not include adjacent suburbs. It is known, for example, that Esarhaddon, Sennacherib's son, built a contiguous community called Kar Ashur-ahi-iddina. Very likely the city's increasing importance constantly demanded new additions even in his father's time.

Excavations have uncovered the remains of an ancient wall in the form of an irregular trapezium totaling about eight miles around the inner city. Traces of a longer outer wall have been found to the northeast. Within the eight-mile circuit two mounds rise, Kouyunjik, toward the southwest, near the village of Rahmanijah, and the smaller mound, Nebi Yunus, with the village of the same name about one mile to the south of Kouyunjik, both mounds covering part of the inner wall. Fourteen miles to the northeast of Kouyunjik is the mound covering Khorsabad, the capital of Sargon (721—705 B. C.), called by him Dûr Sharrukin; and approximately the same distance to the southwest, near the confluence of the Tigris and the Upper Zab, at the modern Kalah, is Nimrud, another royal city. Layard [59] is of the firm opinion that the edifices, of which remnants exist at Nimrud, Kouyunjik, and Khorsabad, once formed part of the same extended community. He believes that the temples were centers of separate districts in the one city. Nimrud, he holds, was the original site of Nineveh, the temples of Kouyunjik and Khorsabad having been erected later. If the objection is raised that not many archaeological evidences of occupation have been found in the triangle formed by the Tigris, the Zab, and the line through Khorsabad connecting the two rivers, these answers are to be given: First, much of the intervening territory was probably occupied by natives who built small, simple homes of dried mud, bricks, and straw. The ravages of time could completely obliterate their

[59] *Popular Account of Discoveries at Nineveh* (1857), p. 313. But Thompson and Hutchinson, *A Century of Exploration at Nineveh* (1929), p. 113, hold: "It is not improbable that Kouyunjik represents early Nineveh."

remains. Travelers in Iraq recount how today native villages are soon leveled with the ground. In the second place, however, this entire territory is replete with evidences of habitation. Layard reports: "Scarcely a husbandman drives his plow over the soil without turning up the vestiges of former habitations." [60] Besides, numerous mounds in this territory have never been investigated, and the few that have been uncovered, for example, Balawat, southeast of Nineveh and northeast of Kalah, have yielded surprising returns.[61] Since the line of the outer wall is only partially known, it is impossible at present to compute the area within this greater limit.

2. *Palace Construction.* Nineveh had a royal residence before Sennacherib's day, but almost with inscriptional disdain he refers to the smallness of its dimensions. Full of pride in the newness and immensity of his architecture, he built "The Palace with No Rival"; and indeed, this structure was unparalleled throughout Assyria until that time. His annals speak of its cedar, cypress, alabaster, its guarding lions in bronze, its bull colossi cut out of white marble, its many sculptured slabs. The great hall in the royal abode measured forty by one hundred and fifty feet.

3. *Defense Program.* To protect the city against invasion, Sennacherib devised a double line of walls. The inner wall, according to *in situ* investigators, seems to have been completed. According to the dimensions in the royal inscriptions, the bulwark was forty courses of brick wide, one hundred and eighty courses high. Today, after twenty-six centuries, the ruins still tower

[60] Op. cit., p. 316.

[61] All writers of antiquity who discuss the size of Nineveh are agreed in ascribing vast proportions to it. Diodorus Siculus (II, 9) says that the city was 150 stadia long and 90 standia broad, making the entire dimensions of the quadrangle 480 stadia. Quintus Curtius (V, 1) agrees with Diodorus Siculus in maintaining that the Babylonians sought to restrict the severity of siege by creating enough farmlands and orchards within the walls to make the city self-sustaining.

Perhaps the Assyrians at Nineveh had the same policy. Jonah's reference to "much cattle" (4:11) points to the necessity of large pasture lands. That prophet (3:3) calls Nineveh "an exceeding great city of three days' journey." Remarkably, Jonah's three days' journey corresponds to the sixty miles of the geographer.

seventy feet. Fourteen gates were built in the walls, and at some of these, as Nahum indicates, were river gates, where the water entered the city. At the Gate of the Quay, for example, the Khosr flowed directly under the palace walls. Outside this inner fortification, moats dug when the clay bricks for the walls were made, added to the city defenses. Whether the Tigris River actually flowed by the city at this time is a debated question.

The outer wall, as excavators report, was not completed in its entire course. However, as far as it went, it was a formidable structure, significantly called *Bad-nig-erim-huluhha*, the one "which terrifies the enemy."

Besides, Sennacherib built an armory. Its construction, including the removal of dilapidated buildings on its forty-acre terrace, required six years. In this large storehouse weapons of war: bows, arrows, quivers, chariots, wagons, armor, horses, mules, their harness and equipment — everything required for the maintenance and enlargement of his domain, was kept in lavish quantities.

4. *Road Building.* Sennacherib extended Nineveh's streets and enlarged especially the dimensions of the Royal Road. It was seventy-eight feet wide, more than twice the breadth of the average paved thoroughfare in our country.

5. *Irrigation and Water-Supply Projects.* To provide water for irrigation ditches and for defense moats, as well as to bring fresh, sweet water into the city, since the Tigris was muddy, Sennacherib first of all, changed the course of the Tebiltu. This necessitated the razing of a small palace and the construction of a mound for the new residence mentioned above. It has been estimated that this operation required the services of 10,000 men for twelve years, but such tremendous undertakings cost relatively little in Nineveh, since the work was done by slaves from captive countries and by forced labor. The Tebiltu could become a turbulent water course, especially when heightened by the spring

freshets, and more than once it had destroyed buildings and property.

A system of dams to the west of the city regulated the waters of the Tigris, and another series of dams in a flood-control system on the east restrained the Khosr River. An irrigation canal brought water to the city's orchards from Kisir, 40 (?) miles away.

Nineveh, as reorganized and extended by Sennacherib, was a center of magnificence for those days. So well had his planning and building been executed that we read relatively little of further construction during the reigns of his son and his grandson, Esarhaddon and Ashurbanipal. The former recounts chiefly that he built a new suburb in Nineveh and enlarged his father's armory. Among the vassal kings who contributed material for this stupendous structure was Manasseh of Judah.

Ashurbanipal restored Sennacherib's inner walls. As he recounts:

> The wall in the midst of the city of Nineveh . . . whose base through the abundant showers and heavy rains that Adad had yearly sent down upon my land during my reign had become shaky so that its turrets were on the verge of falling — that wall, which had grown old and whose foundation had become dilapidated — I cleared away its fallen portions, I discovered its retaining walls [I made its] base [o]f mount[ain] stone [. . . .] of that wall [. . . .] [. . . .] I attained [. . . .]. From its foundation to its cornice I built (it) completely.[62]

Perhaps it was the Babylonian revolt against Assyria that thus turned Ashurbanipal's thoughts to the defense of his capital. He also restored Ishtar's E-mashmash sanctuary and enlarged the court of Ninib. The temple of Nabu, younger than Ishtar's sanctuary, which previously had been renovated by Adad-nirari III (788 B. C.), then by Sargon (721—705 B. C., who calls it the temple of Nabu and Marduk), was likewise rebuilt. Here part

---

[62] Edition D, VIII, 64 ff. See Piepkorn, *Historical Prism Inscriptions of Ashurbanipal* (1933), p. 99.

of the famous Kouyunjik library was preserved. Most of this unique collection was housed in the new palace which Ashurbanipal erected. During the early part of his reign he lived in the restored *bît-ridûti*, House of Succession, and then temporarily in the Southwest Palace of Sennacherib. The *bît-ridûti* was completely razed and then rebuilt on a much larger, more majestic scale. This, Nineveh's last great palace, became Ashurbanipal's official residence.[63]

Here, then, was the Nineveh against which Nahum spoke in prophetic denunciation, a city of cruelty and crime, oppression and slavery, falsehood and lust, where Oriental paganism displayed its ugliest traits. Before the end of Ashurbanipal's long reign the decline of Assyrian power had set in. After his death in 626 B. C. and the further deterioration during the reign of the three inconsequential kings, Ashur-etil-ilani, Sin-shum-lishir (a usurper), and Sin-shar-ishkun, the city fell in 612 B. C. as Nahum had prophesied. This is one of the foremost dates in the human record; and while it is futile to speculate on the *ifs* of history, the consequences that would have resulted from a victorious Assyria spreading its influence beyond Greece, to even more remote parts of the Mediterranean world, are almost immeasurable in their potentialities for widespread disaster and the restriction of Hellenistic culture.

The city never rose from its debris, although straggling settlements mushroomed temporarily on its site. But the tradition that Nineveh was buried beneath the mounds opposite Mosul survived throughout the following centuries. Xenophon may have passed the covered ruins of Nineveh without recognizing its identity, and Niebuhr may have crossed the mounds without knowing that he was traversing the site of the Assyrian capital; but subsequent writers, particularly among the Arabs, recorded the tradition which placed Nineveh on the Tigris opposite Mosul.

---

[63] For a detailed description of the palace, featuring the building plan and its various sculptured slabs, see Olmstead, *History of Assyria*, pp. 496—503.

Nineveh's Exploration and Excavation

No doubt remains that the ancient capital stood on the left bank of the Tigris, opposite Mosul, with Nineveh proper represented chiefly by the two mounds Kouyunjik and Nebi Yunus, together with the adjacent territory within the outer walls. This identification has been made certain by the excavations at this place, which have uncovered the temples and palaces of kings who reigned there, with adequate identification of the place as Nineveh. To these excavations, begun more than 100 years ago, we owe our detailed acquaintance with Assyrian kings, priests, soldiers, and people, as well as our knowledge of the Assyrian policies, morals, religion, culture, architecture, and warfare.

Early travelers who made their way through the forbidding Tigris territory left impressive, if not always accurate, descriptions of the ruins near Mosul. Among them were Edward Ives, J. Kinneir, and James Silk Buckingham. Claudius James Rich, who became British consul at Baghdad, visited the site of Nineveh in 1820, investigated and measured the mound, secured numerous archaeological specimens, and also mapped the ruins.

In 1842 the first real excavation was undertaken by Paul Emile Botta, the French consul at Mosul. In December of that year he started to dig into the Kouyunjik mound. The yield was quite limited, and in March 1843 he transferred his activity to Khorsabad, fourteen miles northeast. Almost from the outset he was remarkably successful in uncovering inscriptions, bas-reliefs, and the remains of a palace. Perhaps it was the immensity of these ruins which made Botta report that Nineveh had been rediscovered. Instead, he had found the palace of the Assyrian monarch Sargon II (721—705 B. C.). The survey of this expedition issued by Botta and his artist, E. Flandin, the five-volume, impressive *Monument de Ninive,* 1849—1850, also presents the results of the initial three months' work at Nineveh itself.

In 1845 Austen Henry Layard started his operations at the

Nimrud mound (the site of the ancient Kalah), about twenty miles southeast of Kouyunjik on the Tigris. Within twenty days after his arrival a bas-relief was uncovered, and despite difficulties with officials and financial limitations the excavations at Nimrud, which were to continue with interruptions until 1847, yielded remarkable results. Contradicting both local tradition and facts soon to be revealed, Layard prematurely concluded that Nimrud covered the remains of ancient Nineveh. Strengthened by this success, he began to excavate the southern corner of Kouyunjik, which Botta claimed as French property. The sand and debris here proved much deeper than at Nimrud, and after a month Layard stopped his work to return to the richer prospects in the south. The heat of the summer soon drove him back to Mosul and gave his eager restlessness the opportunity to work again at the nearby Kouyunjik. This time he succeeded in uncovering the northwest gate of the city wall and found two winged figures. His program at Nimrud completed in 1847, he returned to resume excavations on the south section of the Kouyunjik mound. Soon undreamed-of success followed: Sennacherib's palace was found.

Layard left Mosul for England in January 1847, and the trustees of the British Museum authorized Ross, who had ably assisted him, to carry on the excavations. In 1849 Layard returned to resume work at Kouyunjik, now with the help of the British government. The palace of Sennacherib at Kouyunjik was carefully uncovered; hundreds of bas-reliefs depicting that monarch's wars and hunting trips were systematically laid bare. Two rooms were found containing hundreds of clay tablets in cuneiform script, the Kouyunjik library, one of the most remarkable discoveries in all Mesopotamian archaeology. Subsequent excavations brought other similar tablets to light. The whole library collection, as numbered by the British Museum, now totals about 30,000.

In April 1851 Layard, as he himself recounts, "with a heavy heart turned from the ruins of ancient Nineveh." But the diggings at this former empire capital were to continue. Hormuzd Rassam, a native Christian whose brother was British vice-consul at Mosul, had worked with Layard in the 1849-1851 excavations and was selected by the trustees of the British Museum to expand the work. He started in 1852, and after uncovering perfect sculptures, monuments, and part of Ishtar's temple, he began secret operations on the north corner of Kouyunjik, a section reserved by Botta. After four nights of excavation Ashurbanipal's great palace was uncovered, and an abundance of bas-reliefs, battle records, religious sculptures, as well as several thousand tablets from the royal library, came to light. Botta relinquished his claim to this part of Kouyunjik, and Rassam continued the exploration until April 1854, when William Kennett Loftus and William Boutcher, an artist, took Rassam's place, clearing many important sections of the palace.

Then the excavations at Nineveh were halted for almost two decades, until May 1873, when George Smith, sent to Nineveh by popular demand, once more began operations at Kouyunjik in Sennacherib's palace and later on in Ashurbanipal's. After his funds ran out, he returned to England; but early in January 1874 he was back at Kouyunjik. Near the southwest palace gate he found inscriptions of Shalmaneser, Tukulti-Ninurta, his son, and Ashurnasirpal, besides adjacent temple restorations. He was also rewarded with many tablets of the type Layard and Botta had unearthed. In 1876, while planning his third excavation, he died near Mosul, as other gallant archaeologists before and after him, a martyr to science. Two years later Hormuzd Rassam again undertook the work at Kouyunjik, but on a smaller scale, and continued until 1882. He brought out the celebrated prism of Ashurbanipal and more tablets from the royal archives.

It might seem that after these repeated diggings in the course of forty years Nineveh would be completely excavated; but Ernest Budge, sent to Kouyunjik by the British Museum, for the seasons of 1888—1889 and 1890—1891, reported that two immense palaces were buried beneath the dirt dug by previous explorers. Twelve years later, in 1903, Leonard King, defraying the expenses of his own expedition, attacked the Kouyunjik mound once more, disclosed the remaining rooms of Sennacherib's palace in the southwest section, and brought to light new sculptures and archives. Similar results were obtained in Ashurbanipal's northern palace. Sinking forty-foot shafts in sections of the mound not yet investigated, King was able to reveal the various levels of early and late Assyrian epochs. He found a new eastern palace, presumably built by Sennacherib. R. Campbell Thompson continued King's excavations in June 1904 and was successful in uncovering the courtyard of the long-sought Nabu temple.

For two years Kouyunjik remained untouched by any official expedition. In October 1927 R. Campbell Thompson and R. W. Hutchinson resumed excavating near the site of Nabu's temple, tracing almost the entire ground plan of that sanctuary. Besides, a ninth-century palace was uncovered, likewise a palace built by Sennacherib for an unnamed son. Thompson's work continued until 1932.

The last archaeologists to work at Kouyunjik report:

Very much, however, remains to be done. Neither Sennacherib's palace, nor that of Ashurbanipal, is completely cleared, although their extent is fairly well known; the Temple of Ishtar, with the adjacent Temple of Kidmuri and the temple-tower, has, we think, been partly located, but only a portion excavated; and consequently, as this is the chief building in Nineveh, going back long before we have any record of a palace, with its very goddess Nina giving her name to the ancient site, there can be no doubt about the supreme interest of excavations at this spot. . . . Nineveh is not yet by any means a squeezed lemon, and no site in Iraq can claim to be of more importance.[64]

The force of this statement is emphasized by the fact that one of the two prominent mounds at Nineveh, Nebi Yunus, the

[64] Thompson and Hutchinson, *A Century of Exploration at Nineveh* (1929), p. 10.

reputed site of Jonah's tomb, has remained untouched by the excavator's spade out of deference to the Mohammedans, who there maintain a mosque and a graveyard.

Nineveh's Picture in the Prophet Nahum

The Nineveh of Ashurbanipal is faithfully portrayed by Nahum. The prophet beholds its broad streets (2:5), concerning which Sennacherib makes special entries in his *Annals*. He sees the highly praised city gates as centers of pivotal attack (3:13). He envisions the emergency manufacture of bricks for the walls (3:14). He knows the haughty eagerness with which the Ninevite kings sought to have their name perpetuated. The weeping palace maidens (2:8), the cowardly nobles (3:17), the bartering merchants (3:16), the carousing officials (1:10; 3:11), are pictured in pointed reference.

Especially, however, does Nahum know the Nineveh of military might, war, and blood. He portrays the capital as the center from which wickedness has passed over to the surrounding nations (3:19). At the heights of Assyrian power, Ashurbanipal ruled, either directly by conquest or indirectly by tribute, Egypt, Memphis, Lais, Tanis, Athrebis in upper Egypt (667 B. C.); Thebes and other localities in lower Egypt (664 B. C.); Arabia (the land of the Indri, Arabi, and Nabaati, east of Ammon), Moab, and Syria (648 and 647); the Ararat country (655 B. C.); Babylon (652—648 B. C.); Elam (655—652 B. C.); Asia Minor, the territory of Hilakku, of Tebal and of Lydia (dates uncertain); the Manni (fourth or fifth expedition); the Medians (fourth and fifth expeditions); Mesopotamia (no date given); Phoenicia (667 B. C.), Syria, and Palestine (Manasseh of Judah); the Gimirri and the Umman Manda (no date given), northern enemies.

The empire had been built by blood and torture, cruelty and massacre, destruction and devastation, sacking and plundering, such as history has seldom seen. When Nahum calls Nineveh "the bloody city" (3:1), he expresses his whole-souled resentment against the calculated cruelty practiced by the Assyrian conquerors. That brutality for which Ashurnasirpal had been infamous almost two and one-half centuries earlier was perpetuated in Ashurbanipal's reign, sometimes in precise repetition. Enemies were impaled, flayed, the walls of cities covered with their skins. Their heads were cut off and hung around the neck of the captives or displayed at Nineveh's gates. Bones of enemies were publicly crushed "before the gate in the middle of Nineveh" by the sons of the deceased enemy. The tongues of those who had spoken disrespectfully of Ashurbanipal's gods he tore out, the grand monarch records. The wide, indiscriminate slaughter of rebels and the complete destruction of enemy territory (often featured in the stereotyped sentence, "That district I conquered, devastated, burned with fire"), these were part of the accepted procedure in practically every conquest.[65]

Equally characteristic of Assyrian procedure was the systematic booty and looting. Even if we allow for conventional exaggerations, the quantity of spoil brought back to Nineveh is startling in its immensity. Sennacherib, for example, recounts that after his first campaign: "I returned to Assyria with 208,000 captive people, a huge spoil, 7,200 horses and mules, 11,073 asses, 5,230 camels, 80,050 cattle, 800,100 ewes. — This does not include the men, asses, camels, cattle, and sheep which my troops had carried off and parceled out among themselves."[66] From Thebes, the strongly fortified city to which Nahum refers (3:8 f.), Ashurbanipal took, according to his own inventory: "Silver, gold, precious stones, the goods of his palace, all there was, brightly colo[red] (and) linen garments, great horses, [the people,] men

[65] For Ashurbanipal's own record of his barbarities, see Piepkorn, *Historical Prism Inscriptions of Ashurbanipal* (1933), pp. 37, 50 ff., 66 ff., 73, 75 f., 83 f., 92 ff.

[66] See Luckenbill, *Ancient Records of Assyria and Babylonia* (1926 to 1927), II, 133.

and women, two tall obelisks, fashioned of glittering electrum, whose wei[ght] was 2,500 talents [placed at the gate] of the temple, [I re]moved from the[ir] positions and to[ok] off to Assyria. Booty, heavy (and) [countless, I carried away] fr[om The]bes." From the Arabians the Assyrians took so much live-stock that camels could be purchased at a trivial price. His Historical Prism boasts: "Cattle, shee[p], asses, camels, [and] slaves without number they took. The whole territory of my land in its entirety they filled (with them) to its farthest border. Camels I distributed like sheep, [divi]ded [them] among the people of Assyria. Throughout my land camels [were bo]ught for a shekel and a half of silver at the gate of barter. The *sutammu* as pay, the brewer for a tun [of beer], the gardener as wages, received [cam]els and slaves."

Most conspicuous in the list of war's conquest was the human booty. When Ashurbanipal in his eighth campaign "covered the Gambulu like a storm," he records: "His wife, his sons, his daughters, his concubines, his singers, male and female — I led (them) forth and counted (them) as spoil. . . . The officials who stood before him, (his) smiths, his quartermasters — [I led forth] and counted (them) as spoil. All [their] arti[sans,] [al]l there were, the bond of city and country — I led (them) forth, I counted (them) as spoil. . . . The people of his land, male and female, small and great, without exception, the warriors (as well) — I led (them) forth, I counted (them) as spoil." Practices like this helped fire the spirit of the prophet to denounce Nineveh as "the mistress that selleth nations." (3:4)[67]

Nineveh is denounced by Nahum as a city full of lies and robbery (3:1). Oriental treachery reached low depths in Assyrian statecraft. Sennacherib's spokesman before the walls of Jerusalem

---

[67] For Ashurbanipal's own report on the human and material spoils carried off by his troops, see Piepkorn, op. cit., pp. 41, 71, 73, 83.

(2 Kings 18:17 f.), with his studied falsehoods, was doubtless typical of Assyrian officialdom. The display inscription, Olmstead summarizes,[68] simply lists the various conquests for the greater glory of the monarch. That they are to be used with caution is obvious. The annalistic inscriptions are often proved unreliable by comparison with parallel tablets and Old Testament references. The number of those slain in one battle is variously listed as 14,000, 20,500, 25,000, 29,000 in various parallel tablets. The 1,235 sheep captured according to the original account became 100,225 in a revised report. The prefixing of a huge round number to a fairly small number in the original was a fairly common trick among the scribes. Internal emendations also disprove the reliability and historicity of the annalistic inscriptions.

Accompanying this falsehood, oppression, robbery, and massacre was the overbearing pride which provoked some of Nahum's denouncements. The royal arrogance is typically reproduced in the introduction to Ashurbanipal's Historical Prism: "I, Ashurbanipal, the great king, the mighty king, king of the universe, king of Assyria, king of the four world-regions, offspring of the loins of Esarhaddon, king of Assyria, duke of Babylon, king of the land of the Sumerian and the Akkadian, grandson of Sennacherib, king of the universe, king of Assyria — [when as my fate] the great gods in their council decreed a favorable destiny, they gave me a broad comprehension, caused my mind to grasp all of the scribal art, exalted my name in the assembly of princes, magnified my rule." [69]

Even more bombastic and egoistic is Esarhaddon's self-praise: "I am powerful, I am all-powerful, I am a hero, I am gigantic, I am colossal, I am honored, I am magnified, I am without equal among all kings, the chosen one of Assur, Nabû and Marduk, called of Sin, favorite of Anu, beloved of the queen,

[68] *Assyrian Historiography* (1916), p. 7.
[69] See Piepkorn, p. 29.

Ishtar, goddess of all [the world]; the unsparing weapon, which utterly destroys the enemy's land, am I." [70]

At the same time gross idolatry covered the land. The temples, the graven images, the molten images, the houses of the gods (1:14) to which Nahum refers, are the evidence of idolatry constantly featured in Ashurbanipal's inscriptions. For example, he boasts: "The sanctuaries of the great gods, my lords, I restored, with gold (and) [silver] I decked. Tutelary deities, storm-bird gods, lofty columns I erected in their gates. Êšarra, Êmašmaš, Êgašankalamma, Êhulhul I made shine like the writing of heaven. Every kind of gold (and) silver adornment of a temple I [ma]de, I ad[ded] to that of my royal ancestors." [71]

In a single cylinder, Rassam's, he pays repeated homage to Adad, Ea, Bel, Nabu, Sin, Shamash, Ninurta, Nergal, Marduk, Nusku, Enlil, Ninlil, Irra, Girra, Anu, and, above all, to Ashur and Ishtar, mentioning these seventeen favorite gods 326 times. Ashur appears by name seventy-nine times and is called "the great god who begat me." Above all others, however, does Ishtar, the patron of Nineveh, receive recognition. She is often referred to as "the Assyrian Ishtar," "Ishtar of Nineveh," "Ishtar of Arbelah," or simply as Ishtar, and is featured ninety-five times. She is given these titles: "The Mistress," "Queen of Kidmuri," "Revered Queen, the Daughter of Enlil," "Lady of Ladies," "Goddess of War," "Mistress of Battle," "Queen of the Gods," "Heroine Among the Gods," "the Exalted of the Gods," "NANA the Glittering." The royal cult of many gods was expanded by the common people.

The knowledge of Nineveh which Nahum thus shows and his acquaintance with the imperial palaces are so impressive that some commentators have sought an Assyrian location for Elkosh, his native city. This conclusion is not necessary. The fame of

[70] The Senjirli Stele. Luckenbill, *Ancient Records of Assyria and Babylonia* (1926—1927), II, 226.

[71] See Piepkorn, p. 29.

the capital, the dread reports of its cruelty, the evidence of its tyranny, had reached to the far corners of the East. Nahum was a well-informed student of human affairs. Besides, he was God's prophet.

THE FULFILLMENT OF NAHUM'S PROPHECIES

The harmony which exists between Nahum's prophecy and its fulfillment in Nineveh's exit from history must corroborate the truth that the seers were guided, not by *Ahnungsvermögen,* that ability to anticipate which keen-minded students of human affairs sometimes display, but by a divinely inspired, prophetic genius. That a Judean author, at a time when Assyrian armies, flushed by heaped triumphs, were crashing through African and Asiatic opposition to record new victories, should foretell the complete destruction of the Tigris metropolis is amazing in itself. So unexpected was the demolition of the city that Nineveh's collapse has been called "one of the greatest riddles of world history." But that Nahum's prevision foresees in detail a score of the notable occurrences which marked the Assyrian capital's end cannot be explained on purely human premises. His predictions, as the force of their fulfillment emphasizes, are the products of divine revelation.

To understand the startling agreement of Nahum's prophetic delineation with its counterpart in historic actuality, it is necessary to compare with his book the composite picture which secular history draws of Nineveh's last days, hitherto largely a dark, uncertain period.

The Greek Sources

Until the close of the last century the chief sources of information regarding the fall of Nineveh were Greek. Thus Herodotus (484—425 B. C.) in his *History* (I, 103, 106, 178) reports that Phraortes, king of the Medes (ca. 647—625 B. C.), attacked Assyria but was killed and his army defeated. Cyaxares, son and successor of Phraortes, filled with a desire to avenge his father, moved energetically against Nineveh. At first success crowned his efforts. The Assyrian capital was cut off and besieged; but a formidable army of Scythians led by Medyes, son of Protothyas, drove him away and lifted the siege. The exact date of this ill-fated campaign is not known. Probably it was about 620 B. C. A few years later, it seems, Cyaxares defeated the Scythians and soon began a second campaign against Assyria.

Ctesias, Greek court physician to Artaxerxes Mnemon, claims to have consulted documentary sources in the Persian royal archives while writing his *Persica,* a chronicle of Assyria and Persia in 23 books. Only fragments of this work survive, especially in the *Chronicles* of Diodorus Siculus (ca. 20 B. C.). This author draws the following picture of Nineveh's end: The Assyrian king was Sardanapalus, an effeminate and thoroughly corrupt monarch. Arbakes, a general of the Medes, and Belesys, a Chaldean official, vassals of Assyria, met in Nineveh. Arbakes gained admittance to the royal quarter of the palace, witnessed the depravity of the king, and determined to organize a rebellion of the conquered countries against him, especially since Belesys had predicted that Arbakes would capture Sardanapalus' empire. At first Sardanapalus was successful over the rebel army consisting of Persians, Medes, Babylonians, and Arabians; but victory in these battles made his people careless, and Arbakes attacked them stealthily at night while the Assyrian soldiers were feasting and drinking. After their defeat the inhabitants of Nineveh were tightly locked within their walls. The siege extended over two years, for Sardanapalus had provisioned the city beforehand. Inordinately heavy rains raised the river to such a level that the walls collapsed. This was regarded as the fulfillment of an ancient oracle to the effect that Nineveh would fall only when the river itself declared war against it. Therefore Sardanapalus built a huge mound containing gold and silver objects, royal apparel, and placing his concubines and eunuchs in the midst of this funeral pyre, destroyed himself, his dependents, and his palace by fire.

As the flames arose, the rebels stormed the city, captured it, and made Arbakes king.[72]

Pompeius Trogus (ca. 20 B. C.), Nicolaus Damascenus, Velleius Paterculus (19 B. C.—A. D. 31) and later authors perpetuate the tradition that Sardanapalus, the last Assyrian king, was a degenerate and an effeminate ruler.

Admittedly the light which Greek sources shed on the last days of Nineveh is meager and disappointing. However, they agree in this, that the Medes were prominently connected with the capture of the city. The accounts generally center in Sardanapalus, a mythical, composite figure with the effeminate characteristics of Ashurbanipal, whose legendary end is reminiscent of Shamash-shum-ukin's (668—646 B. C.) or Sin-shar-ishkun's (612 B. C.) suicide by fire. The Median general who is pictured as opposing him bears the name Arbakes or some similar designation and plays the role later actually filled by Cyaxares.

On the other hand, the statements of the Greek historians cannot be completely discarded, and some Assyriologists now find a germ of truth in certain declarations. Recent investigations seem to point to the possibility and, in a few instances, to the credibility of some of their assertions. A long siege, the prominence of the Medes in the assault, the devastation by fire, the complete obliteration of the city, are recognized parts in Nineveh's debacle. The facts of the destruction in some respects also present the background required for certain episodes transmitted by Greek historians. The possibility that Nineveh's walls broke because of the rising river is endorsed by known instances of such collapse as well as by the seasonal height of the river at the time of the city's fall. That Ashurbanipal, despite his frequent claims of prowess, was a lily-livered coward who more than once shrank from active fighting is recognized by modern historians. The drunkenness associated with the city's end was not an exceptional vice, as bas-reliefs from Nineveh, picturing drinking scenes, testify.

[72] Diodorus Siculus, *Bibliotheca historica,* II, 24—27.

Cuneiform Sources

Much more important are the cuneiform records with their older and better witness to Nineveh's destruction. These cuneiform accounts are the following:

1. Nabopolassar's (625—605 B. C.) inscriptions summarize boastfully yet vaguely: "As for the Assyrians, who since distant days had ruled over all the people and with heavy yoke had brought misery to the people of the land, from the land of Akkad I banished their feet and cast off their yoke." The same king also boasts: "I killed the Subaraean (the Assyrian) and turned his land (variant: the enemy land) into rubble and ruins." [73]

2. The Stele of Nabu-naid. This is a semicircular basalt inscription found in 1895 at Mujelibeh, near the modern Hillah, and dates no later than the middle of the sixth century B. C. In the second of the ten preserved columns its ancient record offers a cuneiform summary of the Assyrian Empire's end. The city of Nineveh is not specifically mentioned, and the tablet is broken at several points of vital context; but lines 14 to 19 ("the king of the Umman Manda, the fearless, destroyed their sanctuaries, those of the gods of Assyria, in their totality") as well as the inferences summarized by Messerschmidt and Gadd [74] leave no doubt that this section of the stele deals with the destruction of the Assyrian Empire. Gadd believes that this passage has nothing to do with the fall of Nineveh, "but is concerned with the wars against the neo-Assyrian kingdom at Harran, in which the Umman Manda took the leading part." The language of Nabu-naid's record, however, is too sweeping and comprehensive

---

[73] Stephen Langdon, "Die Neubabylonischen Königsinschriften," in *Proceedings of the Society of Biblical Archaeology* (1912), pp. 17 ff., 67, and 68.

[74] Leopold Messerschmidt, "Die Inschrift der Stele Nabunaids," in *Mitteilungen der vorderasiatischen Gesellschaft* (1896), pp. 55 ff., and Cyril John Gadd, *The Fall of Nineveh* (1923), British Museum Tablet 21901, or the *Babylonian Chronicle,* p. 20.

to eliminate Nineveh. The stele seems to be a telescoped account of Cyaxares' operations throughout Assyria before and after the city's fall.[75]

3. British Museum Tablet 21,901. The contents of this remarkable document were published in 1923 in Cyril John Gadd's *The Fall of Nineveh*. Although the tablet is not dated, its neo-Babylonian characters show that it is part of the chronicle literature which originated in the earlier years of the Achaemenid period (550—330 B. C.). The references pertaining to the fall of Nineveh are partially fragmentary on account of the damage which the tablet has suffered, and even the complete sections, written in the annalistic style of the *Babylonian Chronicle*, contain relatively meager information regarding the city's capture. But in summarizing the events from Nabopolassar's tenth year until the beginning of his eighteenth year (616—609 B. C.) this tablet offers invaluable data concerning the preliminary siege of the city and its subsequent destinies.

The beginning of this document pictures Nabopolassar, the founder of the neo-Babylonian empire, in open rebellion against the Assyrians, who were fatally weakened by the attacking Scythian hordes. These anti-Assyrian efforts, which may have begun a few years before, centered in the 616 B. C. battles for certain Assyrian provinces; but in 615 B. C. Nabopolassar launched his offensive against the heart of the Assyrian Empire and besieged Ashur, ancient capital. This campaign appears to have been too ambitious. Relief troops from Nineveh helped the Assyrian forces at Ashur throw the Babylonians into hurried flight. In the autumn of that year the Medes, seemingly on their own responsibility, without alliance, attacked one of the Assyrian provinces. In 614 B. C. the lines of military operation were drawn more closely about Nineveh, and the siege of the city was begun

---

[75] This assumption is based on the premise that the Umman Manda here are the Medes. See Maximilian Streck, *Assurbanipal und die letzten assyrischen Könige*, I, CCCLXXV f.

by the Medes, under Cyaxares. A sector of the suburban territory was taken, but a break in the tablet perhaps removes the reason for the escape of Nineveh itself. When the cuneiform record continues, it recounts the capture of Ashur by the Medes, its destruction, the brutal massacre of its inhabitants, and the ominous alliance made between Cyaxares and Nabopolassar. The year 613 B. C. produced the lull before the storm, a period marked in the annals only by a notice regarding a provincial revolt (with Assyrian support) against Babylon and the consequent punitive expeditions. With 612 B. C. the doom arrived. Apparently (the lines are partially obliterated) the Babylonians, the Scythians, and the Medes were allied, marching up the left bank of the Tigris, against Nineveh. The Chronicle indicates that Cyaxares and his Medes played the major part in the subsequent attack and that under his leadership the Babylonians and Scythians assumed the minor role. The siege of the city itself lasted almost three months. While the precise presentation of the Chronicle and its mutilated condition preclude the possibility of learning the details of the siege,[76] it seems apparent that three battles were fought before Nineveh fell in the month of Ab (April-May), 612 B. C. The city was "turned into a mound and a ruin"; yet before the bloody end, in which Nineveh's "chief men" were killed and plunder beyond counting was taken, a company of Ninevites seized an appropriate opportunity to escape the vigils of the besiegers and under the leadership of one Ashuruballit established a petty Assyrian kingdom at Haran.[77]

[76] That the broken tablet at this place treats of Nineveh's capture can be established only by deduction, since the signs for "Nineveh" are quite vague and partially uncertain. However, Gadd, p. 20, correctly maintains: "That this section actually deals with the fall of Nineveh would be certain even if the name had completely disappeared, since (1) the end of Sin-shar-ishkun is expressly indicated; (2) the Babylonian king receives in Nineveh the spoil of Assyrian provinces; and (3) henceforth the kingdom of Assyria and the struggle against it are transferred to the west."

[77] See Gadd, op. cit., pp. 39, 40.

Old Testament Sources

Prophetic references to the destruction of Assyria besides those of Nahum are the following: Is. 10:12-19; 14:24, 25; 30:31-33; 31:8, 9; Zeph. 2:13-15; Zech. 10:11; Ezek. 31:11-16 and 32:22, 23.

The Excavations

In addition to the inscriptional material afforded by cuneiform sources, the results of excavations at the site of Nineveh bear important relation to the predictions of Nahum's oracles. No other ruins in the Assyrian Empire have been investigated as repeatedly as those beneath the Kouyunjik mound opposite Mosul, which covers part of the ancient metropolis. In the investigation of the city's palaces, fortifications, and walls, the historian is furnished with the decisive material by which certain of the prophet's statements may be checked as to their accuracy. Thanks to the labors of archaeologists, uncovered Kouyunjik gives definite answer to such questions: Was Nahum correct when he prophesied that the city would be burned? Was he right when he foretold destruction by water? Is there any evidence for the complete devastation of Nineveh during the Assyrian rule? Were the temples and their images destroyed? Was "an utter end" made of the city? Is its present site waste and ruin?

Nahum's Prophecies Compared with Historical Sources

A comparison of Nahum's predictions with the statements of these sources suggests the following points of contact and agreement: [78]

1. Nahum implies a long siege before the destruction of

[78] Clearly the following pages disprove the statement by Streck: "Naturally one cannot expect of such a prophecy as Nahum to be instructed by it regarding the actual course of the catastrophe. . . . Only a few details . . . might be interpreted as individual features." (Op. cit., I, CDXX)

the city.[79] Nineveh is ironically directed to draw water, strengthen its defenses, prepare bricks and mortar (rather than hastily thrown-up earthworks) for the emergencies of the protracted siege. (3:14)

The *Babylonian Chronicle* tablet offers direct testimony to the fulfillment of this forecast. Nineveh was not taken by immediate storm, for the final siege lasted "from the month of Sivan to the month of Ab," approximately three months. Diodorus, indeed, preserves the hazy tradition that "the siege dragged on for two years" and, as he proceeds to show, went on into the third year. If the operations from 614 to 612 B.C. are grouped together (see 2 below), this tradition has been proved almost literally correct. Some have believed that the "three months occupied by the final siege had been expanded by tradition into three years." Gadd, who suggests this possibility, admits, however: "Against this is the invasion of the 'Bactrian' (i. e., Scythian) army, which seems to demand a longer time, and it is therefore probably better to accept the three years as correct, on the understanding that the war was by no means continuous." [80] The *Babylonian Chronicle* thus "has a remarkable interest as at least a partial confirmation of the tradition which survives in Diodorus that the siege of Nineveh extended into the third year."

2. Nahum warns that "all thy fortresses are fig trees with the first-ripe fruit. When they are shaken, they fall into the eater's mouth" (3:12), i. e., the many Assyrian fortresses surrounding the city (see the context) shall be captured with ease.

The *Babylonian Chronicle* tablet, obverse 11, 24 ff., offers remarkable confirmation of this prophecy in its record for 614 B.C. While the capital city sustained the first assaults in that year, the fortified towns in the environs began to fall. The tablet mentions particularly Tarbis, the present-day Sharif-Khan, north-

---

[79] In contradiction to Andrew Bruce Davidson, *The Cambridge Bible for Schools* (1920), p. 40: "Nahum does not seem to anticipate a lengthy resistance."

[80] C. J. Gadd, *The Fall of Nineveh* (1923), p. 17.

west of Nineveh. If fortifications protected the territory between Nineveh and Ashur, they, too, seem to have fallen quickly; for in the same years Ashur was speedily destroyed.

3. Nahum seems to indicate two stages in the operations against the city. In the first place, the attackers are pictured, not quietly awaiting the end of the siege, but as preparing to give battle outside the city. Vividly the prophet portrays the hostile troops, particularly their cavalry: "Chariots are in fiery steel on the day of His preparing, and the cypress spears are swinging. Chariots career madly in the streets. They overrun one another in the squares." (2:4, 5)

The British Museum tablet seems to imply such battles outside the city, for it records: "From the month of Sivan to the month of Ab three battles (?)...." (Reverse 1, 42)

4. In the second phase of the operations against Nineveh, Nahum foretells, the city itself will be subjected to heavy assault. After the futile attempt to drive the attackers away, the Ninevite warfare outside the city collapses. The enemies "hasten to her wall" and set up their siege machinery (2:6). Disorder reigns within the city. The Ninevites, perhaps in flight, "stumble over their corpses," for there is "a multitude of dead bodies." (3:3)

Briefly the *Babylonian Chronicle* summarizes this second stage of the operations: "A mighty assault they made upon the city." (Reverse 1, 43)

5. Anticipating the attack and siege, Nahum tells the Ninevites: "Strengthen thy fortifications," and he directs the besieged to prepare bricks and mortar for emergency defense walls. (3:14)

Corroboration for the literal fulfillment of these predictions foretelling the final, frantic efforts to strengthen the defenses is furnished, not by inscriptional material but by the ruins of the capital. The Ninevites did fortify their stronghold. They did erect defense walls; for on the basis of topographical researches made by archaeologists at the site of Nineveh, Olmstead [81] mentions the traces of walls quickly erected by the inhabitants "on the line where ran the city defenses before the rebuilding by Sennacherib." He reports: "To the south of the gate, the moat is still filled with fragments of stone and of mud bricks from the walls, heaped up when they were breached."

6. Nahum foresees the city gates, the pivotal points of entrance, attacked and completely destroyed; for he writes: "To thine enemies the gates of thy [Nineveh's] land are open wide." (3:13)

Archaeological reports have stressed the significance of Nineveh's gates as the objectives of assault and have inferentially shown the accuracy of Nahum's prophecy. Olmstead remarks: "The main attack was directed from the northeast and the brunt fell upon the Hatamti gate at this corner. . . . Within the gate are traces of the counterwall raised by the inhabitants in their last extremity." [82]

7. Describing the final chapter in Nineveh's history, the prophet predicts that while the Ninevites are drunken, they shall be consumed. (1:10; 3:11)

The mock security of intoxication which Nahum beheld in his prophetic vision survives in traditional recollection. Herodotus (I, 106) has a story of defeat after drunken debauch in the day of Cyaxares, immediately before the fall of Nineveh. But Diodorus (XXVI, 4) more correctly associates this directly with the destruction of the city. We are told: "Meantime the Assyrian king . . . gave way to negligence and distributed to his soldiers meats and liberal supplies of wine and provisions in general to make merry upon. While the whole army was thus carousing, the friends of Arbakes learned from some deserters of the slackness and drunkenness which prevailed in the enemy's camp and made an unexpected attack by night."

81 Olmstead, *History of Assyria* (1923), p. 637.   82 Loc. cit.

8. Nineveh's capture is assured. Nahum confidently exults: "Desolation and devastation and dilapidation" (2:11). "Nineveh is laid waste," the passers-by cry out. (3:7)

The specific and historical account of the manner in which this startling prediction, made at the heyday of Assyrian power, was fulfilled is offered by the *Babylonian Chronicle* tablet. In this record Sin-shar-ishkun is the king of Assyria residing at Nineveh at the time of its downfall. The city is attacked by a coalition of the Medes under Cyaxares, the Scythians, and the Babylonians under Nabopolassar. The operations against Nineveh began in 614 B. C. They continued, with interruptions, until 612 B. C., when, in the month of Ab, Nineveh was captured. Inferential evidence indicates that the brunt of the assault was borne by the troops of Cyaxares and that the Babylonians were not prominent in the attack.[83]

9. Three times Nahum predicts that Nineveh is to be destroyed by a flood. He prophesies: "With an overrunning flood He [God] will make an end to its place" (1:8). How this inundation is to come upon the city is told in his augury: "The gates of the rivers are opened, and the palace sways" (2:7). As a consequence, the prophet declares: "Nineveh is like a pool of water." (2:9)

This triple emphasis on inundation is more than figurative, and the expressions "gates of the rivers," "overrunning flood," "pool of water" cannot be described away as poetic imagery. These predictions came true, we may well conclude. To be sure, the *Babylonian Chronicle* makes no reference to this inundation; but the terseness of its annalistic style precludes the detailed mention of any episode in the strategy of the siege. However, the Babylonian tablet inferentially offers an acceptable background for the fulfillment of Nahum's prophecies. According to its chronology, Nineveh fell in the month of Ab. The season of the

[83] See Gadd, op. cit., p. 14.

heavy rainfall in Nineveh occurs normally in March, while the rivers attain their greatest height in the months of April and May, the period roughly parallel to Ab.

More positive is the actual evidence of flood submergence found at Nineveh. Badger writes: "The fact here recorded literally fulfills the prophecy of Nahum and accounts for a stratum of pebble and sand which has been found a few feet below the surface in the mounds of Koyoonjuk and Nimrood." [84] Layard likewise calls attention to evidences of inundation. These *in situ* investigations contradict the disparaging opinions that the excavations at Nineveh furnish no evidence that floods destroyed any portion of the walls.

Tradition also speaks forcefully in support of the fulfillment of Nahum's flood prophecy. Diodorus, recalling the manner in which the river allied itself with the besiegers, recounts: "The siege dragged on, and for two years they pressed their attack. . . . But in the third year, after there had been heavy and continuous rains, it came to pass that the Euphrates (!), running very full, both inundated a portion of the city and broke down the walls for a distance of twenty stades. At this the king, believing that the oracle had been fulfilled, and that the river had become plainly the city's enemy, abandoned hope for saving himself." [85]

In the *Anabasis* (III, 4, 12) Xenophon connects the capture of the city with terrifying thunder and therefore doubtless with a storm.

Besides the topography of Nineveh, as far as it may now be reconstructed, shows how the high waters of the contiguous rivers might have undermined the walls and flooded large lower areas in the city. As far as we now know, three rivers come into consideration. The first is the Tigris. The exact course it took has been debated. On the one hand, investigators like Thompson

[84] George Percy Badger, *The Nestorians and Their Rituals* (1852), I, 78, 79.

[85] *Bibliotheca historica*, II, 26, 27.

and Hutchinson maintain that the river did not flow immediately past Nineveh's walls "except perhaps at the time of high floods in spring." Instead they hold that the Tigris took essentially its present course, which is 1—1½ kilometers west of the city walls. They maintain that it was the Tebiltu, an offshoot of the Tigris, that flanked the southwest side of the city.[86] On the other hand, the majority of scholars have held that the Tigris flowed directly past the city on the west.[87] Indeed, it appears that the course of the river was gradually changed through the centuries. It may well be that the annual heavy alluvial deposits which the Khosr (see below) brought into the Tigris slowly pushed this river westward. Belck and Lehmann report: "Our most important observations concerned themselves, as already indicated, with the course of the Tigris. We came to the conviction that this must have changed very greatly, and we found that the Tigris must have flowed directly past the walls of Nineveh. Thereby the reports in Nahum and the weak notices in the classical accounts . . . receive their confirmation."[88] Similarly Layard relates that he could trace the old bed of the Tigris in the adjacent alluvial deposit.[89] Thus, as capable historians have conceded, the Tigris could have been the river which turned Nineveh into "a pool

[86] Thompson and Hutchinson, in *A Century of Exploration at Nineveh* (1929), pp. 122 f., insist that if the Tigris flowed along the southwest city wall, the gates in that section would certainly bear a name indicating their connection with the river. They point out that the two gates in the southwest which have such indication are near the Tebiltu and the Khosr. This is only a secondary consideration, however, as the gate names may have been changed or need not, even originally, have reflected the river location.

[87] Karl Ritter, *Die Erdkunde* (1822—59), p. 224. Sir Austen Henry Layard, *Nineveh and Babylon* (1875), p. 77. Felix Jones, "Nineveh's Location," *Journal of Royal Asiatic Society* (1855), XV, 316, 323. F. E. Peiser, "Tigris to the East of Nineveh," *Mitteilungen der vorderasiatischen Gesellschaft*, III, 277, 278. C. F. Lehmann and Paul Haupt, *Israel, seine Entwickelung im Rahmen der Weltgeschichte* (1911), p. 149. M. Streck, *Assurbanipal und die letzten assyrischen Könige* (1916), I, CDXXXIX. Claude Hermann Walter Johns, "Location of Tigris," in *Encyclopaedia Britannica*, 11th ed. (1911), XIX, Col. 3, 421.

[88] W. Belck and C. F. Lehmann, "Reisebriefe von der armenischen Expedition," in *Mitteilungen der geographischen Gesellschaft in Hamburg* (1900), XVI, 67.

[89] Austen Henry Layard, *Nineveh and Babylon* (1875), p. 118.

of water." Gadd concludes: "The truth doubtless is that Kyaxares simply took advantage of the devastation caused by an abnormally high Tigris in the preceding spring to press home his assault upon the only place in the walls which accident had rendered vulnerable." [90] Again, in his studies of Nineveh's collapse, Friedrich holds that the city was captured after the swollen waters of the Tigris and its tributaries had swept away sections of the wall and flooded the capital.[91]

The second river which could have caused "the overrunning flood" was the Khosr (Assyrian: Husur; Arabic: Hausar). This seems to have entered the city from the northeast, through the Ninlil Gate. It took a circuitous course through southwest Nineveh and, cutting through the city walls near the Quay Gate, joined the Tigris. The Khosr was capable of swelling to such proportions that its overflow could cause wide damage.[92] Therefore Sennacherib records: "To assuage the flow of these waters I made an *agammu*," [93] a pool, or a reservoir. Thompson reports on Sennacherib's *agammu*. "Some two miles north of Kouyunjik the Khosr, only thirty yards wide, runs through the Ajilah gorge. . . . Here on the river are two massive dam walls, the upper about 150 yards upstream of Ajilah, the lower about 250 yards downstream." [94] At both of these dams, constructed in the typical Assyrian style, the investigators believe, there was originally a gate or sluice to regulate the water flow. How easy, then, for the besieging army to impound the Khosr River at this place, close the sluices of the *agammu,* cut off this source

[90] C. J. Gadd, *The Fall of Nineveh* (1923), p. 18.

[91] Thomas Friedrich, "Ninevehs Ende u. die Ausgänge des assyrischen Reiches," *Festgaben zu Ehren Max Büdingers von seinen Freunden u. Schülern* (1898), p. 31.

[92] Olmstead's map (*History of Assyria,* p. 327) makes the Khosr take an almost straight line through the city. Topographical evidence seems to indicate that the river bent decidedly, particularly near the present Kouyunjik mound.

[93] Cylinder EI, col. VIII, 47. Luckenbill, *The Annals of Sennacherib,* p. 115. But Luckenbill translates *agammu* as "swamp."

[94] Thompson and Hutchinson, *A Century of Exploration at Nineveh,* page 131.

of water supply (the water of the Tigris was not drinkable), and then, opening the river gates (see 2:7), let the mass of dammed waters sweep down on the doomed city, carry the river gates away, flood the lower sections of the city, and thus help spell the beginning of Nineveh's end! Even today, at the supposed site of the Ninlil Gate in the city's walls, the Khosr broadens to recall the prophet's words: "Nineveh is like a pool of water" (2:9). The ruins of the *agammu* indicate that this section of Sennacherib's water works did not collapse simply through neglect, but was destroyed, doubtless by enemy action.[95]

Lehmann-Haupt propose another theory by which the Khosr wrought the fatal havoc. They hold that the enemy, once within the outer walls, closed the sluice gates which had diverted the high waters of the Khosr into side canals. This action, they explain, gave the swollen river the irresistible, tearing power by which it broke the walls.[96]

Local tradition, also recorded by Lehmann-Haupt, likewise maintains that the Khosr River destroyed the walls and expedited Nineveh's capture. They write: "Today the place may still be seen where the water broke through; and the natives informed

---

[95] Thompson and Hutchinson, op. cit., p. 132, call attention to one of the gates in the inner wall, the *Mushlalu* Gate, frequently explained as the "River Wall Gate." They suggest that this may be so named because of its association with the "river wall" *(mushlalu)* about one mile below the *agammu*, a second dam at the bend of the Khosr. Great boulders, they report, have the appearance of being placed there. This arrangement would lend additional force to the hypothesis suggested above, because it puts the city in direct connection with the *agammu*.

[96] C. F. Lehmann and Paul Haupt, *Israel, seine Entwickelung im Rahmen der Weltgeschichte* (1911), p. 149: "Nineveh lay on the left bank of the Tigris, whose waters directly washed its walls on the west, as even today personal inspection shows. A left-side stream of the Tigris, the Khosr (today the Chausser), divides the city into two halves. Its course and conjunction with the Tigris were well regulated by dam installations. The besiegers succeeded in capturing the higher installations (situated within the outer walls of the city). They closed the drainage sluices through which the water of the Khosr, highly swollen at the time of the melting snow, could be diverted into the moats of the fortress and the side canals; and through the dams, as through the opening of the safety sluices in the Khosr, the river was given such violence that it overflowed its regular bed, inundated the territory of the city, and broke down the walls of Nineveh toward the Tigris, after which the summer high water of the Tigris did the rest."

me — it should be noted, without my suggesting this through questions — that this was the work of the Khosr. But, as one observes only too frequently in the Orient, they transposed the occurrence into a much-too-recent past. In this way Nineveh actually perished through floods of water, as the contemporary prophet Nahum (2:7 ff.) and the later classical passages in harmony with him (Diodorus II, 26 ff.) have announced. Only ignorance of the local conditions and of the change in the flow of the Tigris — the Tigris now, in consequence of century-long floods, flows past the walls of Nineveh at a distance of a half kilometer — help them misunderstand the long period of time." [97]

The third river, whose gates could have been opened or whose waters could have produced the overrunning flood, is the Tebiltu. This stream, as its name implies (it is significantly derived from the Assyrian verb *tabâlu,* "to take away," "to tear away") could become a raging torrent. Its course has not been traced satisfactorily. Olmstead [98] makes the Tebiltu run parallel with the Khosr for some distance outside the city walls, and then he has it enter Nineveh from the north and flow through the city, joining the Tigris on the west at the Water Gate. Thompson and Hutchinson attack this topography and maintain that the course of the Tebiltu suggested by Olmstead would make the river flow uphill. [99] They hold that the Tebiltu was an offshoot of the Tigris; that it entered the city through the northwest wall near what was later the Nergal Gate; that originally it flowed close to the northwest slope of the present Kouyunjik mound and then turned to the southwest to continue until it joined the Khosr. This original course was altered by Sennacherib, who to protect the burial grounds and the foundation of the small palace rechanneled part of the Tebiltu, inside

[97] Ibid., p. 149.

[98] Olmstead, *History of Assyria,* p. 327.

[99] Thompson and Hutchinson, *A Century of Exploration at Nineveh* (1929), pp. 122—124.

the city, so that it flowed to the west corner of the inner wall and then washed the entire southwest wall until it reached its old bed southwest of Kouyunjik. If this was the course the Tebiltu took in 612 B. C., it could the more easily play havoc with the city walls.

The Assyrian inscriptions give ample testimony to the Tebiltu's devastating violence. Sennacherib, Ashurbanipal's grandfather, complained that the river not only rose above its bank repeatedly during the centuries, but also undermined the foundations of some palaces and probably was the cause for their demolition. In his days the river constituted such a menace that he changed its course, perhaps removing some of the bends in order to expedite its flow. He also strengthened the foundations of the temple with "mighty slabs of limestone," so that "its platform might not be weakened by the flood of high water." If, as we have reason to believe on the basis of topographical studies by Thompson and Hutchinson, the Tebiltu ran inside the city along the southwest section of the wall, it could have become, if swollen artificially or naturally, the agency for the destruction of large portions of the wall. Is there any significance to the fact that in this section the defenders sought to erect a secondary wall? [100] Had the city wall been destroyed? [101]

Thus the time of Nineveh's fall, the high-water season,

[100] See Olmstead, *History of Assyria,* p. 637.

[101] See Sennacherib's building records, Bellino Cylinder, written in 702 B. C. (after Luckenbill, *Annals,* p. 99):

"46. The Tebiltu-river, a raging, destructive stream, which at its high water, had destroyed the mausoleums inside the city and had exposed to the sun their tiers of coffins (lit. piled-up coffins),

47. and, from days of old, had come up close to the palace and with its floods at high water had worked havoc with its foundation and destroyed its platform:

48. that small palace I tore down in its totality. I changed the course of the Tebiltu, repaired the damage, and directed its outflow

49. through its covered channel (bed) . . .

51. . . . along the Tigris, I filled in a terrace, and made a careful survey of it . . .

52. That in days to come its platform might not be weakened by the floods at high water, I had its sides (lit. walls) surrounded with mighty slabs of limestone, and (so) I strengthened its structure."

as well as the evidence of inundation found at Kouyunjik, and the traditional recollections of a river flood, all point to the fulfillment of Nahum's startling, threefold prophecy. In addition, topographical investigation reveals that either the Tigris, the Khosr, the Tebiltu, or these three rivers conjointly (note the plural in 2:7: "the gates of the rivers") could have made the proud capital "a pool of water."

10. Nahum repeatedly predicts that Nineveh will be destroyed by fire: "They shall be consumed as stubble fully dry" (1:10); "I will burn her chariots in the smoke" (2:14); "Fire consumes thy bars," he continues (3:3); and he repeats, "Fire will devour thee." (3:15)

Destruction by fire, as frequent as it was in the ancient Orient, was not the inevitable destiny of every captured city; yet Nineveh was assigned to the flames. The *Babylonian Chronicle* is again silent regarding this detail, which was of no particular moment in its brisk annalistic summary; but this silence is not shared by Diodorus (II, 27), who records that Sardanapalus (regarded as Nineveh's last ruler), "despairing of his fate" (but resolved not to fall into the hands of his enemies) . . . prepared a gigantic pyre in the royal precincts, heaped up all his gold and his kingly raiment as well upon it, shut up his concubines and eunuchs in the chamber he had made in the midst of the pyre, and burned himself, his family, concubines, eunuchs, and palace.

Abydenus echoes the same tradition when he speaks of Sarakos (Sin-shar-ishkun), who "burned himself and his royal palace." [102]

Whatever actual history may lurk behind this dramatic denouement, the excavations upon the site of Nineveh have revealed the truth of Nahum's double prophecy concerning destruction by fire. Layard reports: "The palace (Sennacherib's) had been destroyed by fire. The alabaster slabs were almost

[102] Eusebius, *Chronicon,* I, 28, 35, 37, 130.

reduced to lime, and many of them fell to pieces as soon as uncovered. The places, which others had occupied, could only be traced by a thin white deposit, like a coat of plaster, left by the burnt alabaster upon the wall of sun-dried bricks." [103] Rawlinson summarizes: "The recent excavations have shown that fire was a great instrument in the destruction of the Nineveh palaces. Calcined alabaster, masses of charred wood and charcoal, colossal statues, slit through with the heat, are met with parts of Ninevite mounds and attest the veracity of the prophecy." [104]

Similarly other explorers have noted the unmistakable evidence of conflagration at Kouyunjik. When Hormuzd Rassam began his investigations at the north corner of Kouyunjik, he first of all came upon a ruined wall; and when that ended, "there was nothing except ashes, bones, and rubbish." In 1903 L. W. King reopened the diggings at Nineveh, particularly in the southwest, and found in the debris covering the great court of the palace "charred cedar" timber, and in the rooms of the devastated structure, sculptures the surface of which "had been cracked by fire." In 1927 Thompson and Hutchinson completed excavating the temple of Nabu and reported: "There was no question about the clear traces of the burning of the temple (as also in the palace of Sennacherib), for a layer of ash about two inches thick lay clearly defined in places on the southeast side above the level of the Sargon pavement." [105]

The catastrophic intensity of the fire is also corroborated in the report by Thompson and Hamilton.[106]

[103] Layard, *Popular Account of Discoveries at Nineveh* (1857), p. 321.

[104] Sir Henry Rawlinson, *The History of Herodotus* (1862), p. 448, note.

[105] Thompson and Hutchinson, *A Century of Exploration at Nineveh* (1929), pp. 45 and 77.

[106] R. Campbell Thompson and R. W. Hamilton, "The British Museum Excavations on the Temple of Ishtar at Nineveh, 1930—31," in *Annals of Archaeology and Anthropology* (Liverpool, 1932), XIX, Nos. 3, 4, p. 73. For a further report on the devastation of fire see R. Campbell Thompson and R. W. Hutchinson, "The Excavations on the Temple of Nabu at Nineveh," in *Archaeologia* (Oxford, 1929), LXXIX, 106, 107.

11. The capture of Nineveh, so Nahum prophesied, was to be attended by a harrowing slaughter. He draws this vivid picture: "A host of slain, and a multitude of dead bodies; and there is no end of their corpses; they stumble over their corpses." (3:3)

Through subsequent centuries the memory of the carnage at the capture of Nineveh persisted. Diodorus (XXVI, 6, 7) relates: "In two battles fought on the plain before the city the rebels defeated the Assyrians, slew Salaemes (the Assyrian general) on the field, slaughtered many of the opposing forces in the pursuit, and, as for the rest, cut off as they were from the retreat to the city and compelled to cast themselves into the Euphrates (!), they slew them all with few exceptions. So great was the multitude of the slain that the flowing stream, mingled with their blood, changed its color for a considerable distance."

Once again the *Babylonian Chronicle* does not pause to relate any particularly brutal details of the slaughter in connection with Nineveh's capture. But if the operations from 614 to 612 B. C. are regarded as a continued offensive against the capital and if we picture the attack on adjacent cities as typical, even the chronicler was impressed by this vicious destruction, for after the capture of the city of Tarbis, "in the district of Nineveh," he records his dismay at the bloody butchery practiced by the Medes.[107] It is quite possible that Diodorus, in his story of the blood-tinged Euphrates, has preserved the tradition of the terrifying massacre envisioned in Nahum's prophetic panorama.

12. Nahum also draws a picture of the plundering and pillaging which will mark the overthrow of the capital. Apostrophizing the city's enemies, he shouts: "Seize booty of silver! Seize booty of gold! For there is no end to the store, an abundance of all desirable articles" (2:10). After the looting has subsided, he looks upon Nineveh and predicts: "Desolation and devastation and dilapidation." (2:11)

[107] Rev., lines 26, 27. He employs the term *limnish,* lit., "in an evil manner."

The booty taken when Nineveh fell was so staggering that the Babylonian chronicler uses an expression not employed in any other campaigns from 616 to 609 B. C. In full harmony with the prophet he states (reverse 1, 45) "the spoil of the city, *a quantity beyond counting,* they plundered." Striking indeed is this agreement between Nahum's prediction: "There is no end to the store," and the chronicler's record: "The spoil of the city, a quantity beyond counting." Diodorus remarks that Arbakes removed many talents of gold and silver from the destroyed capital. Significantly, too, little precious metal has been found in Kouyunjik.

13. As Nahum foresees the city's fall, he predicts: "Behold, thy people in thy midst are women" (3:3). This has usually been interpreted to the effect that the defenders of the city would show unmanly cowardice and flee. Others have read more dire implications into this expression. However, a statement by Athenaeus, following Ctesias, which may have a significant bearing, has hitherto escaped attention in this connection. This compiler, discussing the luxury of nations, cities, and individual rulers, expatiates on the degeneracy of Sardanapalus and recounts: "Arbakes, a Mede by birth and one of the generals of his realm, entered into intrigue with a eunuch named Sparameizes to obtain a view of Sardanapalus; and the king reluctantly giving his consent, an audience was permitted him; when the Mede entered, he saw the king with his face covered with white lead and bejeweled like a woman, combing purple wool in the midst of his concubines and sitting among them with knees uplifted, his eyebrows blackened, wearing a woman's dress and having his beard shaved close and his face rubbed with pumice (he was even whiter than milk, and his eyelids were painted), and when he looked upon Arbakes, he rolled the whites of his eyes." [108] Most authorities, including also Duris, record that Arbakes, outraged to think that such a person should be their king, stabbed him to death. But Ctesias

[108] Charles Burton Gulick, ed., *Athenaeus* (1933), I, 528, 529.

says that the king got into a war and, after collecting a large army, was defeated by Arbakes and died by setting a fire to himself in the palace; he heaped up a pyre four hundred feet high, on which he placed a hundred and fifty gold couches and an equal number of tables, these also of gold.

Nicolaus Damascenus, who wrote two centuries before Athenaeus, has perpetuated a similar tradition; he emphasizes the effeminacy of Sardanapalus but leaves undetermined the connection which this perversion bore to the fall of Nineveh. The wide persistence of such legends may be seen in the references found not only in Ctesias, Athenaeus, Nicolaus Damascenus, but also in similar statements by Duris, Diodorus Siculus, Pompeius Trogus, Velleius Paterculus, Justinus, Orosius, and others.

While popular tradition easily magnifies every abnormality, the more recent historical evidence, however, tends to corroborate the picture of Ashurbanipal as a weakling. Olmstead calls him "a frightened degenerate who had not the stamina to take his place in the field." [109] Under the impress of this enthroned effeminacy, it is without particular difficulty that we can reconstruct the last years of Nineveh's existence in harmony with the prophet's prevision.

14. Nahum predicts the precipitous flight which follows the city's capture. "They are in flight," he declares, and when bystanders, seeking to quell the panic, cry out: "Stand, stand!" "no one turns around" (2:9). Even the officials of Assyria are "as the locust," and the military leaders as "grasshoppers" that "flee." (3:17)

Ample testimony corroborates this flight. Diodorus, for instance (XXVI, 8), preserves the tradition, which coincides remarkably with the prophet's forecast of Nineveh's royalty in hasty retreat. "Sardanapalus," so he relates, ". . . sent away his three sons and two daughters with much treasure into Paphlagonia, to the governor of Kattos, the most loyal of his subjects."

[109] *Assyrian Historiography,* p. 7.

The *Babylonian Chronicle* (reverse 1, 46) is even more emphatic, for, though mutilated, it indicates that "(the king) of Assyria before the king (i. e., of Media or Babylonia) escaped." We may well expand the brevity of this notice by assuming that during the siege a number of the Assyrians, including, as Nahum has specifically prophesied, officials and military leaders, made their escape in an unexpected moment, fled as the locusts to distant localities, beyond the reach of the besiegers.

15. Nahum lays repeated stress on the fact that in the siege and fall of Nineveh the Assyrian nobles play an ignominious role and are doomed to defeat. Ironically he warns: "Thy guards are as the locust, and thy scribes as a swarm of grasshoppers which alight on the wall on a cold day. The sun riseth, and they flee, and their place is not known. Where are they? Thy shepherds slumber, King of Assyria; thy mighty ones rest in death."

Part of one of the nine lines which the British Museum tablet devotes to Nineveh's downfall records that "a great havoc of the chief men was made." It does not weaken the force of this prediction and its fulfillment to observe that a similar statement is made when, at the capture of Ashur, Cyaxares made "cruel havoc" of the chief men. Nahum, in prophetic preview, sees an inglorious defeat for the Assyrian nobility, and the *Babylonian Chronicle* in historical review pauses to recount this very fact.

16. Nahum specifically foretells that in the overthrow of the city Nineveh's temples and their images will be desecrated. He repeats Yahweh's decree: "From the house of thy gods I will cut off graven image and molten image." (1:14)

The stele of Nabu-naid lays this striking emphasis on the general overthrow of the Assyrian temples: "The king of the Umman Manda, the fearless one, ruined all the temples of the gods of Assyria; and he ruined the cities on the border of Akkad . . . and did not leave one of their sanctuaries."

Especially decisive is the report by Thompson and Hutchinson on the complete destruction of the temple of Nabu at Nineveh. These investigators write: "The temple, like the rest of the buildings on the mound, was burnt in the general *debacle,* the ash strata being obvious, particularly on the top of the Sargon courtyard . . . where the fallen *libn* of the walls was marked in a well-defined mass 2' thick above the ash. . . . Outside the temple . . . ash lay thick, and near the southeast doorway . . . the ash was 6" thick and about 1' 6" *below* the level of Ashur-banipal's pavement. . . . *This ash confirms all the traditional accounts of the destruction.*"[110] (Our italics)

Other details concerning the temple devastation in Nineveh are told in scientific survey by Thompson and Hamilton.[111] Not merely by chance, but directly in fulfillment of Nahum's prophecy, the statue of the mother goddess Ishtar, bombastically dedicated centuries previously by Ashur-bel-kala, was literally "cast out," so that it lay headless and humiliated in the debris. How the Assyrian temples were desecrated is shown by Hormuzd Rassam's report on a vandalized temple at Nimrud (19 miles south of Nineveh and probably destroyed about the same time that Nineveh fell): "At Nimrud my researches also proved of some importance by the discovery of what has been proved to be the temple of Assurnasirpal. Everything in it was found in fragments, with the exception of a marble altar and the marble chairs; and it shows that the enemy was determined not to leave one stone upon the other, when he destroyed it. Hundreds of beautifully painted and enameled tiles and knobs (which I believe belonged to the ceiling of the temple), inscribed marble tablets, pieces of

110 Thompson and Hutchinson, *The Excavations on the Temple of Nabu at Nineveh,* p. 106. Note also observations like these on p. 73 concerning the condition of the Nabu temple: "A very small portion of the W corner was so destroyed as not to be worth excavation." "The inner walls (of the chamber, the shrine and the library) had collapsed in the general destruction" (p. 74). "We found few traces of walls standing." (P. 44)

111 Thompson and Hamilton, *The British Museum Excavations on the Temple of Ishtar at Nineveh* (1930—31), pp. 55 ff.

marble tripods, and other small objects were found in utter confusion, scattered all over the floor of the temple." [112]

17. Nahum predicts that "Huzzab is stripped. She is brought up, and her handmaidens are moaning, as with the sound of doves. They are taboring upon their breasts" (2:8). This unusually difficult verse (see commentary) is most frequently so interpreted that Huzzab becomes the queen of Nineveh and that she is led away captive together with her lamenting handmaidens. However, commentators have had trouble in expressing the action indicated in "she is brought up." Most frequently it is regarded as equivalent to "she shall be led away." But the Hebrew is too specific for that. In the original the verb meaning "brought up" is used in the conjugation here employed, only in two other passages: 2 Chron. 20:34, in the sense "to be mentioned," "to be recorded" (which obviously does not fit here), and Judg. 6:28, for "to bring up a sacrifice on the altar, as a burned offering." This, I suggest, is the interpretation which should be accepted here. Nahum foresees that at the fall of the city Nineveh's queen is "brought up" (on an altar, or elevated structure). Now, do any traditional recollections shed light on the queen's fate and indicate how she was "brought up"?

Athenaeus, quoting Ctesias as his authority, gives this significant account: "The king [Sardanapalus] was defeated by Arbakes and died by setting fire to himself in the palace; he heaped up a pyre 400 ft. high, on which he placed 150 golden couches and lay down; and not only he, but *his queen with him*" [our italics]. Athenaeus continues to relate that the flames lasted for fifteen days and that the people of Nineveh, when they saw the smoke, thought that Sardanapalus was offering "sacrifices."

It may well be that tradition has retained in a garbled form the very event which Nahum's prophecies have forecast. The

[112] Hormuzd Rassam, "Utter Destruction of Nineveh," *Transactions of the Society of Biblical Archaeology*, VII, 57; *Excavations and Discoveries in Assyria*, pp. 37 ff.

queen is featured only in this Ctesias-Athenaeus account, but the towering pyre in the royal precincts (which harmonizes strikingly with the otherwise difficult "brought *up*") is also described by Diodorus, by Pompeius Trogus, and by Justinus in Eusebius.

Nahum foresees that the queen's maidens will accompany her, striking their breasts in lament. The Ctesias-Athenaeus account specifically relates: "The concubines were on other couches" and were likewise consumed by fire. This prophetic forecast and this traditional review may describe the same event. Diodorus, Pompeius Trogus, and Justinus also feature the concubines as perishing in Sardanapalus' suicidal flames, and it requires little imagination to see them striking their breasts, as the prophet pictures them, when, with the queen, they are "brought up" on the towering pyre.

18. Though Nineveh is to be destroyed, Nahum does not embrace the entire Assyrian nation in his dire prophecy. It is almost an axiom of history that while empires vanish, cities remain. Nahum, however, by implication, predicts the opposite. The royalty and the leaders have fled; yet the last two verses of the book are formally addressed to "King of Assyria" (3:18). Nineveh, the prophet implies, will be wiped out, but its king remains, albeit a *roi fainéant,* whose "nobles rest" (in death) and whose people are "scattered on the mountains, and there is no one to gather them." (3:18)

In one of its most distinguished services the *Babylonian Chronicle* seems to substantiate directly the details of this remarkable prediction. Reverse 1, 46 apparently indicates that "(the king) of Assyria before the king escaped." It may be that one of the leaders who fled to safety was Ashur-uballit. He is mentioned in the annals of the sixteenth year (610 B. C.) as occupying "the throne of Assyria" in the city of Haran (reverse 1, 60) and of the seventeenth year (reverse 11, 66 ff.), when he is specifically called "king of Assyria" and described as an ally of Egypt.

Inferences drawn from the *Chronicle* and the subsidiary evidences of other sources indicate the weakness of Ashur-uballit's reign, the dispersion of his people, and the general fulfillment of the prophet's prediction.

19. Dispersion is likewise predicted. When the city falls, the *"people is scattered on the mountains, and no man gathereth them"* (3:18). Not all captured and devastated cities have suffered this fate. Babylon was laid completely waste by Sennacherib with a massacre regarded as bloody and horrifying even in those cruel days; but the citizens of Babylon returned, rebuilt their city; it flourished for a century and a half to acquire an unparalleled glory in the neo-Babylonian period. Jerusalem was besieged and captured by Nebuchadnezzar; masses of its people were led into captivity; but they returned and rebuilt the city, which has been perpetuated ever since. The captive and dispersed citizens of Nineveh, however, never returned to restore the capital. Its inhabitants disappeared so completely that they have left no impress on subsequent ages. No people have lost their identity more completely and quickly than did the Ninevites, confirming Nahum's prediction. *Cambridge Ancient History,* III, 130, declares: "The disappearance of the Assyrian people will always remain an unique and striking phenomenon in ancient history."

This prediction becomes the more remarkable when the scope of its time is understood. Even those critics who maintain, against the internal evidence, that the prophecies are *post eventum* cannot explain, even on their own theories, how Nahum with its long-range view, covering all subsequent centuries, could declare that no man would gather the scattered remains of Nineveh; yet 2,500 years of history have strikingly corroborated this forecast made before the city collapsed.

20. Nahum writes the finis for Nineveh. Not only will it be destroyed, but the Lord will make "an end" (1:9). Its posterity will be cut off, for, said Yahweh to Nineveh: "I will

make thy grave" (1:14). The voice of Nineveh's "messengers shall not be heard again." (2:14)

With few exceptions every large ancient city in the Orient has been destroyed; but many of them have been rebuilt, and some have perpetuated themselves until our day. However, Nahum visualizes the "utter end" of Nineveh, which in his day was the metropolis of the Middle East. How, the modern reader may well pause to ask, could the prophet know that a city with the wealth, power, and dominance that were Nineveh's would be utterly extirpated as a consequence of the assault which his book describes? How could he conclude that Nineveh would never be restored, unlike the city of Babylon, destroyed by Sennacherib in a campaign that was ruthless even for the Assyrians, yet rebuilt by the Babylonians immediately thereafter? The answer is found in the assurance of Amos (3:7): "Surely the Lord God will do nothing but He revealeth His secret unto His servants the prophets."

The Babylonian chronicler records that the assaulting enemies "turned the city into a mound and a ruin" (reverse 1, 45). It has remained desolate and unoccupied ever since. About 200 years after its devastation, Xenophon passed by its site without realizing that the ruins were the remains of haughty Nineveh (*Anabasis* III, 4, 10—12). He calls the territory Mespila. Lucian (*Charon,* c. 23) declares: "Nineveh has perished, and there is no trace left where it once was." Strabo (XVI, 1, 3) writes that Nineveh soon disappeared forever after the destruction of the Assyrian Empire. In 1776, when Niebuhr came to the site of the destroyed city, he thought the mounds were natural eminences. Only since 1842, through Botta's excavations and Layard's subsequent work, were the mounds of Kouyunjik definitely identified as covering parts of ruined Nineveh.

Layard, reviewing his excavations, on the eve of his return to Nineveh, writes: "We have been fortunate enough to acquire the most convincing and lasting evidence of that magnificence, and power, which made Nineveh the wonder of the ancient world, and her fall the theme of the prophets, as the most signal instance of divine vengeance. Without the evidence that these monuments afford, we might also have doubted that the great Nineveh ever existed, so completely has she become 'a desolation and a waste.' " [113]

Kuenen endeavors to discredit Nahum's prediction of Nineveh's "utter end" by insisting that the city was perpetuated. He writes: "It stands assured that Nahum foretells and describes the destruction of Nineveh as though it were already taking place. . . . Nineveh was depopulated and became a desolation comparatively quickly, but still not all at once. . . . She must thus have quickly sustained a swift and irreparable blow by the rise of Babylon, but she was not altogether annihilated." He also cites Tacitus (*Annals,* XII, 13) and Ammianus Marcellinus (xxiii, 6).[114] Similarly George Smith maintains: "It should always be remembered that the site of Nineveh has been inhabited from the fall of the city until now." [115] Likewise Streck declares that centuries later a small city arose on the ruins of Nineveh.[116] These are specious technicalities. Imperial Nineveh was destroyed forever. Excavators are agreed that "for the next three hundred years at least [after 612 B. C.] there is nothing to show that there was any occupation at all on the site." [117] Nineveh disappeared; as far as is known,

[113] Austen Henry Layard, *Popular Account of Discoveries at Nineveh* (1857), p. 351.

[114] Abraham Kuenen, *De Profeten en de Profetie onder Israel* (1875), I, 152, 153.

[115] George Smith, *Assyrian Discoveries* (1875), p. 139.

[116] Maximilian Streck, *Assurbanipal und die letzten assyrischen Könige* (1916) I, CDXLIX, note 1.

[117] Thompson and Hutchinson, *A Century of Exploration at Nineveh,* p. 138; also Thompson and Hamilton, *The British Museum Excavations on the Temple of Ishtar at Nineveh,* p. 74: "After the destruction in 612 there appears to have been no occupation at least until the 3rd century B. C. and perhaps not until the 2nd or even 1st." And Layard, *Discoveries in the Ruins of Nineveh and Babylon,* pp. 590 ff.

no sixth-century or subsequent Babylonian record, no Persian text, mentioned the extinct capital. Herodotus, I, 193, identifies the Tigris as the river "on which the city of Nineveh formerly stood." The varying fortunes of the settlements which sporadically arose after the Macedonian era, during the Seleucid, Greek, Roman, Sassanian, and the later periods, are traced, almost layer by layer, in *A Century of Exploration at Nineveh*.[118] These isolated settlements, however, are not the perpetuation of the Assyrian Nineveh, and none of them has maintained its existence. The impartial verdict of history, substantiating Nahum's predictions, declares: "Other, similar empires have indeed passed away, but the people have lived on. . . . No other land seems to have been sacked and

[118] Pp. 139 ff. The authors, R. C. Thompson and R. W. Hutchinson, who excavated at Nineveh, state that "the first sign of civilized re-occupation appears to be after the Macedonian conquest. Layard, *Nineveh and Babylon*, p. 592, speaks of relics of the Seleucidae and the Greek occupation from Kouyunjik. . . . In 1904—5 on the site of the Temple of Nabu a Greek inscription on a column came to light which would appear to belong to the second century. . . . We have found fragments of red pottery which may be attributed to the first century B. C. Next Meherdates captured Nineveh (called 'Ninos' by Tacitus, *Annals* XII, 13) in 50 A. D. and during the Roman period a castle appears to have stood on the site. . . . Claudius (A. D. 41—54) may perhaps have made Nineveh into a Roman colony. . . . We found some fragments of *Terra sigillata* of the first century A. D. on the site of the Nabu Temple, and two lamps of the third century. . . . The Sassanian period is marked by a few Pehlevi gems, fragments of pottery, and coins (quoted by Layard, ibid.), and by a hoard of Sassanian coins of the fifth century found by us on the Temple site. The sixth and seventh centuries may be marked by the fairly numerous fragments of pottery ornamented with stamped medallions of animals, etc., in relief, often with Christian emblems. The eighth—tenth centuries roughly marked by fragments of Barbotine ware, the prototype of this decoration apparently being on some metal jugs of either Late Sassanian or Early Post-Sassanian work, of the type figured by Sarre. From this point onwards — say from the ninth to the fourteenth centuries — the site of the Temple of Nabu appears to have been occupied by a succession of five or perhaps six buildings, chiefly marked by cement floorings and solid cemented wall. The stratum in which they lie is not more than 3½ feet thick, and consequently does not mark a very long period. . . . From the name Nineveh a bishop of the Chaldean Church derived his title according to Assemani. At the end of the fourteenth century Timur hunted the Christians from Mosul, and this may well mark the last occupation of this group of buildings." — These sporadic occupations, however, betray no disharmony with Nahum's prediction. The prophet does not declare that no one will ever inhabit the site of the city. He does assert, however, that the Assyrian Nineveh is gone forever. See also D. A. Lincke, *Continuance of the Name Assyria and Nineveh After 606—607 B. C.*

pillaged so completely as was Assyria." [119] Sayce agrees: "Nineveh, 'the bloody city,' fell, never to rise again, and the doom pronounced by Nahum was fulfilled. For centuries the very site of the imperial city remained unknown, and the traveller and historian alike put the vain question: 'Where is the dwelling place of lions, and the feeding-place of the young lions, where the lion, even the old lion, walked, and the lion's whelp, and none made them afraid?' " [120]

21. Not only will the city be destroyed forever, but it is to be "waste" (3:7). "Desolation and devastation and dilapidation," the prophet exclaims (2:11) as he surveys the smoldering capital. Not all devastated cities are marked by hideous, repulsive ruins. Time often deals kindly with them. Their tottering walls become the objectives of pilgrimages, their mossy slopes the impulse to poetic picture. But Nineveh, according to the *Babylonian Chronicle,* was turned into "a mound and a ruin" (reverse 1, 45). As Nahum foresaw the desolation, so Zephaniah (2:13-15) predicted: God "will stretch out His hand against the North and destroy Assyria; and will make Nineveh a desolation and dry like a wilderness. And flocks shall lie down in the midst of her, all the beasts of the nations. Both the cormorant and the bittern shall lodge in the upper lintels of it; their voice shall sing in the windows; desolation shall be in the thresholds; for He shall uncover the cedar work. This is the rejoicing city that dwelt carelessly, that said in her heart, I am, and there is none beside me. How is she become a desolation, a place for beasts to lie down in!" [121]

22. Though Nineveh is destroyed forever and its site a perpetual, desolate waste, yet the memory of its wickedness and its

[119] *Cambridge Ancient History,* III, 130, 131.

[120] Archibald Henry Sayce, *Assyria: Its Princes, Priests, and People* (1926), 2d ed., p. 171.

[121] For a description of the desolation that reigns over Nineveh's ruins and that recalled Nahum's prophecies to its author see Sven Hedin, *Bagdad-Babylon-Nineveh* (1918), p. 367.

universal oppression still lingers among posterity. As Nahum closes his oracles, he surveys the events following the destruction and predicts: "All who hear the message concerning thee will clap [their] hand over thee" (3:19b). This joyous applause will be provoked by the reflection on Nineveh's widespread iniquity, for the prophet concludes his book with the question: "Upon whom hath thine evil not passed over continually?" (3:19c)

Expression of the rejoicing which the prophet foresaw is recorded in the brief, contemptuous, but exultant obituary by Nabopolassar, king of Babylonia, as he indicts Assyria's "wickedness," its heavy yoke, and the multitude of misery it caused.

Thus practically every phase in Nineveh's fall was predicted at the very heyday of the Assyrian Empire's power.

The harmony between prediction and fulfillment is so clear and startling that some recent writers have declared the book to be a *post eventum* record of the fall. Thus Humbert says that the passages describing the fall of Nineveh are so precise and vivid that they were written after, rather than before, the event. But Nahum's book, even according to the critical consensus, is a preview rather than a review, and as such it constitutes one of the most dramatic and electrifying instances of divine prophecy in the OT.

Commentary on
THE BOOK OF NAHUM

Chapter 1

v. 1 The Burden of Nineveh
The Book of the Vision of Nahum, the Elkoshite

As customary in prophetic writings, Nahum's oracles are introduced with a superscription. Unique for the OT, however, is the double title.

The first part of this compound heading labels the book as "the burden of Nineveh," the heavy weight of doom resting on the Assyrian capital. This city came into prominence before 2000 B. C. and attained the zenith of its power in Sennacherib's reign (705—681 B. C.). During almost two centuries preceding Nahum, tyrannical Nineveh had first threatened, then subjugated the north country, Israel. In 724 B. C. Shalmaneser IV began the siege of Samaria, and in 722 B. C. the city fell to his successor, Sargon II (722—705 B. C.), who put an end to the political existence of the Ten Tribes. The first Assyrian contact with Judah came in the Syro-Ephraemitic war (731 B. C). Ahaz, spurning divine assistance, invoked Tiglathpileser's armed aid; but the Assyrian war lord demanded a heavy price: Judah became a vassal state. Sennacherib invaded Judah in 701 B. C., took many towns, encircled Jerusalem, but left without capturing the royal city, although his annals claim that he received heavy tribute payment from Hezekiah. In Esarhaddon's reign (681—668 B. C.) Assyrian troops again overran portions of Palestine, and now, as Nahum takes up his prophecy, Ashurbanipal (668—626 B. C.) holds

143

Judah in servile subjection, a small segment of his vast empire extending from Egypt to the sub-Caucasus country.

Against Nineveh, capital of this rapacious realm, characterized by sadistic cruelty and blood-stained magnificence, Nahum raises his inspired voice to foretell "the burden" of the destruction which divine justice has decreed. Today the ruins near the Tigris River opposite modern Mosul reveal traces of the city's former grandeur, emphasizing the heroism of the Judean prophet who dared predict devastation for that proud, imperious world center in the heyday of its power.

In the second part of the title the prophecies are called "The Book of the Vision of Nahum, the Elkoshite." The term "book" is not otherwise found in a superscription of this kind; but no cogent reason can be adduced for its removal, as demanded by critics. Its presence, however, does not justify an older explanation (Keil) to the effect that Nahum simply penned his predictions without orally proclaiming their messages. His oracles are called a "vision," a frequent and technical term. See Is. 1:1; Obad. 1; 2 Chron. 32:32, for the occurrence of this term, as here, in the title to prophetic writings. Originally the word denoted a literal "beholding," for its verbal root means "to see." However, it was employed figuratively in a wider sense, without any necessary connotation of actual physical seeing. Yahweh's messenger might receive "a vision" through words which God spoke to him. Used in the broad sense of "prophetic perception," the term here implies both revelation and inspiration. It embraces the entire contents of the book; and since there is no assurance whatever that three chapters were given as a single vision, it may well be translated as equivalent to a plural, especially since the plural form does not occur. By its own declaration, then, the book is a "vision," not a compilation of liturgical material, as now frequently maintained.

The first verse offers direct testimony to the Nahumic authorship in the words "of Nahum, the Elkoshite." Both the prophet's name and his birthplace are significant. During the dark days when Assyria's ruthlessness crushed God's people, Nahum was to bring his countrymen no program of political expediency, no plan of military technique, no strategy for secret revolt, but the promise of consolation which would come with the overthrow of their oppressors. That this comfortbringer lived in an unheralded South Judean locality rather than in the national capital shows impressively how God chooses "the weak things of the world to confound the things which are mighty." (1 Cor. 1:27)

Nothing is otherwise known of Nahum, his family, profession, livelihood, and achievements. Such total absence of biographical detail emphasizes that those who enjoy high spiritual privileges and fulfill vital religious missions have often lacked the recognition with which mediocrity is sometimes exalted in our times.

No valid reason exists for assuming that the prophet did not add the superscription himself. It was customary to affix headings (see the titles in such passages as Is. 38:9). Admittedly these two statements, "The Burden of Nineveh" and "The Book of the Vision of Nahum, the Elkoshite," correctly summarize the contents of these prophecies.[1]

מַשָּׂא — Some uncertainty attaches to the precise meaning of this word. It occurs frequently in the superscription of prophetic writings and at the beginning of prophetic books, Hab. 1:1; Mal. 1:1; or at the beginning of independent oracles, Is. 13:1; 14:28; 15:1; 17:1; 19:1; 21:1, 11, 13; 22:1; 23:1; 30:6; Zech. 9:1; 12:1. It has been translated in the following ways: (1) "Burden" by AV, RV, and some of the ancient versions, chiefly Ⓥ, which offers "onus"; similarly Ⓣ. Ⓖ in Nahum offers λῆμμα, "lifting up," but elsewhere renders the

---

[1] "The essential accuracy of the superscriptions is generally acknowledged. The first, stating the contents of the book, accords perfectly with the bulk of the subject-matter; while the second . . . must be given the benefit of every doubt." J. M. P. Sm. "The first part of the title is necessary . . . but the second part, too, could hardly be dropped," says Or.

noun in a variety of ways, though λῆμμα is the most prevalent. Luther offers "Last," "burden," which is unquestionably the meaning of the word in other connections, where it denotes the burden carried by animals (2 Kings 5:17; Neh. 13:15; Is. 46:1) and by men (Jer. 17:21, 22) as well as the weight of suffering and sorrow (Num. 11:11, 17; Deut. 1:12). The interpretation of Nahum's prophecy as predictive of the burden which doomed Nineveh must bear is appropriate for the oracles which it introduces, and this explanation is adopted by Hngs., Stnh., and others. (2) The term has also been translated as "pronouncement," "utterance," "oracle," by many modern interpreters, e. g., Dr., J. M. P.Sm., Sel., Jnk., Bev., who derive the noun from the verb נָשָׂא, "to lift." This verb means "to take up" in connection with a parable (Num. 23:7), a lamentation (Amos 5:1), a proverb (Is. 14:4), a prayer (Is. 37:4), an announcement of doom (2 Kings 9:25). Consequently it comes to mean, in effect, "to speak" (Ex. 20:7). It is in this sense that Ⓖ (predominantly), Θ, and Σ translate the term.

The choice between the two translations is difficult; but the meaning "burden" is preferable. For (1) מַשָּׂא, in the overwhelming preponderance of instances outside the prophetic titles, has this sense as its chief meaning. (2) The parallel usages at the beginning of Hab. and Mal., as well as the similar occurrences in Isaiah's serried prophecies against foreign nations (13:1 ff.), unquestionably introduce burden-bearing statements against oppressive, sinful peoples. The occurrence in Zech. 9:1 and 12:1, the only instances in which the burdensome element is not conspicuous at first glance, need not be an exception. The preposition עַל may there be translated "concerning," to give this sense, "the burden of the word of Yahweh concerning Israel." Zechariah's statements in the following verses center in Israel and are indeed a burden to the unbelieving nations.

In rejecting the meaning of מַשָּׂא as "utterance," "pronouncement," we submit that this is a much less colorful word than would be expected in Nahum's vivid style. Bev.'s equation of "raising the voice" with "indictment," "proclamation against," is unfounded. (1) If מַשָּׂא has the meaning "pronouncement," "utterance," it is strange that it is never found with the genitive, indicating the author of the statement. How different the usage with נְאֻם, which demonstrably has the meaning "utterance"! (2) If the word is translated "utterance" here, it should be so reproduced in other prophetic titles. But, as Hngs. points out (*Chris.,* III, 339), this rendition does not fit in several such instances. Thus, if in Is. 15:1 "utterance" is used, the statement becomes tautological or mediocre. (3) The meaning "utterance" is uncertain at best. In all instances נָשָׂא (with or without קוֹל) denotes an unusual utterance. Ex. 20:7, an apparent exception, is to be explained by the fact that the mere pronouncing of Yahweh's name is no common speaking.

חָזוֹן — It is objected (Stnh.) that "this wider meaning of the term "vision" came into use after the prophet's time; but Is. 1:1 employs the word with the same connotation. Likewise the objection has been raised that "the prophet would not use the term 'vision,' 'revelation,' in reference to his utterances"; but this is contradicted by Hab. 2:2, where the prophet, writing his vision, himself employs the term as Nahum here does. Gray (*International Critical Commentary,* "The Book of Isaiah," p. 2) holds that the use of חָזוֹן, "vision," may be ascribed to a later conception by which "the prophecies of Isaiah, Nahum, Obadiah may have been . . . not so much or at all, the teachings of these prophets to their own age, but a record of events seen in vision (i. e., literally seeing in vision) several centuries before they actually happened." However, it will be shown that Nahum speaks directly to his contemporaries in Judah and that his prophecy is "no revelation of the final stage of history," as Gray suggests.

The authenticity of the double title has been contested and generally rejected. Nahum, it is asserted, is the only OT book with two superscriptions. To the critical mind nonconformity is suspicious evidence which indicates "the superscription in whole or in part to be of late origin" (J.M.P.Sm.). While most critics agree in questioning the authenticity of the two titles, they vary in their opinion as to the origin of the two parts in this verse. J.M.P.Sm., for example (ibid.), holds that the last three words, translated "the vision of Nahum the Elkoshite," cannot possibly qualify as the original record of the prophet. Nor does he concede that Nahum is responsible for these three words. To his mind, "it is more likely that the older portion of the heading ('the vision of Nahum the Elkoshite') came from an editor than that it came from the prophet himself." More recent critics, e. g., Ehr., Stnh., are willing to admit that these three words "may have been added by the prophet himself." Jnk., however, holds that only מַשָּׂא נִינְוֵה was prefixed by Nahum. All such objections are built on assumptions. They penalize originality by labeling an unusual double title as suspicious. They deal with unfounded generalities when they state (J.M.P.Sm.): "The addition of superscriptions, as a matter of fact, seems to have been a favourite form of editorial exercise." Instead of offering a plausible explanation for this title in its present form, they submit a series of conjectures. Besides assuming hypothetical editors, Ehr. introduces a reader who capriciously adds the first half of the title. Similarly Ries. says that the first two words of this verse are a gloss motivated by 3:7. The removal of the title as a whole leaves the prophecies headless; the excision of one of the two halves elides an element necessary for their full understanding.

v. 2 A zealous God and an Avenger {is} Yahweh.
An Avenger {is} Yahweh, and wrath is His.
An Avenger {is} Yahweh for His adversaries,
And He {is} a Reserver {of wrath} for His foes.

The initial verse of the prophetic oracles ascribes to Judah's God the absolute righteousness which must finally demand Nineveh's end. The destruction of the Assyrian capital will not be accidental or the result of merely human forces. It will come from the Almighty. "Yahweh" is mentioned three times in the opening verse and ten times in the first chapter with all the stress inherent in such repetition. From the outset the prophet is at pains to emphasize that religious and moral degeneracy necessitate Nineveh's doom; therefore he prefaces his forecasts, not with the description of the divine nature in general, but with the restatement of the specific truth that God rebukes all who rise up against Him.

"A zealous God . . . is Yahweh," Nahum begins. This simple, majestic introduction, besides exalting Yahweh's strength, pictures the divine zeal, which is finally responsible for the collapse of the haughty metropolis. The AV and RV rendition of the Hebrew term as "jealous," if accepted in the popular sense, being "suspicious or morbidly fearful of rivalry," "distrustfully watchful," is incorrect. The Hebrew original, when used of God, denotes first of all the attribute which demands exclusive devotion and is utterly intolerant of rivalry. Ex. 20:5; 34:14; Deut. 4:24; 5:9; 6:15. Also implied is the anger in which this attitude expresses itself. The unusual Hebrew adjective employed by Nahum *(qannō')* occurs besides here only in Joshua 24:19, a description of God's wrath; but the associated noun *(qin'āh)* frequently designates His consuming anger. See Num. 25:11; Deut. 29:20; Ezek. 5:13; 16:38, 42; 23:25; Zeph. 1:18; 3:8; Ps. 79:5. The OT conception of Yahweh as "jealous" often (like the now archaic AV English) involves divine zeal, picturing the energy of the Almighty, who, unlike the idols of the heathen, is not silent or passive in matters of righteousness and truth. Thus God is described as zealous in the defense of His people. See 2 Kings 19:31; Joel 2:18; Zech. 1:14; 8:2; Is. 9:61; 37:32.

These three aspects are basic for Nahum's presentation of his "zealous" God: First, He will have no one beside Him, and Assyrian idolatry has bowed before many idols. Second, Yahweh will direct His wrath against all who oppose Him, and Nineveh has long resisted Him. Third, God will vindicate His people, and they have been crushed to earth by tyranny entrenched on the Tigris. Since this zeal is frequently associated with the announcement of impending punishment (Deut. 4:24; Joshua 24:19), it is eminently fitting in the introduction of an oracle forecasting Nineveh's overthrow despite its greatness and glory.

This celestial eagerness to execute judgment shows itself in the fact that God is "an Avenger." No wickedness or oppression, however securely enthroned and however long its triumphant course, can elude His retributive reach. Since He is Righteousness in its perfect essence, He must arise to rebuke every violation of His will, especially the abhorrent, deep-rooted evils with which Nineveh has long increased its guilt. If His people are unjustly tyrannized and despoiled, crushing punishment must be meted out in return even against supernations like Assyria, which for centuries rebelled against the Lord and terrorized nations. Such avenging power, and the relief it brings to God's sufferers, is a frequent subject of Scriptural discussion. Is. 63:4 announces: "The day of vengeance is in Mine heart, and the year of My redeemed is come." See also Is. 34:8; 61:2; 59:17; Jer. 11:20; Ezek. 25:14, 17; Ps. 94:1. This execution of justice, however, is not to be explained as the expression of an unrestrained human passion, but as the predetermined payment which the Almighty demands for every unforgiven infraction of His Law. Yahweh alone can exact such penalties. "To Me belongeth vengeance,"

Deut. 32:35 (Rom. 12:19). While men are commanded to re-frain from carnal, hate-filled revenge, God in His holiness (and the OT restricts the execution of such retribution to Him) must vindicate His name.

"An Avenger is Yahweh," the prophet repeats with the solemnity and force of intentional restatement, "and wrath is His" (literally, "He is the Possessor of wrath"; AV and RV: "full of wrath"). God is not only marked by occasional indignation, He controls divine anger; He directs it when, where, and against whom He pleases, as He exacts complete punishment.

With unusual emphasis Nahum repeats: "An Avenger is Yahweh for His adversaries." The threefold mention of divine retribution is not an indication of three major injuries inflicted on Israel by Assyria (Abrabanel) or of the triple vengeance which Yahweh will demand for Israel (Rashi). Nahum's per-vading theme is the Lord's punishment of Nineveh, and forcefully does he introduce his discourse with the emphatic cry, "Vengeance! Vengeance! Vengeance!" Significantly Nineveh, Judah's enemy, by implication is here implicitly regarded as God's adversary. Well does Lu. (XIV:1338) conclude: "This is a very rich comfort for the believers, when they hear that the Lord calls those His enemies who set themselves against the believers. . . . So He here calls the Assyrians His enemies, who were enemies of the people of Judah."

Finally, in listing God's attributes, exhibited as the divine finger writes history (and soon to be witnessed in the haughty Assyrian citadel), Nahum concludes: "He is a Reserver of wrath for His foes." Yahweh's ire is held in reserve. It may appear that He suffers one indignity after another without rising up to crush His foes, that heathen nations blaspheming the Almighty have triumphed; "but," Nahum implies in warning, "take a long-range view, and be sure Yahweh consistently maintains His wrath and will finally give full expression to His anger." As page after page of the human record is completed, the prophet asserts, one truth stands out boldly: the Almighty reserves wrath for His enemies; in the divinely appointed hour He will pour out His fury. For the NT restatement and individualized application, see Rom. 2:5, 6. However, as the verse indicates, only against God's enemies is His wrath thus stored. Yahweh promises penitent Israel, "I will not keep anger forever" (Jer. 3:12). For the same phraseology, expressing similar compassion, see Ps. 103:9; Jer. 3:5.

It has been overlooked, especially by those who say that the opening verses have nothing to do with Nahum's prediction of Nineveh's end, that this verse, in its threefold emphasis on divine vengeance, actually presents the theme of the book: the atrocities committed by the Assyrian capital are to be avenged — and (this likewise has not been properly recognized) avenged when Nineveh is made to suffer the agony, disgrace, and destruction she has inflicted on others. She has taken kings captive; now her own royalty will be led away (2:8). She has besieged a hundred enemy cities; now she will suffer siege (3:14). She has spoiled others; now she is to be spoiled (2:10). She has massacred masses of foes; now the multitude of her own slain is staggering (3:3). Her troops have desecrated the temples of vanquished peoples; now her own sanctuaries will be violated. She has set fire to almost uncounted cities; now the flames are to devour her own palaces and homes (3:15). She has ruined cities by flooding water; now she is to be inundated (2:7). Her troops have left conquered capitals in ruins; now "desolation and devastation and dilapidation" are to overtake her (2:11). Ruthlessly has she scattered people in exile; now she is to be dispersed beyond regathering (3:16-18). She exhibited captives as a spectacle to her people; now she herself is to be a gazingstock (3:6). She made others flee for their lives; now her own leaders must seek safety in flight (3:17). Nineveh has boasted that she has forever destroyed her opponents' capitals; now "an utter end" is to be made of her (1:8). — With such drastic, startling

etaliation will Yahweh be avenged of His enemies, chiefly —
o Nahum implies — Nineveh.

אֵל — Ges., Hwb., in two notes attached to the article אֵל,
"God," lists the several etymological explanations of the
term which have been advanced, together with the names of
the respective authors and the pertinent literary references.
אֵל has been derived (1) from אוּל, "to be strong." This
meaning, though apparently only secondary to the root, is
supported by the occurrence of another term, אַל, meaning
"power," "strength," as in the expression יֶשׁ־לְאֵל יָדִי, "it is in
the power of my hand," Gen. 31:29; Micah 2:1. (2) From
אוּל, "to be first." (3) From אָלָה, "to be strong." However,
no definite occurrence of the verb in this sense can be cited.
(4) With less probability the noun is associated with the
preposition אֶל, "unto," making the term mean really "the
goal," or "him after whom one strives." But the frequent
Assyrian *ilu,* "god," seems to preclude this derivation. While
no final etymological decision can be reached, the association
with the roots in (1) and (3) above, both of which mean
"to be strong," seems most appropriate. Although the term
may theoretically be used of the true God and of heathen
gods (a fact which helps account for the frequent addition
of the definite article, suffixes, or qualifying words yielding
combinations like אֵל אֵלִים, אֵל עוֹלָם, אֵל הַכָּבוֹד), it is prevalently
employed without the article, tantamount to a proper noun;
for example, אֵל חַי, אֵל עֶלְיוֹן, אֵל שַׁדַּי. In poetical language,
as here, אֵל, without article or nearer definition, is a regular
designation of the true God.

קַנּוֹא — Occurs only here and Joshua 24:19. The usual
form is קַנָּא.

וְנֹקֵם יהוה — Some (Mrt., Du., Hpt., and others) omit וְנֹקֵם.
Du. drops יהוה. Ries. rejects the entire verse thus far. — For
the emphasized predicate in the first place see Ges., Gra., 141 *l.*

נקם יהוה — J.M.P.Sm. and Hst., who follow Wllh., Gun., Hap., No., Du., in omitting this phrase (Mrt., Hpt., Stk., G.A.Sm., K.-G., Sel. drop only the tetragrammaton), appeal to the similar Ⓖ rendition in support of the allegation that נקם יהוה is a dittography. However, ἐκδικῶν κύριος, "avenging is the Lord," is found in א Corrector, Lucian Recension, Catena, and Marchalianus Corrector. Ehr. objects to the second יהוה and substitutes הוא, declaring: "The prophet would hardly have written נקם יהוה three times consecutively without variation." Why not? See Is. 6:3, קדוש קדוש קדוש, and Jer. 22:29, אֶרֶץ אֶרֶץ אֶרֶץ.

ובעל חמה — Ⓖ μετὰ θυμοῦ, "with anger"; Aq. and Σ: ἔχων θυμόν, "having anger"; Ⓥ, "habens furorem." These versions and Ⓢ agree in dropping the *Waw*, an omission which Gun., No., and Hap. accept. On בַּעַל in this construction, see Ges., Gra., 128 *s* and Prov. 22:24; 29:22; 2 Kings 1:8.

נקם יהוה — Sel. transfers this part of the verse to v. 9 as "an antiphonal response."

ונטר — This term is used several times with the meaning "to guard," "to keep" (Cant. 1:6; 8:11, 12). In a developed sense it here means "to keep," "to reserve," and its object must be implied, just as "wrath" is supplied in the similar ellipsis of Lev. 19:18; Ps. 103:9; Jer. 3:5, 12. For similar omission in the instance of the synonymous שָׁמַר see Jer. 3:5: הֲיִנְטוֹר לְעוֹלָם, "Will He keep [His anger] forever?" Against this interpretation Hpt. would connect נטר with the Assyrian *natāru*, "to be wrathful." But the root meaning and the elliptical usage in other passages substantiate the accepted rendition. Ⓖ renders καὶ ἐξαίρων, "He lifts out his enemies," perhaps confusing נָטַר with נָטַל.

Modern criticism has dealt drastically with this verse. Some have placed the entire verse after v. 9a, making the introductory ode commence with v. 3; but even Sel. calls this a *Miszgriff.* Since v. 2a starts with an *'Āleph,* it is generally retained in this initial position. But the advocates of the acrostic differ in their disposition of v. 2b and further complicate the situation by uniting vv. 2b and 3a. Bi. places v. 3a and v. 2b (in this order) after v. 9. Most critics place v. 2b after 9, because v. 2b starts with a *Nun,* the letter required there by the alphabetic theory. J.M.P.Sm., who follows this realignment, justifies the procedure with the assertion that v. 2b breaks "the continuity of the acrostic" and that it "belongs alphabetically" in this relocated position. How, then, the question presents itself, can modern criticism account for this drastic misplacement? Sm. suggests: "Some editor, not recognizing the alphabetic structure, placed the line where it seems to belong logically." This is highly improbable. No evidence whatever exists to show that editors thus arbitrarily rearranged, nor that, with the meticulous scrutiny to which the text was subjected, they would have ignored the alphabetic acrostic had these lines been originally written in that sequence. Besides, the portion excised from the verse belongs logically, as by literary emphasis and agreement of critics, at this place, whereas in its proposed new position, after v. 9 (which is demanded merely by the necessity of providing the initial letter *Nun*), the statement "Yahweh takes vengeance on His adversaries and reserves wrath for His foes" comes as a weak anticlimax. Stnh.'s attempt to vindicate this procedure fails to convince. Even Htz. protests: "Nahum begins very beautifully with a general sentence. . . . He pictures Jehovah with those characteristics through which Nineveh's fall is now produced."

> *v. 3 Yahweh {is} long-suffering, but great in power*
> *And will assuredly not leave {the guilty} unpunished*
> *Yahweh — in whirlwind and in tempest {is} His way*
> *And clouds {are} the dust of His feet.*

The prophet now qualifies the repeated emphasis on God'
avenging power. Divine retributive justice is neither weakened
nor set aside by apparent delays. Beholding Nineveh's continued
prosperity, Nahum's countrymen might infer that Yahweh could
not punish a city of its magnificence and proportions; yet such
a conclusion, this third verse proceeds to show, would be utterly
unwarranted; for postponement comes only from the Almighty':
wisdom and forbearance.

Therefore Nahum, adopting an ancient and frequent ex
pression of celestial tolerance (Ex. 34:6; Num. 14:18; Jer. 15:15
Joel 2:13; Jonah 4:2; Ps. 86:15; 103:8; 145:8; Neh. 9:17) de
clares "Yahweh is long-suffering" [lit., "long of anger"]. Con
scious of His superiority, He calmly waits His own time before
inflicting punishment. His forbearance has been exercised, so this
verse must be interpreted, not toward Judah but toward Nineveh
Had it not been for this divine restraint, the Assyrians would
have been wiped off the earth long before.

For Yahweh is "great in power" (Num. 14:17). — His
tolerance must not be attributed to impotence. This greatness in
might cannot refer to His "understanding," as suggested by
Dav.-Lan., who cites Job 36:5 to justify this usage. However,
this passage has the word "understanding," which is missing in
our text. Nor does "great in power" denote the Almighty's
"moral strength" (J.M.P.Sm.) and set forth "that Jehovah's
self-control is too great to permit Him to act on the impulse of
sudden outbursts of wrath." The Hebrew word for "power" is
not used in this sense. Again, the prophet does not here describe
God as "great in patience," as Htz. originally asserted, who
equated "might" with "patience." The passages he adduces, Job

5:11, 12 and Ps. 22:16, certainly do not show this meaning.
Nor does Ehr.'s reference to Num. 14:17 justify the meaning
"patience." The term has its normal meaning here, implying that
although Yahweh may delay while His wisdom and mercy plot
His program, nevertheless His omnipotence is unimpaired. The
Almighty has been long-suffering toward the Assyrian metropolis,
as the Book of Jonah emphasizes; but since the city has continued
in iniquity, it cannot escape unscathed.

Nahum now proceeds to the chief point at issue: patient
yet powerful, God "will assuredly not leave the guilty unpunished," i. e., treat them as innocent, leave them guiltless. It may
appear that Nineveh's hauteur remains unrebuked, but the prophet
protests in strong syntactical construction (for the same or similar
phrase see Ex. 20:7; 34:7; Num. 14:18; Deut. 5:11; 1 Kings 2:9;
Jer. 30:11; 46:28; Job. 10:14) that Yahweh will by no means
permit iniquity to escape its penalty.

Both the power and the destructiveness of divine punishment are now explained, as Nahum continues to exult, "Yahweh — in whirlwind and in tempest is His way." [2] This is not
merely the description of God's approach in a theophany and
"the convulsion of nature at the manifestation of divine presence"
(Stnh., J.M.P.Sm.). Nor are the words intended to imply that
Nineveh's overthrow is to be marked by physical upheavals. The
context suggests that the reference to whirlwind and tempest be
regarded as poetical description of God's exalted power in its
devastating punishment. He sweeps down upon the transgressors
with the irresistible, unrestrained fury of a death-dealing tornado.
Similar references to siroccos, it is true, are found in connection
with theophanies (Judg. 5:5; Is. 29:6; Zech. 9:14; Job 38:1;
40:6); here, however, the emphasis is laid, not on the Almighty's

_____

[2] Sel. asserts that 1 Kings 19:11 ("but the Lord was not in the wind")
opposes the statement "His way is in whirlwind and in tempest." This is a specious
objection. God was not in the particular strong wind which preceded His comforting appearance to Elijah; yet this was a special, individual instance for a purpose
altogether different from that motivating His approach in judgment.

appearance but on His power. To understand the full force of the picture, we must realize with what impact of devastation whirlwind and tempest (the same combination is found Is. 29:6; Ps. 83:16) sweep over Palestine.[3]

The parallel thought the prophet continues, "Clouds are the dust of His feet." The picture is commonly interpreted as representing "the fine dust stirred up by the feet of Yahweh as He passes along in His wrath" (J.M.P.Sm.; similarly Stnh.). This misses the point. Apparently the comparison implies that a human warrior momentarily raises dust as he hastens to battle (Ezek. 26:10). God is so immeasurably superior that in His exalted stride, approaching in whirlwind and tempest, He stirs up great clouds across the heavens. It is beside the point to observe that "one of the principal features of the sirocco are the clouds of small dust which it occasions" (Stnh.). The prophet's emphasis is not on dust clouds but on dust in general, and there is no evidence that the Hebrew term for "dust" is ever used in the sense of "dust clouds." Certain it is that the clouds associated with the Almighty's appearance and the manifestation of His power are not dust clouds but vaporous clouds (Ex. 16:10; 19:15 ff.; Num. 9:15 ff.; Deut. 4:11; 1 Kings 8:10 f.; Is. 19:1; Ezek. 1:4; 10:3; Ps. 97:2; 104:3). His strides cover the vast areas of extenuated clouds.[4] His movements are marked by the

[3] Thomson, *The Land and the Book*, 1910, (pp. 200, 201) gives this account, illustrating the catastrophic force of Palestinian whirlwinds: "This plain of Ijon has lately been rendered famous by a most extraordinary storm. . . . Some friends of mine . . . were coming down the hill by Kefr Keely . . . when one of them called their attention to tall columns of mist over the marsh of the Huleh. They came this way very rapidly, and soon broke upon them with awful fury. . . . Those who attempted to reach Khyam perished in the plain, although it is not more than two miles wide, and in full view of their houses. Thus ten men died in a few minutes from the mere chill of this wonderful wind. There was no snow, no frost, and not much rain; but the wind was perfectly awful, driving and upheaving everything before it. These cold winds draw out all animal heat with amazing rapidity. Not only were these men chilled to death almost instantly, but eighty-five head of cattle also perished before they could be brought to the village."

[4] In the Ras-Shamra Tablets, the expression *rokeb-'aripôt* (rkb-'rpt), "he who rides on the clouds," occurs repeatedly in the mention of Aleyn Ba'al. J. W. Jack, *The Ras Shamra Tablets*, p. 50, says that this is "a term descriptive

darkening of the heavens as the whirlwind sweeps and the tempest howls.

Gun., Wllh., No., and other advocates of the alphabetic order have omitted v. 3a as "an ameliorating gloss from Num.14:17." It is maintained that these words "break the continuity of the acrostic." Nahum did not write acrostically. It is also objected that the present text offers "an abnormally long line" (J.M.P.Sm.). Yet some of the lines which Sm. accepts are equally long or even longer. See, for example, the *Zayin* and *Lāmed* lines. Finally Stnh. maintains that the point of view expressed in this verse is that of one "who wrote later than Nahum in a time of distress and despondency, when Israel was beset by adversaries, and hard thoughts were being entertained about Jehovah." According to this opinion, the first part of the verse shows God's long-suffering attitude toward Israel. "It is not against His people, but against their adversaries that Jehovah directs the full force of His wrath; towards His people, on the contrary, He is slow to anger." This reads foreign elements into the text; for the whole presentation of the opening verses features the universality of God's judgment, righteousness, and long-suffering, without any indication of distinction between Israel and the rest of the world. However, Bev. summarizes the general critical opinion: "This verse seems to have been inserted as an afterthought to attenuate the vengeful aspects of God's justice in the preceding and following verses." But Nahum does not soften. The omission of this verse section would result in the loss of essential truth and the interruption of the prophet's thought. It would weaken the introduction leading to the theme of Nineveh's destruction and set aside the prophet's

---

of the servants or messengers of Aleyn, eight in number." More usual, however, is the explanation that this phrase designates Aleyn Ba'al himself. Cp. H. Bauer, *Zeitschrift für die AT Wissenschaft*, X, 1933, p. 88. See also Zellig S. Harris, *Annual Report of the Smithsonian Institution*, 1937, p. 498. But Nahum's description, "Clouds are the dust of His feet," is not parallel to these Ugaritic references and is much stronger.

argument to the effect that the Assyrian capital has been permitted to stand until this time because of God's long-suffering patience. Other critics, in protest, believe that this verse, in whole or in part, is original but misplaced. Thus Du. begins his rearrangement of Nahum's prophecies with this verse: Mrt., Hpt., Kent, and Stk. use the last clause of the first half, וְנַקֵּה לֹא יְנַקֶּה יהוה, acrostically to complete the alleged *Mem* line, v. 9. Hst. places the entire first half of this verse, together with v. 2b, after v. 9. Such disagreement casts a significant light on the trustworthiness of the critical reconstruction claims. Through such arbitrary excision and realignments it is possible, with the aid of profuse emendations, to have Nahum say almost anything.

יהוה — This is the subject of a compound sentence. On this construction see Ges., Gra., 143 *a*. Hst. transposes this to follow כֹּחַ as subject. K.-G. drops the tetragrammaton.

אֶרֶךְ אַפַּיִם— Literally, "long of face," a physiological reflection of a benign, compassionate attitude. This is an epexegetical genitive, showing a quality otherwise expressed by an adjective. Htz. mistranslates, "lengthening himself in regard to anger." The meaning is literally reproduced in the Greek μακρόθυμος. The opposite, "short, quick of anger," is found in Prov. 14:17.

וּגְדוֹל— The Kethibh reads normally גְּדוֹל. The *Qerē* asks for גְדָל־.

כֹּחַ — J.M.P.Sm. here presents a typical illustration of higher critical inconsistency and employment of the circle argument. First he attacks the reading "great in power," because, he says, this is an idiom which occurs nowhere else. How can it be an idiom if it occurs nowhere else? Must we elide all phrases which occur only once? However, see Num. 14:17 for the similar phrase יְגְדַּל־נָא כֹחַ. Having decided that Ⓜ is unreliable because it is unique, Sm. proceeds to substitute "great in mercy." This substitution is made without any semblance of versional or MS suggestion, but in keeping with Gun., No., K.-G., and others, who are agreed that since the phrase "great in mercy" is found in a few passages, it must have been the original here. But why not substitute "great in wisdom," a frequent phrase? Then, after assuming that "great in mercy" should be substituted, Sm. concludes that this reading cannot be original, but must be attributed to a glossator who "felt the need of a reference to the patience and mercy of God." Dav.-Lan. seeks to change Ⓜ by the utterly unjustified charge "The meaning of the phrase, 'great in power,' is not clear." Sel. objects to this change and keeps כֹּחַ, but (like Ries., who wants כֹּחוֹ) in the sense of "patience."

לֹא יְנַקֶּה — On the use of the infinitive absolute with the finite verb of the same root, see Ges., Gra., 113 *l*. On the position of the negative see ibid., 113 *v*. On the form יְנַקֶּה: instead of the ending in Seghol see ibid., 75 *hh*, with the unsatisfactory explanation that this is imitative of Aramaic formations. Ⓖ, ἀθῷῶν οὐκ ἀθῳώσει, "absolving, He will not absolve." Ⓥ, "et mundans non faciet innocentem." On נִקֹּה with an accusative of person see Ex. 20:7; with an accusative of thing, Joel 4:21; without object, Ex. 34:7; Jer. 25:29.

יהוה is omitted by Gun., Hap., Mrt., K.-G., and Stnh. as a gloss; Hpt. weakens the verse by substituting עָזוֹ. Supporters of higher critical reorganization declare that the line starting with יהוה is also misplaced. In the words of Stnh.: "The line introduces the *Beth*-couplet of the original acrostic. According to the Hebrew text, it is prefaced by Jehovah, but the LXX connects this with the preceding clause, perhaps correctly; in that case it will have been inserted not by the editor but by the glossator." All this is pure conjecture.

בְּסוּפָה — Ⓖ, ἐν συντελείᾳ, "in completion," perhaps mistaking סוּפָה for סוּף, "end."

בְּשְׂעָרָה — This occurs also in Job 9:17 and is probabl
derived from שַׂעַר, equivalent to סַעַר, the action of a destruc
tive storm.

דַּרְכּוֹ — Ehr. unnecessarily demands דְּרִכוֹ, "His striding."

וְעָנָן — Ⓖ has the pl., νεφέλαι, "clouds"; Ⓥ also, "nebulae."

אֲבַק רַגְלָיו — Gun. and No., followed by Bi. and v.Ho., un
profitably change to וְאָבָק לְרַגְלָיו, "clouds and dust are at Hi
feet," but this removes the point of the picture. Sel. prefixe
only the *Waw*.

v. 4 *He rebuketh the sea, and He drieth it up.*
And all the rivers He maketh dry.
Bashan droopeth and Carmel,
And the bloom of Lebanon droopeth.

God's avenging power spreads terror over nature even ir
its mightiest manifestations, so that oceans and rivers are emptied,
green pastures and mountains wilt. Elaborating this thought
Nahum declares, "He rebuketh the sea, and He drieth it up."
All-powerful Yahweh, controlling even the unmeasured oceans
needs only speak to them, and their depths disappear. The rebuk
ing of the sea may, however, be an allusion to Israel's miraculou:
deliverance from Egypt. The similar language of Ps. 106:9: God
"rebuked the Red Sea also, and it was dried up," points to such
reference. Yet divine omnipotence is not limited to that one
historical occurrence. Yahweh can dry up any or all seas and
oceans. See Is. 50:2: "Behold, at My rebuke I dry up the sea
I make the rivers a wilderness"; 51:10: "Art Thou not it which
hath dried the sea, the waters of the great deep?" Ps. 66:6:
"He turned the sea into dry land; they went through the flood
on foot." Stnh. is incorrect in asserting that the prophet describes
"the common experience of the effect of a whirlwind on rivers
and watercourses, or as he witnessed it beating down on the sea

and driving back its waves." The language and the repeated "drying up" are far too strong. Despite Ex. 14:21, v. 4 is logically independent of v. 3. The prophet's point of view here restricts itself to the assertion that Yahweh (regardless of wind or other agency) can turn sea into dry land. H. Zimmern (*Die Keilin- schriften und das Alte Testament,* 3d ed., p. 508) finds here an eschatological reference to the ocean as an enemy of God. Others maintain that "the old myth concerning the battle of the light-god with the chaos-monster shimmers through here." But the text is innocent of this complication.

As further evidence of the divine dynamics Nahum records: "All the rivers He maketh dry." If the oceans represent depth and power, the rivers may be said to picture length, extent, national defense. Yet though these streams, like the Nile, run hundreds of miles; though like the Euphrates they irrigate proud empires or, like the swift Tigris, course by the banks of Nineveh and the Assyrian cities, God can dry them up. As He made a pathway through the Jordan, so He can lay all the river beds bare. Ps. 18:15 declares: "Then the channels of waters were seen, and the foundations of the world were discovered at Thy rebuke, O Lord, at the blast of the breath of Thy nostrils."

Turning now to the plateau and mountain countries, the prophet continues, *"Bashan droopeth and Carmel, and the bloom of Lebanon droopeth."* *Bashan* (etymologically the name denotes a fertile, stoneless plain) was the Transjordanic country which extended from Mount Hermon in the north to Gilead in the south and from Salchah in the east to Geshur and Ma'aka in the west (Deut. 3:10 and 13; Joshua 12:4 ff.; 13:12). It was gen- erally coincidental with the modern Nukra and was noted for its rich pasture lands, Micah 7:14, for its steers, cattle, and rams, Deut. 32:14; Amos 4:1; Ps. 22:13, especially for its mighty hills, Is. 2:13.

Carmel, the fertile mountain that juts out into the Mediterranean to the south of the Bay of Acre, takes its name from the attractive, gardenlike appearance which its projecting ridge assumed. Dean Stanley writes of Carmel that because of its beauty "its protracted range of eighteen miles in length, bounding the whole of the southern corner of the great plain, is marked out from the surrounding scenery. Rocky dells, with deep jungles of copse, are found there alone in Palestine. And though to European eyes it presents a forest-beauty only of an inferior order, there is no wonder that to an Israelite it seemed 'the Park' of his country — that the tresses of the bride's head should be compared to its woods — that its 'ornaments' should be regarded as the type of natural beauty — that the withering of its fruits should be considered as the type of national desolation." Scriptural appraisal of Carmel's beauty or productivity is found in Is. 33:9; 35:2; Jer. 50:19; Cant. 7:5.

Lebanon denotes the high, "white" mountains forming the northern boundary of Canaan (Deut. 1:7; 3:25; 11:24; Joshua 1:4; 9:1), noted for their snow (Jer. 18:14), their mountain streams (Cant. 4:14), particularly for their forests (Is. 10:34) with cedars (Ps. 29:5; Judg. 9:15; 1 Kings 5:14; 2 Kings 14:9; Is. 2:13; Jer. 22:23).

These three districts (also combined in Is. 33:9) are mentioned, not because this part of ch. 1 dates from the late Syrian dominion and the territory of the Damascus tyrants is threatened (Hap.); nor because Bashan, Carmel, and Lebanon represent the extreme east, west, and north, and therefore (?) the whole country; nor (Bev.) because "they are all frontier heights" where "the enemies of the Chosen People are meeting with destruction as they reach the border of Palestine," but because these three districts are fertile, forest-clad, well-watered territories, ordinarily immune to drought or blight. Again, the mention of Bashan, Carmel, and Lebanon may be a historic reference to the defeat of mighty peoples east and west of the Jordan, conquered by

God's miraculous intervention (Ex. 15:14 ff.). Now, Yahweh's power is so penetrating that even snow-capped Lebanon, garden-like Carmel, and Bashan in its bounty must droop and die before the manifestation of His omnipotence. For a similar reference, see Amos 1:2. If oceans, torrents, plateau countries, and mountain ranges can be wiped out, should Yahweh choose to remove them, what coalition of conquerors, even Assyria itself, can hope to thwart His purposes?

גּוֹעֵר — Wllh. and several others substitute the perfect גָּעַר, the form found in a few MSS. However, the participle is syntactically strong and adds to the vividness of the description, since it denotes continuity in the present and thus obviates the sole reference of the verb to the drying up of the Red Sea, Ps. 106:9.

וַיַּבְּשֵׁהוּ — The imperfect with consecutive *Waw* also denotes the present, either of contemporaneous action or of permanent characteristic, and describes the activity which follows that of the participle. Mrt., No., and v.Ho. call for וַיְיַבְּשֵׁהוּ as the regular *Pi''el* of יבשׁ, but Ges., Gra., 69 *u* shows that "in the imperfect Pi''el syncope of the first radical *Yodh* sometimes takes place," and cites וַיַּבְּשֵׁהוּ as shortened from וַיְיַבְּשֵׁהוּ. See also Lam. 3:53, וַיַּדּוּ for וַיְיַדּוּ. Gun., following Stk., suggests יִבַשׁ, "and it dries up," but the parallel causative construction makes this improbable. Without any support Wllh., Sel., K.-G., and Hst. demand וַיְבַשֵּׁהוּ, "and He causes it to dry."

אֻמְלַל, from אמל, *Pu''lal,* Ges., Gra., 55 *d,* means "to dry up," "wither," "wilt." It is used of plants, Is. 16:8; 24:7; Joel 1:12, and here; of oil, Joel 1:10; of the world, Is. 24:4; 33:9; of a country, Jer. 14:2; of a city, Lam. 2:8; of a childless woman, 1 Sam. 2:5; of those robbed of hope, Is. 19:8; Hos. 4:3. J.M.P.Sm. and others would replace אֻמְלַל by דָּלַל (Sel., דַּלְלוּ, or perhaps דָּאֲבוּ), "to pine." The reasons given for these radical changes are (J.M.P.Sm.): (1) "The acrostic calls for an initial *Daleth* here." This, of course, is a circle argument and proves nothing. (2) The versions, Sm. maintains, differ from Ⓜ, which has אֻמְלַל both at the beginning and end of the verse, by employing two different verbs. Ⓖ offers ὠλιγώθη, "it was diminished" and ἐξέλιπεν, "it failed," but as Sm. concedes, Ⓖ's employment of different verbs for the same Hebrew term is a "not infrequent usage." Nevertheless Sm. argues that the two different terms in the versions here cannot be cited as evidence of a desire for variation and presupposes two different Hebrew terms, because (1) "the translators were not zealous for variety, for in 1:6 זַעַם and חֲרוֹן are rendered by the same word by both Ⓖ (ὀργή, 'anger') and Ⓢ." Yet in 3:19, where the Hebrew has שֹׁמְעֵי שִׁמְעֲךָ and where, if Sm.'s principle were followed, it should have ἀκούοντες τὴν ἀκοήν σου, "hearing thy report," it uses two different words for the same Hebrew term and offers, ἀκούοντες τὴν ἀγγελίαν σου, "hearing thy message." (2) Sm. contends that "the variety exists in *all* the versions." Again, in other passages all the versions use words that differ from the Hebrew original. (3) Finally Sm. objects that Ⓖ and Ⓢ use verbs for אֻמְלַל which never occur elsewhere as its equivalents. However, both verbs appearing in the versions in a general way reproduce the meaning of אֻמְלַל. See also Num. 4:15, 19, 27, 31 for four different Ⓖ translations of the same Hebrew word. — Now Sm. assumes that the second אֻמְלַל (Ⓥ *elanguit*) is genuine and the first spurious; and in search of an appropriate term, he, with Du., Sel., Hst., and others, selects דָּלַל, "to be poor, lowly," because this word is frequently found as the Hebrew basis for ἐκλείπειν, the Ⓖ translation for the second אֻמְלַל. However, this would place *Daleth* "at the end of the line instead of the beginning, where it is needed." Sm. extricates himself from this difficulty by the following tenuous explanation: "When the oldest versions (Ⓖ, Ⓢ) were made, it is quite clear that the opening word of the line was אמלל, for the renderings of these two bear indisputable testimony to that fact. But, if a scribe depended largely upon his memory, not slavishly eying his copy, the resemblance in both form and meaning between 'א and 'ד might easily have occasioned their interchange." Besides indicting painstaking copyists on the count of "slavishly eying" the original, Sm. presupposes the necessity of a *Daleth* line. No reason exists either for the charge or for the assumption. The line, as it stands in (M), gives a forceful sense. Other critics have not been satisfied with this explanation. Buhl offers אָבַל, "mourn." Gun., followed by Bi., Wllh., Or., Hpt., v.Ho., proposes דַּאל, "to faint." Arnold suggests דֻּכְּאו, "they are struck." Jnk. wants דָּמַם (or the pl. דָּמְמוּ), "it became speechless." K.-G. substitutes דָּאַג, "he is concerned about." In short, אֻמְלַל has provoked a dozen conjectural alterations, not because it is objectionable textually or in meaning, but because an initial *Daleth* is required by those who adhere to the unproved alphabetic scheme of the first chapter. It should not be overlooked that the twofold occurrence of אֻמְלַל may be due to what Gesenius calls a striving after chiasmus. See Ges., Gra., 114 *r*, note.

Ries. unfoundedly concludes that the last two statements of the verse, mentioning Bashan, Carmel, Lebanon, are glosses induced by the mention of mountains in v. 5!

> *v. 5 Mountains quake on account of Him,*
> *And the hills melt,*
> *And the earth lifts itself before Him.*
> *Yes, the world and all who dwell in it.*

The argument of the preceding verse is here intensified. Not only do the heights wither before Yahweh's approach, but also, as the prophet declares, "mountains quake on account of

Him." The shaking of the towering peaks is ascribed to "the vibrating effect of thunder or perhaps of an earthquake or volcanic disturbance" (Stnh.); and the assertion is made that "earthquakes or volcanic disturbances were apparently familiar phenomena to the Hebrews and furnished the materials in large part for their descriptions of theophanies." Others (Dav.-Lan.: "The earth seems to lift itself up, when the ground trembles at the heavy thunderbolts") ascribe the quaking mountains to the hurricane presupposed in v. 5. But the prophet's focus is not on theophanies as such. His theme is still God's all-consuming, devastating, resistance-crushing power. Even mountains, regarded as ancient, permanent supports for the world (Job 9:5, 6), collapse under His impressive tread and move before His majesty. The same acknowledgment is expressed in Micah 1:4; Hab. 3:6, 10; Ps. 114: 4-7; Job 28:9; Judg. 5:4 f.; Is. 64:11; Jer. 4:24; Zech. 14:4.

"The hills melt," Nahum continues, and these words are said to describe, "in a fine figure, the rushing hill-torrents swollen by the heavy rain of the passing storm" (Stnh.). Dav.-Lan. finds this meaning: "The streams rushing down the mountains on all sides seemed as if the mountains themselves had become fluid." Similarly Dr. calls the whole description "plainly hyperbolical" and forgets its potential nature. The prophet's picture, however, includes far more than mountain rivulets, swollen by cloudbursts. The rocky hills themselves, symbolic of fastness, melt, flow away, and disappear before His presence — so powerful and all-consuming is the Lord.

Rising to a climax, the prophet exults, "And the earth heaves before Him." It is not necessary to assume with some interpreters that this sentence continues the picture of the storm. The text, independently of the previous emphasis on the whirl-wind and tempest, declares that when God approaches, the ground is lifted up, as in seismic quake, Is. 13:13. Perhaps Nahum envisions the earth's rise and fall as a gesture of homage and adoration. Ultimately, however, the emphasis here, as in the entire verse, lies on the divine dynamics.

"Yes, the world and all who dwell in it" (Ps. 24:1; 98:7), the verse concludes, will be raised before the Presence. The reference to the productive, inhabited world as well as to all men and creatures found in it extends the sphere of the Almighty's power from the realms of nature to the domain of man and beast. These in their totality, despite human pride, regardless of brute strength, will be moved by Yahweh's approach for judgment. The prophet does not indicate when these upheavals will be produced. He may be thinking theoretically of the omnipotence that can manifest itself in these stupendous demonstrations; or he may behold prophetically the catastrophic consequences of the Final Judgment, typified by every major disaster. Most likely this presentation of God's shattering energy should be connected with the impending ruin of Nineveh. The stress in these verses of adoration lies on the Almighty's absolute supremacy, in comparison with which the strongest forces of the entire world are puny and helpless. How, then, can even Assyria successfully resist Him?

הָרִים — Ⓖ, τὰ ὄρη; Ⓣ likewise definite. This has led Mrt., No., Kent, Du., K.-G., Sel., Stnh., Ries., and others to read הֶהָרִים. No MS authority exists for this addition, and the definite article is not required by its presence in הַגְּבָעוֹת. Frequently in parallelism one noun has the article, while the other has not.

רָעֲשׁוּ — The verb is used for the shaking of a mountain here and in Jer. 4:24; Ps. 46:4.

מִמֶּנּוּ — The preposition has causal connotation.

וְהַגְּבָעוֹת — Gun., followed by No., Hst., and others, removes the *Waw* for metrical reasons and prefixes וְכָל־. This proposal is destitute of support, despite the analogy with Amos 9:13.

הִתְמֹגֵנוּ — The *Hithpōlal* occurs also in Amos 9:13: "The hills shall melt," and Ps. 107:26: "Their soul is melted."

Yet Ⓖ offers ἐσαλεύθησαν, "they are swayed"; Ⓥ, "desolati sunt," "they lie waste."

וַתִּשָּׂא — This is the *Qal* imperfect of נָשָׂא, to be translated, "the earth lifts itself up," Ps. 89:10; Hos. 13:1. The verb should be retained in this sense to describe the action of the earthquake just mentioned; yet this interpretation has been attacked. Commentators hold that "Ⓜ calls for an intransitive rendering of נָשָׂא" and that the intransitive meaning is doubtful. Neither objection should stand. The intransitive meaning of נָשָׂא occurs in Hos. 13:1: "Ephraim . . . lifted himself up"; Ps. 89:10: "in the day of the rising of His waves"; Hab. 1:3: "contention shall arise." Sm. seeks to remove the intransitive force of these passages, but his presentation is not convincing. Nevertheless the form must be changed by critical decree, and among the proposed substitutes these are to be noted: (1) Stnh. chooses וַתָּשֹׁם, "is desolated," from שָׁמֵם; but the thought that the entire world with its inhabitants is to become desolate at the approach of Yahweh is too comprehensive for the prophet's present purpose. (2) Du., whom Sel. follows, suggests וַתִּשַּׁח, "and the earth sinks," from שָׁחַח; but in the *Niph"al* this verb occurs otherwise only with persons. (3) The majority of critics, Gun., Mrt., No., and others, want וַתִּשָּׁא (apparently after Ⓣ), from שָׁאָה, "the earth is laid waste." This reading involves only the change of the שׂ to a שׁ. It is, therefore, possible, but neither necessary nor advisable. The only other passage in which the term occurs in this sense is Is. 6:11, which speaks of spoliation by military destruction. With all the noise of such devastation that passage appropriately uses שָׁאָה, which denotes the tumult of annihilation and hence is employed of noisy waters in Is. 17:12, 13. Note the conception of noisy destruction in the derivatives שָׁאוֹן and שְׁאִיָּה. K.-G. wants the masc. form וַיִּשָּׂא. V.Ho. and Ehrl. keep the verb שָׁאָה but ask for the imperfect *Qal* form וַתִּשְׁאֶה; Bi. and No. propose וַתִּשָּׁא. (4) Hap. reverts to נָשָׂא but pro-

poses the *Niph"al* imperfect וְתִּנָּשֵׂא, "and the earth is lifted up,"
while Oo. secures the passive by reconstructing וְתֻּשָּׂא, although
the *Hoph"al* never otherwise occurs. (5) Grz. radically alters
the word to read וַתִּנְעַשׁ, "and [the earth] sways." These changes
are unnecessary, for the Ⓜ form of וַשֵּׂא, which has consistent
MS support, well fits the picture of the earth raised in quake
and upheaval. The versions generally support this thought,
for Ⓖ has ἀνεστάλη, "it was raised up"; Aq., ἔφριξε, "it shiv-
ered"; Σ, ἐκινήθη, "it was moved"; Ⓥ, "contremuit." These
renditions offer little support to the critical alterations. Only
Ⓣ seems to be based on שָׁאָה. J.M.P.Sm.'s objection: "We
should expect נָשָׂא, if intransitive, to be followed by מִתַּחְתָּיו,
instead of מִפָּנָיו," is overdone. The older interpretation, that
the earth "goes up" in smoke or that its voice "goes up"
in terror, would demand qualifying and descriptive additions.

וְתֵבֵל — Ⓖ, ἡ σύμπασα, "the entire," scil., γῆ, "earth." Is this
a mistaken reading for הַכֹּל? Otherwise Ⓖ translates תֵבֵל
as ἡ οἰκουμένη, "the inhabited (earth)." Wllh., followed by
many of the commentators, objects to the *Waw* in וְתֵבֵל,
which is missing in Ⓖ and Ⓢ. But note the use of the *Waw*
as equivalent to "yea," denoting a higher or detailed conception, 2 Sam. 1:23; Hos. 8:6. See Ges., Gra., 154, note b.
Two preceding clauses of the verse are introduced by *Waw*,
and it would be natural to expect the copulative here. This
may also be an instance of the double *Waw*, "not only the
earth but also all who dwell in it." See Gen. 36:24; Num.
9:14; Jer. 13:14; Ps. 76:7. The asyndeton of Ⓖ is not significant. Hst. arbitrarily demands as substitute for תֵבֵל the verb
וְאָבְלוּ and points to Amos 8:8; 9:5 as parallel constructions.
Yet why should the Hebrew require the concept of "mourning" with every mention of "those who dwell in it"? For the
same combination that Nahum records, minus the association
of "mourning," see Ps. 24:1. ·

> *v. 6 Before His anger, who can stand?*
> *And who can maintain himself in the burning ire*
> *of His fury?*
> *His wrath is poured out like fire,*
> *And the rocks are torn down by Him.*

Having exalted the all-consuming divine power, Nahum begins to draw specific conclusions as he approaches his theme. God can not only annihilate the mighty forces and factors of nature, but His wrath also directs destruction toward all human opponents. His hatred of men's sins and His indignation over individual as well as national evil necessitate His ultimate retributive intervention. If oceans dry up before Him and mountains melt; if the earth itself quakes at His approach, how can wicked nations hope to save themselves from the onslaughts of His rage? This is the rhetorical question which the prophet asks in the double interrogative: "Before His anger, who can stand? And who can maintain himself in the burning ire of His fury?" No one, not even the Ninevites, brazen in defiant self-sufficiency, can keep their arrogant stand against God. His wrath is so hot that it consumes all who resist Him. It is utterly impossible to face the avenging Lord. (Jer. 10:10; Mal. 3:2)

"His wrath [5] is poured out like fire," the prophet continues, as he describes the devastating force of divine vengeance. Fire is mentioned, not because of its "purificatory effects," neither is the picture limited to volcanoes (as Henderson maintains), which belch forth flame and break the rocks with lava. Nor is there any connection with the Persian fire worship, as J.M.P.Sm. suggests. Above all, we search in vain for an allusion to a fire-deluge myth which Sel. finds in this verse. Fire is featured because of its destructiveness, its sweep, and the completeness of its devastation. Together with other OT writers (Deut. 4:24; 9:3; 32:22;

[5] The use of four different words for "wrath" in this verse illustrates the wide use of synonyms sometimes found in OT Hebrew, which has ten distinct terms expressing "anger."

Jer. 7:20; 42:18; 44:6; Ezek. 22:21; Amos 7:4) Nahum makes the red flames an apt picture of God's consuming wrath.

Once more tribute is paid to divine omnipotence in the words "The rocks are torn down by Him." Some have conjectured that this havoc is the effect of the fire's heat, making the prophet imply that as the flames leap over the crags, the rocks themselves are split asunder. Stnh. follows Dr. and finds in this phrase "the masses of rock loosened in a thunder-storm." But the prophet has a more graphic picture in mind. He visualizes the Almighty's irresistible approach as He makes ready to exercise justice and retribution, and before His coming even the rocks, typical of that which is hardest and strongest, crack into pieces. For historical occurrence see 1 Kings 19:11, and for a similar thought, Jer. 23:29; 4:26; 51:25, 26; Micah 1:4.

לִפְנֵי זַעְמוֹ מִי יַעֲמוֹד — Most of the critical commentators transpose the sentence order at the beginning of this verse and read, וְזַעְמוֹ מִי יַעֲמד לְפָנָיו. Candidly Stnh. admits that this transposition and the resultant alteration are introduced "in order that the line may begin with the letter Zayin." Sel. accepts this inversion as a "natural" change, but Hebrew syntax recognizes nothing "natural" in this unusual order. Arn. properly objects that the sentence thus reconstructed must be translated, "His anger, who can stand before Him?" since the pronominal suffix of the third person sing. masc., when affixed to the word פָּנִים, throughout the other verses refers to God. Arn. then changes יַעֲמוֹד to יָכִיל, "he grasps," but even J.M.P.Sm. regards this as "too violent." In considering the changed order proposed for the first four words of the verse, we ask immediately: How could an editor be so stupid or perverse either carelessly or willfully to change the word sequence and to destroy the alphabetical order? Arn. believes that the writer of Ⓜ did not copy here, but quoted erroneously from memory. This is pure theory, discredited by the care which copyists are known to have exercised. Ⓜ here is exalted Hebrew and should not be changed.

וּמִי — The *Waw* is arbitrarily dropped by J.M.P.Sm. and others, leaving מִי a proclitic, to be pronounced with יָקוּם, for the improvement of the hypothetized metrical pattern. Such excisions are contradicted by definite OT usage, e. g., in Ps. 24:3: מִי יַעֲלֶה בְהַר יהוה וּמִי יָקוּם.

נִתְּכָה — This is the *Niph"al* of נָתַךְ, "to flow," "to melt." The versions generally support this meaning, Ⓖ offering τήκει, "it melts"; Aq., συνεχωνεύθη, "it was melted down"; Σ and Θ, ἔσταξεν, "fell in drops"; Ⓛ, "fluere fecit." Nevertheless, the well-authenticated Ⓜ reading is not acceptable to many. Wllh., followed by Ries. and others, objects that the translation "His wrath flows like fire" "is impossible." Therefore he suggests in place of נִתְּכָה a verb which means "to burn," and in place of the following נִתְּצוּ he reads נִתְּכוּ, translating: "His wrath burns like fire, and the rocks melt before Him." This alteration is unjustified, however, for the verb נָתַךְ, which Wllh. finds incompatible with the mention of fire, is actually used in this association in Jer. 7:20: "Mine anger and My fury shall be poured out . . . and it shall burn," as well as in Jer. 44:6: "My fury and Mine anger was poured forth and was kindled."

בַּחֲרוֹן — Ehr. maintains that the preposition does not fit here and proposes changing the phrase to בֶּחָרוֹת, Ps. 124:3; but the inappropriateness of בְ is not obvious.

נִתְּצוּ — This (assonant with נִתְּכָה) is the *Niph"al* of נָתַץ, which has a wide usage. It may designate the tearing down and destruction of houses and cities, Jer. 1:10; 18:7; 31:27; Lev. 14:45; Judg. 9:45; 2 Kings 10:27; 23:7; 25:10; Is. 22:10; Ezek. 26:9, 12; of walls, 2 Kings 25:10; Jer. 4:26; 39:8; 52:14; of an altar, Ex. 34:13; Deut. 7:5; Judg. 2:2; 6:30-32; 2 Kings 11:18; 23:12, 15; of a *massebah*, 2 Kings

10:27. It may well be used for the tearing down of rocks. However, one Kennicott MS reads נִצְּתוּ, the *Niph"al* perfect of יָצַת, "to flame up," "to be burned." This is given preference over all other MSS, which here are identical with Ⓜ, by Gun., Bi., No., and others. But the picture of kindled rocks is highly unusual and has no justification here. Stnh. admits: "It is not very natural to think of rocks as being kindled by fire." Ries., following Hal., wants נִתְּכוּ.

בָּאֵשׁ — Ⓖ, ἀρχάς, "beginnings," probably based on a mis-reading of בָּאֵשׁ as רֹאשׁ. The error is shared by Ⓛ, but it in no way authenticates Grz.' substitution רֹאשׁ.

מִמֶּנּוּ — Ⓢ has the fem. pronominal suffix, which Gun. and Bi. prefer; the reference, however, is to God.

Ries. says that this verse consists of two added notes which refer to v. 5; but not even the radical among the other interpreters have accepted the large-scale excisions demanded by this Roman Catholic school of thought.

v. 7 Yahweh {is} good
As a Stronghold in a day of affliction,
And He knoweth those who trust in Him.

The prophet's message, however, is not an unrelieved de-nunciation. While the annihilating power of God's wrath is terrifying to contemplate, this anger is reserved for His foes. Because of His righteousness and faithfulness the Almighty offers divine succor for those who seek refuge in Him. Turning abruptly to this comforting thought, Nahum voices the assurance: "Yahweh is good as a Stronghold." God is good, the only Source of absolute, perfect goodness. There is nothing good besides Him. Men are evil and treacherous; but God is "good," not only in the moral sense of His sinlessness, but here chiefly in His faithfulness, as

He fulfills His pledges; in His mercy, as He remembers His ungrateful children; and in His help, as He hastens to support and defend His own. Nahum stresses this assurance of divine shielding when he emphasizes God's goodness. Amid dire warnings of destruction and insistent prophecy of doom, this blessed conviction exults triumphantly. Yahweh offers the protection which a fortified citadel grants the soldier. Through faith the child of God finds safety and strength. In a world of tumult and sorrow, where oppression seems securely enthroned and persecution the believer's lot, Yahweh in truth is "a mighty Fortress," the specific comfort repeated throughout the OT; for example, in Is. 17:10; 25:4; Jer. 16:19; Joel 4:16; Ps. 27:1; 28:8; 31:5; 37:39; 43:2; 46:2; 52:9; 144:2; 2 Sam. 22:33.

Such heavenly aid becomes apparent "in a day of affliction" (2 Kings 19:3; Is. 37:3; Jer. 16:19; Obad. 12 and 14; Hab. 3:16; Zeph. 1:15; Ps. 20:1; 50:15; Prov. 25:19; 27:10). As these passages show, "a day of affliction" is not to be restricted to a single, specific judgment, "the day of Yahweh" (Sel.), "which makes the heathen feel the anger of God but Israel experience divine deliverance" (K.-G.). It is rather any time of distress and anguish, particularly the long years of suffering under the tyranny of overbearing Nineveh, when it seems that even Yahweh has become indifferent to His people's sorrows.

Finally, the prophet reveals this blessing for all believers: "He knoweth those who trust in Him." This celestial knowledge embraces not only mere theoretical acquaintance but also the intimate understanding of close relationship, by which Yahweh recognizes and provides for all who trust in Him. God knows those who are His because He has created and redeemed them; He shows this knowledge by the uninterrupted concern for their welfare and the divine direction of their lives. Because Yahweh knows them, they have the assurance of His help — a truth restated in Gen. 18:19; Ex. 33:12; Deut. 2:7; 34:10; Ps. 1:6;

2:12; 18:30; 34:9; 37:18; 46:2; 144:2; Jer. 1:5; 16:19; Hos. 13:5; Amos 3:2. Lu. exults (XIV:1342): "Such conviction [that God knows] defeats sin, hell, death, and all afflictions."

To be blessed by this divine acquaintance, men must "trust in Him," that is, come to Him penitently with their sins, accept His promises as true, and build their hope on His forgiving, sustaining love. The prophet emphasizes the benediction of such true faith. All who take God at His word will find that they are no strangers to His omnipotence, but that He knows them, loves them, guards them.

This assurance of a divine Stronghold for the day of trouble was directed especially to Judah and Jerusalem during the Assyrian tyranny, amid the groaning under Nineveh's oppression. Judah was to look patiently, with undiminished faith, to the divine Refuge. No other sacred book of any age emphasizes the sustaining comfort of reliance on divine goodness as repeatedly and in the face of such apparently hopeless factual contradictions as the Scriptures. Other creeds may plead for action or contrariwise for stolid resignation. But during the long night of the Assyrian domination Israel was asked to trust hopefully in the all-knowing God as its never-failing Stronghold.

טוֹב — Bev. omits this, translating against all authority, "God is the Lord." But why should Nahum emphasize this truth, self-understood by him?

לְמָעוֹז —Stnh. deletes this and reads simply, "Good is Yahweh." Most modern commentators transpose the word to the next clause and change the text to read טוֹב יהוה לְקוָֹיו, "God is good to those who wait for Him." This alteration, accepted by Bi., Gun., Wllh., and most other modern critics, partially also by Bev. (Wllh. asserting, "The language of the psalms begins to emerge here"), is supported by these arguments: (1) The Ⓖ reading τοῖς ὑπομένουσιν αὐτόν, "those who wait on Him." Although Ⓥ's "confortans" opposes Ⓖ, critics pre-

fer the Greek translation to the Hebrew original. Stnh. (who
here does not hesitate to suggest the possibility that Ⓜ is
a corruption of the Ⓖ reading!) asserts, following Wllh.:
" 'Good' in such cases is more closely defined" and "usually
stands in connection with a word denoting the class of persons
to whom Jehovah shows His kindness." But goodness is often
associated with objects, rather than persons, so that the present
Hebrew construction is not without repeated analogies. See
Gen. 3:6; 49:15; 1 Sam. 25:8; 2:24; 2 Sam. 18:27; Esther
8:17; 9:19, 22; Ps. 84:11; Hos. 4:13. (2) It is further maintained that Ⓣ, which translates "to Israel," probably had לְקֹוָיו
for a basis. This is pure speculation, however, void of all
probability, since יִשְׂרָאֵל and לְקֹוָיו have only one consonant in
common. (3) The real reason for this change is indicated
by J.M.P.Sm.'s statement that there is "need of another beat
in the line." Here again the supposed metrical pattern becomes
the arbitrary and inexorable standard for the establishment
of the correct text. This altered reading is not justified by
the fact that טוֹב לְקֹוָיו "occurs also in Lam. 3:25." Nor do the
other passages cited by Sm., Ps. 25:3; 37:9; 69:7; 86:5; Is.
40:31; 49:23, prove anything more than that the participle of
קָוָה is used at these places. Other critics have suggested contradictory and unsupported changes. Hap. offers לְעֹזִי בּוֹ לְמָעֹוז,
"to those who take refuge in Him as a stronghold"; similarly Bi. V.Ho. proposes לִמְקֹוִים לוֹ מָעֹוז הוּא, "to those who
wait for Him He is a stronghold." Du. wants לִמְקַוָּו לְמָעֹוז,
"for those who wait for Him as a stronghold." — As to the
formation of מָעֹוז, also found in 3:11, it seems to be derived
from עֹוז with a prefixed מ denoting place. It may also have
association with עוז. See Ges., Hwb., under מָעֹוז.

וְיֹדֵעַ — Because they desire another accent, many critics who
espouse the metrical theory add יהוה. Or., Dr., Du., Sel., and
Jnk. refuse to make this addition but omit the *Waw*. V.7b

is ascribed to an editor by Stnh. and transposed so that it follows v. 8a, because "the line introduced the *Yodh*-line in the original acrostic." However, even J.M.P.Sm. retains the Ⓜ order at this place, although with most critics he drops the conjunctive *Waw* for alphabetism and adds the tetragrammaton. Stnh.'s radical rearrangement requires a series of changes and disturbs the message of comfort with which the prophet fills the verse.

חֹסֵי בוֹ — τοὺς εὐλαβουμένους αὐτόν, "those who reverence Him"; Ⓥ, "sperantes in se." Many modern critics, against all MS authority, draw the first two words of v. 8 to this sentence. Thus Sel., followed by Hst., adds יַסְתִּירֵם, which plus the beginning of the next verse yields "and hides them in the overflowing flood." Jnk. completely changes the end of the verse, similarly draws the first words from v. 8, makes further alterations, and then reads, "They will be rescued in the flood that approaches." Ries. again arbitrarily removes the entire verse. All these departures from Ⓜ are without cause or benefit, being motivated by a desire to start the next line with the כ in כָּלָה.

v. 8 But with an overrunning flood
He will make an end {to} its place,
And His enemies He will pursue with darkness.

After showing that Yahweh is good to those who trust in Him, the prophet now, by contrast, begins his theme proper, the destruction of Nineveh. "But with an overrunning flood He will make an end to its place," he predicts. Devastation mentioned by flood is frequently recorded in the OT, as literal (Ps. 32:6; Job 38:25; Is. 8:7; 54:9) and as figurative (Prov. 27:4; Dan. 9:26; 11:22). Both interpretations have been proposed for this verse. Thus the "overrunning flood" is said to denote a hostile invasion (Htz., Keil). The verb of the same root as the noun "flood" is used in this wider sense by Is. 8:8 (to depict the unrestrained invasion of Palestine by the Assyrian army); 28:15; Jer. 47:2; Dan. 11:26, 40. Others have adopted a more general interpretation, suggesting an "overrunning flood" of undefined evils. It is preferable, however, to take the "overrunning flood" literally (Hab. 3:10). The assumption of actual flood and inundation, perhaps also not without a certain emphasis on suddenness, as the mountain streams quickly become raging torrents in the spring, agrees with the general thought in Greek tradition. Diodorus Siculus (II, 27), for example, says that the Euphrates (!) flooded its banks and made twenty-one furlongs of Nineveh's walls collapse. This afforded the enemy entrance and fulfilled an ancient oracle to the effect that the city would not fall until the river became its enemy. Of much more force than tradition is the fact that the excavations reveal indubitable evidence of destruction by water. Besides, Nahum distinctly foretells the flooding of the city in these two additional passages: 2:7: "The gates of the rivers are opened, and the palace sways"; 2:9: "Nineveh is like a pool of water." How remarkably does the prophet foresee this startling factor in the city's defeat!

Through this inundation "He will make an end to its place." With inspired clarity the sacred seer predicts here at the beginning of his indictment of Nineveh, as at the end, 3:19, that the city will soon face complete, final doom. Although these words were written in the heyday of Assyrian power, their forecast of the city's entire, permanent extinction was fulfilled to the letter.

When the city is thus flooded, we are told, "His enemies He will pursue with darkness." While Nineveh lies buried in its own debris, God's surviving adversaries will be relentlessly pursued. Since He is Light (Ps. 27:1; 36:9; 43:3; Is. 2:5) and His wicked enemies darkness (Is. 8:20; 60:20; Job 38:15), the Assyrians will retreat in unilluminated flight. They are doomed to stagger blindly in the lightlessness that symbolizes defeat and death (Is. 8:22; Prov. 20:20; Job 5:14; 15:33; 18:18). Because of the darkness they are unable to find the right path and must ultimately perish.

Such statements accurately foresee the final destiny of the remnant surviving Nineveh's demise. The fugitives sought to re-establish the nation in Haran, and for a few years they succeeded in maintaining themselves; but God pursued them with darkness. Their petty kingdom was wiped out, and the last evidences of Assyrian glory enshrouded in perpetual night.

וּבְשֶׁטֶף עֹבֵר — Ⓖ καὶ ἐν κατακλυσμῷ πορείας, "and in an upheaval of the way." Bev. declares without explanation, "The initial 'but' is . . . not easy to justify." Following other critics, he overlooks the evident contrast between vv. 7 and 8. Or. omits the conjunction entirely, erroneously connects the closing words of v. 7 with the opening of v. 8, and translates, "He knows those who trust in Him when the flood overthrows." But the Hebrew does not permit the resolution of this participle into a temporal clause, and the verse separation of the MSS opposes this division. Other critics have generally held that these two words are the beginning of a sentence which is "evidently incomplete." Some have therefore added a verb implying deliverance. Thus Bi. (in an altered opinion) and v.Ho. supply יְמַלְּטֵם, "He will rescue them." Gun. adds (and he is followed by Wllh. and others) either יְמַלְּטֵם or יַצִּילֵם, "He will rescue them," "He will snatch them away." Du. changes עֹבֵר into יַעֲבִירֵם, "He will bring them across." Similarly Bev. translates, "and bringeth them safe through cataclysms." Hap. omits עֹבֵר. Sel. proposes and Hst. accepts יִסְתִּירֵם, "He protects them." Similarly Stnh. suggests: "The rendering should be, 'But in an overrunning flood,' the verb being supplied. The missing verb may be *ya"azor* [He will help], which accidentally fell out from the text by homoioteleuton after the preceding *obher.*" However, J.M.P.Sm. points out correctly that the picture of a flood is used for destruction; therefore he conjectures that to the words "with an overflowing flood" should be added, "He will destroy the wicked," the opposite of deliverance. Yet only metrical preconceptions and devotion to a theory of alphabetic sequence have thus ruled out the natural, literal, forceful interpretation. "With an overrunning flood He will make an end to its place." Despite critical insinuation this thought is absolutely complete.

מְקוֹמָהּ — The evident address is to Nineveh, which even Htz. concedes. Yet J.M.P.Sm., presenting the critical point of view, objects: "There has been no mention of Nineveh thus far in the poem; hence the suffix 'her' is without any antecedent." But if the title in v. 1 is original, as we maintain, the suffix can clearly refer to Nineveh. Nevertheless J.M.P.Sm. accepts the alteration originally suggested by Buhl and followed in substance by practically all modern critics, according to whom קָמָיו, "his adversaries," has been substituted for the textual מְקוֹמָהּ, "its place." Buhl's contention (loc. cit.), which is followed by K.-G., that "make an end," כָּלָה, is not otherwise construed with a second accusative, is not decisive, as Neh. 9:31 and Ezek. 20:17 show. J.M.P.Sm.'s extended defense of this alteration, which he bases on the similarity of the initial letters בּ and מ, is not convincing. The accidental or intentional interchange of these two consonants in proper nouns by the *Qerē,* Greek translators and Assyrian forms, does not prove that any similar change has occurred in this verse. Sm.'s appeal to the versions which, with the exception of Ⓢ, are united in giving מְקוֹמָהּ a personal interpretation (Ⓖ, τοὺς ἐπεγειρομένους, "those who rise up"; Ⓥ, "consurgentibus") is not decisive. These translations lack uniformity and contradict the reading which all OT MSS have perpetuated.

Fatal to the acceptance of בְּקָמָיו is the fact that וּמ in itself is a neutral term. It receives the connotation of hostility through construction. All passages in which it denotes a hostile rising up (except in the difficult Deut. 33:11) have a preposition such as, e. g., עַל or אֶל. Here such prepositional direction is missing, and בְּקָמָיו can therefore be correctly translated only as "among those of his who arise." How much stronger the Ⓜ prediction of the complete devastation of Nineveh: "He will make an end of its place"! Similarly to be rejected are other unnecessary substitutions and emendations.

יְרַדֶּף־חֹשֶׁךְ — For the translation "He will pursue His enemies *with* darkness," see Ges., Gra., 118 *e.* Theoretically it is possible to translate: "He will pursue His enemies *into* darkness," Job 18:18 (AV, Stnh.) or: "Darkness will pursue His enemies" (Ⓖ, Ⓥ, Ⓢ, Calvin, Dav.-Lan., Hap., and others). Since, however, Yahweh is the acting power in the preceding sentence, it is more natural to translate as above, particularly since His direct action is stronger and more dramatic than the pursuit by darkness itself. Instead of the graphic picture thus offered by Ⓜ, Bev. translates, He "rushes His enemies into dark room." Sel., similarly Hst., offers, "And His enemies He thrusts into darkness." These are variations of the transitive action required by Gun.'s emendation, "He will thrust into darkness." This rendition, also suggested by Wllh. and followed by many others, is based on an arbitrary alteration, which against all MS indication reads, instead of רדף, "to pursue," הָדַף, "to thrust into." Even J.M.P.Sm. admits that this change "seems unnecessary," and Stnh. concedes: "It is doubtful whether one is justified in emending a text which offers a satisfactory sense. Moreover, הָדַף is found nowhere else construed with an accusative of motion: cf. Job 18:18, where the preposition 'unto' is inserted."

> *v. 9 Why do ye meditate concerning Yahweh?*
> *He Himself is making an end.*
> *Oppression will not rise up a second time.*

At the time Nahum writes, Nineveh's power is so imposing and widespread that some may wonder whether the Almighty can prove His superiority in this protracted day of affliction. Therefore, as the people of Judah behold the increasing Assyrian might and feel the yoke of its oppression more heavily, the prophet turns to them with a question which is to produce two strengthening answers: "Why do ye meditate concerning Yahweh?" i. e., "What makes you doubt?" All uncertainty should vanish.[6]

Therefore in emphatic reply comes the prophet's answer, "He Himself is making an end." There would be reason for apprehension if mere men were asked to break the Assyrian tyranny. But emphatically does Nahum explain that God Himself with all His invincible might and His irresistible destruction will make an end of His enemies. The promise of v. 8 is thus repeated. Assurance is added to assurance. Judah need not tremble, nor should it doubt the divine promise. Nineveh is doomed to complete divinely directed extinction.

With redoubled comfort the prophet adds, "Oppression will not rise up a second time." The most appropriate meaning for this much-discussed phrase seems to be this: Judah here receives the assurance that Nineveh will be so totally devastated that it cannot overrun Israel again as in the past, particularly

---

[6] This verse, thus interpreted, is additional testimony to the early authorship. Judah would not be driven to question Nineveh's ultimate end had the book been written immediately before 612 B. C., as most interpreters now assert. At that time the Assyrian Empire was drastically reduced, and the whole nation was in dissolution. Invading armies were besieging the capital. For a number of years its kings had maintained themselves only for short, shadowy reigns. The prophet's question, "Why do ye meditate concerning Yahweh?" would certainly be out of place under such circumstances. If, however, these verses were written earlier, about the middle of the seventh century, when the Tigris tyrant was at the zenith of its power, the question concerning the security of the Assyrian dominion is graphic and timely.

under Sennacherib. Others (Wllh. et al.) have found this closely related thought: The visitation which Nineveh suffers is so overwhelming that a second punishment from God will not be necessary, 1 Sam. 26:8. Yahweh does not have to strike twice. The former explanation seems preferable, since "oppression" is more aptly employed in reference to Judah. See 2 Sam. 20:10. This is not a promise that God's people will never be harassed again, but it is a pledge that the same sorrows which have burdened it during the sway of Assyrian tyranny will not be repeated in a second reign of terror under Ninevite kings like Belial-Sennacherib.

This verse offers a glaring instance of uncurbed critical extravagance. First of all, J.M.P.Sm. inverts the order of these utterances, making the sequence 9c, 9b, 9a. *Bouleversement* of such radical scope predicates either willful alteration or senseless miscopying on the part of the Hebrew scribe, who, under this assumption, threw the lines into reverse order. Critics like Dav.-Lan., reviewing this rearrangement, have candidly admitted: "As far as sense goes, this is certainly no improvement." No convincing explanation can be offered for this procedure. Why, it may well be asked, should the Ⓜ sequence of the three sentences be reversed? Sm. answers: "The exigencies of the acrostic structure require the placing of this line (v. 9c) here rather than where it is in Ⓜ." With this apodictical pronouncement, yet without a syllable which seeks to account for the change, the issue is regarded as closed, although the versions clearly testify to the Ⓜ order. As every radical rejection of Ⓜ involves further complications, so here the relegation of the question, מַה־תְּחַשְּׁבוּן, to the last place leaves no reply to the query. Sm. is forced to admit: "The answer to this question, or whatever else it may have been that formed the original conclusion of this line, is now lost." After this rearrangement of the words, and the assumption that a vital section has been lost, critics begin to tear the torso of the verse into shreds by a series of drastic textual changes. When finished, they have produced an artificial verse and disrupted the forceful connection of Ⓜ. Sel., however, is far more radical. He rearranges the verse with subsequent changes and additions from earlier verses. Tactics of this sort discredit the entire critical procedure and invalidate its claims.

מַה — On its use, not in the sense of "what?" but of "why?" see Ex. 14:15; Ps. 42:12; 52:3.

תְּחַשְּׁבוּן — Ⓖ, λογίζεσθε, "you plan," "devise," (1:11) as Ⓥ and Ⓢ have it. On the ending see Ges., Gra., 47 m. Interpreters are sharply divided on the question of the addressees in this verse. One group holds that the author here speaks to Nineveh or Assyria. Others believe that the verse is directed to Judah. This second opinion is preferable, but not for the reasons advanced by critical writers. Particularly the preceding context makes the allocation to Judah probable. In v. 7 those in Judah to whom Nahum addressed his book are told that Yahweh is a Stronghold in a day of affliction (צָרָה), and in v. 9, after the rhetorical question, the same people are assured that affliction (צָרָה) will not reappear. In v. 8 the promise is recorded, "He will make an end" (כָּלָה), and in v. 9, as if in echo, comes the asseverative statement, emphatic in its unusual order and pronominal emphasis, "an end (כָּלָה) He Himself will make." The rhetorical force of this closely knit context is significant.

מַה־תְּחַשְּׁבוּן has been translated (1) "What are you thinking of Yahweh?" — (so, in effect, Wllh., Dr., G.A.Sm., No., and others translate). But this is too nondescript, especially when regarded as spoken by the enemies. (2) "What are you devising against Yahweh?" (J.M.P.Sm.) But this verse is not addressed to Yahweh's foes, and its emphasis is not on "the futility of all human desires aimed against the great God."

(3) "Why do you meditate concerning Yahweh?" Those who reject this translation (e. g., Sm.) maintain that the verb חשׁב in the *Pi"el,* when used with אֶל or עַל, "always means 'to plot or plan against.'" But אֶל and עַל can be contradictory prepositions, and the only passages which merit consideration are those in which the *Pi"el* of חשׁב is used with אֶל, the preposition in this verse. As a matter of record, this construction occurs otherwise only in Hos. 7:15, and there the idea of plotting or planning lies not in the verb but in the noun רַע, "evil": "They meditate evil against Me." Gun. and No. recognize this usage by adding רָעָה here too. Similarly Stnh. offers: "How dost thou imagine (or devise) wickedness?" mistakenly believing that the words are addressed either to Nineveh or Assyria. In order to secure hostile direction for חשׁב, Gun., Hpt., and Du. replace אֶל by עַל. The verb חשׁב is in itself a neutral verb and can be used *bono sensu* or *malo sensu.* In the latter case the idea of plotting or planning against someone is indicated either by the use of the preposition עַל, "against" (Dan. 11:24), or by the addition of some explanatory noun, as in Hos. 7:15. Two verses later Nahum himself employs the construction חשׁב עַל in the same sense of "plotting against." Besides, the last clause in v. 9 does not fit into the interpretation that Assyria and Nineveh are here addressed. The point of the verse is not: "What are you, the people of Nineveh, plotting against Jehovah? How do you propose to resist Him or to avert the destruction which He has resolved to bring upon you? Don't you know how hopeless all this is, since our Lord is God?" (Stuart), but: "Why do you, people of Judah, meditate, entertain doubt and uncertainty concerning God's ability to make an end to Assyria and to prove Himself on the day of affliction?" Dr. objects: "The intensive conjugation (to *think much, ponder, meditate*), is against the rendering 'What *think ye* with regard to Yahweh?'" But the usage in Ps. 73:16; 77:6,

is parallel in the same conjugation. Bev. stresses the liturgica
theory, declaring as he summarizes the contents of this verse
"We . . . have here a dramatic appeal to the Jewish nation
or perhaps to the worshipers in the Temple, to thank Go
for the divine intervention as depicted in these chapters.
He adopts the textual change to תְּשַׁבְּחוּן (from שָׁבַח, "to sin
a hymn," "to praise," Ps. 145:4; 147:12), and translate
"Why do you sing praise to Jahweh?" He finds the chorus
or the congregation's liturgical response in v. 8: "He wil
make an utter end." This does not fit into the context an
necessitates further changes. Sel. finds the congregational o
choral response in v. 2b, which he transposes to this place
Such radical reorganization patently invalidates the whol
claim.

כָּלָה הוּא עֹשֶׂה—The sentence sequence (object, subject, verb
is an intentional stressing of the answer to the question "Wh
do you meditate concerning Yahweh?" This reply echoes the
similar statement in the preceding verse. The text also of thi
section of v. 9 has not remained unchallenged. No. reads the
finite יַעֲשֶׂה for the participle and drops the pronoun. J.M.P.Sm
wants כִּי עַד כָּלָה הוּא עֹשֶׂה, "for unto complete destruction He
is about to work." He admits that Ⓜ here "yields good
sense," but charges that it "lacks any formal connective with
the preceding half of the line." He overlooks entirely the
fact that this clause, "He is Himself making an end," is the
answer to the rhetorical question in the preceding part of
the line. Besides, he arbitrarily decapitates v. 10, transposing
its first two words to this section of v. 9 and turning the
entire verse topsy-turvy. Stnh. apodictically asserts that Ⓜ
cannot be correct and by devious procedures secures "an utter
end will I make of His (Jehovah's) place," i. e., Zion, words
which he puts in the mouth of the Assyrians.

לֹא־תָקוּם—Critics reject תָקוּם, from קוּם, and ask for יִקּוֹם, from
נָקַם, "to take vengeance." This is not justified by the inexact

Ⓖ ἐκδικήσει, "He will avenge," yet the translation "He will not take vengeance" (twice on His enemies) is adopted, in effect, by Gun. and many other commentators. It should be noted, however, that Σ's οὐκ ἀνθυποστήσονται, "they shall not undertake for," and Ⓥ's "non consurget" reflect an original קום, which some critics (e. g., v.Ho., Bev., Hst.) have retained. In an attempt to justify the substitution of נֹקֵם for קמו, the following issues have been raised. First of all, it is stated that Yahweh is the subject in the parallel clause, which J.M.P.Sm. changes and translates: "For unto complete destruction He is about to work." Therefore, it is asserted, Yahweh should be the subject also in this clause. A glance at the parallelism of the Psalms shows that Yahweh is often the subject in the first member of the verse but not in the second. See Ps. 1:6; 3:5; 4:8; 10:16; etc. Then it is alleged that "no close analogy for the Ⓜ phrase is known." This is not decisive. If valid, it would require that the entire OT should contain no instance of the same thought similarly or synonymously expressed in two places. The Hebrew of Ⓜ is clear and unmistakable; see 2 Sam. 12:11. Finally the entire Ⓜ expression is called "too abstract and colorless." But the numeral is complete, and the promise that no second oppression will arise is anything but colorless. Stnh. concedes, "The Hebrew gives an admirable meaning."

צָרָה — Despite clear MS evidence, Gun., No., and others read בְּצָרָיו, "against his enemies," or "upon his adversaries." Jnk., following Hpt., wants מִצָּרָיו, "from his enemies," and Hst. and Bev. read simply צָרָיו, "his enemies." This not only contradicts the versional rendition (Ⓖ, θλίψει, "adversity"; Ⓥ, "tribulatio") but also breaks the connection with צָרָה of v. 7. Hst. adds this sentence to make his reconstructed parallelism complete: וְאֹיְבָיו לֹא יַעֲמְדוּ עוֹד, "And His enemies shall arise no longer." Such license condemns itself.

Ries. again summarily rejects the whole verse as an addition.
Stnh. declares that with this verse "the original prophecy of
Nahum began" and that it is "no part of the acrostic." Many
critics disagree with him and regard additional verses of
chapter 1 as originally part of the acrostic and therefore
non-Nahumic. It is significant that even a conservative critic
like Stnh. is ready to remove more than half of the first
chapter as a later addition.

> v. 10 For {they shall be} like thorns entangled
>   And drunken when they carouse.
>   They shall be consumed
>   As stubble fully dry.

This verse (which Wllh. regards as corrupt and impossible
of full interpretation) is one of the most difficult in the entire
book. It likewise shows that Nineveh, careless, carnal, carousing,
will be destroyed completely. The Assyrians, Nahum continues,
"shall be like thorns entangled." Various meanings have been
attached to this picture. Some (Htz.) find the point of comparison
in the fact that the OT (Ezek. 2:6) employs thorns to symbolize
wicked enemies; but this offers only a weak explanation. The
Ninevites were more than "wicked"; besides, the verse deals with
the punishment which will overtake them and not merely with
their moral delinquency. Again, the entangled thorns, as explained by Sel., are the habitat of lions; but the animals come
into the text only by radical, uncalled-for emendation; and Jer.
4:7, to which Sel. takes recourse, does not mention the thorns
of our text. The emphasis has also been placed (Htz., Ew., Keil,
Bev.) on the impenetrable barrier presented by a bramble thicket
(see 2 Sam. 23:6; Micah 7:4; Is. 7:19, 23-25). Yet the conception of Nineveh as inaccessible, difficult of approach and capture,
is not brought out by this or any other statement. The passages

cited are not parallel in word or subject. Like most other translations, this rendition neglects the force of the "entangled" and misinterprets the consonantal construction of the words. Once more, it is held (J.M.P.Sm.) that the Assyrians are "as a patch of thorns laid low by the sickle and ready for the fire." This is based on an arbitrarily emended text. Another translation, originally offered by Kimchi, is: "Like drunkards who fall into the flames as though desiring so to do, they will be consumed." — This is too involved and stilted; besides, it does not reproduce the text. Much to be preferred is the explanation that the entanglement indicates the confusion of disaster which overtakes Nineveh; that as thorns entwined form an inextricable mass which need not be destroyed one branch after another, but can be consigned en masse to the flames, so the Assyrian capital will fall in confusion, but with completeness. In some passages which speak of thorns and ruin, the point of comparison is the worthlessness represented by the brambles and the ease with which their destruction will be accomplished (Is. 9:18; 10:17; 27:4; 33:12; Eccl. 7:6). Both of these thoughts may likewise be involved in the comparison, as the second half of the verse specifically emphasizes. — What sustaining comfort this prediction must have brought Israel! Their inveterate enemies, tyrants of long centuries, are only hopelessly entangled "briars and brambles," which will be wiped out altogether and quickly! [7]

Similarly difficult is the continuation: They shall be "drunken when they carouse." The prophet may express a double point of view in these words. First, he may indicate the feeling of carnal security with which the Ninevites approach disaster, picturing them as so self-confident that they engage in carousal and drink all danger away. Perhaps even more prominently, however, he may predict the complete impotence of the Assyrians, asserting that they shall be as helpless as a thoroughly intoxicated

[7] On the Palestinian thorn growths see Dalman, *Arbeit und Sitte in Palaestina* (1933), II, 139, 310, 315 ff., 320, 322 f., 329, 355.

man. For the utter weakness of drunken warriors see Jer. 25:27:
"Drink ye, and be drunken, and spue, and fall." According to
tradition, Nineveh was taken when the defenders were engaged
in riotous drinking. Diodorus and others relate that while Assyrian armies were celebrating their former victories in lavish
banquet, the enemy assailed them unexpectedly by night and
defeated them.

Entangled thorns are easily destroyed, drunken warriors
readily overcome. Therefore the fate of Nineveh is foretold:
"They shall be consumed as stubble fully dry." The picture of
stubble swept by fire (frequent in the Scriptures; see Ex. 15:7;
Is. 5:24; 47:14; Jonah 2:5; Obad. 18; Mal. 3:19) is here doubly
heightened, first, by the addition of "dry," and then by the
adverbial qualification "fully." In the same completeness with
which a field of dry stubble is swept by flames, Nineveh will
be burned out of existence. This is the first of three specific
predictions involving fire as agency of devastation. See 3:13;
3:15. The ruins of Nineveh reveal heavy deposits of ashes and
other widespread evidences of conflagration.

Most critics use this verse as the *Kaph* couplet and arbitrarily transpose it to follow v. 8.

כִּי — This is best explained as a causal particle, motivating
the statement in the preceding verse that for Judah affliction
will not rise a second time from the hands of the Assyrians.
The translation of this conjunction in the concessive sense is
unnecessary and complicates the basic meaning. The versions
preserve the causal relation.

עַד — The use of this preposition indicates degree, and it
is found in comparisons, e. g., 1 Chron. 4:27. Despite un-
grounded changes by critics, it should be translated as "as,"
"like." Hst. drops כִּי עַד; Jnk. reads the two together, changing
the last consonant and creating כְּיַעַר, "as a forest"; Sel. wants
"woe to (the) city," maintaining that כִּי עַד is a mistaken gloss
on הוֹי עִיר in 3:1.

סִירִים סְבֻכִים, "thorns entangled." Interpreters have often despaired of securing the meaning of these words and have claimed that the text is "hopelessly corrupt" (Ehr.); "wholly unintelligible" (J.M.P.Sm.); "much corrupted" (Stnh.); "cryptic . . . probably a proverb" (Bev.). Consequently this phrase and the following words have become an almost incomparable field for radical alteration. (1) Gun., K.-G., Sel., and others read סִירִים כְּסוּחִים, "thorns cut off." J.M.P.Sm., accepting the same reconstruction, thus explains the process by which this substitute is secured: "Ⓜ seems to be due to corruption and conflation. It embodies two efforts to restore a corrupt text. One, interpreting סִירִים as 'thorns,' restored סבכים; the other, taking it as 'pots,' restored וכסבאם וסבאים, on the basis of Hos. 4:18. The reference later in the context to stubble and burning makes the interpretation 'thorns' much more probable. Starting with this, we can restore כסחים, on the basis of Ⓖ, the remnants of Ⓜ, and Is. 33:12: so Gun., Mrt., Stk. (though Mrt. and Stk. add כֻּלָּם). The further correction וצמאים presupposes a confusion of מ and ב . . . and of צ and ס . . . and drops כסבאם as due either to a gloss or to dittography." It is difficult to suppose that even the most stupid or careless scribes would have followed a procedure as devious and complicated as this. Even Sm. admits that his emended translation "rests upon a text which is confessedly largely conjectural and, as with all guesses, the chances are against it." (2) Stnh. arrives at this: "Like a thicket of thorns are they consumed"; but his version simply eliminates the difficult words. (3) Hst. proposes: "His enemies are intertwined thorns." (4) Grz., following Ⓢ, reads: שָׂרִים סְבוּאִים וּבְסָבְאָם, "princes drunken in their wine." (5) V.Ho. substitutes סְבוּכִים כְּסִירִים, "interwoven as thorns." (6) Oo. changes to כְּסוֹדִים סְבוּכִים כְּסֹבֶךְ, "foundations interwoven like a thicket." (7) Ries. similarly reads, "for they are destroyed to their foundation," makes other uncalled-for changes, and then declares

the whole verse a gloss! (8) Du. suggests סִירִים סְבוּכִים אַךְ לוֹ,
"interwoven thorns will surely be to him." (9) Such alterations are moderate in comparison with Hpt.'s procedure. He
arrives at "soaked though they be as toss-pots" and explains
his translation as follows: "The noun סִיר means both *pot* and
thorns, cf. Eccl. 7:6. The glossator who added סְבָכִים (instead
of סְבָאִים) understood סִירִים to mean *thorns,* whereas סירים סבואים
means *wine-jars,* lit., *jars wined,* i. e., *filled with wine.* (Cf.
toss pot, swill pot, swill bowl, swill tub, etc.). After סירים
סבואים we must add כי המה, *although they.*" It should be noted,
however, that סִיר is never used in OT in the sense of "wine
jar." Prevalently it denotes a metallic pot to which fire can
be applied. Again, the pl. of סִיר is normally סִירוֹת. Hpt. also
finds a deeper significance here. The wine jars represent
Antiochus Epiphanes and Demetrius I, his nephew, both
noted as drunkards. On the rejection of the Maccabean
authorship see p. 37. All these alterations are uncalled for
and unsupported. The versions are confused. Ⓖ reads for
כִּי עַד־סִירִים סְבָכִים, ὅτι ἕως θεμελίου αὐτοῦ χερσωθήσεται, καὶ ὡς
σμῖλαξ περιπλεκομένη, "For unto its foundation shall it be left
waste and like a plant entwined." This may rest on a confusion of *Daleth* and *Resh,* whereby a form of יָסַד, "to found,"
"to establish," was read for סִירִים. This conflation is retained
by Ⓛ, which offers: "[quia] ad fundamentum usque suum
[funditus] sicut spinae se invicem complectuntur." Ⓢ has the
equivalent of "thy princes are rebels," as in Is. 1:23. Σ reads:
ὁμοίως στοιβῇ συμπεπλεγμένη, "like an intertwined plant."

וּכְסָבְאָם סְבוּאִים —Ⓖ omits this phrase. Σ reads: καὶ τὸ
συμπόσιον αὐτῶν συμπινόντων ἀλλήλοις, "and the drinking bout
of those who are drinking together with one another."
Ⓥ: "sic convivium eorum pariter potantium." The כ indicated time and should be translated as "when." סָבְאָם is the
infinitive construct of סָבָא, plus the suffix. The phrase is

dropped by Gun. and Hst. as dittography. Jnk. offers
וּכְסוֹבְאִים סְבוּאִים, "and drunken like drunkards." Du. makes radical changes to secure סְבַךְ לִבְיָאִם מָלֵא, "the thicket full of lions." These alterations condemn themselves.

אֻכְּלוּ is used in the sense of "consume," "devour by flames," Ex. 3:2; Neh. 2:3, 13. ⒢, βρωθήσεται, "it will be eaten up," or in some MSS: βρωθήσονται, "they will be eaten up." Σ: ἀναλωθήσεται, "it will be consumed." Mrt. adds כֻּלָּם, "all of them," after אֻכְּלוּ. Gun. wants יִמְלוּ, "they are filled." Jnk. requests יֵאָכְלוּ.

יָבֵשׁ — Hap. wants the plural, יָבֵשׁוּ. Mrt., Hpt., and others want to substitute בָּאֵשׁ, "by fire," but this weakens the picture. ⒢ has ὡς καλάμη ξηρασίας μεστή, "as a reed full of dryness." ⒧: "et quasi stipula exsiccabitur."

מָלֵא — Most critics follow Wllh. in changing this to הֲלֹא and prefixing it to v. 11. This is contrary to all MSS and versional evidence. ⒢ does not reproduce מָלֵא. Stnh. finds the rendering of מָלֵא as "fully" "only just possible," and finally he offers: "like dry stubble from before fire." Nevertheless it is a legitimate adverbial accusative and used as a neuter in the sense of "with fullness." See Jer. 12:6 and Ges., Hwb., *sub* מָלֵא. Sel. offers מִלְּאוּ. ⒮: "They filled themselves."

v. 11 From thee went out one
Who plotteth evil against Yahweh,
A counselor of Belial.

In unconnected dramatic address the prophet now turns to Nineveh and, citing her past hostility to the Almighty, shows by implication how devastation like the horror it had projected for God's people is to overtake the haughty city itself. "From thee went out one who plotteth evil against Yahweh," Nahum tells Nineveh.[8] Various identifications have been offered for the one who "went out" from Nineveh, i. e., at her instigation, with her support. It is proposed that the term "be taken collectively of all the Assyrian monarchs who had oppressed or would oppress the people of God" (as Htz., Sel., and recently many others take it). Most commentators pointedly prefer a reference to Sennacherib, who "went out" of Nineveh against Judah and Jerusalem. This association has the advantage of mentioning specifically the largest and most disastrous invasion, besides re-calling a familiar event of personal experience for some still alive when Nahum penned his prophecies. Especially did this defeat of Assyria's king show Yahweh's power. The record of Sen-nacherib's invasion and his besieging Jerusalem in Hezekiah's days is found in 2 Kings 18:13 ff. and the parallel in Is. 36:1 ff.[9] According to the Ninevite monarch's own account,[10] he pillaged and plundered with wide, cruel devastation, capturing Lachish and Eltekeh, cities of Judah, besides forty-six fortified towns. He boasts that he carried away 200,150 people, in addition to

[8] The Hebrew for "went out" is also used technically for military expedi-tions and invasions. See, for example, 1 Sam. 8:20; Is. 42:13; Zech. 14:3; Job 9:21. Interpreters are therefore quite agreed in assuming that the word refers to a hostile campaign. The Hebrew for "from thee" may also denote the source or impulse of action, Gen. 24:50; Hos. 8:4; Is. 30:1.

[9] Stnh. holds that the reference to Sennacherib's invasion (701 B. C.) would not be recent enough for Nahum and adds: "It is quite possible that he is thinking of the Scythians. . . . There is reason to believe that they entered Pales-tine as allies of Assyria in order to preserve the loyalty of this part of her empire." This introduction of the Scythians is speculative at best. If the Book of Nahum was written, not in 625 B. C., as Stnh. supposes, but twenty-five or thirty years earlier, as we have outlined, the destruction under Sennacherib would have occurred only forty or fifty years before. Besides, the immense losses sustained by the As-syrians in that invasion would have been recalled for generations. Again, if our dating of these prophecies is correct, the book was written twenty-five years before the Scythians assumed a powerful role as Assyrian allies. Moreover, Stnh. himself feels the difficulty involved in calling the Scythians "one who plans evil against the Lord." No evidence whatever remains to show that at this time they rose up against Yahweh or harmed Judah. Finally, the role assumed by the Scythians in later Assyrian history is still obscured by uncertainty.

[10] For Sennacherib's own story of his "going out" from Nineveh to Judah see *Annals,* col. III, 11, 18—49 (Luckenbill, *The Annals of Sennacherib* (1924), pp. 33 f.).

multitudes of horses, mules, camels, asses, and sheep. From Hezekiah he received tribute to the extent of thirty talents of gold, 800 talents of silver, precious stones, couches of ivory, thrones of ivory, elephant hides, rare woods of various kinds, a vast treasure, as well as Hezekiah's daughters, women of his palace, and others.

Nahum's direct charge against Nineveh, from which this vicious destroyer went forth, lays more than the brutality of destruction to Sennacherib's charge. He is described as "one who plotteth evil against Yahweh." The Assyrian conqueror was God's marked enemy.[11] The taunting words of Rabshakeh, 2 Kings 18:30 ff., doubtless expressed the attitude of Sennacherib and Assyrian officialdom in their sneering ridicule of God.

Sennacherib not only sought the defeat of Judah and Jerusalem, he also proposed to transplant the people (Is. 36:17) — another evil plan against Yahweh, since it implied the desecration of the temple and the violation of God's ordinance for His children.

Because of this evil strategy against the Almighty, Sennacherib was also called "a counselor of Belial," the one who advises worthlessness and wickedness. The etymologically uncertain term "Belial" ("worthless" and by implication "wicked") is eminently appropriate for the defeated Assyrian ruler. The final failure of Sennacherib's Palestinian campaign, the destruction of his army before Jerusalem, the uprising in his empire, his death in one of his temples and at the hands of his own sons, show that the last year of his life and his final destiny were truly "without profit."

11 Higher critics here find a conflict between Nahum and earlier prophets. Thus J. M. P. Sm. asserts: "When he (Sennacherib) fought against Israel, he was in reality fighting against Yahweh, thought Nahum. Yet Micah certainly, and Isaiah probably, thought of the Assyrians as Yahweh's agents or tools in the work of punishing sinful Israel." This raises a misconceived objection. It is quite possible for Assyria to be the rod of Yahweh's anger, the instrument used in punishing Israel, and at the same time for Sennacherib to counsel evil against Yahweh.

K. places this verse, emended, after v. 2!

מִמֵּךְ — ⒢, ἐκ σοῦ. The complicated critical attempts to rearrange the verses of ch. 1 alphabetically have made the literary analysts ask for a conjunction at the beginning of the verse. Thus Stnh., who wants a *Kaph* here, conjectures: "It is probable that this verse was originally introduced by *for* [כִּי]." Sel. and others make the same addition. The insertion of conjunctions when ⒨ offers none, and their removal when the text has one (v. 14), is evidence of critical arbitrariness. Du., who calls for an initial *Mem,* changes the fem. suffix in מִמֵּךְ to the masc. מִמְּךָ. Htz. unnecessarily restricts מִמֵּךְ, interpreting it as "out of thee, thou queen of Nineveh," in the sense "thou hast borne." He finds a parallel in Gen. 17:6. From the fact that in vv. 12b and 13 Judah is mentioned in the second person and Nineveh in the third some have concluded that the address here is to Judah. However, מִן in מִמֵּךְ denotes the source of action. See Gen. 24:50; Hos. 8:4; Is. 30:1. The emphasis is therefore more than local. It denotes Nineveh as the power which originated and which sustains the assaults of evil.

יָצָא — ⒢, ἐξελεύσεται, "he shall go forth"; ⒱, "exibit." These futures perhaps assume the imperfect יֵצֵא. Following the tense of the versions, some translate, "will have gone forth"; but the translation of יָצָא as a future perfect is not indicated. Besides, v. 10 mentions the complete destruction of Nineveh, and the statement that Judah's foes will depart would here come as an appended anticlimax.

חֹשֵׁב — ⒢, λογισμός, "consideration" (perhaps an error for λογιζόμενος, "considering"); but B, א, Marchalianus, Lucian Recension and Catena have the reading βουλευόμενος, "taking counsel," also Aq.

רָעָה — "evil" in the sense of "calamity," "catastrophe." Arbitrarily Hst. drops this and the preceding word.

יעץ — Ⓖ, λογιζόμενος, "considering"; Ⓥ, "mente per-
tractans."

בְּלִיַּעַל—The etymology of this term is unclear, but the
following are the more important attempts at explanation
(see Ges., Hwb., and *International Critical Commentary*,
Judges, p. 419): (1) בְּלִיַּעַל is composed of two elements,
בְּלִי, "without" and probably "advantage," "benefit," "useful-
ness." (2) Hupfeld finds as a second element the term עָלָה,
"coming up," that is, "to one's advantage," so that this combination would similarly mean "without profit." (3) Lagarde,
"one who does not permit to ascend." (4) Stnh. holds that
it "is best regarded as a diminutive formation from בָּלַע,
"to swallow up." The meaning under this association would
be "engulfing ruin." This definition, while meaningful in
our passage, does not seem to be appropriate in view of the
other passages in which the term is employed, particularly
in the phrase "the sons of Belial." (5) Jerome, in translating
the phrase "absque iugo," offers the etymology בְּ . י עֹל, "without a yoke." But too much must be read into this suggestion
to make it conform with Scriptural usage. (6) George Foot
Moore (*International Critical Commentary*, Judges, p. 419)
regards these various etymological steps as dubious and finds
no association for the term in Hebrew. Amid these conflicting attempts at explanation it seems that the first and
most widely accepted derivation, "without value," "no advantage," "worthless," has the simplest and most acceptable
basis. Ⓖ otherwise translates בְּלִיַּעַל by ἀνόμημα, "transgression
of the Law," "illegal act"; ἀνομία, "lawlessness"; ἀποστασία,
"desertion," "falling away"; λοιμός, "hunger," "famine";
παράνομος, "lawless"; ἁμαρτωλός, "a transgressor." Yet in
Nah. 2:1 it is rendered as εἰς παλαίωσιν, "for old age" and
in this verse as ἐναντία, "opposite, contrary things." Obviously
Ⓖ translators had only uncertain and contradictory interpretations. Aq. offers κακίαν βουλευόμενος ἀποστασία, "one who

plans evil by means of a falling away." Ⓛ translates here, "cogitans contraria," but in 2:1 reads "in vetustatem" and elsewhere treats it as a proper noun. Ⓢ has the equivalent of Belial. In the OT the term, besides denoting "worthlessness" and "evil," or the results of such a state or condition, sometimes has a concrete and personal meaning. It is, therefore, translated in the Greek as a proper name, Prov. 16:27; Job 34:18. It was regarded as the name for Satan in the *Testimony of the Twelve Patriarchs,* the *Ascension of Isaiah,* the *Book of Jubilees,* and in the *Sibylline Oracles,* where it designates Nero. In the NT it is reserved as a title for Satan, 2 Cor. 6:15. St. Paul here accepts a usage of the term which was current in the Jewish literature of his time. ⒼA, in Judg. 20:3; Θ, in Judg. 19:22; and the versions occasionally (RV regularly) reproduce it as a name.

> *v. 12 Thus saith Yahweh: Even if {they were} complete*
> *and so numerous*
> *And so protected, yet did they pass away.*
> *I afflicted thee;*
> *Not will I afflict thee again.*

This difficult verse begins with the impressive "Thus saith Yahweh." The phrase, used only here in the entire book, is more than an introductory formula; it is the prophet's guarantee that the predictions which follow are not merely human conjecture but the *dicta* of the infallible God Himself. At the same time this "Thus saith Yahweh," unique in Nahum's oracles, is likewise the prophet's open declaration that his utterances are inspired, that he, as God's mouthpiece, speaks the message of divine, unchangeable truth.

To show the Almighty's power, the prophet begins: "Even

if [they (the Ninevites) were] complete and so numerous and so protected." [12] The reference of v. 11 continues as Sennacherib and his invasion of Judah remain the subject of discussion. In that time of Judah's trial God says, "Mine enemies are *complete,* intact, not reduced in complement or size." How complete Sennacherib's forces were is shown at Lachish, subsequent to Sennacherib's first approach to Jerusalem. The account reveals full military equipment, with archers, slingers, spearsmen, equipped with ladders, battering rams, and machines. A picture of Sennacherib's camp at Lachish reveals similar evidence of minute preparedness.

These enemies of God's people are "numerous," Yahweh declares, and Judah knew to her sorrow their overpowering proportions. With allowance for propaganda exaggerations, the armies in Sennacherib's expedition must have reached formidable numbers. While few specific figures have survived concerning the actual size of the Assyrian host,[13] the distance to be traversed from Nineveh to Palestine, the time required in these campaigns, the extent of the military operations, the capture and the transportation of heavy booty, all demanded a large army.

In the third place, God says, the Assyrian armies are "protected," literally, "mailed." This translation, suggested for the first time, rests on a legitimate consonantal exchange explained below. If this interpretation is accepted, the Assyrians are described as not only numerous and completely supplied but as also well armored.

All this the people of Nahum's Judah and Jerusalem understood only too well. Some of them had witnessed the siege

---

12 The AV and RV translation "quiet" misses the prophet's argument and misleads the reader. The basic concept of the Hebrew selemim is "completeness," "fullness." See, for example, Deut. 25:15 and Prov. 11:1, "full, complete weight and measure"; Gen. 15:16, "full, complete measure of sins"; Amos 1:6, 9, "full, complete deportation"; Ruth 2:12, "full, complete compensation."

13 The casualties among Sennacherib's hosts before Jerusalem totaled 185,000, 2 Kings 19:35.

of Jerusalem as children. Now God's messenger reminds them: "Even if [they were] complete and so numerous and so well equipped, yet did they *pass away*." With all the pomp and boasting of his armies the Assyrian monarch was defeated before Jerusalem and died an ignominious death.[14]

With a new strengthening message the divine oracle continues, "I afflicted thee." Sennacherib's invasion in 701 B.C. and the subsequent Assyrian tyranny were indeed heavy visitations for Judah, the penalty paid for its ingratitude toward God.[15] Now, however, the last years of the scheduled penalty are approaching, and Yahweh declares, "Not will I afflict thee again." This promise pledges the cessation of sufferings originating in Nineveh, for the next verse assures Judah that the Assyrian taskmaster's rod and shackles are to be broken.

כֹּה אָמַר יהוה — Although found many times in OT, particularly in the Prophets, this is its only occurrence in Nahum. Such sparing usage lends emphasis. Nevertheless Gun., Hap., No., and others are unwilling to concede that the phrase is genuine here. They brand it as a later addition, doubtless because it is out of harmony with their plan of metrical structure. Yet if it is removed, the promises in the first person which follow in the remainder of the verse would be unintelligible. Even Sel. protests against this excision. V.Ho arbitrarily changes it to נְאֻם יהוה to secure a line starting with *Nun*. Stk. transfers this to the beginning of v. 11.

Ⓜ for this verse is generally regarded as so unintelligible "that it defies all explanation" (Sel.). The extent to which

[14] On the use of *ābhar* in this sense see Ps. 37:36; Job 33:18; 34:20; 36:12. Htz. interprets it as "fly away" and cites Jer. 13:24; Is. 40:24. But this is not conclusive.

[15] It is frequently objected that Nahum entirely overlooks his people's sins. However, the phrase "I afflicted thee" implies the punishment with which Judah was visited for its rebellion against God. Significantly the verb reproduced as "afflicted" is used for the retribution with which the Almighty visits transgression of His Law and rejection of His grace. See Deut. 8:2, 3, 16; 1 Kings 11:39; 2 Kings 17:20; Is. 64:11; Ps. 90:15; 119:75; Lam. 3:33.

some reconstructions have gone may be seen in Stnh.'s alteration, which reads: "Thus saith Jehovah, Though thou rulest over peoples . . . and many be designated by thy name, yet the glory of thy power shall pass away, and the report of thee shall no more be heard." Bi. produces this: "The pride of tyrants is a flood. It disappears quickly and runs off." Ru. reaches this: "I shall cause mighty waters to flow, and the sound of thy name shall no longer resound." To show the further divergence of critical opinion, one need only compare Mrt.'s final offering (which J.M.P.Sm. follows): "Verily, the days of my contention are completed; yea, indeed, they are over and gone."

אִם שְׁלֵמִים וְכֵן רַבִּים—Various substitute readings have been proposed. Thus (1) Gun. and Mrt. have offered this version, accepted by No., Kent, and alternatively by J.M.P.Sm.: אַךְ שָׁלְמוּ יְמֵי רִיבִי, "Verily the days of my contention are completed." (2) Sm., however, also suggests the possibility of אַךְ שָׁלְמוּ יָמִים רַבִּים, "Verily, many days have been completed." (3) Wllh., followed by G.A.Sm. and in essence by Dr., alters to אִם שָׁלְמוּ מַיִם, "If many waters are ever so full." (4) Hpt. changes to אִם מַיִם מְלֵאִים, "if the waters are filling." (5) Jnk. reconstructs אִם שְׁלֵמִים וְאִם רַבִּים, "if they are complete and if they are numerous." (6) V.Ho. proposes מֹשֵׁל מָרוֹם, "the ruler of the heights." (7) Ru.: אֲמַשֵּׁל מַיִם רַבִּים, "I shall cause many waters to flow." (8) Hap.: מֹשֵׁל מַיִם, "He rules the water." (9) Ries.: מֹשֵׁל מַיִם רַבִּים, "the ruler of great waters." (10) Bi.: "The pride of tyrants is as high water." Similarly Sel., followed by Hst.: הִנֵּה מֹשְׁלִים מַיִם רַבִּים, "Behold, tyrants are mighty waters." The picture, Sel. declares, is this, as Bi. outlines: Tyrants, like powerful waters, are dangerous; but they run off quickly and pass away. (11) Du., after radical omissions: אִם שָׁלֵם יוֹם עֻנֹּתָךְ, "if the day of thine affliction is complete." (12) Stnh.: "Though thou rulest over peoples."

(13) T. H. Gaster: "what though great waters gushed." He asserts that the first two consonants in שְׁלֵמִים are to be read as שְׁלוּ, from the neo-Hebrew root שְׁלַל, related to Arabic šalla "to gush." With further changes he continues the verse: "yet they have ebbed and passed o'er." This likewise is artificial and foreign to the context. What comfort could Judah receive from this: "As the rushing torrents ultimately subside, so will God cause all previous disasters to vanish away"? In the first place, not all rushing torrents subside. Then, מַיִם רַבִּים without qualification cannot specifically denote raging torrents. The reference to water as disaster would lose force if applied figuratively to Judah and then literally to Assyria. Finally, "gushing" is not an apt symbol of devastation. — In all these differences, critics approach agreement only in omitting וְכֵן as a dittography, and in substituting מַיִם or some other form. Thus J.M.P.Sm. and others ask for אִכֵּן. Gun. regards כֵן as a noun meaning "place," "socket," "foundation." The versions compound the difficulty. ⒢ offers κατάρχων ὑδάτων πολλῶν, "ruler of many waters," which rests on a mistaken division of words and resultant false combinations. "Even if [they were] complete and so numerous." J.M.P.Sm. objects to this translation on two counts. First he asserts that שְׁלֵמִים, in the sense of "complete," is "somewhat forced." However, beside the etymological association from the root שָׁלֵם, which means "to be uninjured," "whole," "complete," the emphasis on the fullness (see also above) is found in Gen. 33:13, "uninjured": Deut. 27:6; Joshua 8:31, "whole stones." See also 1 Kings 8:11; 11:4; 15:3, "a perfect heart." Thus the term here may refer to their sincerity, their completeness of number, their unimpaired strength. Likewise he objects that "the pronouns 'they' and 'he' are loosely related to the context, the former in particular finding no satisfactory antecedent." The whole tenor of the

verse in its context, particularly v. 10, should leave no doubt
that God's enemies in Nineveh are meant. The change of
number from the pl. to the sing., as disturbing as it may be
in English, is not infrequent in Hebrew. But see below.

וְכֵן נָגֹזּוּ — The customary derivation of the verb is from גָזַז,
"to shear." Obviously this meaning does not fit here, for
נָגֹזּוּ is parallel with the conception of completeness and number.
The whole periodic construction emphasizes Assyrian power
or preparedness. May we not assume that by interchange of
related consonants the verb גזז may have the same meaning as
קָשַׂשׂ? The root of this verb occurs in Biblical Hebrew only in
קַשְׂקֶשֶׂת, "scale," Lev. 11:9-12; Deut. 14:9; Ezek. 29:4, where
it is used of fish scales. Singularly enough, however, 1 Sam.
17:5 employs the term to describe Goliath's brass "coat of
mail," the armor which was made up of small, overlapping
metallic scales, fastened on leather or cloth, a familiar part
of ancient military equipment. Bas-reliefs of heavily armed
Assyrian infantry and cavalry clearly show armor of this type.
In equating גזז and קָשַׂשׂ the mutation of the two sibilants is
typical of a frequent interchange. For example, both עָלֵז
and עָלַס mean "to rejoice." Nor is the equation of ג with ק
unparalleled. It occurs in גָבִיעַ and קֻבַּעַת, both meaning "cup,"
"goblet." — Ⓖ translates נָגֹזּוּ as διασταλήσονται, "they shall be
scattered"; Ⓛ, "dividentur"; AV, "even so shall they be cut
down"; Luther, similarly. But these versions do not reproduce
the second וְכֵן. Radical interpreters, of course, have not
permitted נָגֹזּוּ to stand. Thus (1) J.M.P.Sm., following others,
wants the form גָזוּ, "they shall pass away." (2) Wllh. and
Sel. suggest the imperfect, יָגֹזוּ, "they shall pass away."
(3) New. emends to יָגֹל, "he tears away." (4) Hap. reads
נִגְזָרוּ, "they shall be cut off." (5) Gun. asks for נָגֹז, "cut
off." (6) Del. proposes נָגֹחוּ (גוח Niph"al), "they are destroyed."
(7) Wllh. alternatively changes to יִזֹּרוּ, "they disappear."

Stnh. changes וְכֵן to וְכִנּוּ, claiming "the root כנה is used in the *Pi''el* in the sense of 'to give a title or cognomen.'" But it is so used in bestowing honorable names. These alterations are arbitrary and altogether unnecessary in view of Ⓜ's good sense when translated as suggested here.

וְעָבָר — Ⓥ has the future, "et pertransibit." The word is dropped or changed by most critics. J.M.P.Sm. says that the word is "not improbably a gloss on the rare word גִּז and justifies its elimination by the omission of it in Ⓖ. The other versions, however, retain the word, Ⓢ and Ⓣ changing the form to the pl. The sing. after the pl. is difficult and has been interpreted as a collective which embraces the many troops in one large army or as expressive of an indefinite group. For a somewhat similar usage of the third sing. masc. in the sense of indefinite "they," see Ges., Gra., 144 *d*. Much to be preferred to the general and collective interpretation of the sing. is the assumption of a personal subject, the one who plans evil against Yahweh, the counselor of Belial mentioned in the preceding verse. Even if his armies were complete, numerous, and mailed, yet did he pass away. See below. On the use of the *Waw* before עָבָר see Ges., Gra., 112 *gg*. See also Num. 21:9.

וְעִנִּתִךְ לֹא אֲעַנֵּךְ עוֹד — Ⓥ, followed by Lu., Or., Stk., G.A.Sm., Jnk., and others, omits the *Waw,* but Ⓖ has it in its present position. This tends to invalidate J.M.P.Sm.'s transportation of the *Waw* from עִנִּתִךְ to לֹא. Otherwise Ⓖ has missed the sense, translating καὶ ἡ ἀκοή σου οὐκ ἐνακουσθήσεται ἔτι, "the report of thee shall no longer be heard." The copulative *Waw* is difficult. We would expect a conditional or concessive clause; yet there seems to be no justification for the "though" in the AV. May the *Waw* in וְעִנִּתִךְ not have been misplaced by wrong spacing, so that it actually belongs at the end of עָבָר, the original text having read עָבְרוּ עִנִּתִךְ? This at the same

time would remove some of the difficulty in connection with
the singular עֹבֵר preceded by the pl. The context shows that
the address is not to Nineveh, as Ew., Htz., Wllh., G.A.Sm.,
Dr., and others have assumed. In defending this position,
J. M. P.Sm. declares: "As the text stands in Ⓜ, the more
natural rendering is, 'and I will afflict thee so that I need
not afflict thee again,' in which case the address is to Nineveh
or Assyria and the meaning is that Yahweh is about to
destroy Nineveh utterly, once for all." Essentially the same
position is adopted by Htz., Wllh., G.A.Sm., Dr., and others.
Similarly RV suggests: "So I have afflicted thee that I will
not again afflict thee," that is, the affliction will be complete,
final. But the Hebrew offers no justification for the translation "so that." On the joining of final and consecutive
clauses with *Waw,* see Ges., Gra., 165, 166. It is not true
that up to this time God has emphatically afflicted Assyria
and that in the future He will refuse to afflict it again. Not
only will Nineveh be humbled and afflicted, it will also be
destroyed, and that in the days yet to come. The address is
to Judah, as Keil, Or., Gun., Mrt., Jnk., and others also hold.
Stnh. asks for "and the report of thee shall no more be heard,"
a translation prompted by Ⓖ. Hap. reads עִנִּתִם לֹא אֲעַנֶּם עוֹד,
"I have afflicted them, not will I afflict them again." Hst.
proposes the infinitive absolute construction עַנֹּה עִנִּתִךְ, "I have
oppressed you hard." Although most critics have given up
the attempt to secure alphabetic sequence here, the following
acrostical claims have been made: The *Nun* line is found
here in נִוּוּ (Hap., who eliminates vv. 11 and 12a). The
Shin line is secured by omitting אִם and starting with שְׁלֵמִים
(Arn.). The '*Ayin* line was discovered by Sel., who in his
first edition started the verse with וְעָבַר, omitted the *Waw,*
changed the form to the plural, and introduced other alterations. All this vanished in his second edition.

v. 13 And now
I will break his rod from off thee,
And thy bonds I will tear apart.

For further assurance that no more affliction from Assyria will overwhelm Judah, God makes a double promise. First He pledges, continuing the address to His people, "And now I will break his rod from off thee." The "now," besides indicating the immediacy of Israel's liberation, also expresses the contrast between the past oppression and the future freedom. The "rod" implies a rod-bearer with an uplifted club, despotical Nineveh, which had mercilessly beaten Judah.[16] Nahum does not here have the Ten Tribes in mind and their deportation after the capture of Samaria (Htz.); his interests center in Judah, which, particularly under Tiglathpileser, Sennacherib, Esarhaddon, and now Ashurbanipal, was subjected to Ninevite cruelty. When the Assyrian rod is broken, its cruel power is shattered (1:14), and Judah is free (2:1). For the similar picture of the taskmaster with an upraised club towering over a slave see Is. 9:4; 10:5, 24; 30:31; Ps. 2:9.

In the second place, God promises, "Thy bonds I will tear apart." The figure is that of a prisoner whose hands or feet have been fettered and who has thus been rendered helpless. A related thought is expressed in Is. 52:2; Jer. 2:20; 5:5; 30:8; Ps. 2:3; 107:14; 116:16. Until the dawn of the promised deliverance, Judah will bear the bonds of serfdom, but the hour will soon strike when Yahweh Himself, tearing these emblems of servitude apart, will set His people free. Deliverance is expressed by the same picture in Lev. 26:13; Is. 10:27; 28:10; Ezek. 34:27.

[16] How incongruous is the statement of J.M.P.Sm.: "The oppressor referred to is the power that happened to be in dominion over Judah at the time this was written; perhaps it was Persia"! Sm. incorrectly regards 1:13 as a later addition. Therefore he departs from the theme of the prophecies and finds a post-exilic taskmaster. Contrarily Stnh. holds that the verse was written "probably towards the close of Josiah's reign, as Assyria's end approached."

This verse casts a significant light on the date of the book. Evidently Judah and Jerusalem are still under Assyria's rod, languishing in the bonds Nineveh imposed. When, we ask pertinently, did Jerusalem suffer under the Assyrian yoke? Not particularly during Josiah's last years (639—609 B.C.), but definitely in Manasseh's reign (698—642 B.C.). To follow most critics in dating the book, including this passage, at 614 B.C. is as incongruous as to assume that an address to the people of our country, promising them independence from British rule, could have been written in President Andrew Jackson's administration.

Wllh. (followed by Hpt.) maintains concerning 1:13 to 2:3: "In the verses with even numbers Ashur of Nineveh is addressed, in those with uneven numbers Judah or Zion. This change of address, verse after verse is intolerable . . . 1:13; 2:1-3 . . . are added." But this overstates the case. V. 12 is addressed to Judah, and there is no address in 2:3. The remaining interchange of person is dramatic and easily understood. Dav.-Lan. echoes Wllh.'s assertion that this verse is spurious, stating, without reason or explanation, "V.13 might be an interpolation or marginal note." Ries. also drops this verse.

וְעַתָּה — The initial *Waw* is omitted by Gun., Hap., and v.Ho. to furnish the ע line of the acrostic.

מֹטֵהוּ — The *Qerē* in some text editions asks for מֹטֵהוּ, but the change is not necessary, since מוֹט occurs in the sense of "rod," "staff." It is clearly so used in Num. 13:23 as the "staff" on which the two spies brought the immense cluster of grapes, and in Num. 4:10, 12 as a "bar" on which the temple equipment is carried. Though the picture of a long, heavy pole fits strikingly here, AV offers "yoke." This, however, is not substantiated elsewhere, מוֹטָה being the word for "yoke," Jer. 27:2. Objection is also taken (Wllh. and others) to the pronominal suffix ־הוּ, which, it is said, presupposes the form

מַטֶּה, since the ־הוּ suffixes are characteristic of *Lamed He* nouns. This objection is not decisive, for the OT has the forms אוֹרֵהוּ, "his light," Job 25:3; לְמִינֵהוּ, "after its kind," Gen. 1: 12, 21, etc.; פִּילַגְשֵׁהוּ, "his concubine," Judg. 19:24. Ⓖ, τὴν ῥάβδον αὐτοῦ, "his rod," and Ⓥ, "virgam eius," could reproduce מוֹט in the sense of "pole," "rod." Hst. and Stk., after Du., arbitrarily ask for the pl. מוֹטוֹת; Wllh., מוֹטוֹ; Or., מוֹטָתוֹ; Gun., מֹטוֹתֶיךָ; Mrt. and K.-G., מוֹטוֹתָיו; v.Ho., מַטְּךָ. Most agreed are the critics on מַטֶּהוּ. But all these changes are unnecessary, since Ⓜ is good (if somewhat less usual) Hebrew and furnishes striking sense.

מֵעָלֶיךָ — Ⓥ, "de dorso tuo." Hpt., claiming to find an interpolation within an interpolation, as well as K.-G. and v.Ho., omit this. Du. and Stk. change to עֻלֵּךְ, "thy yoke." Ⓜ should stand. The suffix refers to Judah. Ehr. denies this and changes the text to read מטות עֻלֵּךְ, "the hooks of thy [Nineveh's] yoke." However, this is apodictical exegesis. The address to Judah comes naturally and forcefully after the conclusion of v. 12.

> *v. 14*   *And Yahweh hath ordained concerning thee:*
>   *No more of thy name will be sown.*
>   *From the house of thy gods I will cut off graven*
>   *image and molten image.*
>   *I will make thy grave, for thou art despised.*

To the promise of freedom for Judah the prophet joins a series of direct threats against Nineveh. In an impressive introduction he says, "And Yahweh hath ordained concerning thee." Once again, as in v. 12, Nahum deliberately speaks in the capacity of a divine messenger, charged with proclaiming God's sentence on the doomed city. The predictions to follow are not the mere expressions of fallible men; they are rather the immovable decrees of the Eternal. "Everything that happens, happens according to the direction of God's Word," says Lu. How majestical Yahweh appears here as the Sovereign of all peoples, whose utterances decree the destiny of every nation! The Assyrian capital (probably not the king), representative of the empire, is warned, "No more of thy name will be sown." The figure of no further sowing, in the sense of no more propagating or perpetuating, implies not only that Nineveh will be cut down, but also that for all times the city will remain extinct. Nations may be said to perpetuate themselves by sowing the seed from which the future continuance of their name and growth sprout, as generation rises against generation. But Nineveh will have no descendants to keep its name and fame alive. It faces permanent annihilation. For similar pictures see Is. 14:20-22; 40:24; Jer. 31:27; Hos. 2:23; 1 Sam. 24:21; Deut. 7:24; 29:20.

Here the retaliation motif appears. Nineveh's kings were constantly concerned that their names and their families be perpetuated. Ashurbanipal, following the general plan of his predecessors, closes his annals with the request that the son who follows in rule preserve his father's name on the building inscription, and with a warning that anyone who removes his, Ashurbanipal's, name will be judged by Ashur, Sin, Shamash, Adad, Bel, Nabu, Ishtar of Nineveh, Ishtar of Arbela, Ninurta, Nergal, and Nusku, the eleven most powerful deities in the Assyrian pantheon.

Nahum's dire sentence is enlarged to include the prophecy that Assyrian temples will be violated, Assyrian idol-gods broken. "From the house of thy gods I will cut off graven image and molten image." It was customary for Nineveh's conquering hordes to desecrate the altars and temples of their vanquished foes, to deport their idols, and thus to emphasize the supremacy of Ashur, Ishtar, and the gods worshiped in Assyrian shrines. Now the haughty city itself is to experience the same defamation which it repeatedly inflicted on others. In singling out "the house of thy gods," Nahum refers perhaps particularly to one of the two outstanding temples in Nineveh, the sanctuary of Ishtar (*Ê-mash-mash*) and the temple of Nabu (*Ê-zida*). These were glorious structures on which one king after another lavished royal bounty. The Ishtar temple at Nahum's time looked back on almost 1,500 years of existence with constantly increasing importance as the center of Nineveh's worship. The threat that these temples would be destroyed was, therefore, not only a disparagement of polytheism but also a body blow to Assyrian pride and ancient tradition. Nahum speaks of "a molten image" and "a graven image," the same combination found in Deut. 27:15; Judg. 17:3 f.; 18:14. The Assyrian temples abound particularly in stone figures and sculptured bas-reliefs depicting the higher and lower gods as well as grotesque tripartite guardian spirits and demons. Molten statues, although not as frequently preserved in the ruins (because of their metallic value they were highly prized booty), have likewise been found.[17] These images are to be cut down in a striking demonstration of their utter impotence.

Excavators have commented on the complete devastation which marks Nineveh's sanctuaries. It seems as though the invaders sacked the temples with particular vengeance. Some sections of the Nabu temple were so completely overturned that competent investigators decided further exploration of these sites would not pay. Slabs written by Ashurbanipal have been found at Nineveh in both temples, Ê-mash-mash and Ê-zida. On one with official repetition the king asks Ishtar [and Nabu on the

---

[17] Is. 46:6, 7: "They lavish gold out of the bag and weigh silver in the balance and hire a goldsmith; and he maketh it a god; they fall down, yea, they worship. They bear him upon the shoulder, they carry him, and set him in his place," thus mentions these idol statues made of metal. See Is. 44:10-12. The metal idols in Babylonia (Jer. 10:9; Dan. 5:4) were probably made in the same way as those found in Assyria. A bas-relief unearthed by Layard in the southwest ruins of Nimrud pictures idols, sculptured or of metal, carried in procession by Assyrian warriors.

other] "For all time, O Ishtar, look upon it [the temple] with favor." The utter devastation of this sanctuary only fourteen years after Ashurbanipal's death proved Ishtar's impotence. Likewise does the violence wreaked on their costly shrines re-emphasize the retaliation which divine justice decrees for Nineveh's war lords. They wrecked the temples of other nations; now their own temples are to crumble in debris.

Again, God warns, "I will make thy grave." Nineveh is not to be temporarily incapacitated; it is to die and be buried. Her end is at hand. When the gods in whom the city has placed its false trust are destroyed, the mass interment will follow. Nineveh in its totality will lie buried in ruins. Its tomb will be marked by the tells that rise over its waste.

Summarizing the reasons for this fatal rejection, the prophet continues, "For thou art despised," namely, by almighty God (Gen. 16:4 f.; 1 Sam. 2:30). Nineveh's iniquity has been so deep-rooted and protracted that the Holy One of Israel can contemplate the city only with the contempt which must result in its unalterable collapse.

The order of this verse and its place in the prophecy is changed by critical caprice. J.M.P.Sm. inserts it, together with 1:11 and 2:2, 4-14, into a special section called "The Fall of Nineveh." Stnh., however, asserts, "The v. connects with v. 12." Ries., who regards only the first seven words as genuine, connects them with v. 12b. Sel., on the other hand, separates the section 1:12-14 and 2:1, 3, which he calls "The Prophecy of Deliverance to Judah."

וְצִוָּה — Ⓖ, καὶ ἐντελεῖται, "and He will command." The *Waw* is not consecutive, introducing the future, as maintained by Stnh.; it is simply copulative (as in Gen. 15:6; 28:6) and connects the promise of Judah's freedom with the prediction of Assyria's destruction. Nor should the *Waw* be omitted, as Wllh., Gun., Hap., and others propose. This is gratuitous and removes the thought that the Almighty has long conceived the plan which will soon go into effect. Dr.'s assertion that "the v. would be much more forceful without" the *Waw* is typical of the literary superrefinement and would impose Western standards on the Semitic mind.

עָלֶיךָ — These oracles of doom are pronounced, directly or indirectly, on Nineveh, since the address in the second person singular masculine, "concerning thee," can be understood only as a reference to the doomed city, the defeated nation, its king, or a personification of the capital. Pusey and Henderson assume that Sennacherib is addressed, but the book was written too late for this assumption. Michaelis holds that God speaks to Ashurbanipal, but this view would limit the prophet, whose messages throughout predict not merely a change of dynasty but also the destruction of a city and the final collapse of an empire. If Nineveh is thus addressed, it is not necessary with Grz., Mrt., No., and others to "read all the suffixes in the verses as feminine with the Syriac." Neither MS authority nor syntactical necessity exists for this procedure. Ⓥ's "inhonoratus es" and the context discredit the switching of gender. Equally unnecessary are Hap.'s change of number, for the singular עָלֶיךָ to עֲלֵיהֶם, and Sel.'s (similarly Bev.'s) change of person to עָלָי.

לֹא יִזָּרַע מִשִּׁמְךָ עוֹד — Ⓖ, οὐ σπαρήσεται ἐκ τοῦ ὀνόματός σου ἔτι, "there shall not be sown of thy name." Mrt., No., K.-G., Sel., and others read לֹא יִזָּכֵר, "there shall not be remembered." More recently interpreters like J.M.P.Sm. and Stnh. protest that this "emendation is unnecessary," that the original Ⓜ "is much more suggestive and in keeping with the poetic feeling of Nahum." No grammatical difficulty attaches to the phrase. The מִן in מִשִּׁמְךָ, which most critics drop, is partitive and normal, Ex. 16:27; 2 Sam. 11:17. Other abortive attempts at emendation include Mrt.'s לֹא יִזָּכֵר בִּשְׁמָם, "he will

not remember their name"; Du.'s יַעַד, "he will go away";
Hpt.'s יֻרֶה שֶׁלֶמְךָ, "thy remains (corpse) shall be scattered";
Hst.'s לֹא יֻזְרְעוּ שְׁמַנֶּיךָ, "thy fat lands will not be sown."

מִבֵּית אֱלֹהֶיךָ —Ⓖ A adds καί before ἐξ οἴκου, "from the house."
Mrt. reads the plural, "from the houses." No. and Hap. omit
מִבֵּית אֱלֹהֶיךָ. K.-G. and Hst. want בְּתֵּי, "houses." As a gloss
Du. suggests, "from the house of thy father." No good
purpose is served by such toying with the text.

מַסֵּכָה —a cast, or molded image. Ⓖ, χωνευτά, "cast or
molded things." Dav.-Lan. and Or. find an implied second
object and translate, "I will make it [the house of thy god]
thy grave." This prediction, it is declared, has enjoyed a general fulfillment, inasmuch as the Assyrian idols proved a means
of the people's destruction. Specifically it is alleged that
a temple became a grave when Sennacherib was murdered
in one of his idolatrous shrines, Is. 37:38. Against this
reading adopted by Ⓣ and Ⓢ, also widely accepted by older
interpreters, it must be observed that no second object is
expressed. As Keil points out: "Were a second object to be
assumed, it would be necessary to find it in 'a molten image
and a graven image,' which hardly offers an acceptable
translation. No alternative offers itself, and this translation
is necessary, 'I will make thy grave.'" J.M.P.Sm. insists,
however, that the expression "make thy grave" is not "used
elsewhere as the equivalent of 'put to death,' or 'bury thee.'"
But these passages with a markedly similar point of view
should be noted: Is. 53:9; Ezek. 39:11. After altering the
preceding verb, Grz. arbitrarily offers אָסִיר מִקִּרְבֵּךְ, "I will
remove from thy midst." Oo. alters Ⓜ to secure אֶשָּׂא מִקִּרְבֵּךְ,
"I will lift up from thy midst." Gun. and Hap. propose
אַשְׁמִיד קִבְרָם, "I will destroy their grave." Sel. and Hst. want
וְאָשֵׁם קִבְרֵךְ, "And I will destroy thy grave."

כִּי קַלּוֹתָ —This means, etymologically, "thou art light." It

is here used morally. See the related thought in the Aramaic
of Dan. 5:27, "weighed in the balances and . . . found
wanting." The translation here suggested, "thou art despised,"
is that indicated by the use of the same verb in 1 Sam. 2:30
and Gen. 16:4, 5. It has also been reproduced, "Thou art
become insignificant," but this statement affords no motivation
for blotting out the city. Nineveh will be destroyed, not
because she has become unimportant, but because God
despises her. Ⓥ's "inhonoratus es" reproduces the sense better
than ὅτι ταχεῖς, "because swift," or the similar Ⓢ and Ⓣ.
Literary critics have gone to devious extremes in connection
with the closing words of this verse. J.M.P.Sm., following
Wllh. and others, omits כִּי and translates, "I will make thy
grave a dishonor" (substituting קָלוֹן for קַלּוֹתָ), and explains:
"As emended the text marks the climax of misfortune for
Assyria in that instead of being held in honour after she
has ceased to live, the memory of her is to become an
occasion for insult and reproach." It should be noted, however, that the Semitic desecration after death was either
exposure in the absence of burial (Ps. 141:7; Rev. 11:9)
or the opening of the grave and the scattering of the remains
(Is. 14:19; Jer. 8:1). Sm. here follows metricists in giving
two accents to the dissyllabic אָשִׂים. Sel. and Hst. read קַלְלְתָּ,
"thou art accursed," though Sel. regards this as a gloss.
However, Stnh. admits, and K.-G. agrees generally: "We
seem to need some clause like 'for thou art,' etc., to round
off the verse; and the rhythm (kina) of these lines, moreover,
appears to demand it." Bi. (similarly Gun.) produces an
Aramaic word, קִיקָלוֹת, "dung-heaps," and changes the rest
of the verse. Grz. reads וְנִכְלַמְתָּ, "thou hast been disgraced."
V.Ho. substitutes קִיקָלוֹן, "disgrace," while Del. and Sel. want
the Hiph"il of שָׁמֵם, Del. in the sense of "devastate," Sel.
with the meaning "I made solitary," which, he asserts, rather
inconclusively, is supplied by 2 Sam. 13:20; Is. 54:1.

Chapter 2

v. 1   Behold!   On the mountains feet of a herald proclaim-
ing peace!
Celebrate thy festivals, O Judah!   Pay thy vows!
For Belial will not again pass through thee.
He is altogether destroyed.

So positive is the prophet of God's deliverance that in this
new section, beginning with the sudden "Behold!" he foretells
the fulfillment of the threats announced in ch. 1. "On the
mountains" (not those "in the direction of Nineveh," but the
Judean highlands) "a herald" is discerned. He is visualized as
poised on a ridge, not because of the "custom of signaling tidings
from one hilltop to another" (the passages J.M.P.Sm. cites to
show this: Is. 5:26; 13:2 ff.; 49:22, are not decisive), but
because his words can be heard far and wide from this vantage
point (see Is. 40:9), particularly also because a messenger coming
with news from Nineveh would first be seen on the hills of the
horizon. The herald's "feet" are specified, probably as the members
active in running (Acts 5:9).

The messenger comes "proclaiming peace," i. e., the end
of Nineveh and with it — tranquillity. The sufferings inflicted
by the oppression of the tyrant on the Tigris are over now that
the capital of international crime is destroyed. Instead of groaning
under Assyrian serfdom, Judah can enjoy not merely the cessation

217

of warfare, but, with the liberation from paralyzing fear, also peace, progress, prosperity.

Consequently Judah is urged (either by the herald or by the prophet): "Celebrate thy festivals, O Judah!" At the very beginning of their recovery God's people should express their gratitude for heaven's aid. Implied, perhaps, in this appeal is the inference that now through the reign of peace the possibility of observing the religious festivals is restored. The inhabitants of Judah had been in no mood to gather for joyous celebration as long as Nineveh's tyranny exacted its relentless tribute; and the hostility of the Assyrians discouraged or entirely interrupted public worship. The threat that one of Sennacherib's successors might return to take the temple and suspend all worship is over because of the divinely bestowed and decisive victory which the prophet envisions. Significantly, his first thoughts seek to secure God's recognition and to give Him thanks for the deliverance.

Besides, the liberated nation is urged, "Pay thy vows!" During the long years of servitude many a prayer had been raised to the Almighty, vowing the fulfillment of certain voluntary pledges after the deliverance dawned. Now, the night of oppression ended, these obligations were to be met. The deliverance comes from God; He must be thanked.[1]

The reason for the peace proclamation is found in the added assurance, "For Belial will not again pass through thee." The term "Belial" (see 1:11) may employ the abstract for the concrete, "worthlessness" for "the worthless one" (1 Sam. 25:25; 30:22; 2 Sam. 16:7), thus viewing the hostile power of evil not as an individual, but personified as the embodiment of wickedness, Nineveh itself. In much the same way the mention of enemies

[1] No one was required to make a vow, which in its sacrificial aspect is classified as a freewill offering (Deut. 12:6). Yet when a votive pledge was made, it had to be kept, and, if involving a sacrifice, paid according to the formal prescription of the Law, Lev. 22:18 ff.; 27:1 ff.; Num. 15:3 ff. On the early occurrence of the vow, see Gen. 28:20 ff.; Judg. 11:30 ff.; 1 Sam. 1:11 ff.; 2 Sam. 15:7 ff. Later references occur in Is. 19:21; Jonah 1:16; Job 22:27; Ps. 22:25; 50:14; 56:12; 66:13; 116:14, 18; Prov. 20:25.

under specific titles is met in Hos. 5:13; 10:6; Jer. 25:26; 51:41. The enemy of God will no longer march destructively through Judah (Zech. 9:8; Joel 3:17), for "he is altogether destroyed." This defeat is no casual disaster or temporary rebuff. The final disintegration is at hand.

Nahum's exultation not only reflects the general picture in Is. 40:9: "O Zion, that bringest good tidings, get thee up into the high mountain"; it repeats almost literally the thought of Is. 52:7: "How beautiful upon the mountains are the feet of him that bringeth good tidings, that publisheth peace!" The Isaianic passage directed to God's people in exile foresees the Messianic triumph and predicts the spread of the Gospel, as both the context and the citation by St. Paul in Rom. 10:15 indicate. This coincidence with Isaiah's language is probably too marked to be accidental; and Nahum employs the earlier prediction of spiritual peace in his own forecast of temporal tranquillity. As Isaiah's promise is found in a section which makes the release from the Babylonian Captivity a pledge of deliverance from sin's captivity through Christ, so Nahum, repeating the older Messianic oracle, finds in the destruction of Assyrian iniquity and the pledge of peace a foregleam of the Messiah's victory and the resultant joy.[2]

[2] This Messianic force was recognized by the early church. The verse is quoted in *Tertullian Against Marcion*, IV, 13, a section in which Christ's connection with the Creator is emphasized. Among the many OT citations quoted as predictive of the Messiah, these words of Nahum are specially adduced. (*Ante-Nicene Fathers*, III, 364). Lu.: "We all are of the conviction that there is not a single one of the prophets who in his prophecy did not insert something of the coming Christ and of the grace which would be revealed in Christ. In this prophet I would like to interpret this passage of Christ, for there is otherwise in this prophet no passage which can be understood as referring to Christ" (XIV: 1350). However, Lu. also explains: "If he has not here spoken of the Gospel, which through Christ should be spread throughout the world, then this is nowhere expressed in this prophet. Nevertheless, I will not force Christ in where He has not inserted Himself. I hold fast to my opinion that the prophet here speaks especially of the Good Messenger, through whom it should be announced that the enemies are defeated, the booty secured, the peace restored. . . . He who in a general way wants to interpret the passages as referring to Christ's Gospel may do so. I have nothing against it." (XIV: 1390—91)

הִנֵּה — This has been transposed by Gun. and Hap. t follow מְבַשֵּׂר or changed to הִנָּם (v.Ho.). No cogent reaso justifies these alterations, each of which involves furthe changes.

מְבַשֵּׂר — Hpt. omits this word as superfluous, but its occu rence in Is. 52:7 is warrant for its inclusion here.

מַשְׁמִיעַ — V.Ho. omits this, although it is required for th reason just stated. Ries. drops the entire verse thus far.

שַׁלְמִי — Gun., Hap., and K.-G. add יְרוּשָׁלַיִם as vocative. Why The latter admit, "because of the meter."

יוֹסִיף — ⑤, προσθήσωσιν. On this basis Ries. substitute the pl. יוֹסִיפוּ.

לעבור — The *Kethībh* read לַעֲבוֹר, while the *Qerē,* becaus of the *Maqqeph,* wants לַעֲבָר־. ⑤ erroneously reads לַעֲבֹד, "t serve." Despite the fact that this is a clear infinitive construc *Qal,* Gun. and others make it a *Hiph"il* and Hap., an im perfect *Qal.*

בְּלִיַעַל — ⑤, εἰς παλαίωσιν, "for old age"; Ⓛ, "in vetustatem. These versions somehow connect the Hebrew noun with th root בָּלָה, "to become worn" or "old." Hst. arbitrarily ask for כְּדִבְלַיַעַל. Stnh. maintains that this clause originally fol lowed 1:13.

כֻּלֹּה — On the form of the suffix see Ges., Gra., 91 *e.* Wllh Gun., No., and others read this as כָּלָה (⑤, συντετέλεσται "it has been corrupted") and translate (so Sm.), "He wil be destroyed, cut off." But כָּלָה in the *Qal* means "to b finished," "to be at an end," and it would be redundant i inserted before נִכְרַת. Sm. tries to justify the substitution o כָּלָה for כֻּלֹּה by stating, " כֹּל with suffix usually follows it verb rather than precedes it"; but a usage which is onl "usually" observed should not be made the decisive basi for textual alteration. Hpt. reads כָּלֹה, "he has been ended."

נִכְרָת — This is the pausal perfect. ⑤, ἐξῆρται, "he ha been removed."

Criticism has thrown caution to the wind in dealing with
this verse. Bi. leaves only a few words of the entire verse
and places before them רַגְלֵי to secure the ר line. V.Ho. starts
with רַגְלֵי, omitting much of the preceding and following,
or transferring it. Gun. likewise starts the ר line with רַגְלֵי,
transposing the previous words, and makes the שׁ line begin
with שְׁלֹמִי and the ת line with an artificial ת. Even J.M.P.Sm.
summarizes: "By proceedings like these, any poem might
be transformed into an acrostic." Yet Sm. believes that this
verse, together with 1:12, 13 and 2:3, is "a later addition
to the prophecy of Nahum." Stnh. ascribes this verse to
a "prophetic editor." Yet all the while the Hebrew text as
it stands yields striking sense in dramatic continuity.

v. 2   *A disperser is come up before thee. Guard {the}*
         fortress!
     Watch {the} way! Strengthen {the} loins!
     Make {thy} strength mighty to the utmost!

Having broadly foretold utter destruction, the prophet
advances to the details of the supercity's extinction. How will
the Assyrian capital be overthrown? Nahum answers; and by
a sudden change of person (as in 1:11, 12, 13, 14) the address
shifts from Judah to the doomed capital. He announces, "A disperser is come up before thee." The haughty citadel of crime
is to suffer a doubly ignominious destiny: it is not only to be
crushed, but its surviving inhabitants, unlike those of many
other conquered cities, are to be driven away and scattered abroad.
The capital which boasted of its stability is to face "a disperser."
As Nahum otherwise expresses this dominant, repeated prediction,
its people are in flight (2:9); they are "scattered on the mountains, and there is no one to gather them" (3:18).

Hitherto in the prophecy the hostility against Nineveh has come from Yahweh. Now a specific foe is introduced — a "disperser," who remains anonymous. He may, therefore, be the enemy personified or God Himself. It should not be overlooked that the OT recognizes only the Almighty as the Disperser of the nations. The Hebrew verb and conjugation here employed are used, in connection with national affairs, otherwise only of God; and the assumption that Yahweh is the "Scatterer" fits strikingly into the context. The fact that the "disperser" — if a human enemy — is not mentioned by name [3] may point to the early date of the book; for if the critics are right in placing the prophecies from 614 to 612 B. C., the identity of the attackers would have been known and could have been mentioned.

This advance against Nineveh is so certain that the author says: He "is come up" (used technically of hostile military operations, Judg. 1:1; 1 Sam. 7:7; 1 Kings 15:7; 20:22; Is. 7:1, 6; 21:2; Jer. 50:21; Joel 1:6; Hab. 3:16) "before thee," i. e., before the capital. Historians have been astonished at the total dispersion of the Ninevites. Not only did its citizens turn to flight, the city's military leaders fleeing as locusts (3:17), but the people were so completely scattered that the metropolis was never rebuilt.

[3] Many commentators identify this "scatterer" as an individual leader. Older interpreters suggested Sennacherib, who could hardly be the "scatterer" of his own Ninevites, or Nebuchadnezzar and Cyrus, who are excluded because of their date. The modern tendency is to find "the shatterer" (the unwarranted critical substitution) in Cyaxares, King of Media, founder of its empire, who in 625 B. C., it is affirmed, besieged Nineveh. J.M.P.Sm. supposes that Nahum wrote on the verge of this campaign, if not after it had been begun, and holds that the author "may have intended to characterize Cyaxares as 'the hammer,' or 'shatterer,' cf. the title Judas 'Maccabaeus.'" The actual and earlier date for Nahum eliminates the possibility that the author here thought of Cyaxares. Why rob these oracles of their prophetic, semivague character, when they feature undefined personifications, like Belial, the counselor of evil (1:11 and 2:1), and here the "disperser"? Likewise to be rejected is Bev.'s argument. First he finds difficulty with the sing., "disperser," contending that more than one enemy assailed Nineveh. Then, however, he condescends to say: "As Nahum is writing poetry, he does not need to distinguish the *two* foes who were assaulting Nineveh, the Babylonians and the Medes." The singular, the "disperser," is not justified by poetic license, but by the fact that the Babylonians played only an insignificant role in the city's downfall, while the Medes under Cyaxares really took the city.

n accounting for the disappearance of Nineveh and later of the
ation, which during long centuries controlled vast areas, we
hay accept these two considerations urged by *Cambridge Ancient
History*, III, 130 f. "First, even in lands where, as Gibbon has
emarked, the people are of a libidinous complexion, the Assyrians seem to have been unduly devoted to practices which can
nly end in racial suicide; the last years of their history can only
e explained by a loss of manpower not entirely accounted for
by civil wars. Secondly, it is certain that the Medes carried off
into their own country large numbers of the *ummâne*, the crafts-
nen who worked in metal and in stone. Many of the glories of
Persepolis and Ecbatana were wrought by workmen trained by
he guilds of Nineveh; the art of seal-cutting was taught to their
masters by Assyrian slaves."

Now follow four sharp commands in unconnected con-
truction. Because the "disperser" has come up, Nineveh is first
of all told to "guard the fortress." [4] The defenses must immediately be placed under careful control so that the city can protect
tself against the foe gathering before its walls. Its watchmen
must scan the horizon to observe every approach of the besiegers.
Therefore the second command reads, "Watch the way!" i. e.,
urvey each road so that no surprise attack overtakes the Assyrian
capital. More than watchfulness and prepared waiting are necessary, however. The morale of the city's troops must be strong;
each one must be ready for unyielding resistance. "Strengthen
he loins!" is the cry that rings through the city. This may be
a general appeal for the exercise of physical power (Job 40:16:
"His strength is in his loins," and, by contrast, Nah. 2:11) or an
indication that the loose, flowing, Oriental garb must be tied up
for action. G. A. Smith holds that it may be "a call to attention,
he converse of 'Stand at ease.'" Finally, the Ninevites are told:
"Make thy strength mighty to the utmost." Every means of

[4] On the various phases of attacking and defending a besieged city, see
Billerbeck-Jeremias, *Der Festungsbau im Alten Orient* (1903), pp. 170—188.

resistance is to be adopted. All possible provisions for with
standing the siege are to be employed. Each rampart and fortres
must be made more redoubtable.

How were these four commands to be understood? Man
(including J.M.P.Sm.) have treated the words as ironical. Other
take the imperatives as "the cries of the frenzied inhabitants o
the doomed city" (so, alternatively, Stnh.). However, neithe
irony nor frenzy appears indicated. Nahum here reproduces, a
it were, the very cries which echo throughout the attacked city
the terse, pointed commands of military officials. The fact tha
the author leaves the outcome of these efforts in doubt for a fev
verses adds to the dramatic force of his presentation.

מֵפִיץ — *Hiph"il* participle of פוץ, denoting "one who dis
perses." AV and RV offer, "He that dasheth in pieces." The
verb is frequently found in the sense of "to disperse," e. g.
Is. 24:1; Jer. 13:24; 18:17; 2 Sam. 22:15; Hab. 3:14; Ps
18:15; 144:6. Significantly in all occurrences of the *Hiph"i*
(save Jer. 23:1) God is the subject. Despite the fact tha
the verb repeatedly refers to a dispersion of nations simila
to that which overtook Nineveh, the Ⓜ reading has beer
widely attacked, often without better reason than the inde
cisive desire for a better word. Stnh. declares apodictically
that "scatterer" is not suitable. Instead, the majority of com
mentators propose reading מַפֵּץ, "hammer," or מְפַץ, "ham
merer," "shatterer." Prov. 25:18 has מֵפִיץ, which is usually
translated as "hammer," "maul" (AV). Sel., who substitute
מַפֵּץ, "hammering," "destruction," Ezek. 9:2, yet translates "the
destroyer," gives this reason for departing from Ⓜ: "Destruc
tion, not dispersion, is the theme of the song." However
dispersion is an emphatic theme of Nahum's oracles, as 3:18
clearly shows. Besides, the nation which is dispersed is de
stroyed. Nor can any solid evidence be advanced to suppor
Sel.'s further contention, "The term is a motif-word in the

dragon battle." Hap. departs from the critical consensus by proposing הַפֹצֵה, "he who rescues." Ries. asks for מֵפִיחַ, "fiercely snorting." These alterations are neither necessary, demonstrable, textually grounded, nor versionally supported. Ⓖ, ἐμφυσῶν, "blowing hard," "scattering," and Ⓥ, "qui dispergat coram te," both emphasize the concept of dispersion, not of destruction.

עַל־פָּנַיִךְ (Grz. subjectively מֵעַל) has emerged from critical scrutiny with these changes: (1) It is read as פָּנָיו by Ew., Htz., Stnh., Dav.-Lan., No., Jnk., the fem. suffix discarded in favor of the masc. (2) Perles (*Analekten*) asks for פִּנַּיִךְ: Ru. for the same word, but with the masc. suffix, פִּנָּיו; Sel. and Bev. similarly for "battlements." The interpretations derive the form from פִּנָּה, "corner," "cornice," which with the pronominal suffix would normally be פִּנָּתֵךְ, sing., or פִּנּוֹתַיִךְ, pl. No reason suggests itself for the emphasis of the cornices. Ehr. retains Ⓜ, but insists that עַל־פָּנַיִךְ must be translated "at once," "immediately"; but Deut. 7:10 and Job 1:11, which he cites to prove this idiom, are not conclusive. The original conception of "face" has been stressed in explaining that Nineveh's was a hard, set, obstinate countenance. However, the prepositional phrase should be interpreted as usually, in the sense of "before," "in front of." The few Ⓖ MSS which have the equivalent of פַּיְו are not important.

Ⓣ and Jewish medieval commentators held that the address of v. 1, to Judah, specifically to Hezekiah, who died about a half century before Nahum wrote, is continued here. Their opinion is shared by Jerome and some later commentators. The exponents of this view call attention to the fact that v. 1 emphasizes the past destruction of Nineveh, but hold that by a prophetic change of time Nahum could here go back to the era in which Nineveh was not devastated. Contextual evidence shows that Judah cannot be addressed, since in v. 3 it is spoken of in the third person. After v. 3, which is a sort of parenthetical statement, vv. 4, 5, 6 amplify this second verse by describing the approach of the attacking armies. On the other hand, modern commentators tear this verse from its Ⓜ connection and make it follow 1:11, 14, chiefly because these two verses also have the second person in address to Nineveh. This radical realignment of the text, destitute of all MS or versional support, overlooks the abruptness which characterizes the change of person in vivid, realistic presentation.

נָצוֹר and the following infinitives absolute function as imperatives. See Ges., Gra., 113 *bb.* There is no reason for changing these infinitives to imperatives. Ⓖ offers erroneously: ἐξαιρούμενος, "choosing"; σε is added in ⒼA and Lucian Recension.

מְצוּרָה — Ⓖ, ἐκ θλίψεως, "out of tribulation." This mistaken translation probably arose from a confusion with מִצְרָה, which, in turn, contributed to the final Ⓖ version, "A shatterer came up against you, your deliverer from tribulation." Ⓥ prefers "qui custodiat obsidionem." Isolated MSS have נְצוּרָה, the *Qal* feminine passive participle of נָצַר, or מְצוּדָה "citadel," "fortification," which is adopted by Hpt. Wllh., followed by G.A.Sm., K.-G., No., Jnk., and Hst., wants נְצֹר מַצְרָה, "guard (the) watch!" Ru., Mrt., Stk., and Du. accept this reading but keep the infinitive absolute instead of changing to the imperative. However, the word מַצְרָה is coined for this occasion. These alterations are conjectural and unnecessary. Even Sm. concedes that מְצוּרָה "is a well-established word and there is nothing inherently inconsistent in the idiom נָצוֹר מְצוּרָה; words of similar sound but of different roots are not infrequently associated in Hebrew for the sake of assonance."

חֻזַּק מָתְנַיִם — J.M.P.Sm. translates this as "brace the loins" and adds, quoting Dr.: "The call is . . . for a keying up of the spirits of the besieged to the highest pitch; they must exhibit both 'bodily prowess and mental intrepidity.'" This is beside the point, for the phrase "strengthen the hips" does not occur in the sense "brace the loins." The verb is used otherwise of the arm, Ezek. 30:24; Hos. 7:15. In Is. 22:21 the *Pi''el* of חָזַק is found in connection with the girdle, meaning, "to tie firmly about," "to gird."

> v. 3 *Because Yahweh hath cut off the pride of Jacob,*
>   *As the pride of Israel;*
>   *Because plunderers have plundered them*
>   *And spoiled their vine branches.*

The Disperser, against whom Nineveh has just been warned, will destroy the city, "because Yahweh" will avenge Judah. The people of God are defeated and prostrate. While the ultimate cause of their affliction is their own pride, the immediate means of their punishment has been tyrannical Nineveh. Though Yahweh Himself "hath cut off the pride of Jacob, as" He cut off "the pride of Israel," His wrath is directed against the leaders in Nineveh, who plundered God's nation, which this verse pictures as a vine.

This interpretation differs from other explanations of this verse hitherto advanced because it reproduces the Hebrew verb translated by AV as "turned away" and by RV as "bringeth again," in the rare and Biblically unparalleled (although otherwise clearly supported) meaning "hath cut off." The translation here proposed also renders the term frequently translated "excellency" as "pride," its prevalent connotation, as, e. g., in Amos 6:8; Zech. 9:6. Again, our interpretation regards Jacob as Judah, and

Israel as the Northern Kingdom. It differs in this respect from other translations, which make both Jacob and Israel refer either to the whole nation or to the Southern Kingdom. (For Jacob as the equivalent to "Judah" see Micah 3:1, 8; Is. 43:1; 44:1; Obad. 18; also Is. 2:5 ff.; 8:17; 10:20; 29:22; 46:3; Jer. 2:4; 5:20, "house of Jacob.") The statement "Yahweh hath cut off the pride of Jacob" describes a past historic punishment which Yahweh has visited upon Judah, the prophet's home, because of its haughty rejection of the Almighty. Nahum may be thinking of the devastation wrought by Sennacherib, who boasted that he had ravaged Judah.

This divine judgment which God permitted to overtake His people was "as" His judgment on "the pride of Israel." The haughty arrogance of the Northern Kingdom had been punished by its utter defeat and complete destruction under Shalmaneser and Sargon. While Judah had not been utterly destroyed, the havoc wrought in its midst resembled the sweeping devastation which crushed the Ten Tribes. Thus interpreted, the first half of the verse does not state, as various commentators maintain, that God will make His people prosperous, that He will return to Judah, that He will restore both the Northern and the Southern Kingdom (there is no reason for taking the verbs as futures), but that, in the past, as He had cut off Israel, so He also punished Judah, which because of its arrogance now has been beaten into helplessness by Nineveh, the rod of His anger. (Is. 10:5)

Yet while the Assyrians were the divine instrument in punishing God's people, they, too, are to feel that brunt of His anger. For a similar thought see Is. 47:14; 48:14 ff.; Jer. 25:12; 50:17, 18. They were the "plunderers" who "have plundered them" (God's people). The prophet reviews the series of Assyrian invasions from the days of Shalmaneser, Tiglathpileser, Sargon, Sennacherib, Esarhaddon, and the early threats of Ashurbanipal. How fitting the description of these tyrants as "plunderers"! Their systematic looting of defeated nations, the heavy booty in men, animals, and property brought to Nineveh from their invasion of Judah, the heavy tribute they exacted — all this flashes across the prophet's mind as he recalls that "plunderers have plundered" God's people. See Is. 24:1, 3; Jer. 5:10.

Besides, these ravishers have "spoiled their [Judah's] vine branches." In a not-uncommon figure God's people are pictured as a vineyard. Isaiah's entire fifth chapter discusses the vineyard of God, which v. 7 identifies in these words: "The vineyard of Yahweh of hosts is the house of Israel." In similar language Jer. 12:10 states: "Many pastors have destroyed My vineyard." Ps. 80:8 declares: "Thou hast brought a vine out of Egypt." Now Judah as a vine has not only been emptied (Hos. 10:1: "Israel is an empty vine"), its grapes removed, but it has been broken and its branches destroyed. Attempts have been made to identify the branches as the various communities of Judah, or as individuals within the nation; but the point of comparison does not go that far. The sorry plight of Judah in general is well symbolized by the picture of the vine, robbed of its fruit, its branches cut off, with only the trunk remaining.

The description of conquered Judah, under the symbol of a spoiled vineyard, may shed additional light on the dating of Nahum's prophecies. If this verse is a contemporary description of Judah, not merely a historical reminiscence, then Nahum could well have been written during the long reign of Manasseh, when Assyrian plunderers came into the country and took that king captive. Esarhaddon (681—668 B. C.) reports: "I overthrew Manasseh, king of Judah." Ashurbanipal (668—626 B. C.) records that in his third campaign he conducted a devastating expedition to the Phoenician cities on the boundaries of Palestine. 2 Chron. 33:11 even states that "the captains of the hosts of the king of Assyria . . . took Manasseh . . . and bound him with fetters and carried him to Babylon." These two records, one cuneiform and the other Biblical, may be connected. At least

Manasseh was a vassal of Ashurbanipal during the early years of that king's reign. How effective Nahum's word, if applied contemporaneously to the broken stem and the spoiled branches of a once glorious vineyard!

Bev., following Dr., Ries, and other critics, says that this verse "appears to be a gloss, so loosely appended in the margin at the end of this poem that it came to be inserted *after* 2:2 instead of *before* it."

כִּי — This connects, not with v. 2a (Keil), but with v. 2b, and inferentially gives the reason for the Scatterer's appearance before Nineveh and the capital's destruction.

To secure the ח acrostical line, v.Ho. inserts a תַּחַת before the כִּי. Bi. omits the כִּי to find in שָׁב the שׁ line. All this is artificial and unwarranted.

שָׁב — The key to the interpretation of the verse lies in this verb. It has generally been derived from שׁוּב "to return," and reproduced transitively. Thus (1) AV: "The Lord hath turned away the excellency [margin: 'pride'] of Jacob, as the excellency [margin: 'pride'] of Israel." (2) "the Lord bringeth again the excellency of Jacob, as the excellency of Israel." Similarly Ⓥ, "superbiam reddidit"; Ⓢ, "I am about to turn." Translating thus, Ⓥ means that God will restore "the material prosperity of His land." (3) The Lord "has turned the pride of Jacob like to the pride of Israel," G.A.Sm. (4) "For Jehovah restoreth Jacob, the pride of Israel," Stnh. This translation omits half of the verse on flimsy reasons like these: First, "The Hebrew yields no satisfactory sense," a common critical exaggeration! The meaning of the full unabridged verse is striking. Second, "the occurrence of *excellency* in successive lines is inelegant." But if every adjacent recurrence of a word were branded a dittography, hundreds of lines would have to be elided. For a similar repetition of a term, even in qīnāh rhythm, see, e. g.,

Lam. 1:12; 16:22; 2:1; 5:10; 4:9; 15:18. Note especially this striking instance, where גָּאוֹן occurs in parallelism very similar to that of this verse. Ries. translates similarly, but changes שָׁב to הֵשִׁיב. (5) "Restore, O Yahweh, the vine of Jacob," Hst. This interpretation requires unwarranted omissions and the substitution of the *Hiph"il* הֵשִׁיב. (6) "Yahweh will restore the vine of Jacob, likewise the vine of Israel," J.M.P.Sm. and Jnk. Under this interpretation we have here "the hope of the restoration of both branches of the people." But to secure this reading, Ⓜ is deliberately and unjustifiably altered. However, Sm. seeks to endorse the radical changes here involved in this way: First, although he has just protested against the double occurrence of "excellency," he claims that the mention of the vine branches in the second part of the verse "demands the mention of a vine here in the first part as the antecedent of its thought." What chaos would result if in OT parallelism or in compound verses the thought or figure of one part would of necessity be projected into the other! With equal force the mention of the vine branch in Num. 13:23 would necessitate the elimination of the pomegranates and of the figs in the rest of the verse. In the substantially parallel passage, Is. 17:10, by the same process, the mention of the vine plants, "slips," would demand a vine instead of a rock in the preceding section of the verse. In the second place, Sm. finds antecedent probability for the interchange of גָּאוֹן, "pride," and גֶּפֶן, "vine," maintaining that the two words "in Hebrew vary in only one consonant; hence, confusion in copying was easy." But in many cases where similarity of words is much more pronounced, Sm., and many others who accept this emendation, adhere to the original text. One cannot avoid the suspicion that in such alterations where every extant MS and version supports this Ⓜ reading, the critical school has betrayed its determination to follow predisposed conjecture. (7) "For the excellency of Jacob will be restored as the vine of Israel," Sel. This is the passive version of the previous proposal and besides requires radical omissions.

All these emended translations suffer under fundamental difficulties. Thus (a) they assume the transitive use of שׁוּב, in agreement with the versions, Ⓖ, ἀπέστρεψεν, "He turned away"; Ⓥ, "reddidit"; similarly Ⓢ and Ⓣ. But Hngs. has shown that the transitive meaning ascribed to the *Qal* of שׁוּב here, as in Ps. 85:5; Job 39:12; Is. 52:8; Num. 10:36, is unwarranted. Nor does the frequent שׁוּב שְׁבוּת prove the transitive use. (b) Some of these translations regard שָׁב as a prophetic perfect and translate it as a future (e. g., J.M.P.Sm.) although the following verbs, also in the perfect, are referred to the past. (c) Some of these renditions are based on the assumption that the verse voices "the hope of the restoration of both branches of the people," a thought utterly foreign to the prophet's purpose at this place. He is not concerned with the restoration of the extinct nation in the north, the Ten Tribes, which paid for their unbelief at least three quarters of a century before Nahum wrote. J.M.P.Sm. claims that this hope of restoration "was vivid in postexilic Israel" and assumes that the verse probably reflects some postexilic period. This position is contradicted by the evident dating of the prophecies and the integral, essential argument this passage offers. (d) Some of these translations offer no adequate basis for the comparison of "Jacob" and "Israel." Thus Keil explains that both "Jacob" and "Israel" refer to the entire nation, in this way, that the verse pronounces the divine return to Jacob (the historical name of the people) as to Israel (its theocratic name). But this is difficult and complicated.

If, therefore, the transitive meaning of the verb שׁוּב is unacceptable at this place, how is the difficulty to be solved? Hpt. cuts the Gordian knot by omitting יהוה אֵת, thus making the verb intransitive; but this disregards all MS and versional evidence. The text may be preserved and a fitting sense secured by assuming that שַׁב is derived from שָׁבַב (root I), "to cut off," "to destroy," "to smite," perhaps originally "to splinter." The pointing שַׁב is not decisive against this interpretation, for this may be only an assumed vocalization. This would be the only instance in which שָׁבַב (root I) is found in Biblical Hebrew; but its meaning is assured by the Arabic *sabba*, "to cut"; by the occurrence of this root in New Hebrew; by the Jewish-Aramaic noun שִׁבָּא, "a splinter," "a chip"; and probably by the Hebrew word שְׁבָבִים, Hos. 8:6, "chips," or "splinters" of wood. The following considerations favor this derivation: (a) this gives a verb with inherent transitive force; (b) this takes both perfect verbs in the same past tense; (c) it parallels the phrase "I will cut off the pride," Zech. 9:6; (d) this provides an acceptable sense in the context. Why has the Scatterer come up before Nineveh, as the preceding verse announces? Because Judah ("Jacob" here, as Micah 3:1) has been smitten, as Israel was. Now, since Judah has been severely stricken, as the northern tribes were, God intervenes to punish Nineveh; and although the Lord has permitted Judah to be afflicted for pride and arrogance, yet Nineveh, which made Jerusalem a vassal capital, even as it subdued Samaria, will in turn be punished by the Almighty.

גְּאוֹן — This has been interpreted in two ways: (1) as "excellency," "glory." Ges., Hwb., lists this meaning in Is. 14:11; 23:9; Jer. 13:9; Amos 6:8; Zech. 9:6; 10:11; but in each of these instances it could also be translated by "pride." The uncontested meaning, "excellency," "glory," is found in Is. 4:2; 13:19; 60:15; Ps. 47:5; Job 40:10; and as applied to God, in Ex. 15:7; Is. 2:10; 19:21. This meaning is also found in the interpretation of the term as the land of Canaan, Ps. 47:5; Amos 6:8. (2) As "pride," "arrogance." This is the prevalent connotation and occurs in Lev. 26:19; Is. 13:11; 16:6; Jer. 48:29; Ezek. 7:20, 24; 16:49, 56; 24:21; 30:6, 18; 33:38; Joshua 5:5; 7:10; Zeph. 2:10; Ps. 59:13; Prov. 8:13; 16:18; Job 35:13. The explanation of שֹׁב accepted above points to this second meaning, "pride," which is also supported by the versions, Ⓖ, ὕβϱις, "pride"; Ⓥ, "superbiam." Note the striking parallel in Jer. 13:9: "After this manner will I mar the pride of Judah and the great pride of Jerusalem." See also Amos 6:8; Zech. 9:6; 10:11.

כִּגְאוֹן — Stnh., who ascribes the verse to a fictitious second editor, drops the כ. Most radical interpreters (Gun., No., Mrt., et al.) substitute כְּגֶפֶן, "as the vine." Du. reads וּגְפֶן. Gun., No., Dr., and Hst. omit כִּגְאוֹן as a gloss. These elisions and alterations sacrifice the point of the verse.

כִּי בְקָקוּם בֹּקְקִים — Stnh., as others, finds the Hebrew text and the conventional translation objectionable because "the line is metrically too short. Moreover, some closer parallel to the object in the following line is desiderated." He suggests, "For devastators have devastated their vineyards," all without MS or versional authority, as without necessity or proof. Ⓖ offers ἐκτινάσσοντες ἐξετίναξαν, "they have shaken very violently." Ⓥ, "quia vastatores dissipaverunt eos." Ⓢ, "They will trample upon the tramplers." Gun. omits בֹּקְקוּם, while Du., whom Hst. follows, reads בְּקָקוּהָ, "they have plundered her."

וּזְמֹרֵיהֶם — Instead of "vine," Stnh. substitutes "olives," with this motivation: "The Hebrew for this word zemôrēhem is peculiar. It is generally understood to be the pl. of זְמוֹרָה, 'branch,' and rendered, 'their branches'; but in this case we would expect the form zemôrôthehem; moreover, a pl. of zemôrā occurs nowhere else, nor is it obvious why '(vine-) branches' should be especially thought of. The text is no doubt slightly in error; and we should read zēthehem, 'their

olive yards.' " This insertion of "olive yards" is to be rejected
for the same reason Stnh. employs in rejecting "vines,"
namely, it is not obvious why "olive yards" should "be
especially thought of." No MSS or versions suggest this
change. Du. and Hst., following Gun., unnecessarily change
the text to זְמֹרֶיהָ, "her vines."

> v. 4 *The shield of His mighty ones is reddened.*
>   *Men of might are in scarlet.*
>   *Chariots {are} in fiery steel on the day of His*
>   *preparing,*
>   *And the cypress spears are swinging.*

The equipment, preparation, and speed, particularly of the
attacking chariotry, are described in vv. 4 and 5. As Nahum
envisions armies marching against Nineveh, he sees four flash
views, of which this is the first: "The shield of His mighty ones
is reddened." The antecedent of the pronoun in *"His* mighty ones"
has been variously identified. Church fathers as well as some
modern interpreters hold that the address is to the unnamed
Assyrian king. But aside from the vague, unheralded introduction
of the monarch, the language seems far better adapted to the
attackers than to the attacked. Most recent commentators make
the pronoun refer to the "Scatterer" (2:2); and for this reason,
among others, 2:3 is torn out of its present position and assigned
to various places by different critics. If the pronoun is given the
reference suggested by the present arrangement of the verses, its
antecedent would be Yahweh, and the statement would describe
His mighty ones, the enemies of Nineveh. The attitude by which
God calls the forces attacking Assyria His own is not without
Scriptural parallel. In Is. 13:3, for example, Yahweh says: "I have
also called My mighty ones" for the assault on Babylon; and in
v. 4 Yahweh of hosts musters the nations for the attack on the city.

Shields were usually made of wood or wicker, often covered with leather (which could be treated with oil, 2 Sam. 1:21; Is. 21:5, to make them more pliable). Job 15:26 mentions thick metal bosses on the shields.

No specific explanation for the redness is given. We may assume that the shields were red because they were stained with blood. Against this interpretation it has been urged that gore-stained shields would imply the fighting of battles at Nineveh, while the presentation of this verse is said to describe "the appearance of the foe before the battle" or (Stnh.) "the *preparation* for the onslaught rather than the onslaught itself." This objection is not valid, since the author may here picture the veterans of many bloody campaigns, whose leather shields were literally stained with the life fluid of many assailants (Is. 63:2, 3). Others (e. g., Htz., Or., J.M.P.Sm.) assume tentatively that the redness refers to the metal covering of the shields, particularly as this was reflected in the sunlight. Such burnished shields are mentioned in 1 Macc. 6:39 and Josephus, *Antiquities,* XIII, XII, 5. Xenophon, *Cyropaedia,* VI, 4, 1, speaks of Cyrus' Persian army that "flashed with bronze," because of the chariots' side armor and the horses' breastplates and thigh pieces. The prevalent usage of the Hebrew term for "reddened" denotes a process of making red by dyeing or coloring, and this could hardly be true of copper shields. Instead of "reddened" we would expect adjectives or verbs denoting the equivalent to "burnished," "shiny," "glittering." See Ezra 8:27. Nor is there any evidence that copper shields were customarily used in the seventh century B. C. Stnh. holds that the leather of the shields "was dyed or painted red, in order, it may be supposed, by the brilliancy of colour, either to give their bearers a more formidable appearance or else perhaps to conceal their wounds." This is possible, but not indicated.

The appearance of the attackers is further described by the second flash picture in these words: "(His) men of might are in scarlet." Since the verse refers to several classes of the fighters, the mention of "men of might," according to OT usage in Gen. 47:6; Judg. 3:29; 1 Sam. 31:12; 2 Sam. 11:16; Ex. 18: 21, 25; and Is. 5:22, would seem to preclude the entire army (against J.M.P.Sm., who translates "soldier" or "fighter"). The expression otherwise denotes outstanding men selected from the masses. They were uniformed in scarlet or painted in that color.

Cyrus' army is described as "resplendent in purple" by Xenophon, *Cyropaedia,* VI, 4, 1. Other references to the reddish dress of soldiers in the ancient world are found in Aelian, *Variae Historiae,* VI, 6, 6. It should be observed, however, that the Hebrew term employed is "scarlet" and that no evidence has been adduced for the wearing of scarlet clothing. The difficulty in assuming that uniforms of this color are meant here is not the objection raised by J.M.P.Sm.: "Purple and reddish garments were very costly; hence . . . such garments would scarcely be worn by an entire army." Sm. himself concedes the weakness of this statement when with v.Ho. he concedes that cheaper grades of cloth might have been used. Besides, if "men of might" does not designate the whole army but selected heroes or leaders, this objection would likewise fall. In discussing the royal or official apparel of the Babylonians, Ezek. 23:14, 15 mentions vermillion and dyed head attire. It may be assumed that the leaders were signalized in this way. Others (Hal., Hpt.) explain the scarlet color as the result of many bloody stains. This color would fit the period during and after the assault of Nineveh better than the time of "preparing." The term "in scarlet" or "made scarlet" may refer to the application of scarlet war paint. At best it is a difficult term, and perhaps modern interpretation has been on the wrong track in seeking a specific reference for this color. Luther translates: "His army looks like purple."

A hint suggested by the verse itself should not be overlooked. The besiegers are pictured as brandishing cypress spears. Cypress wood is of a reddish hue, and the spears of that material, when swung quickly, could help produce the scarlet impression.

Whatever the specific interpretation may be, scarlet uniforms, scarlet paint, or a general scarlet appearance, the words describe the awe-inspiring impression created by the besieging forces.

The third picture focuses attention on the cavalry, in the words: "Chariots are in fiery steel on the day of His preparing." The acknowledged difficulty in this interpretation lies in the proper rendition of the word translated "steel." If this meaning is retained, the phrase poetically describes the attackers' metal chariotry, which fairly blazed under the Assyrian sun. This explanation appears the least difficult; for it is now well known that metal-covered chariots were in vogue before Nahum's time. No doubt should attach to the propriety of using "fire" for the reflected flash and glare of the sunlight; for Ezek. 28:14, 16 mentions "stones of fire," i. e., scintillating gems. Some who accept this rendition believe that the "fire of steel" may refer to iron or steel decorations on the chariots; but this would appear to be an insignificant statement in a vivid context. Others find here an indication of chariots armed with scythes, one of the most terrifying implements employed in ancient warfare; but these were in vogue only much later. The steel of these burnished chariots glistens "on the day of His preparing," i. e., for battle, Jer. 46:14; Ezek. 7:14; 38:7. The pronominal suffix "His" refers to Yahweh (see above) and shows that these gleaming armies with their glittering chariotry are advancing because it is His day, His preparation for Nineveh's decreed destruction.

In the final flash picture presented by this verse the action of the approaching army is described in the words "the cypress spears are swinging." The term translated "cypress spears" literally designates "pieces of cypress wood." The word may also describe objects made of this material (2 Sam. 6:5, musical instruments of wood), and in this military context the meaning "weapons of wood" suggests "spears," because their shafts were made of cypress. This wood was hard, densely grained, and of a reddish color. It was highly prized in the ancient world and used especially for poles, because its durability could well serve military purposes. These spears, the text continues, are swung or brandished, either in military drill or in wild charging. Under either interpretation the terror-inspiring appearance of Nineveh's enemies is again graphically described.

מָגֵן — Ⓖ ὅπλα, "shields." Ru. arbitrarily substitutes סִנְּנוּ, "they mocked."

גִּבֹּרֵיהוּ — For the unusual pronominal suffix, found otherwise 1 Sam. 30:26; Ezek. 43:17, see Ges., Gra., 91 *l.* Grz. and Hap. change the sing. suffix to the pl. גִּבֹּרֵיהֶם, appealing to Ⓖ, δυναστείας αὐτῶν, "of their kingdom," and Ⓢ, "their heroes," as corroborative evidence. But Ⓥ has correctly retained the sing., "fortium eius." Stk.'s rejection of the suffix is not justified.

מְאָדָּם — On the form see Ges., Gra., 52 *q,* with other examples of the *Pu"al* in *o* instead of the usual *u.* In offering ἐξ ἀνθρώπων Ⓖ patently confuses the verb אָדַם and the noun אָדָם. Ⓥ with "ignitus" approaches the sense if not the specific meaning. The *Pu"al* of אדם occurs otherwise only in the six passages Ex. 25:5; 26:14; 35:7, 23; 36:19; 39:24, where it denotes "being made, or dyed, red."

מְתֻלָּעִים — This is related to תּוֹלַעָה, "coccus worm," and to תּוֹלָע, "cloth dyed with coccus." The verb which occurs only here denotes in the *Pu"al* "being made scarlet" or "being clothed in scarlet." Ⓖ with ἐμπαίζοντας, "playing," "mocking," evidently mistakes the root for עָלַל. Ⓥ offers correctly "in coccineis." As difficult as this term is, it offers no reason for the substitutions suggested by Hap. and others.

בָּאֵשׁ — Most modern interpreters ask for כָּאֵשׁ, which is found in a few Hebrew MSS. However, Ⓜ is more forceful. Ru. changes this to בָּאִישׁ and translates, following Ⓖ on the previous words, "The valiant men mock at man," a puny, mistaken substitute.

פְּלָדוֹת — Ⓖ, αἱ ἡνίαι, "the reins"; Ⓥ, "habenae"; Ⓢ and AV, "the torches." However, the root is well known in classical and vulgar Arabic and in Syriac. If the term, which occurs only here in OT, has the same meaning in the Hebrew, it denotes steel or iron, and it is to be translated with the preceding construct, "in a fire of steel," i. e., in the reflected flare of the steel. The Persian origin of the word, even if it could be demonstrated conclusively, would not invalidate the possibility of this loan word's being employed by the Hebrew. It would not necessarily be "too late to be found here" (Dav.-Lan.). Jnk. concedes: "Cultural productions migrate with their names from nation to nation," and reports an association of this term with the Arabic. Nevertheless some interpreters hold that בְּאֵשׁ פְּלָדוֹת is a gloss. Thus J.M.P.Sm. maintains that when these words "are removed, the line becomes of normal length." He finds difficulty in connecting the phrase either with that which follows or with that which precedes. Why should it be connected? He concludes erroneously, but following Wllh. and others, that Ⓜ is practically untranslatable. Others take recourse to subjective alteration. Thus (1) Greve offers פְּלָכוֹת in the sense of "axles," although פֶּלֶךְ does not occur with this meaning. Bev. accepts the translation "axles," i. e., the "axle-bosses of the chariots," and maintains that "this is a new explanation." It is neither new nor acceptable, as his final version shows: "The axles of the chariots are like fire, as when they were new." (2) Ru. reads פְּלָצוּת, "terror." (3) Hap., J.M.P.Sm., and others ask for לַפִּידוֹת, "torches." However, the pl. of לַפִּיד is לַפִּידִים, which Hst. requires. Sm. cites instances of nouns with two genders, but this would not authenticate the use of פִּידוֹת? in v. 4 and of לַפִּידִים in v. 5. (4) Du.'s פְּתִיחוֹת, "drawn swords," is unsupported. (5) Ries. on the basis of Ⓖ asks for פְּרָדוֹת, "reins."

בְּיוֹם — J.M.P.Sm. adds the article to make the word an absolute and a demonstrative, "that day"; yet, as if not convinced of his own proposal, he suggests, "with less likelihood הוּא must be supposed to have dropped out of the text at a very early date." His reference to Judg. 13:10 does not prove the permissibility of changing the text here and translating בַּיּוֹם "in that day." Stnh. in agreement with other critics maintains that this word "is probably a gloss."

הֵכִינוּ — This, too, is regarded as a gloss (Stnh., Hst., and others) or emended (J.M.P.Sm. and Sel.) to הָכִינוּ, "they will make ready." But this would require a conversive *Waw* and is contradicted by strong versional testimony, Ⓖ offering ἐν ἡμέρᾳ ἑτοιμασίας, "in the day of preparation," and Ⓥ, "in die preparationis eius." The reasons adduced for the critical change of the phrase are not decisive. Thus Sm. states that the words "on the day of his preparing" are "rather lame." Stnh. insists that Nahum would hardly "have paused, in his vivid description of the forces ready to attack, in order to point out that what he described referred to the day of their preparation." This objection overlooks the fact that the singular suffix, "in *His* preparation," refers to Yahweh, as shown above. Again, it is asserted that "the infinitive construct of the *Hiph"il* stem of כּוּן nowhere else has the intransitive or passive force involved in the rendering 'preparation,'" J.M.P.Sm. The context does not demand an intransitive or passive force. 2 Chron. 26:14; Ps. 7:14; Jer. 46:14; Ezek. 7:14 have the active sense required here. Sm.'s final translation, "They will make ready the chariots on that day," is weak and unwarranted. Similarly emaciated is Sel.'s, "As the fire of torches they make the wagons ready," הָרְכָבִים הֵכִינוּ.

וְהַבְּרֹשִׁים — AV, "fir trees"; Ⓖ (similarly Ⓢ), καὶ οἱ ἱππεῖς, "and the horsemen." This is probably based on a misreading of Ⓜ as וְהַפָּרָשִׁים, "the riders." Are such confusions of the ב with פ to be regarded as evidence that the Ⓖ copyists had the text read to them? Ⓥ offers "et agitatores." Most modern critics give Ⓖ preference over Ⓜ and translate, "horses," "chargers." However, בְּרוֹשׁ (Assyrian *purušŝu*) denotes "cypress," and the pl. designates articles made of this wood. Here in a military scene the context suggests weapons of wood, and the term has well been translated "spears," "lances," "javelins," with special reference to their shafts made of cypress wood.

הָרְעָלוּ — AV, "are shaken terribly." The meaning of this *hapax legomenon* is derived from the cognate Aramaic and Syriac רעל, "sway," "stumble," and from the related nouns רַעַל, Zech. 12:2, a "stumbling" or "swaying," and תַּרְעֵלָה, Is. 51:17, 22; Ps. 60:5, with a similar sense. The versions are not decisive. Ⓖ, θορυβηθήσονται, "they shall be confounded"; and Ⓥ, "consopiti sunt." If the meaning "sway," "swing," is retained, the action may refer to military exercise and drill, or, more vividly, to the wild brandishing of weapons. Those who reject בְּרֹשִׁים in favor of פָּרָשִׁים translate (so J.M.P.Sm.) "the chargers will tremble," i. e., the high-spirited war horses will "quiver with excitement, eager for the fray" (Stnh.). They are "prancing" (Bev.). Hpt, appealing to an Arabic root, proposes: "They are frenzied," "They run amuck." Aside from the etymological difficulty involved in this association, the context, with its emphasis on military preparation, seems to preclude such disorganization.

Similarly unacceptable are Sel.'s "They let their steeds rage" and Jnk.'s "The riders wildly jump to and fro." Ru. finally secures: "And the horses rattle in the street and the chariots rage." Hst. proposes, "The chargers are decorated," connecting the verb רעל with the noun רְעָלָה, "veil." Ri. believes that the original reading was יִתְהוֹלָלוּ, which was then somehow transferred to the beginning of v. 5. Ries., who permits only the second and fourth statements of this verse to remain and changes these, translates, without explanation, "and the horses stamp."

> *v. 5 Chariots careen madly in the streets.*
> *They overrun one another in the squares.*
> *Their appearance {is} like torches.*
> *As flashes of lightning they speed to and fro.*

Most impressive to Nahum are the charging chariots of the besieging enemies. He continues, "Chariots careen madly in the streets." To him, as a prophetic observer, the wagons of war seem to bolt in wild frenzy (Jer. 46:9; 2 Kings 9:20). The original Hebrew for the term translated "streets" primarily means "the outside." While it most frequently denotes the "street," it has a supplementing sense, "open country," "field" — Prov. 8:26; Job 5:10, territory outside the city; Ps. 144:13, the pasture land for sheep.

Based on these varied meanings, two locations for the scene of this verse have been suggested. Some (J.M.P.Sm., Htz., and others) hold that the locale is in the broad fields outside the city, where the enemy musters his chariots preparatory to the attack. Cogent reasons should be offered for departing from the normal sense, "streets." Besides, we have no basis for assuming that large fields adapted to cavalry movements lay immediately outside the city. Nineveh was surrounded by suburbs. Therefore the usual connotation, "streets," seems preferable and may include the avenues and the suburban highways about Nineveh and leading to the city,[5] for the context describes an attack that gradually leads to the city's walls. The phrase would, then, not refer to a mustering of the chariotry, but to their raging charge through Nineveh's environs. The areas of such streets harmonize better with the verbs than do unrestricted open spaces. Besides, the word translated "squares" in the parallel statement "They

[5] J.M.P.Sm. seeks to remove this possibility with the statement: The streets of a suburb are not "adapted to cavalry maneuvers." However, the reference is not to maneuvers but to the enemy's irresistible onrush toward the city walls. Topographically this advance would cut through suburban Nineveh. Sel., however, concedes that the streets were those leading to the city and cites in corroboration Esther 4:6; Neh. 8:1, 3; Prov. 22:13.

overrun one another in the squares" is characteristically used to designate intersections of the streets. Squares are the wide, open places within a city, Deut. 13:17; 2 Sam. 21:12, and usually. Larger cities had many of them, Jer. 5:1; 9:20; 49:26; 50:30. Particularly mentioned are the wide, open spaces at the gates (Neh. 8:1, 3) and before the temple (Ezra 10:9) and before the palace (Esther 4:6). At these open places people congregated (Job 29:7), children played (Zech. 8:5), travelers lodged (Gen. 19:2; Judg. 19:15). The term is used, as here, in connection with "street" in Jer. 5:1; 9:20; Prov. 5:16; 7:12; 22:13; 26:13 to denote the thoroughfares and wider intersections of the city. This frequent association with "street" seems to preclude the interpretation which places the chariots in the broad fields outside Nineveh. Here, too, the prophet's description conceals a disparagement of Nineveh. The streets and squares of Nineveh were the object of Assyrian pride. Sennacherib, for example, records, "I widened its [Nineveh's] squares, made bright the avenues and streets and caused them to shine like the day" [Bellino Cylinder, 1. 61]. Now these very streets and squares are overrun by enemies.

Others (e. g., Umb., Kl.) limit the chariot charge to the city and its squares, holding that the second half of the verse reflects the reaction of the besieged. The wagons of war racing madly through these thoroughfares were so numerous and speedy that when they came to the street intersections, they ran over one another and so put fear into the Ninevites. This effect seems precluded by the second part of the verse, "Their appearance is like torches. As flashes of lightning they speed to and fro." In no way do these words indicate terror in the hearts of the besieged; instead, they describe the movements of the enemy cavalry. Bolting from one line of attack to another, the metal-covered chariots gleaming in the sunlight seem to be flaming torches, strokes of lightning, because of their flashing swiftness.

יְתְהוֹלְלוּ from הָלַל, "to be mad"; *hithpō''ēl*, "to rave," "to rage." For similar usage, see Jer. 46:9. Ⓖ, συγχυθήσονται, lit., "they will be poured together." A few MSS have הִתְהַלְלוּ. A similar misassociation with the root הָלַל, "to rejoice," "to praise," may help account for Ⓢ, "they glory." Ⓥ, "conturbati sunt."

הָרֶכֶב is omitted by Wllh., Sel., Bev., and others. The last-named explains, it "is awkward here with a plural verb"; but he is forced to admit, "still it does seem that the chariots are in question." However, רֶכֶב is a collective, and Ges., Gra., 145 *b,* authenticates the use of the pl. verb either preceding or following a collective. Besides, רֶכֶב is essential to the picture of the whole verse. How weak in comparison is Sel.'s "they behave in the streets as distracted!"

יְשְׁתַּקְשְׁקוּן from שָׁקַק, "to overrun." The *Hithpalpēl* means "to overrun one another," Ges., Gra., 55 *g*. Ⓖ, συμπλακήσονται, "they shall be woven together"; Ⓥ, "collisae sunt." Ⓢ, "they boast." Ries. apodictically drops the first half of the verse.

מַרְאֵיהֶן — On the form see Ges., Gra., 93 *ss*. The feminine ending is unusual, but it is not necessary to follow Wllh. and most critics in changing this to the masculine suffix form מַרְאֵיהֶם. The use of the third person feminine plural suffix is relatively infrequent, and alleged harmonizing changes should not be introduced hastily. רֶכֶב is a collective, and many collectives are regarded as abstracts, hence as feminines. The suffix may also refer to the entire picture, as a neuter.

לַפִּידִים — Ⓖ, λαμπάδες, "torches." The origin of this term is uncertain. It may be connected by metathesis with the Assyrian *dipâru,* "torch." Apparently it has radical associations with the Greek λαμπάς. K.-G. removes this phrase as a gloss on v. 4, but for no decisive reason.

יְרוֹצֵצוּ — This is the only *Pōlēl* occurrence of the verb רוּץ, "to run," but it should not be changed for this reason into יָרֻצוּ (so Grz.), nor into יְנוֹצְצוּ "they flash" (Ehr.), which does not occur in the *Pōlēl* and has no MS authority here. The *Pōlēl* primarily denotes intensity; hence the verb may be rendered, "they run swiftly" (Hpt.), or, "they run to and fro."

Ries. without a word of explanation drops the entire front half of this verse.

> v. 6 *He remembereth His mighty {ones}*
> *They stumble {over themselves} in their advancing.*
> *They hasten to her wall,*
> *And the protection is set up.*

The attack moves on, beyond the suburbs, to Nineveh proper, and this verse records, "He remembereth His mighty [ones]." The prophet speaks of God, although Sel. and J.M.P.Sm. make "the shatterer," and most critics the Assyrian king, subject. As the divine remembrance in Gen. 8:1 and Ps. 98:3 indicates, Yahweh shows that He keeps those in mind who serve His purposes, by helping and sustaining them. The "mighty ones" (RV, "worthies") are therefore not "satraps commanding in the different provinces who are summoned to the relief of the capital" (Bev.), nor necessarily "the nobles" (J.M.P.Sm.); neither can we satisfy the term by asserting that they are "leaders and men alike, just as we might speak of a troop of soldiers as a fine set of men" (Stnh.). These "mighty ones" (lit., "glorious," "preeminent" ones) are the heroes of v. 4, the intrepid captains assailing Nineveh.

The verse also emphasizes the vast numbers engaged in the assault. So many rush forward in the eager attack that "they stumble over themselves in their advancing." It is quite possible, as indicated below, that the verb originally meant "to crowd," "to push one another over" (3:3). This would offer better sense than "stumble," which Htz. interprets as a sign of weakness.

As the text approaches the climax, we are told that after the first encounters are over, "they [Yahweh's mighty ones] hasten toward her [Nineveh's] wall." They have crossed through suburban districts, wiping out all opposition. The outposts have been taken, and the final attack, centered on the walls, begins. As the shock troops encircle the city, "the protection is set up." It is difficult to identify the military equipment described by the Hebrew *sôkhēkh*. The root meaning is that of "protecting," "covering." The term probably denotes some sort of shelter by which the besiegers shielded themselves, perhaps against the heavy missiles thrown down from the vantage point on the city walls. Thus the *sôkhēkh* is probably not in first instance an instrument like the battering ram (so Stnh. and tentatively J.M.P.Sm.), since the idea of protection appears to be dominant in the term. Apparently, as the versions emphasize, it is a covering during assault and may have been used in connection with siege machinery. It recalls the *testudo* of the Roman armies, or the movable towers depicted in the cuneiform bas-reliefs employed for the covering of both soldiers and siege apparatus. Thus in one verse the advance of the troops, their crowding eagerness, their arrival at the walls, and the setting up of their military equipment is graphically described.

יִזְכֹּר — The normal meaning is, "He remembers." Although this gives good sense, it has been rejected in favor of many other renditions, including the following: (1) G.A.Sm., J.M.P.Sm., and others translate, "He summons his nobles" (for a council of war). But יִזְכֹּר is not demonstrably used in the sense of "to summon." Job 14:13, cited to prove this usage, is not decisive. Nor is there any validity to J.M.P.Sm.'s vague assertion, "Some such sense seems to be demanded by the context." (2) יִזְכֹּר is dropped by Mrt., Hpt., and others, yet without reason and against versional testimony. (3) Grz. arbitrarily asks for יִשְׁכְּרוּ, "they are intoxicated." (4) Oo., without proof, reads יְמַהֲרוּ "they hasten." (5) Ru. departs radically and offers וְחֵילָךְ, "and your infantry." (6) Du. alters to יִדְהֲרוּ, "they rush forward." (7) Bev., without any explanation, wants, "he runneth over the list of his mighty defenders." (8) Stnh. arbitrarily reads יֶאֱצוּ, "his majestic ones press forward." (9) K.-G. wants יִפְקֹד, "he musters," but this is destitute of proof or warrant. (10) Ehr. emends to וּמִבְחַר אַדִּירָיה, "and the best of their brave." Other critics retain the verb זכר, yet refuse to accept the Ⓜ reading. Thus (11) v.Ho. suggests the pl., יִזְכְּרוּ, "they remember"; (12) Jnk., יַזְכִּיר, "he urges"; (13) Hap., on the basis of Ⓖ, καὶ μνησθήσονται, יִזָּכֵר, "and he is remembered"; (14) Sel., Ries., Hst., יִזָּכְרוּ, "they are remembered," i. e., his nobles are called up. The variety and mutual exclusiveness of these emendations testify to their unsoundness, while Ⓜ's sense is concrete, progressive. The subject of the verb is not the disperser of v. 2 (Sel.) or the Assyrian king (Lu., Keil, most critics), but Yahweh, v. 3.

אַדִּירָיו — Ⓖ, οἱ μεγιστᾶνες αὐτῶν, "their great ones"; Ⓥ, "fortium suorum." These versions, together with Ⓣ, have a pl. suffix, which is hardly in keeping with the singular subject of יִזְכֹּר under the interpretation accepted above. Yet Ru., Ries., and Hap. prefer Ⓖ to Ⓜ. V.Ho. reads אַדִּירָיה.

יִכָּשְׁלוּ is used reflexively, "they stumble over themselves." This should be accepted in preference to the unauthorized contradiction of the text demanded (1) by Stnh., "they stumble not"; (2) by J.M.P.Sm., "they [the nobles] take command." This translation is further elaborated with the explanation: "The commanding officers after a council of war take charge, each of his own division of the army, and lead in the attack upon Nineveh." Sm. thus changes יִכָּשְׁלוּ to יִמְשְׁלוּ, "they rule over." (3) Sel. (who in his first edition asked for יְיַלֵּשׁוּ, "they hurl themselves forward," which K.-G.

accepted, now, followed by Hst.) reads יָשֹׁכּוּ, "they duck."
Bev. adopts this, explaining, "Perhaps 'dive down between'
would best give the meaning," and finally he secures, "They
stand among the embankments." (4) Du. proposes, "His
nobles gallop straight in their course." However, the text
should not be altered, since, as it stands, it presents an
acceptable picture, the eager assailants of Nineveh stumbling
over one another. Note the *Niph"al* as expressive of reciprocal
or mutual action, Ges., Gra., 51 *d*. J.M.P.Sm. objects that this
eager stumbling "is hardly applicable to the movements of
a body of men eagerly advancing to overthrow a city"; yet
it is no more objectionable than the parallel statement in v. 5,
the chariots "overrun one another." Nor can we refer the
stumbling to the defenders (as many of the older commentators do), who "being suddenly called out and badly
disciplined stumble over each other as they hasten to the
defense." This is improbable in itself and destroys the climax.
Perhaps יִכָּשְׁלוּ is to be translated in the sense of "to crowd,"
"to jostle." This, Ges. suggests, may have been the original
meaning.

בַּהֲלִכָתָם — The *Kethîbh* would have us read בַּהֲלִכוֹתָם, "in
their goings," the *Qerē*, בַּהֲלָכָתָם "in their going." The pl.
of the *Kethîbh* seems to fit more appropriately than the
sing. of the *Qerē*. Ⓖ completely misunderstands this part of
the verse and translates, καὶ φεύξονται ἡμέρας καὶ ἀσθενήσουσιν
ἐν τῇ πορείᾳ αὐτῶν, "and they shall flee by day and faint in
their way." Ⓖ is evidently conflated, for Ⓥ reads: "ruent in
itineribus suis." Nevertheless Ⓖ is accepted by Grz. as re-
flecting a lost original, and he adds וְנָסוּ בַיּוֹם, "and they shall
flee in that day." Ru. and v.Ho. ask for מְנוּסָה יוֹמָם, "flight
by day." Kent wants יַשְׂכִּילוּ בַּהֲלִיכוֹתָם, "they shall be wise in
their journeyings." Gun. reads יְאַשֵּׁרוּ, "they shall go on their
ways." J.M.P.Sm. translates הֲלִכוֹתָם tentatively as "their com-
panies," but admits the difficulty involved by conceding,

"This rendering involves giving to הַלְכוֹתָם a shade of meaning not elsewhere found, viz., 'company of soldiers'; but the closely allied meaning 'caravan' occurs in Job 6:19, and the verb הָלַךְ is used of the marching of soldiers in Jgs. 1:10; 9:1; 1 K. 22:6, 15." However, the last passages do not show הָלַךְ in the sense suggested, and the picture of a militant division is foreign to הַלְכוֹתָם, not substantiated by Job 6:19.

חוֹמָתָהּ — No., Hap., Sel., and others follow Du. in removing the *Mappîq* to secure a *He* directive, "toward a wall." This form actually occurs in a few Hebrew MSS and is reproduced in Ⓢ and Ⓣ. Ⓖᴬ and B have ἐπὶ τὰ τείχη, "to her walls"; Ⓥ, "muros eius." However, we would expect the definite article if the *Mappîq* were dropped and the הָ explained as a directive *He*. The word is an adverbial accusative, answering the question "whither." Although there is no expressed antecedent to the suffix, the whole situation points clearly to Nineveh.

וְהֻכַן — Ⓖ (similarly Ⓢ and Ⓣ): καὶ ἑτοιμάσουσιν, "and they shall prepare." On the basis of this mistaken version Ru., Ries., and Hap. change the passive sing. to the active pl., וְהֵכִינוּ.

הַסֹּכֵךְ is a *hapax legomenon*. Ⓖ puts this, after its incorrect translation of וְהֻכַן, into the accusative, τὰς προφυλακὰς αὐτῶν, "their defenses." Ⓥ, "umbraculum." The opinion that this designates "some kind of engine used in defense, or some kind of breastwork, composed of the interwoven branches of trees erected between the towers on the walls" (cited by Stnh.) is rejected by the fact that the preceding context deals with the besiegers. The primary need of the Ninevites is not "protection"; they required instruments for repelling the invaders. Likewise to be rejected is the assumption (Htz.) that הַסֹּכֵךְ denotes a troop charged particularly with the defense of the wall.

v. 7 The gates of the rivers are opened,
And the palace sways.

After the detailed prophetic picture of the attack which, step by step, has brought the hostile troops to the walls, Nahum devotes the rest of the chapter to forecast the city's capture, spoil, and desolation. The normal strategy of a siege subsequent to the surrounding of the city would require the hammering at the walls, the storming of fortifications. Instead, however, the text suddenly declares, "the gates of the rivers are opened." The interpretation of this prediction involves considerable difficulty and has produced the following attempts at explanations:

1. Hap. maintains that these gates were the fortified bridges spanning the rivers and offering entrance to the city. He holds that as the doors of Lebanon (Zech. 11:1) are the entrance to Lebanon, so the gates figuratively denote the bridge entrances on the river banks. Had the prophet meant this, he would doubtless have been more specific and declared, "The gates of the city are opened." Besides, the verb "to open" is not suitable for bridges, since there is no evidence that drawbridge arrangements were in vogue at Nineveh.

2. Similarly, Jewish medieval commentators, as well as Ew., Keil, and others, identified "the gates of the rivers" as gates located on the banks of rivers or canals. It is now known that five gates of Nineveh opened toward the Tigris, three to the canal on the north, seven to the moats and streams on the south. Stnh., who accepts this explanation, believes the sentence implies nothing more than that a number of these gates were opened, "that the last defences had been captured and that the capital lay henceforth at the mercy of the enemy." However, the verse does not mention the gates of the city but "the gates of the rivers." Would the Hebrew text not have avoided ambiguity and definitely indicated "the city gates at the rivers"?

3. Johns and Hen. suggest the sluice gates in the dams

controlling the city moats. By opening the gates regulating the flow into these ditches, the water would finally rise above the level of the moats and overflow in the direction of the besieging armies, unless the territory on their side were considerably higher than the city walls. — There is not the slightest archaeological evidence or topographical indication in support of this theory.

4. According to Hpt. and Dav.-Lan., the prophet means the points where the Khosr or the canals pass through the city wall. This, as the previous explanations, neglects the exact phraseology, "the gates of the rivers." No historical record exists to show whether these places could be opened or closed.

5. It has been further stated (Kl. and Or.) that these gates were the breaches made in the city walls by the torrential rush of the rivers. Or. says: "Kleinert's explanation is best: The gates of the rivers, which open without help of human hand, are to be understood according to the analogy of the windows of heaven, Gen. 7:11, or of the bars of the sea, Job 38:10, and their opening, according to Gen. 7:11. A higher hand unlooses the watery element by which Nineveh is almost surrounded; and that for its destruction." Unusual, indeed, would be the use of "gates" for the demolished sections of the walls. A stronger term than "opened" would likely be employed to designate disaster caused by devastating floods.

6. The possibility that the expression "the gates of the rivers" is only figurative and that, as Htz. holds, the picture represents the highways along which the people stream, is ruled out by the nonfigurative statements which otherwise characterize this section.

7. We hold that the phrase "the gates of the rivers" must be taken literally as the arrangement which, either open or closed, would help control the flow of the rivers toward the city.[6]

[6] This interpretation is supported by the corresponding term in Assyrian, *bâb-nâri,* literally "the gate of the river," the term applied to a canal gate by Sennacherib.

Fortunately archaeological investigations have helped to clarify the situation. The Tebiltu, e. g., which originally flowed through the city, could become a devastating torrent. It had repeatedly undermined palace foundations and weakened other structures. Sennacherib changed its course and perhaps expedited its flow by straightening its course and removing dangerous bends. In his comprehensive flood-control program this king also dammed the larger river, the Khosr, outside the city, and thus made a reservoir. Thompson and Hutchinson report that the water was restrained by a magnificent double dam with two massive river walls at some distance from Nineveh itself. In the ruins they found traces of the original dam gates, or sluices, by which the water flow to the city could be increased or reduced. Nahum envisions that at the beginning of the siege these dam gates would be closed by the enemy and the river impounded to cut off the city's supply, the waters of the Tigris being undrinkable. Later, the reservoirs completely full, these sluice gates, "the gates of the rivers," would be literally opened and great masses of devastating waters swept down on the doomed city. In consequence of this flood, the gate at which the Khosr entered the city, the Ninlil Gate, and the adjacent wall would be destroyed. The Quay Gate, at which the Khosr left the city, might also be devastated and in the intervening city much serious damage done. After the flow subsided, the entrance to Nineveh would have been made much easier for the besiegers.

In general harmony with this explanation are the well-known traditions.[7] Diodorus recounts how the river became "an enemy to the city" and how, just before Nineveh fell, a succession of heavy downpours swelled the Euphrates (sic), flooded a section of the city, and cast down part of the wall to a length of twenty stadia. Diodorus is palpably incorrect

[7] Nineveh was captured in the month of Ab, the period roughly parallel to the high-water period of the Khosr. This date harmonizes with the above explanation.

in some of the details involved, e. g., in bringing the Euphrates to Nineveh's walls. We may well suppose, however, that his account perpetuates an ancient local tradition concerning the events Nahum here describes.

In the attempt to belittle such traditional reminiscences and to discredit the thought that flooding torrents contributed notably to Nineveh's destruction, J.M.P.Sm. objects: "The excavations on the ancient site of Nineveh thus far have furnished no evidence that any portion of the walls was washed away by floods." Similarly Hst. maintains: "Nineveh's ruins show not a trace of inundation." This in itself is not decisive, since the traces of a short but violent flood are not always pronounced. Besides, Sm.'s statement is contradicted by Lehmann-Haupt's observation that at present one can observe the break in the remnant of Nineveh's wall caused by a torrential stream. Streck declares: "Even today the breach is to be seen, and the people dwelling in the vicinity informed me, without my having revealed my purpose to them, that this was the work of the Khosr."

Once more, then, the text describes the retaliation which the Assyrians suffered. Often their victorious troops would flood a conquered city. Thus Ashurbanipal recounts: "Sha-pî-bêl, his [Gambulu's] stronghold . . . I laid waste by flooding it." The tactics which Nineveh used will be used against it.

J.M.P.Sm. further objects that "when Yahweh co-operates with His people against the enemy in storm and flood, as this view would involve, instead of leaving His part in the victory to be inferred, as would be the case if this interpretation were correct, the prophets always emphasize the fact of Yahweh's aid and give it a large place." This observation is unjustified, in view of the preceding verse, which directly associates God with the attack on Nineveh. Besides, in the entire first chapter, divine omnipotence is ascribed to Yahweh and the destruction of Nineveh inferentially attributed to Him. Sm.'s criticism is further unfounded, since the OT frequently features disaster through natural causes, without pausing to explain that the Lord directs these forces. See, for example, Judg. 5:21: "The river of Kishon swept them away, that ancient river, the river Kishon." [8]

In consequence of the furious river flood after the gates are opened, "the palace sways." This translation, which has been contested, is not only supported but also made probable by the fact that in earlier times the raging river wrought havoc with the palace. How contrary to the context, to assume a radical figure of speech by taking this phrase, with Keil and others, "as descriptive of the dismay and terror that befall the inmates of the palace," who "are overwhelmed with terror and despair." Even Stnh. accepts the meaning "dissolves," "sways," as preferable because of the parallel preceding statement. "Palace" alone is never used figuratively for the people of a palace.

Ashurbanipal had two chief palaces in Nineveh, as far as excavations have revealed. One, the north palace, he built himself. This building, which became the official residence, was surrounded by a royal park and housed part of Ashurbanipal's library. The other palace, in the southwest of the city, was erected by Sennacherib and called "The Palace Without a Rival." This was completely rebuilt and restored by Ashurbanipal, as the excavations, especially by Layard, indicate. Here the greater part of Ashurbanipal's noted library was found. In both palaces the walls were decorated with bas-reliefs which present the best in Assyrian artistry. No cuneiform record has yet been deciphered which deals with the southwest palace, but the record of the north temple shows that Ashurbanipal expected this building, built also by the slave labor of captive kings, to stand for generations. The gods of Assyria were invoked to give strength

[8] Similarly unwarranted is the objection raised by Stnh., who asserts: "It is not likely that he [Nahum] had such exact knowledge as to say how the rivers or canals were planned and regulated. . . . Probably all that he knew was that the city was surrounded by a wall and the wall by moats or rivers and that access and egress were provided for by a sufficient number of gates."

to future kings who lived there. What evidence of his idols' impotence, then, and what proof of God's power, to have this magnificent structure soon fall into complete destruction! Likewise, what striking demonstration of retaliation — the residence of the king who ruined many enemy palaces now pictured as swaying before its fall!

הַנְּהָרוֹת — Ⓖ, τῶν πόλεων, "of the cities," except א Original, which follows Ⓜ with ποταμῶν, "of rivers." The pl. is not to be explained (so Hpt.) as originating under the influence of the construct pl. שַׁעֲרֵי, since only one river comes into consideration.

הַהֵיכָל — By predominant OT usage this denotes God's "palace," "the temple." It comes from the Sumerian ê-gal, "great house," and appears in Assyrian as êkallu, "palace." This is the meaning here and in 1 Kings 21:1; 2 Kings 20:18; etc.

נָמוֹג — Ⓖ, διέπεσε, "fell apart"; Ⓥ, "ad solum dirutum"; Ⓢ, "is shaken."

> v. 8 And Huzzab is stripped. She is brought up,
>   And her handmaidens are moaning, as {with}
>   a sound of doves.
>   {They are} taboring upon their breasts.

Attention is now focused on the women of the palace; the men, it may be implied, being defeated, captured, or killed. Nahum foretells: "And Huzzab is stripped." Unusual difficulty attaches to the Hebrew expressions translated in the AV and RV as "Huzzab." It seems impossible to establish its meaning precisely and definitely. Interpreters have suggested, with slight or drastic changes, that this term be read "the lizard," "the lady," "glory," "the queen," "the goddess Zib," "the mistress," "the river Husur." Others have given the word a verbal form and after certain alterations offer: "she has brought forth," "though firmly established," "made to flow away," "it is decreed," "there was a stand made." These mutually exclusive suggestions (see below) show the uncertainty which attaches to "Huzzab." Probably the word is best explained as a proper noun designating either Nineveh or more likely the Assyrian queen. Below the interpretation of "Huzzab" as originally denoting "the gazelle" is tentatively proposed as a title or emblematic name for the queen. The whole discussion awaits further archaeological and linguistic light.

The stripping indicates that Huzzab is at the mercy of the assailants. She has been subjected to what was apparently a customary indignity: her clothing is torn off, and she is paraded naked before the conqueror. The same treatment is mentioned in 3:5; Is. 47:2, 3; Hos. 2:10. The Assyrians themselves frequently stripped their captives. Now, by divine judgment, Nineveh is to receive the same harsh treatment she meted out to others.

Besides being uncovered, Huzzab, Nineveh or its queen, is "brought up." The exact connotation of this broad term is again difficult. Usually it is explained as meaning "to be removed," "led away" (Jer. 37:11; 2 Sam. 2:27). Billerbeck-Jeremias [9] finds here the queen's going upstairs to lament in her chamber. However, the verb "to go up" occurs in this conjugation (the *Hoph"al*) only in two other OT passages. One of these (2 Chron. 20:34) is hardly of import in our consideration, since it uses the term figuratively in the sense of "to be recorded, mentioned." The other occurrence (Judg. 6:28) employs the word for bringing up a sacrifice. Traditional accounts recall that before the fall of the city the king made a tremendous funeral pyre, on which he and his concubines were burned to death in mass suicide. The Assyrian king is not mentioned in this section of the book. He does not appear until the city has been destroyed and the

[9] *Beiträge zur Assyriologie* (1895), III, 102.

people led away, the inference perhaps being that the monarch, addressed in 3:18, is the new ruler who ascended the tottering throne after the fall of Nineveh. The emphasis laid on Huzzab, the queen (?), may imply that the monarch who unsuccessfully defended the capital has been killed or has committed suicide by self-immolation and that in accord with ancient custom the dead king's wives and concubines are also immolated, as tradition specifically maintains.

While Huzzab is "brought up," "her handmaidens are moaning." Critics who alter the preceding words to create an unauthorized reference to a Ninevite goddess assert that these handmaidens are "female devotees of Ishtar, the women who gave themselves up wholly to her temple service and were given the name *kadishtu* (i .e., 'holy women') of *Ishtaritu* (i. e., 'dedicated to Ishtar')." However, the term here employed does not occur in OT Hebrew in the sense of sacred prostitute, or temple woman. Some (Jerome, Kl., Or., and others), assuming that Huzzab is Nineveh, interpret her handmaidens as the outlying communities which live from the capital city. This again is without OT parallel. In Num. 21:25, 32; Joshua 15:45; Judg. 11:26; Ps. 48:12 cities are said to have "daughters," probably in the sense of dependent communities, but the term "handmaiden" is not demonstrably used to describe such relationship. Keil explains the handmaidens as the people of Nineveh. Commonly inhabitants are termed "sons," Ps. 141:2; Ezek. 23:15; Lam. 4:2; Is. 51:18. Frequently, too, cities and countries are personified in the OT by the Hebrew for "daughter," plus a following genitive; but why would the citizens be called "handmaidens"? If, however, as we have concluded, Huzzab, either an appellative or a proper noun, may denote the queen, the "handmaidens" are literally her personal attendants, the ladies-in-waiting, probably also the king's concubines. These women evidently accompany Huzzab and perhaps are "led up" with her. Diodorus Siculus relates that the concubines of Sardanapalus were placed on the funeral pyre which he had built when he realized that the city was doomed.

These handmaidens are "moaning as with a sound of doves" (Is. 38:14; 59:11). The birds are mentioned, not because of their timidity or helplessness, but because their cooing was thought to resemble the sound of lamentation. This similarity is not too apparent to the Western mind, although our mourning dove, as its name indicates, shows the characteristic which the prophet emphasizes. Probably the sound of the Palestinian dove, more than that of the common American variety, recalls a plaintive note of moaning.

In addition, as part of their lamentations, these handmaidens are pictured as "taboring upon their breasts." The verb "taboring" comes from the noun tabor, a small drum, and means "to drum," "to beat as a drum." The Hebrew root similarly means "to strike cymbals," Ps. 68:25. The picture here, then, is that of grief-stricken court women continually striking their breasts, as Luke 18:13: "smote upon his breast," or Luke 23:48, "smote their breasts." This action is expressive of intense, desperate sorrow and well describes the agony of the palace habitués, when they know that the city must fall and that they themselves are doomed.

וְהֻצַּב—This difficult term has not been adequately explained. The versions are of little help. Ⓖ offers καὶ ἡ ὑπόστασις, "and the structure." Is this a mistaken derivation from מַצָּב? Ⓥ has "et miles," perhaps due to a confusion with צָבָא. Ⓢ translates, "and she raised up." The following are some of the attempts to explain the term.

1. Huzzab is a proper noun. This transliteration appears in AV and in RV in the margin. Ⓣ, Kimchi, and Rashi, as well as many recent commentators, regard Huzzab as the name of the Assyrian queen. No queen of this name is known to history, but this does not remove the possibility. If archaeological records of the past were complete, the

name might be found. Nor is J.M.P.Sm.'s objection decisive, that "her name is not of a formation otherwise found in feminine proper names." Names do not necessarily follow patterns. Patristic writers, as well as some more recent scholars, including Keil, have held that Huzzab is a figurative designation of Assyria or of Nineveh itself, just as Rahab represents Egypt, or Sheshach, Babylon.

2. Related is Htz.'s change in vocalization resulting in הַצָּב, *Hassab*, "the lizard." This, he proposes, is a designation of Nineveh, the capital city, which, like the lizard, can be brought out of its hole only with great difficulty. But the noun is normally construed as a masculine.

3. Dav.-Lan. also reads הַצָּב, but translates "lady," remarking that "in lieu of anything better one might be tempted to think that the litter might mean the woman or lady, just as in Arab. za''inah means a woman's litter and then a woman."

4. G.A.Sm. and others suggest that the word be read הַצְּבִי with the meaning "glory," "splendor," "beauty," as a name for Nineveh. However, this noun is always construed as a masculine.

5. Hen. and others have connected וְהֻצַּב with the preceding verse and offer "(the palace is dissolved), though firmly established." But simple *Waw* is never found in the concessive relation.

6. RV and a number of commentators have the translation "it is decreed," deriving the form from נָצַב, as in Deut. 32:8; Ps. 74:17. However, the verb has this meaning in no other passage, and the presentation would drag in such a vivid context as this if slowed by such a vague statement. The AV margin suggests "that which was established," or "there was a stand made." This comes close to the original meaning

of נָצַב but does not easily and intelligibly lend itself to the context.

Most modern commentators change the consonantal reading of Ⓜ, with the result that a long line of alterations are proposed, none of which can lay claim to versional support. The following are a few examples:

7. Mrt. substitutes הַשֵּׁגָל, "the queen."

8. Stnh. and others replace הֻצַּב by הוּצְאָה, "she is brought forth." This, Stnh. conjectures, may have been followed by "the daughter of the queen." The sense would then be that a princess was led away captive.

9. V.Ho. suggests the translation "the goddess Zib," but without any supporting evidence.

10. Bev. believes that "the word may originally have been Husur, the small river flowing through Nineveh," but himself admits that under this interpretation "the rest of the verse becomes hopeless, and the 'maidens' come in too unexpectedly."

11. Hap. changes the word to מַצָּב or מַצָּבָה, "foundation."

12. We prefer to leave the consonantal text essentially unchanged, but suggest the reading הַצְּבִי, "the gazelle." This presupposes that the form was originally written without the *Yodh*. Many words normally reproduced with *Hireq magnum* are written defectively. Ges., Gra., 8 *k,* seems to deny the propriety of employing a simple *Hireq* at the end of a word, but see 44 *l.* An example of the case in point is found in Ps. 16:2, where evidently אמרת stands for אָמַרְתִּי. In the OT the figure of a gazelle is used to picture that which is beautiful and desirable (Cant. 2:9, 17; 4:5; 7:4; 8:14), and it may be that the same thoughts linger in this name of Nineveh or its queen. Of course, the difficulties in identifying the term may someday be removed by new light, which archae-

ological investigation is constantly shedding on questions like these.

וְנִלְּתָה — Ⓖ, ἀπεκαλύφθη, "she was uncovered"; Ⓥ, "captivus abductus est"; Ⓢ, "her horsemen." This term likewise has been subjected to drastic changes, involving the alteration of either the preceding or the following words. Thus Du., Sel., and Hst. ask for וְנִלְּתָה; Hpt., הֻגְלְתָה. There is neither necessity nor justification for these changes.

הֹעֲלָתָה — On this form see Ges., Gra., 63 p, where it is explained as equivalent to הֹעֲלָתָה. Ⓖ, followed by Ⓢ, offers καὶ αὕτη ἀνέβαινεν, "and she went up." Ⓥ, however, retains the passive "abductus est." Ehr. proposes הַבְּעֻלָה, "the mistress," i. e., Ishtar, the lady of Nineveh. Sel., בַּעְלָתה, "his mistress." Ri. wants עֶרְוָתָהּ, "her nakedness." Thus by the unwarranted change of the first three words, translations like these are secured: "His mistress is led out. She must go into exile" (Hst.). "The mistress is led away captive" (Jnk.). "The daughter of a queen is brought forth" (Stnh.). All these reconstructions are unjustified. The *Hoph"al* of עָלָה, as shown above, means "to be led up for sacrifice." This gives good sense, presents a stronger meaning, and is in harmony with tradition.

מְנַהֲגוֹת — Ⓖ, ἤγοντο, "they led"; Ⓥ, "gementes." Sel., following K.-G. and followed by Hst., reads מְנֻהָגוֹת, "being led away." These and other changes of the text, as well as K.-G.'s and Sel's and Hst.'s addition הֹגוֹת, "sighing," are arbitrary. Although the root נְהַג is a *hapax legomenon,* its meaning "moaning" is sustained by the Arabic and Syriac.

בְּקוֹל יוֹנִים is classified by G.A.Sm. as an apparent gloss, because it "unduly lengthens the v." Most critics refuse to join him.

מְתֹפְפֹת — Ⓥ, "murmurantes"; Ⓖ, φθεγγόμεναι, "sounding forth." On this basis No. and Hap. change the text to מְצַפְצְפֹת,

Pilpel of צָפַף, "to twitter," "to peep"; but this change is uncalled for, since תָּפַף (a denominative verb from תֹּף, "cymbal") is also found in Ps. 68:26 in the sense of "to strike with cymbals" and is here used in the *Pōʿēl,* meaning "to strike."

לְבִבְהָן — For this form Htz., Hst., Ehr., and others unnecessarily want לְבִבְהָן, but the form can stand as it is. See Ges., Gra., 91 *c.*

> *v. 9 And {thus} Nineveh is like a pool of water from*
> *{the} days of lamentation;*
> *And they are in flight.*
> *"Stand, stand!" {they cry,} but no one turneth around.*

Having described the capture of the capital, the prophet now pictures its desolate appearance. "Nineveh is like a pool of water!" he exclaims. This comparison has been understood as indicating the city's size and power at the height of its glory, with her population continually replenished (Keil), just as new waters flow into a pool. Or. says: "Nineveh is like a vast reservoir inasmuch as the men and precious things from all lands come together in it; but now they scatter." Corroboration is sought in Rev. 17:15, in the expression: "The waters which thou sawest . . . are peoples and multitudes and nations and tongues." But this is not the picture employed by Nahum, for in Rev. 17:1 the emphasis lies on *"many* waters." Again, it is held that the phrase has this meaning: "In the abundance of its wealth and the multitude of its inhabitants, Nineveh is compared to a pool of water . . . swelled by an influx from all quarters" (Green, *A Hebrew Chrestomathy* [1877], p. 202). Support for this explanation is sought in Jer. 51:13, where Babylonia is addressed: "O thou that dwellest upon many waters, abundant in treasures."

But, again, Jeremiah indubitably describes the abundant and diversified streams surrounding Babylon, while Nahum's pool, without such qualification, cannot convey this thought. The limited meaning and usage of the term berēkhāh, "an artificial pool," is not apt symbolism for a multitudinous nation. Further, the statement that the capital "is like a pool of water" is regarded as "a reference to the rapid flight of Nineveh's population, which the prophet compares to water rapidly flowing out of a tank or pool" (Stnh.). But this interpretation is based on alteration of the text. Similarly Lu. (XIV, 1359) maintains that previously the city was populous and glorious; now, however, it is only a fish pond, the water of which has run off. It appears more acceptable to assume that actually Nineveh has the appearance of an inundated area. It has been flooded (v. 7); its palace sways (and falls); the captured city looks like a pool. This translation is in harmony with the context and builds a gradual, logical development from v. 7.

This flooding is dated "from the days of lamentation," from this time of wailing and moaning, when the gates of the river were opened, the city flooded, and Nineveh completely destroyed. Dirges of doom marked that day. This translation (as opposed to AV and RV) rests on a new interpretation of the Hebrew, explained below.

A different thought is voiced in the second half of the verse, where Nahum continues, "They are in flight." The question as to who the antecedents of this indefinite subject are has been answered in several contradictory ways, but the development of the prophet's thought is best served if we assume an impersonal subject: they, the people of Nineveh. The capital is pictured not only as inundated by water and deserted, but also as a place from which the inhabitants flee in the unchecked haste of utter panic. Graphically the text presents an undesignated person appealing to the fugitives with emphatic repetition, "Stand,

stand!" in the sense of "Stop, stay here!" "But no one turneth around." Panic has seized the populace. Nahum does not pause to identify the voice thus raised. The reader may think of an official, an army officer, the leader of the defense. Perhaps, though less probably, the prophet ironically taunts the Assyrians. In any case, the mass flight goes on unhalted.

מִימֵי הִיא — This unusual expression is difficult. It has been translated "from her days," or, supplying the relative, "from the days that she has been," which is explained as "from her beginning," "during the entire period of her existence." The AV similarly reads, "Nineveh of old," in agreement with the RV, "Nineveh hath been from of old." This is supported by Ⓣ, but Ⓜ does not say this, and the thought that Nineveh has been great and imposing throughout its history is hardly expressed by בְּרֵכַת מַיִם. Besides, this translation does not readily give evidence of any connection with the subsequent part of the verse. Most recent commentators assume that the text is hopeless and resort to emendations. They declare that מִימֵי הִיא is a case of dittography, which should be corrected to מֵימֶיהָ, "her waters." This is supported by the versions: Ⓖ, τὰ ὕδατα αὐτῆς, "her waters"; Ⓢ, "And between waters is she"; Ⓥ, "aquae eius." Some critics (Wllh., Dr., No., v. Ho., Hst.) omit the words altogether. Or. offers מַיִם הִיא, "the water of itself." By additions or further elisions, translations like these are secured: "Nineveh is like a pool of water fleeing away" (Dr., G.A.Sm., v.Ho., Jnk., Bev.); "Nineveh is like a pool of waters, whose waters roar as they flee" (Stnh. and similarly Ries., who regards the word as a gloss); "Nineveh, her waters were like a pool of waters, and they are running away" (Dav.-Lan.). Such mutually contradictory renditions are not impressive and do not solve the difficulty. J.M.P.Sm.'s translation, "Nineveh — like a pool of water are her defenders," involves a completely subjective alteration. He corrects מִימֵי הִיא to עַמֶּיהָ, "her people," that is, "her defenders." The passages he cites to justify עַם in the sense of soldiers simply show that in obvious contexts the term "people" may be used for the soldiery. Sm. explains: "The point of the comparison 'pool of water' . . . is found in the rapidity with which the defenders of Nineveh disappear, just at the time of greatest need." But this is reading a meaning into the text, and the difficulty with מִימֵי הִיא remains. Our translation suggests that the Ⓜ text be kept, but that הִיא be regarded, not as the personal pronoun "she," but as equivalent to הִי, which occurs in Ezek. 2:10 in the sense of "lamentation." True, the form with the final א is not found otherwise; but see Ges., Gra., 23 i.

וְהֵמָּה נָסִים — Many interpreters (Mrt., No., Stk., and others) drop וְהֵמָּה as corrupt. ⒼA reads τὰ τείχη, "the walls," perhaps mistaking וְהֵמָּה for חֹמַת. This has made some (Sel., Hum.) think of the pool of a wall (Neh. 3:15; Is. 22:11) and hold that Nahum here refers to a pond from which the water flows out through the wall. Hum. pictures a pool like Bethesda (John 5:7). Most others hold simply that the waters are fleeing; yet the verb is too strong for this action.

עֲמֹדוּ — This is an imperative in pause, Ges., Gra., 42 b. Ⓖ omits one of the verbs, rendering οὐκ ἔστησαν, "they did not stand." Ⓢ, Ⓥ, and Ⓣ retain both verbs. Bu., K.-G., Mrt., Du., and others insert a form of אָמַר, "they cry," before עָמְדוּ עֲמֹדוּ, but this is unnecessary and spoils the dramatic presentation, as Sel. concedes. Hpt. adds יָעִיקוּ, "they yell," after the two imperatives. Ries. gives Ⓖ, οὐκ ἔστησαν, preference over Ⓜ and substitutes לֹא עָמְדוּ.

מַפְנֶה — Ehr. without reason alters this to מַעֲנֶה, "one giving answer" (to those who say, "Stand, stand!"). He overlooks the fact, however, that the picture of "turning" is characteristically employed in such contexts. See Jer. 46:5.

> *v. 10 Seize booty of silver! Seize booty of gold!*
> *For there is no end to the store,*
> *An abundance of all desirable articles.*

The prophecy now takes the form of an apostrophe to the conquerors. After Nineveh has been captured, its palace destroyed, its resistance broken, and its inhabitants thrown into flight, Nahum encourages the victorious invaders: "Seize booty of silver! Seize booty of gold!" Rich plunder, particularly vessels, ornaments, and jewelry made of precious metals, awaits the conquerors.

Silver and gold often head the list of tribute which Assyrian kings received or of the booty which they seized. Ashurnasirpal, *Annals,* for example, mentions these two metals together twenty-seven times in his booty inventories. Shalmaneser III states that in his second year he received three talents of gold and 100 talents of silver from the king of the Hattinites, plus one talent of silver annual tribute; 10 talents of silver from Haianu, plus 10 minas of silver annual tribute; 10 minas of gold and six talents of silver from Aromu; three talents of gold and 70 talents of silver from Sangana, plus one mina of gold and one talent of silver annual tribute; 30 minas of silver from Katazilu — all this in addition to 420 talents of copper, 430 talents of iron, 1,000 copper vessels, 1,300 brightly colored woolen garments, 44 talents of purple wool, 1,800 cattle, 18,000 sheep, 500 weapons, 800 cedar logs, 100 daughters of nobles, three kings' daughters with their dowry. This tribute, which was, of course, supplemented by wholesale booty, was received year after year to fill Nineveh with fabulous wealth.

The proportions of the spoil are, figuratively speaking, unlimited, "for there is no end to the store," lit., "to that which has been prepared." Nineveh was the richest city of its day. According to unsubstantiated traditions, some wealth had been smuggled out during the siege, but much fell into the hands of the victors, because in their precipitous flight the Ninevites were able to salvage but few possessions of value.

Through long years Nineveh had exacted huge booty torn from its prostrate foes. Typical accounts of Assyrian plundering are found in these excerpts from royal reports, selected from Luckenbill, *Ancient Records of Assyria and Babylonia.* Ashur-nasirpal (884—824 B. C.) records:

> 250 strong, walled cities of the lands of Nairī I destroyed, I laid waste, into mounds and ruins I turned them. . . . Forty chariots equipped with the trappings of men and horses, 460 horses broken to the yoke, two talents of silver, two talents of gold, 100 talents of lead, 200 talents of copper . . . 300 talents of iron, 1,000 vessels of copper, 2,000 pans of copper, bowls and chaldrons of copper, 1,000 brightly colored garments (of wool) and linen garments, tables of SHA-wood, couches made of ivory and overlaid with gold, the treasures of his [Amma-ba'li's] palace, 2,000 head of cattle, 5,000 sheep, his sister with her rich dowry, the daughters of his nobles with their rich dowries, I received. (I, p. 181)

On the "Black Obelisk" of Shalmaneser III (860—824 B. C.), the reliefs bear these titles:

> Tribute of Sūa, the Gilzānite. Silver, gold, lead, copper vessels, staves for the hand of the king, horses, camels, whose backs are two humps, I received from him.

> Tribute of Iaua (Jehu), son of Omri (mār Humrī). Silver, gold, a golden bowl, a golden beaker, golden goblets, pitchers of gold, lead, staves for the hand of the king, javelins, I received from him.

> Tribute of the land of Musri. Camels, whose backs are two humps, a river ox (buffalo), a *sakēa,* a *sūsu,* elephants, monkeys, apes, I received from him.

> Tribute of Marduk-apal-usur of Suhi. Silver, gold, pitchers of gold, ivory, javelins, *būia,* brightly colored (and) linen garments, I received from him.

> Tribute of Karparunda, of Hattina. Silver, gold, lead, copper, copper vessels, ivory, cypress (timbers), I received from him. (P. 211)

The Nimrud slab inscription of Adad-nirâri (805—782 B. C.) tells, for example, of this booty in the form of tribute received from Mari', king of Aram, in Damascus:

> 2,300 talents of silver, 20 talents of gold, 3,000 talents of copper, 5,000 talents of iron, colored woolen and linen garments, an ivory bed, an ivory couch, inlaid and bejeweled (?), his property and his goods, in immeasurable quantity, in Damascus, his royal city, in his palace, I received. (P. 263)

Tiglathpileser III (745—727 B. C.) records this booty as tribute from a group of western and southern vassal kings:

> Gold, silver, lead, iron, elephants' hides, ivory, colored (woolen) garments, linen garments, blue and purple wool, maple, boxwood, all kind of precious royal treasure, fat (?) lambs, whose wool was purple in color (lit., dyed), winged birds of heaven, whose wings were blue in color (lit., dyed), horses, mules, cattle, sheep, camels, female camels, together with their young, I received. (P. 276)

Sargon (724—705 B. C.) lists this booty as received from defeated Aramaeans:

> His royal tent, his golden palanquin, his royal throne, (his) golden scepter, (his) golden couch, (his) golden footstool, (his) *udini* of gold and silver, his *kurgangani,* weapon(s and) implements of war, I took away from him. . . . The great hosts of Assur plundered for three days and nights and carried off countless spoil. 90,580 people, 2,500 horses, 610 mules, 854 camels — [this does not include] sheep (?), which my army carried off — I received in the midst of my camp. (II, p. 20)

Sennacherib (705—681 B. C.) gives this as the inventory of a successful expedition:

> I returned to Assyria with 208,000 captive people, a huge spoil, 7,200 horses and mules, 11,073 asses, 5,230 camels, 80,050 cattle, 800,100 ewes. — This does not include the men, asses, camels, cattle, and sheep which my troops had carried off and parceled out among themselves. (P. 133)

Esarhaddon (680—669 B. C.) presents this record of exactment from defeated Abdimilkutti, King of Sidon:

His wife, his sons, the people of his palace, property and goods, precious stones, garments of colored wool and linen, maple and boxwood, all kinds of treasures from his palace, in (great) abundance, I carried off. His wide-spreading peoples — there was no numbering them, cattle and sheep and asses, in great number, I transported to Assyria. (P. 205)

Ample allowance, of course, must be made for the exaggerations featured in these inventories. Sycophant scribes, eager to curry royal favor, did not hesitate to add a huge round number to the small figure of the original. Olmstead, *Assyrian Historiography,* p. 8, declares: "When Sennacherib tells us that he took from little Judah no less than 200,150 prisoners, and that in spite of the fact that Jerusalem itself was not captured, we may deduct the 200,000 as a product of the exuberant fancy of the Assyrian scribe and accept the 150 as somewhere near the actual number captured and carried off."

In remarkable agreement with Nahum's prophecy that "there is no end to the store" is the factual account in the *Babylonian Chronicle* that the spoil taken at Nineveh's capture was "a quantity beyond counting." To understand that this statement was not a conventional exaggeration but that the plunder in the city which once plundered the adjacent world was fabulous in amount and value, one need but scan the records of the Sargonide dynasty to find the lists of heavy loot exacted by Nineveh. During Ashurbanipal's long reign the wealth of Babylon, Thebes, and Susa were brought to the capital. Significantly, little gold or silver has been discovered in the Kouyunjik mounds. The city was completely sacked.

To make Assyrian riches, now in the conquerors' hands, appear in their impressive greatness, the prophet summarizes, "An abundance of all desirable articles." The "desirable articles" (AV and RV: "the pleasant furniture") are not only vessels of precious metal, treasures, but comprehensively all things of value, Hos. 13:15, including costly clothing, Job 27:16.

בֹּזּוּ — Ⓖ, διήρπαζον, "they seized." Accordingly, Du. and Ries. arbitrarily replace the repeated imperatives by perfects. The repetition helps emphasize the size of the booty.

כָּבֵד — Written defectively, as in Gen. 31:1. The versions read verb forms: Ⓖ, βεβάρυνται, "they have been made heavy"; Ⓥ, "aggravata est"; Ⓣ, "devour ye!"; Ⓢ, "they are heavy." Wllh., followed by No., J.M.P.Sm., and others, reads כְּבֹד, a construct, but even Ehr. protests that this is not necessary. Du. reads הַכֹּבֶד, "the weight"; Hpt., כָּבֵד "heavy," prefixing וְשִׁלּוּ שָׁלָל, "take heavy booty!" K.-G. inserts "there is found." Stnh. adds, "Lade yourselves with!" Yet even Sel. declares, "This is altogether arbitrary." Nevertheless many follow this addition in a general way. Ries. substitutes כְּבָדִים, translated as "costly."

מִכֹּל — No., Wllh., and others read כֹּל. J.M.P.Sm. explains the omission of the *Mem* on these grounds: "The sense must be 'a glory (or abundance) consisting in (or of) all, etc.,' not 'an abundance out of'; hence מ is dittography of the following." Yet Sel., in opposition, supposes haplography of the מ. Sm. overlooks the distinctive usage of the explicative *min,* Ges., Gra., 119 *w,* note 2, "often to be translated by *namely.*" This is found, for example, in Gen. 7:22, "of all that was," i. e., "so far as it was." The preposition מִן is, therefore, to be retained, and the last words of the verse are to be translated idiomatically, "an abundance of all [that was] desirable articles." This obviates all changes like Du.'s בְּכֹל, Hap.'s לְכֹל, or Stnh.'s and Ries.'s excision of מִכֹּל ("its omission would improve the metre!"). On the force of כֹּל in indeterminate construction see Ges., Gra., 127 *b.* The two words כָּבֵד מִכֹּל are summarily rejected by Hst., who proposes כְּבָדִים מִכֶּם כֹּל, "too heavy for you (are) all." Sel. wants כְּבָדִים מִכֹּל, "too heavy for all." Bev. asks for "too heavy for them are all."

הֲמִדָּה — Ⓖ, τὰ ἐπιθυμάτα αὐτῆς, "her desirable things." Ⓥ, "vasis desiderabilibus," as in Lam. 1:17; Ⓢ, "the vessels of their splendor." J.M.P.Sm. regards the last four words of the verse as an apparent gloss on תְּכוּנָה and asserts: "The phrase is wholly unrelated grammatically to its context and superfluous also in the strophic form." However, the phrase is legitimate as an apposition to the preceding תְּכוּנָה; if it is removed, the verse loses force.

> *v. 11 Desolation and devastation and dilapidation*
>   *And melting heart and smiting together of knees*
>   *and writhing in all loins!*
>   *And the faces of all them gather redness!*

After the ravages of the plundering orgy are over, the prophet once more beholds debris-strewn Nineveh, and the survey of the crushed city draws from his lips a series of seven exclamations which summarize its utter ruin.

"Desolation and devastation and dilapidation!" so we may weakly reproduce Nahum's outcry. No modern language can do full justice to this Hebrew paronomasia, *"búqāh ûmebhûqāh ûmebhullāqāh."* The synonyms, each succeeding one lengthened by the addition of one extra consonant, are chosen for their similarity of sound. For further and similar heaping of related terms, note Jer. 48:43: "Fear and the pit and the snare"; Joel 2:2: "Darkness and . . . gloominess . . . clouds and . . . thick darkness"; Job 10:22: "A land of darkness, as darkness itself; and of the shadow of death, without any order, and where the light is as darkness."

The literal fulfillment of this prediction, made when Nineveh was at the zenith of its glory, is graphically reflected in the impressions which Layard recorded while contemplating the "rude heaps" in the general vicinity of the once-proud city:

"Desolation meets desolation: the feeling of awe succeeds to wonder: for there is nothing to relieve the mind, to lead to hope, or tell of what has gone by. These huge mounds of Assyria made a deeper impression on me, gave rise to more serious thoughts and more earnest reflection than the temples of Baalbek or the theaters of Ionia." The ruins at Nineveh have remained far more desolate than the destroyed sites of other civilizations. Layard remarks: "Were the traveler to cross the Euphrates to seek for such ruins in Mesopotamia and Chaldea as he had left behind him in Asia Minor or Syria, his search would be in vain. . . . He has left the land where nature is still lovely, where, in his mind's eye, he can rebuild the temple or the theater, half doubting whether they would have made a more grateful impression upon the senses than the ruin before him. He is now at a loss to give any form to the rude heaps upon which he is gazing. Those of whose works they are the remains, unlike the Roman and the Greek, have left no visible traces of their civilization, or of their arts: their influence has long since passed away. The more he conjectures, the more vague the results appear."

"A melting heart!" the prophet continues to exclaim, as he turns from national ruin to individual terror. This is a frequent OT expression. As Joshua 2:11; 7:5; Is. 13:7; 2 Sam. 17:10; Ps. 22:15 show, the underlying thought suggests that the terrified heart loses its stability and melts away in fear. "Smiting together of the knees!" he continues. For a similar picture see Job 4:4; Is. 35:3; Dan. 5:6. People seized by terror lose control of their members. Their limbs, instead of remaining strong and firm, are knocked together in the palpitation of fright, as one knee strikes against the other. "And writhing in all loins!" Nahum further exclaims. The term "writhing" (AV, "pain"; RV, "anguish") is etymologically connected with pangs of childbirth, Is. 21:3; Jer. 30:6, but need not be used so and is probably not employed in that sense here, particularly in view of the mention of the loins in 2:2. Elsewhere in the Scriptures (Ps. 69:24; Is. 21:3, and also, by implication, Ezek. 29:7) terror produces pains in the loins.

As Nahum surveys the stricken enemy once more, he cries, "The faces of all them gather redness!" The meaning of this phrase, which occurs otherwise only in the similar construction of Joel 2:6, has been disputed, and the various renditions hinge largely on the meaning accepted for the Hebrew *pārûr*. Most probably the sense is "redness." The entire phrase, "gathering redness," would mean "becoming flushed." Substantiation for this may be adduced from Is. 13:8: "Their faces shall be as flames."

In these last four statements, mentioning melting hearts, shaking knees, writhing loins, and reddened faces, Nahum shows in a practical way the physiological consequences of fear. Inordinate anxiety makes the sympathetic nervous system react on the glands, sending epinephrine or endocrine, the secretion of the ductless glands, into the bloodstream. Almost instantaneously physical reactions appear. The muscles become tense or alternately relaxed and rigid. This latter condition frequently expresses itself in a trembling weakness of the knees. Overrapid breathing is often another consequence of fear. This produces increased heart action and, in aggravated form, palpitation and pounding of the cardiac muscles. As an anxiety neurosis, fear also creates biological effects by which its victim loses control over muscular co-ordination and experiences internal pain. The prophet specifically refers to this when he mentions "writhing in all loins." "The faces" that "gather redness" likewise may show the physiological results of fleeing; particularly, however, do those obsessed with fear show flushed countenances, after the first shock of fright, because of the stimulated heart action and the throbbing blood vessels.

בּוּקָה — Occurs only here. The force of the prophet's exclamation is weakened by the introduction of initial softening words like "there is" (J.M.P.Sm.) or "she is," AV, RV. The

absence of finite verbs in the first part of this verse presents
a text of peculiar force and energy.

מְבוּקָה — Also a *hapax legomenon,* comes, like בּוּקָה, from
the root בּוּק, related to בָּקַק, "to plunder," "to destroy."
Hpt.'s change to בְּקוּקָה is gratuitous.

מְבֻלָּקָה — The root בָּלַק means "to lay desolate," "to destroy."
Elsewhere it occurs only in Is. 24:1, significantly in connection
with בָּקַק, in the statement הִנֵּה יהוה בּוֹקֵק הָאָרֶץ וּבוֹלְקָהּ, "Behold,
Yahweh is destroying the earth and devastating it." The
corresponding Assyrian root is frequent. מְבֻלָּקָה is a fem. *Pu''al*
participle and, as in Arabic, has abstract force.

The three nouns obviously form a paronomasia. Further
examples occur Gen. 1:2; Zeph. 1:15; Ezek. 32:15; 33:29.
Is. 22:5, מְהוּמָה וּמְבוּסָה וּמְבוּכָה, furnishes an interesting parallel
with Nah. Hst.'s elision of one of these three terms weakens
the effect. Ⓖ, ἐκτιναγμὸς καὶ ἀνατιναγμὸς καὶ ἐκβρασμός,
"a shaking and a swinging and a throwing up." Ⓥ, "dis-
sipata est et scissa et dilacerata." Ⓢ, "Crushed, destroyed,
broken."

נָמֵס — This is not the perfect but the participle. Ⓖ, θραυσ-
μός, "breaking." Hpt. and others connect the root מָסַס with
מָסָה and translate, "His heart becomes watery." But note
the frequent association of מָסַס in the sense of "to melt"
with the noun לֵב, "heart." See Joshua 2:11; 5:1; 7:5; Is.
13:7; 19:1; Ezek. 21:12; Ps. 22:15.

פִּיק — Occurring only here, this stands for the more usual
פּוּק, "to totter," "to stumble," "to stagger," Is. 28:7; Jer. 10:4.
For metrical reasons, but against text and versions, Sel. places
פִּיק בִּרְכַּיִם after מָתְנַיִם.

פָּארוּר — This occurs only here and in Joel 2:6. It has been
associated with the root פָּאַר, "to decorate." However, the
versions reproduce the term with their equivalent for "blackness." Ⓖ, πρόσκαυμα χύτρας, "blackening of an earthen pot";
Ⓥ, "nigredo ollae"; Ⓢ, "I blackened like the soot of a pot";

(T), "covered with black like a pot." Probably it was assumed that since pots are sooty, the word means "black." But Judg. 6:19 apparently shows that פָּארוּר need not imply blackness. Objection has been raised to the rendition of פָּארוּר as "redness" (J.M.P.Sm., Dav.-Lan., and others), on the ground that people in fright turn white instead of red. Some who share this opinion seek to find support in the verb קִבֵּץ and translate "withdraw color," that is, "turn pale." But the verb means "to gather," not "to withdraw." Others (Stnh.) derive פָּארוּר from the root פָּאַר in the meaning "to be dazzling," "resplendent," and understand the noun to mean "whiteness." No justification can be found for the elimination of the last four words of this verse as a gloss, misplaced through editorial arrangement (Hpt., K.-G.). Even J.M.P.Sm. asserts: "There is not the slightest ground for eliminating the clause as a misplaced gloss. . . . It is needed here to complete the balance of thought and give the finishing touch to the picture of despair." Hap. nevertheless changes Ⓜ to read: כְּבָעֵר קִבְּצוּ פָּארוּר, "like a flame they gather redness." Ries., contradicting MSS and versions, asks for the pl. פְּרוּרִים and associates this with Arabic *farfara,* "to twitch convulsively."

> *v. 12 Where {is} a dwelling place of lions*
> *And fodder for the cubs*
> *Which a lion went to bring?*
> *There a lion's brood {lived},*
> *With no one to terrify {it}.*

Nahum now interrupts his description of Nineveh's sack to raise the taunt "where is a dwelling place of lions?" This rhetorical question implies that in the age he envisions, the capital no longer exists. Completely convinced of the city's inevitable, utter destruction, the prophet lifts his eyes to the once-opulent metropolis, but now beholds no traces of its grandeur. He pictures the city as a lions' den, not to symbolize the people's bestiality and their degenerate practices (Calvin), but to describe the ferocity and rapacity of a nation which, like a ravenous lion, pounces on country after country. Neither is it his sole purpose to show that as the lion is the king of the beasts, so Nineveh is the monarch of all lands (J.M.P.Sm.). True, if other enemies of God's people or the royalties of heathen nations are specifically called "lions" (Jer. 4:7; 49:19; 50:17; Ezek. 19:2), Nineveh certainly deserved this title. However, the lion was so frequently featured in Assyrian reliefs and decorations that it is particularly fitting as an epithet of the lionlike city. Above all, however, it should be noted that Assyrian monarchs proudly called themselves "lions." In their grandiloquent self-appraisal Adad-nirari and Ashurnasirpal speak of themselves as lions, and Sennacherib boasts of his military fury: "Like a lion I raged." And so the prophet mockingly uses the very term which in picture and inscription symbolized Assyrian might; and he makes it a byword of scorn. It may be assumed that the prophet also calls Nineveh "a dwelling place of lions" because both Assyria and Babylonia had many lions. During Ashurbanipal's reign lions became a public menace, a national plague. This king reports: "By consuming cattle, sheep, and men they [the lions] became ferocious and terrifying. With their roaring they filled the mountain forests (so that) the creatures of the field were terrified. The animals of the field they continually felled, spilled the blood of men. . . . Like a destruction (caused) by Ira [the god of pestilence] the carcasses of (?) the dead, cattle and (sheep?). The shepherds and guards weep." (Streck, II, 214 f.)

"Where," the prophet continues, "is . . . fodder for the cubs, which a lion went to bring?" In plain language this question means: "Where is the plunder which was brought to

Nineveh's citizens when the Assyrian lion went out on expeditions of conquest?" The phrase "which a lion went to bring" emphasizes the premeditated plans for robbery and booty. The composite rhetorical question is not answered, for in the prophet's future Nineveh no longer exists. The pillagers have been pillaged.

The picture reaches its climax in an added representation of brazen security. While the lion went out to bring prey, Nahum says, "There [in the den] a lion's brood lived, with no one to terrify it." Nineveh was so overbearing in its power that the Assyrian armies could wage campaigns at great distances from the capital, instead of being limited to a restricted, adjacent area for fear of the city's safety. A similar picture of supreme confidence is found in Deut. 28:26. A cub which could take care of itself while the parent lions were away on distant forages — that is the prophet's symbol for the Ninevites. Yet "where," anticipating the desolate ruins, he now asks, "is the dwelling place of lions?" The rhetorical question asserts that Nineveh will vanish; and the fulfillment of this prediction is one of the most amazing chapters in ancient history. Soon after the city's fall its disappearance became so complete that travelers did not recognize its site. Not until almost the middle of the nineteenth century could archaeologists definitely identify the mounds which covered its razed buildings. Even today the exact confines of the city have not been determined.

אַיֵּה — Modern criticism, which insists on rewriting Nahum, is not satisfied with the logical and rhetorical force of the prophet's "where." Bev. insists on substituting אוֹי, "woe," but offers no reason.

מְעוֹן — This term usually designates God's dwelling place, but it is also employed of animals. See v. 13.

וּמִרְעֶה has caused considerable difficulty. The word itself has one basic OT meaning, "pasture," "a place of food" for both domesticated animals (Gen. 47:4; Is. 32:14; Ezek. 34:

14, 18; etc.) and wild animals (Job 39:8; Lam. 1:6). The stress in each instance is not on the pasture as a locality (AV: "a feeding place of the lion, where the lion, even the old lion, walked") but on its food. This is emphasized by Ezek. 34:18: "you eat up the good pasture." Hence the word may be used for "fodder" here, which stands figuratively for "booty." Note Jer. 50:6, where the verb רָעָה is similarly used of predatory enemies. See also Ezek. 34:2. However, it has been objected that מִרְעֶה, either as "fodder" or as "pasture land," is not suitable for a lion (Stnh., J.M.P.Sm.). Yet, as noted, Job 39:8 employs the term in connection with wild asses and Lam. 1:16 in connection with the hart. The noun is thus not limited to association with domesticated animals. Following Wllh., practically all modern commentators alter מִרְעֶה to מְעָרָה, "cave." No textual or versional basis for this change exists, and the alteration is unfortunate, since it contradicts Hebrew usage. מְעָרָה is always employed of caves which contain men. Besides, as a fem. noun it would require a fem. pronoun instead of the masc. הוא.

הוא — On the construction, and against those who insist that הוא is a gloss or misplaced, see Ges., Gra., 155 *b*. J.M.P.Sm. comments: "Standing where it does in Ⓜ, הוא converts the whole series of successive clauses into prosaic statements of fact." However, no "whole series" of dependent clauses follows הוא, and it should not be omitted. It may also be treated as tantamount to a copula.

לַכְּפִרִים — Ⓖ, τοῖς σκύμνοις, "for the cubs." The word designates a young lion; and according to Ges., Hwb., one which goes out to seek its own prey. This particular qualification is apparently not observed in the present passage, and it may be doubted whether this connotation is essential to the meaning of the term. Du. pedantically omits the לְ in conforming to the construct state in the first part of the verse.

אֲשֶׁר הָלַךְ אַרְיֵה לָבִיא — This is arbitrarily omitted by Du.

and Sel. as a late variant for אֲשֶׁר שָׁם גּוּר אַרְיֵה. ⒼA renders אֲשֶׁר הָלַךְ as οὐκ ἐπορεύθη, "did not go"; Ⓢ similarly. Most Ⓖ MSS have ποῦ. לָבִיא is translated "lioness" (RV) and "the old lion" (AV), so that the clause, reproduced literally, would read, "whither went the lion, the lioness, the lion's cub." This translation has not been acceptable, and most interpreters have followed Ⓖ, which reproduces לָבִיא by τοῦ εἰσελθεῖν, "to enter," and have altered Ⓜ to read לָבוֹא, and with further emendation, "where is the cave for the young lions, whither the lion entered (or retreated)?" This is a prosaic statement and adds little to the thought. J.M.P.Sm., e. g., suggests that לָבִיא is a marginal note which has accidentally crept into the text. Its elision is also urged because of alleged metrical nonconformity; for, Sm. states, "The first half of the line is too long by one beat, as compared with the second half and the other lines of the context." Therefore the word is dropped with the explanation, "The line reads smoothly 'Whither went the lion, the lion's cub,' with, etc." This procedure is forced and artificial, since it loses sight of the striking force contained in the literal interpretation here accepted. According to this position, לָבִיא does not denote "lioness"; it is rather the *Hiph"il* infinitive construct of the verb בּוֹא, with elision of the *He,* and means, causatively, "to bring." This is not an isolated instance in which Ⓜ has לָבִיא for לְהָבִיא. It also occurs in Jer. 27:7; 2 Chron. 31:10.

שָׁם גּוּר אַרְיֵה — Ries. changes the first word to שָׁם and then creates a parenthetical gloss, added, he implies, by a reader who explains, "Lion (לְבִיא) is the name for young lion." This is sheer assumption and is discredited by the fact that לָבִיא does not mean "young lion." Stnh. similarly holds that גּוּר אַרְיֵה is probably a gloss on גְּרוֹתָיו, v. 13.

וְאֵין מַחֲרִיד — This is a circumstantial nominal sentence, introduced by *Waw,* to be translated, "without anyone to terrify."

> *v. 13* *A lion, tearing prey for the need of his cubs*
> *And strangling for his lionesses;*
> *And he filleth his caves with prey*
> *And his lairs with ripped carcasses.*

The picture in the previous verse is extended. Nineveh is again called "a lion" and described as "tearing prey for the need of his cubs and strangling for his lionesses." The lion has been interpreted as Assyria's king; "his cubs," as his children or nobles; "his lionesses," as the queens. This pl. remains difficult. It may be better not to press the point of comparison beyond stating that as lionesses with cubs depend on the lion, so the opulence enjoyed by the citizens of Nineveh came from the predatory campaigns of the Assyrian monarch and his armies.

Retaining this picture, Nahum figuratively describes the enormity of the booty. The lion "filleth his caves with prey and his lairs with ripped carcasses." The points of comparison are first of all the brutality (implied in the term "ripped carcasses," lit., "torn animals"). Assyrian cruelty stands almost unparalleled in the record of human history. With due allowances for the exaggerations characteristic of the cuneiform chronicles, the extent of the violence and bloodshed to which the Nineveh conquerors resorted is almost incredible. Typical instances from their earlier history will be noted in connection with 3:1; in the *Annals of Ashurbanipal,* contemporary of Nahum, we find memoirs like these:

"The people of Sais, Pindidi, Si'nu, and the other cities, as many as had joined themselves to them (and) planned evil, large and small, they laid them low with their weapons. They left not a single man among them alive. They suspended their corpses from poles, tore their skin off, and affixed it to the city walls." (Col. I, 1. 124 — col. II, 1. 4)

"The remnant of the survivors [in the armies of Shamash-shum-ukin] I laid low at the bullock statues where they had slain Sennacherib, my grandfather, as an offering to his memory. I let dogs, swine, wolves, vultures, the birds of the heavens, and the sweet-water fish devour their cut-off limbs. After I had carried out these actions (and) quieted the hearts of the great gods, my lords, I gathered the bodies of those who had been snatched away by the plague, and (of those) who had died of poverty (and) starvation, and of those whom the dogs (and) swine had left and who now clogged the streets (and) filled the squares; their remains I gathered out of Babylon, Kutha, and Sippar and threw them over the walls." (Col. IV, 11. 70—85)

"The people [of Bit-Imbi] who lived in the city and had not come out and had not acknowledged my rule, I slew. I chopped off their heads and cut off their lips." (Col. IV, 11. 133—135)

"By command of the great gods, my lords, I prepared a dog chain for him (Ammuladi, the king of Kidri) and had him guard the cage." (Col. VIII, 11. 27—29)

"At the command of Assur and Ninlil I bored through his jaw with my cutting dagger (?), pulled a rope through his cheek and the sides of his face (?), and attached a dog chain to him, and let him guard the cage at the east gate of Nineveh." (Col. IX, 11. 104—111)[10]

The second point of comparison in the symbolism of the ravaging lion is the Assyrian lust for plunder (indicated by the heaped booty in the plurality of caves). Nineveh, indeed, had torn its wealth from the four quarters of the earth. Ashurbanipal brought to Nineveh treasures from three of the world's largest and richest cities, Thebes, Babylon, Susa; and there is no clearer testimony to its rapacity than the military reports, which — often with painstaking detail — gloat over booty and

[10] The references are to M. Streck, *Assurbanipal und die letzten assyrischen Könige* (1916), II. Teil, *Texte*.

tribute. Typical inventories of this spoil are in the official *Annals of Ashurbanipal:*

"Their gods [of twenty-eight conquered cities], their inhabitants, their cattle, their sheep, their property, their possessions, the carts, the horses, the mules, the weapons, the engines of war, I carried back to Assyria with me as booty." (Col. V, 11. 59—62)

"I opened their treasuries [of Susa]. Everything of silver, gold, property, and possessions that had been heaped in them; everything which the earlier kings of Elam down to the present day had gathered (and) heaped up, treasures which no other hand had ever touched before me, these I brought out and counted as booty. Silver, gold, property and possessions from Sumer and Akkad, as well as from Kardunias altogether, everything which the former kings of Elam had taken in seven campaigns and had dragged to Elam, (namely) wonderful *sarîru,* shining *ešmarû,* gems, precious treasures, the tokens of royalty, (the articles) which the former kings of Akkad and Shamash-shum-ukin had given to Elam by reason of their treaty of alliance, clothing, costly jewelry, royal adornment, the weapons of war that served as ornaments, each one wrought by the hands of a warrior as adornment. I took away with me as booty to Assyria the entire furnishings of his palaces, (the articles) on which they sat, lay, and from which they had eaten, drunk, washed (and) anointed themselves, their chariots of war, their gala wagons, (?) their carts which were inlaid with *sarîru* and *zahalû,* horses, mighty mules, with harness of gold (and) silver." (Col. V, 1. 132 to col. VI, 1. 26)

"Thirty-two statues of kings which had been made of gold, silver, bronze (and) limestone, from Susa, Madaktu, Huradi; as well as a pillar of Ummanigaš, the son of Umbadarâ; a statue of Ištarnanhundi, a statue of Hallusi, a statue of Tammaritu the second . . . I carried away to Assyria." (Col. VI, 11. 48—57)

Ries. drops the entire verse as a gloss but does not explain the excision.

אַרְיֵה is dropped by K.-G.

בְּדֵי — Ⓖ, τὰ ἱκανά, "that which is sufficient," idiomatic for what is required "for" or "for the need of." It is unnecessary to change this to כְּדֵי with Hpt. Ehr. says the preposition shows the purpose and cites Ex. 10:12 as a parallel.

גֹּרֹתָיו — Du. changes this to גּוּרָיו, "his young lions." However, Hebrew has two distinct words: גֹּר, which occurs here, designating "a lion's cub"; and גּוּר, which may be used of any young animal. In Lam. 4:3 it denotes "a young jackal," though predominantly it stands for "a lion's cub," Ezek. 19:3, 5; Gen. 39:9; Deut. 33:22; Nah. 2:12. גּוּר in this verse is supported by Jer. 51:38, where it appears in the masc. pl.

מְחַנֵּק is technically employed for "strangling," 2 Sam. 17:23. While J.M.P.Sm.'s question is in place: "Is strangling the method of slaughter characteristic of lions?" the appropriateness of this verb in describing Nineveh's stifling and throttling permits its use here.

טְרֶף and טְרֵפָה — These words differ theoretically in this respect, that the first emphasizes the prey, while the second stresses its torn, ripped condition. Here the terms are parallel and do not indicate any fundamentally different classes of lion food. טְרֵפָה may be used to give the verse a full close. There is no evidence to support the claim by Dav.-Lan. for "plunder."

חֹרָיו — Ⓖ has the sing. νοσσιὰν αὐτοῦ, "his nest." Ehr., in unwarranted literalness, objects to the pl., insisting that a lion occupies only one den. The pl. is intentional here, since, as Ehr. concedes, the pl. may refer to the various parts of the den.

מְעֹנֹתָיו — Ⓥ, "cubile suum." The Hebrew broadly designates a dwelling place and is used of God's habitation in heaven, Deut. 26:15; the temple, 2 Chron. 36:15; the place of wild animals, Jer. 9:10; 10:22; 49:33; 51:37, etc., and here.

> v. 14 Behold, I {am} against thee — the oracle of Yahweh
>   of Hosts.
>   And I will burn her chariots in the smoke,
>   And a sword shall devour thy young lions.
>   And I will cut off thy prey from the earth,
>   And the voice of thy messengers shall not be heard
>   again.

At the end of this section the author returns to the thought which pervades the entire book: Nineveh must be wiped off the earth because God has decreed its destruction. This motif is introduced with the familiar prophetic phrase, "The oracle of Yahweh of Hosts." Nahum is convinced that his is no mere human prediction or conjecture, which any well-informed student of international affairs might hazard. Consciously he emphasizes that as God's messenger he brings an unalterable oracle from "the Lord of Hosts" in His omnipotence, with the totality of all existence marshaled under His sovereignty. With this reassuring introduction the prophet announces the divine dictum, "Behold, I [Yahweh] am against thee [Nineveh]." The impressive "I am against thee," repeated five verses later, is a frequent warning in seventh- and sixth-century prophetic writings. See Jer. 21:13; 23:30 ff.; 50:31; 51:25; Ezek. 5:8; 13:8, 20; 21:8; 26:3; 28:22; 39:1. It expresses God's unrelieved hostility toward the overbearing city; and with Yahweh of Hosts on one side and Nineveh on the other, the outcome of the conflict cannot remain in doubt.

The measures taken by the Almighty in directing His warfare against the doomed capital contain a pointed reference to the preceding verses. In the first place, the prophet voices the divine threat: "I will burn her chariots in the smoke." The Assyrian chariots are singled out because they are contrasted in their destruction with the assailants' war wagons in their triumph (2:4,5) or, more probably, because to the observer they represent the outstanding equipment of the Assyrian army. All the chariots are to be burned "in the smoke," because so many are destroyed by the flames that dense, black conflagration clouds cover the city (see Ps. 37:20). The repeated prominence which Nahum attaches to fire as a means of devastation is noteworthy (3:13, 15). With its chariots burned, Nineveh lacks all means of conducting distant expeditions or offensives far removed from the city.

While the smoke of the chariots darkens the heavens, "a sword," so the divine oracle pledges, "shall devour thy young lions." The emphasis on the sword re-echoes the prominence this instrument of destruction has in the Assyrian king's annals. The sharp weapon which the Nineveh armies used against their enemies will now be turned against them. This reversion to the lions, the picture of the immediately preceding verse, is striking, indicating as it does that when Nineveh's military power is overcome, the "young lions" (those, as shown, who are dependent on Nineveh, the civilian and the soldiery, or those who succeed the present generation, as the lion cubs follow their forebears) must also face annihilation. The Assyrian power is to be wiped out forever; its name shall perish.

"I will cut off thy prey from the earth," God's decree continues. This "prey" has been interpreted as a reference to the booty which the lionlike Nineveh has already secured by extortion and conquest (J.M.P.Sm.). More probably, however, the intended sense is secured by translating, "I will cut off your preying from the earth." Nineveh will no longer be permitted to pounce on defenseless nations and helpless vassals.

The utter end is sealed in this sentence of doom: "And the voice of thy messengers shall not be heard again." The haughty city will have no more representative heralds, for no nation remains to be represented. The officials sent to demand submission, to exact heavy tribute, and to rule conquered peoples with iron-handed, Nineveh-directed policy, will no longer raise their voice in imperious command. Messengers like "Tartan and Rabsaris and Rabshakeh," who taunted Jerusalem during Sennacherib's invasion, 2 Kings 18:17 ff.; or like the emissary who threatened Hezekiah, 2 Kings 19:1 ff.; Is. 37:9 ff.; the officials who "reproached Yahweh," 2 Kings 19:23, all these will disappear with the demise of Nineveh.

אֵלַיִךְ — Stnh., following Wllh., No., and others, maintains that the feminine suffix "refers to Nineveh, but all the suffixes in the verse should be changed to the masculine, referring to Assyria." Yet even J.M.P.Sm. answers: "The thought of the city underlies the whole v., and comes to clear expression in the last word; hence the feminine suffix is suitable throughout." Ri. adds נִינְוֵה. Sel. calls the first two words "the challenge for the duel" and finds a parallel in Marduk's summons to Ishtar. So far can caustic criticism veer from the prophet's plain statement!

נְאֻם יהוה צְבָאוֹת — Although these words are supported by the versions, G.A.Sm. says they are "probably a gloss." K.-G. and Stk. want צְבָאוֹת dropped.

וְהִבְעַרְתִּי — Hal. wants this changed to וְהַעֲבַרְתִּי, "and I will cause to pass over." Du. alters to read וְהַעֲלֵיתִי, "and I will bring up."

בֶּעָשָׁן — K.-G. and Sel. substitute בָּאֵשׁ, perphaps on the basis of ⓉⒹ בְּאֶשָּׁתָא "in the fire"; yet Ⓥ, "usque ad fumum."

רִכְבָּה — Ⓖ, πλῆθός σου, "your multitude." Ⓢ reads similarly, but Ⓥ more correctly offers "quadrigas tuas"; similarly Ⓣ. Jnk. and Hst. substitute רִכְבֵּךְ, "thy chariot." Many liberal interpreters, however, change even the root. Thus Hap. and Oo., following the Ⓖ mistranslation, offer רֻבֵּךְ, "thy multitude." No., סְבָכֵּךְ, "thy thicket"; Du., סְבֹךְ, "thicket"; Ries., מַרְבְּצֵךְ, "thine encampment." Many critics, however, follow Grz. in reading רִבְצֵךְ, "thy lair." The reason for this drastic change, which has not remained uncontested, e. g., by Jnk., is given by J.M.P.Sm., who says that "chariot" "does not suit the figure of the lion which continues here, as is clear from the latter part of the line." Bev. condescends to say, "Mixed metaphors are quite tolerable in Semitic poetry"; but the verse contains no mixed metaphor. Sm.'s objection might be valid if it could be shown that each verse deals only with one subject. Scores of other verses demonstrate that the OT writers often combined within one verse two or three widely different subjects, even as this verse also mentions "booty" and "messengers." The real difficulty with Ⓜ at this place is the third-person suffix. This has been explained (Keil) as an instance of abrupt poetical change of address. Why not, however, drop the *Mappîq* and read רִכְבָּה, "riding," in the sense of cavalry, Ezek. 27:20?

כְּפִירַיִךְ — Ⓢ, "thy young ones." Du. drops the suffix to secure הַכְּפִירִים. New. alters to כְּפָרַיִךְ, "thy villages." Hst. and Sel. substitute גִּבֹּרַיִךְ, "thy heroes," the latter claiming that the picture of the lions has been discontinued and that the sword does not fit the hunting of lions. Yet Ⓥ, "et leunculos tuos comedit gladius." G.A.Sm. and K.-G. brand the whole sentence as a probable gloss.

תֹאכַל — Du. arbitrarily changes this to תֹאכְלֵךְ, "will consume thee."

טַרְפֵּךְ — Hal. reads טֹרְפַּיִךְ, "thy plunderers," tentatively endorsed also by Stnh. Ries. asks for טַפֵּךְ, "thy young ones"; Ri., טַרְפֵּךְ — but inserts וְחַיַת הָאָרֶץ before it, an utterly unjustified addition, to read, "and the animals of the field, thy prey."

מַלְאָכֵכֵה — This is translated by Ⓖ: τὰ ἔργα σου, "thy deeds"; Ⓢ: "of thy deeds" — doubtless a mistaken reading which assumes a form of מְלָאכָה, "work." Hap. accepts this and offers מְלַאכְתֵּךְ, "thy work." New.: מְלַאכְתָיִךְ, "thy works"; Bev., who prefers this, explains the terms as denoting "building undertakings, e. g., temple construction with cedar wood from Lebanon"! Ⓥ correctly presents "nunciorum tuorum." Many

interpreters (Grz., Mrt., Stk., and others) require מַלְאָכַיִךְ,
"thy messengers," asserting that the present Ⓜ form has resulted from dittography of the following *Hē*. So also Ges.,
Gra., 91 *l*. Sel. changes the entire word, reading בְּהֵיכָלַיִךְ,
"in thy palaces"; Ehr. proposes מַהֲלָכַךְ "(the noise of) thy
expeditions." Ri. wants הַלְּבִיָּה, "the mother lion." However,
there is a strong antecedent improbability that a scribe whose
original read מַלְאָכַיִךְ would mistakenly produce two *Hē's*,
drawing one back to the preceding word and thus making
an abnormal form, a process which in addition requires the
change of the final *Kaph*. There is an unusual latitude in
the form of the nominal suffixes for the second person
singular. If this person in the masculine may take the ending
כָה ֽ (Ps. 139:5, with the verbal suffix counterpart כָה, Gen.
27:7); if the second sing. fem. suffix may be כִי ֽ (Jer. 11:15,
with the same form for the verbal suffix, Ps. 103:4), or יְכִי
(2 Kings 4:3), is it unreasonable to assume that מַלְאָכֵכֶה
is a unique suffix of the second sing. fem., the gender and
number required by the context? Wllh. maintains that the
form was intended to emphasize the masc. suffix. Mrt. and
No. omit the last part of this verse from לֹא יִשָּׁמַע on. But
J.M.P.Sm. protests: "The clause fits well into the structure
of the strophe."

Chapter 3

v. 1 Woe to a bloody city!
All of it {is} falsehood. {It is} full of robbery.
Prey doth not depart.

The third chief section of Nahum's book contains further oracles against Nineveh, a series of predictions foretelling the inevitable ruin to engulf the city. First, in a series of short, quick ejaculations the prophet pictures the Assyrian capital at the height of her cruel power and then records the assault which will spell her collapse (3:1-3). He commences this denunciation with the word that (as in Hab. 2:6) summarizes his message, "woe," a threat, a taunt, a derision.

This woe is directed against Nineveh as "a bloody city" (lit.: "a city of bloods," the pl. in the Hebrew denoting shed blood or the guilt involved in its shedding, Ezek. 24:9). This epithet well describes the doomed capital, for the Assyrians were among the most cruel and bloodthirsty of all ancient peoples who have left their records.

The cuneiform tablets furnish appalling testimony to the calculated cruelty inflicted by the armies mustered in Nineveh. Ashurnasirpal II (885—860 B. C.), for instance, lists his atrocities on a monument commemorating the first eighteen years of his reign (see Luckenbill, *Ancient Records of Assyria and Babylonia*, I, 142 ff.). Among them are:

290

Great number of them in the land of Kirhi I slew. . . . 260 of their fighting men I cut down with the sword. I cut off their heads, and I formed them into pillars. . . . Būbu, son of Bubā . . . I flayed in the city of Arbela and I spread his skin upon the city wall.

I flayed all the chief men [in the city of Sūru] who had revolted, and I covered the pillar with their skins; some I walled up within the pillar, some I impaled upon the pillar on stakes, and others I bound to stakes round about the pillar; many within the border of my own land I flayed, and I spread their skins upon the walls; and I cut off the limbs of the officers, of the royal officers who had rebelled. Ahiababa I took to Nineveh, I flayed him, I spread his skin upon the wall of Nineveh.

600 of their [the people in the city of Hulai] warriors I put to the sword; 3,000 captives I burned with fire; I did not leave a single one among them alive to serve as a hostage. . . . Their corpses I formed into pillars; their young men and maidens I burned in the fire. Hulai, then governor, I flayed, his skin I spread upon the wall of the city of Damdamusa.

50 of their [the people in the city of Mariru] warriors I put to the sword; 200 of their captives I burned with fire.

3,000 of their [the people in the city of Têla] warriors I put to the sword. . . . Many captives from among them I burned with fire. From some I cut off their hands and their fingers, and from others I cut off their noses, their ears, and their fingers (?), of many I put out the eyes. I made one pillar of the living, and another of heads, and I bound their heads to posts (tree trunks) round about the city. Their young men and maidens I burned in the fire, the city I destroyed.

In the midst of the mighty mountain I slaughtered them, with their blood I dyed the mountain red like wool, with the rest of them I darkened the gullies and precipices of the mountains. . . . The heads of their warriors I cut off, and I formed them into a pillar over against their city, their young men and their maidens I burned in the fire.

I slew the inhabitants [of the city Hudun] . . . their young men and their maidens I burned in the flames.

The city of Kisirtu . . . together with ten cities of its neighborhood, I captured, I slew their inhabitants.

50 of Ameka's warriors I slew in the field, I cut off their heads

and bound them to the tree trunks within his palace court. Twenty men I captured alive, and I immured them in the wall of his palace.

800 of their [the people in Pitura] fighting men I put to the sword and cut off their heads. Multitudes I captured alive, and the rest of them I burned with fire. . . . I formed a pillar of the living and of heads over against his city gate and 700 men I impaled on stakes. . . . Their young men and their maidens I burned in the fire.

1,400 of their [the people in the city of Uda] fighting men I put to the sword, 580 men I captured alive, 3,000 prisoners I brought out. The living men I impaled on stakes . . . of the others I put out the eyes.

The atrocious practice of cutting off hands and feet, ears and noses, gouging out eyes, lopping off heads and then binding them to vines or heaping them up before city gates; the utter fiendishness by which captives could be impaled or flayed alive through a process in which their skin was gradually and completely removed — this planned frightfulness systematically enforced by the "bloody city" was now to be avenged.

Nineveh was not only cruel; it was also a center of deception. "All of it is falsehood," the prophet continues. Modern versions prefer to join this statement with the following and to translate (AV): "It is full of lies and robberies," or (RV): "Full of lies and rapine." This can hardly be the correct rendition, for the Hebrew has no copulative connecting the last two words. It is best to take the two assertions asyndetically and thus to preserve the full force of the prophet's quick, concise denunciation. Here, then, Nahum pictures the city as made up completely of falsehood. The lies include especially the official promises made to secure the submission of the weaker nations. Such assurances, the prophet implies, are complete misrepresentations. The Assyrians do not mean what they say. They break their word as soon as their interests demand. A typical instance of their attractive falsehood is found in 2 Kings 18: 31 ff., where Sennacherib's official tries to make the people of

Jerusalem believe that by refusing to heed Hezekiah and by obeying Assyria's monarch they would eat of their own fig trees; that they would be transported to a land of corn and wine, bread, vineyards, olive oil, honey; that Judah's God would not be able to deliver His people from Sennacherib's hands. However, this charge also includes the common lies and prevalent misrepresentations in Nineveh. From the utterly false statements by its kings, boastfully perpetuated on their records, down to the common prevarications in commerce and business, "all of it is falsehood." "The one tries to get the other's goods wherever and however he can," Lu. (XIV:1362) summarizes. The most prevalent deception in the capital, of course, is its worship of false gods.

Besides, the city is "full of robbery." Nineveh is the robber citadel. It has despoiled other nations, stripped enemy capitals, pillaged unnumbered towns, and, as the prophet has already forcefully implied (2:9), filled its own territory with plunder.

Finally, Nahum concludes, "prey doth not depart." The term translated "prey" denotes a tearing, rending, as a lion rips the carcass of its victims (Ps. 7:3). The city, truly a ferocious animal, continually occupies itself with plundering its victims and heaping booty. This is no exaggeration. Rather does the prophet present a one-sentence synopsis of Assyria's history, with a summary of the practically ceaseless pillaging and endless rapine which marked particularly Tiglathpileser and the Sargonide dynasty.

הוֹי — Du. adds without warrant וְנִוָה. Dr. and Dav.-Lan. translate, "Oh!" maintaining that the word is "an exclamation and not a threat."

דָּמִים — Ges., Gra., 124 n, explains this "as a sort of plural of the result and at the same time of local extension"; it denotes "blood which is shed." Hence the pl. acquired "simply the sense of bloody deed and especially of blood-guiltiness."

כְּלָה — Sel. wants כְּלָה כַּחַשׁ placed at the end of the verse for metrical reasons (to make "two good *qînâ* lines"), certainly not for textual. J.M.P.Sm. arbitrarily transfers the *'Athnāch* from the previous word to this.

כַּחַשׁ in Job 16:8 denotes "sickliness," "emaciated condition"; here, however, as in Hos. 7:3; 10:13; 12:1; Ps. 59:13, it means "falsehood," "deceit."

פֶּרֶק in Obad. 14 means "crossroads" (?) or "place of escape," but here it is translated as ἀδικία, "injustice," by Ⓖ; as ἐξαυχενισμός, "beheading," by Aq.; ἀποτομία, "cutting off," by Σ; "dilaceratione" by Ⓥ; בּוּא, "booty," by Ⓣ. The last association seems the most probable, for the verb פָּרַק means "to tear off," Gen. 47:40; "bring into safety," Ps. 136:24; Lam. 5:8.

יָמִישׁ — This has been interpreted as a transitive verb and translated, "It will not let go of the prey," that is, return it to its rightful owners. In these words there has been found a special reference to Israel, which has been kept in captivity by the proud capital. But the verb is masc., while the references to Nineveh in this verse are feminine; therefore it appears that טֶרֶף, masc., is the subject and the verb intransitive, as Joshua 1:8; Ex. 13:22; Ps. 55:12; Zech. 14:14. The sentence may then be translated, "prey does not depart," or, interpreting טֶרֶף as a noun of action, "plundering will not cease," Jer. 17:8. Sel., following Bev., asks for תָּמִישׁ, "she does not remove." Mrt., followed by No., believes that a parallel clause has been dropped and adds the Hebrew for "and there is no end to the booty." J.M.P.Sm. agrees to some additions (for "conformity to the poetical measure") and insists: "Unless something be supplied, it seems necessary to treat this clause 'plundering will not cease' as a gloss."

These unfounded demands for change and addition illustrate the manner in which criticism has made versification a Procrustean bed. In opposition Sel., who never hesitates to alter a Ⓜ reading, declares: "Nothing has been dropped."

> *v. 2 Crack of whip*
> *And rumble of wheels!*
> *And galloping horse*
> *And jolting chariot!*

From the denunciation of Assyrian cruelty the prophet suddenly turns to a preview of the final assault on the overbearing capital. Again, as in 2:4, 5, he focuses his attention on the outstanding part of the attack equipment, the chariotry. His almost photographic vision is expressed by the ejaculatory construction which in vv. 2 and 3 features nine short exclamations. "Crack of whip!" he begins, picturing the charioteers brandishing the driver's lash and starting their frenzied charge.

Hardly have the whips snapped when the "rumble of wheels" is heard. Each wheel creaking on its own axle, each wagon of war rolling noisily over rutted roads and pitted fields, the air is filled with a thunderous roar.

In a moment the chariots gain momentum; and previewing their undulated onrush, Nahum cries out, "Galloping horse and jolting chariot!" The cavalry is in full swing, as the unbridled chargers pull the chariots along, jolting hard over the rough places and then almost flying through the air.

The progressive action in this picture, starting with the cracking whip and ending with the racing chariots, has not been previously recognized. Tribute has been paid the prophet, however, for the staccato style of this verse and of the entire section. Jerome asserts that this portrayal of the army preparing itself for the battle is so attractive that "every description of mine is inferior." Hen. declares: "The passage is unrivaled by any other, either in sacred or profane literature." Lu. (XIV:1402) acknowledges: "He uses fitting and exceedingly emphatic words to describe the matter clearly and forcefully. . . . Here you see the power of the Spirit in the prophet, who describes the future matter as though he beheld it present, before his eyes."

קוֹל — J.M.P.Sm. summarizes the position of several critics when he asserts that the twofold occurrence of this term is awkward, and maintains that by removing one קוֹל "the metre would be improved." With similar motivation criticism has sought to drop each repetition in Nahum's prophecies. It forgets the effective syntactical use of repetition in Hebrew as a means of expressing the concepts of entirety, Ges., Gra., 123 c; of superfine quality, Ges., Gra., 123 e; and of distribution, Ges., Gra., 123 d. The emphasis on the battle noise is graphically sustained by the recurrence of קוֹל. It is also possible to translate the word interjectionally and to render, "Listen! A whip! . . . Listen! A rumble of wheels! . . ." Ges., Gra., 146 b.

שׁוֹט — ⑥ has the pl. This is uncalled for, since the nominal construction in this verse and the next is entirely in the sing.

רַעַשׁ — J.M.P.Sm. objects: "Though used for 'earthquake,' it is difficult to refer it here to the trembling of the ground as the chariots dash by. . . . It is rather the noise made by the wheels themselves." However, while the basic meaning of רַעַשׁ is "earthquake," the word is also associated with the noise of battle, Is. 9:4; Jer. 10:22. Significantly in Job 29:24 the term describes a fierce, raging horse. Nahum employs the word here particularly to picture the earth-shaking rumble of many chariots.

דֹּהֵר — The exact connotation of this term is uncertain. The root occurs otherwise only in Judg. 5:22, where it apparently designates the prancing of mighty steeds. However, Hpt. associates this term with the Arabic hadara, which means "to neigh," "to snort," and then secondarily, "to exult." In view of the Hebrew root דָּהַר, which denotes the prancing and racing of horses, it seems most appropriate to follow the progressive development of the text and to take this as "galloping," "prancing." Ⓖ offers διώκοντος, "galloping," or "speeding." Ⓥ, "frementis"; Ⓢ, "snorting." Bev., following others, changes דֹּהֵר to the passive דָּהוּר, which is explained as "urged on." He adds: "The slight change to obtain the passive participle seems justified by the sense in general, as also by closer parallelism with the next half-verse." But Bev.'s conjectural emendation is altogether too weak. Why alter the Ⓜ on such flimsy pretexts?

> *v. 3　Rearing rider and flaming sword and flashing spear*
> *And host of slain and multitude of dead bodies!*
> *And no end of the corpses;*
> *They stumble over their corpses.*

The survey of the jolting chariots gives way to swift-moving flashes of battle and to a multipicture montage of the defeat which Nineveh suffers. The victorious assailants are now in the city, and as the prophet foresees the struggle, he beholds a "rearing rider." During the siege the infantry played the important role; now that the walls have fallen, the charging cavalry comes into prominent action. No explanation is offered for the rearing steeds. Horses pitch and rise on their legs both in response to the bit and involuntarily from fright, excitement, or high spirits. Experienced equestrians also know that their steeds shy from corpses. Significantly, Assyrian battle scenes often feature reared chargers.

Nahum, envisioning the armies joined in battle, cries out in report, "Flaming sword and flashing spear" (lit., "and a flame of a sword and a lightning of a spear"), instruments of war brandished against Nineveh's defenders and shining with reflected light as flames of fire. The spears, whirling through the air, seem to be flashes of lightning. For similar pictures see Job 20:25; 39:23; Deut. 32:41; Ezek. 21:21; Hab. 3:11. It is uncertain whether the cavalry is still envisioned here. While Assyrian horsemen are portrayed as wielding bows and spears, they are not usually represented with swords. That weapon was prevalently used by the infantry. Apparently the prophecy here also includes the foot soldiers.

The gleaming swords have not been drawn in vain and the glittering spears not fallen short of their mark. Nor has much time been consumed in battle. The prophet sees "a host of slain and a multitude of dead bodies." Nahum does not pause to identify the dead, but no doubt remains that he describes the toll taken of the Assyrian defenders.

Even these two statements concerning the widespread slaughter are not sufficient. Surveying the battle scene once more, the sacred seer exclaims: "There is no end of the corpses; they stumble over their corpses." We may find a suggestion of ironic echo in "There is no end of their corpses," for Assyrian annals abound with statements claiming the capture of prisoners and booty "without number." The indefinite subject in both sentences helps make it difficult to decide who stumbles; yet the assumption (which seems indicated in the Hebrew) that they are the fugitive, pursued Ninevites appears better than the explanation that the victorious attackers fall over the prostrate enemies — unless, indeed, the verse pictures the whole field of battle so strewn with lifeless warriors that even the assailants' advance was impeded. In 2:6 the conquering invaders appear to stumble in their eagerness.

When Nineveh fell, the destruction of human life announced in this fourfold statement must indeed have been appalling. Viewing the entire campaign against the capital, the Babylonian chronicler interrupts his terse, objective style to record his dismay at the butchery practiced after the capture of Tarbis, a city "in the district of Nineveh." So much blood was shed here that he says the destruction was carried out *limniš*, "in an evil manner."

פָּרָשׁ means (1) "horse," 1 Sam. 8:11; Joel 2:4; Hab. 1:8; Jer. 46:4; etc., and (2) "horseman," 2 Sam. 1:6; 1 Kings 20:20; Jer. 4:29; 46:4; and many other passages. It is sometimes difficult to decide which meaning should be accepted; here, however, the causative verb and the versions indicate "horseman."

פָּרָשׁ מַעֲלֶה — This phrase, which Sel. for metrical reasons draws to v. 2, has been variously rendered. (1) AV: "The horseman lifteth up (both the bright sword and the glittering spear)." The absence of the definite article and of the *nota accusativi* seems to rule this out. Besides, it would be difficult for a horseman to brandish both sword and spear. (2) RV: "The horseman mounting." But the participle does not mean "mount" in the sense of "to lift oneself," and the action in this verse is far beyond the incipient stage of mounting (3) Lu.: "He brings riders up with." However, the subject "he" is not expressed or indicated, and the "bringing up" is vague. (4) Jnk.: "The horse is brought up." But the participle does not have the passive force. (5) Hal.: "Horses bringing up saliva," i. e., foaming horses. But עָלָה is never demonstrably used in this sense. (6) Ew.: "Assaulting horsemen"; but עָלָה, meaning "assault," requires a preposition of hostile direction. (7) Htz. and Oo.: "a horseman going up." Although supported by Ⓖ: ἱππέως ἀναβαίνοντος ("a horseman ascending"), and the Ⓥ: "equitis ascendentis," this would require עֹלֶה. (8) Jnk.: "a rider high on his horse." This assumes gratuitously that the verb is a *Hophˈal*, מְעֻלֶּה. Hst. without reason elides both words. (9) Calvin (similarly Bev.): "The horseman making his horse to ascend." Yet the horse and the horseman are not both mentioned. This translation is nevertheless quite close to the best rendition (10): "a rearing horseman" (so also Sel., Stnh.). This primary meaning of מַעֲלֶה is best served by the picture of the rider who "causes the horse to rise up." See Jer. 46:9; 51:27.

לַהַב — This denotes the flaming point of the edge of the sword (Judg. 3:22) or of the spear (Job 39:23). Ⓥ, "micantis gladii."

לִגְוִיָּה — Ⓖ, τοῖς ἔθνεσιν αὐτῆς, "to her nations," probably mistaking גְּוִיָה for גּוֹי, "nation." Du. and Ehr. unnecessarily change and ask for לַגְּבָרִים.

וְרֹב חָלָל — Ⓖ, πλήθους τραυματιῶν, "the multitude of wounds"; Ⓥ, "multitudinis interfectae."

כֹּבֶד פֶּגֶר — Ⓖ, βαρείας πτώσεως, "of heavy fall"; Ⓥ, "gravis ruinae."

יִכְשְׁלוּ — The Qerē, followed by Ries. (who regards the last two words as a gloss), wants a perfect with Waw, וְכָשְׁלוּ. However, the Kethībh, which is to be preferred (since the verb does not show independent and progressive action), asks for the imperfect without Waw, יִכְשְׁלוּ (which Sel. wants) or preferably יִכָּשְׁלוּ, 2:6, since the Qal imperfect does not otherwise occur. See, however, the Kethībh of Prov. 4:16. Ⓖ, ασθενήσουσιν, "they will be weak."

בִּגְוִיָּתָם — Some (Mrt., No., Stk., and others) drop the suffix and substitute the pl. בִּגְוִיּוֹת, under the claim that the Mem of the suffix is dittography due to the first word in v. 4. Oo. reads בִּגְוִיָּתָה, "over her body." Hal. asks for בַּעֲוֹנָם, "over their sins." None of these changes can be justified objectively. Du. omits the word, and most modern commentators remove יִכְשְׁלוּ בִּגְוִיָּתָם, declaring (with J.M.P.Sm.): "It is probable that these words are a marginal note which has found its way into the text." Two reasons are advanced for this elision: (1) the words are said to be "superfluous in the poetic form." However, this does not hold, even from the point of view maintained by critical reconstruction; for Stnh. protests: "Nor can it be said that the presence of the line interferes with the poetic form of the verse." (2) The clause introduces "a verb for the first and only time into a series of phrases thrown off in ejaculatory fashion, one after the other." Yet v. 1 contains a finite verb and v. 2 a participle. Why should the series not conclude with another verb in v. 3? Sel., in opposition to critical opinion, retains both terms (though with the change noted above). Far from rejecting the twofold occurrence of וּנְיָה (as do Du. and others), he asserts: "The repetition is, however, deliberately planned, in order to paint the gruesome picture fully." See the fourfold repetition in Amos 3:15. Ries. drops the entire final statement.

> v. 4 *Because of the many harlotries*
>   *Of the harlot fair in grace, the mistress of witchcrafts,*
>   *Who selleth nations through her harlotries*
>   *And peoples through her witchcrafts.*

The prophet, advancing to the reason for the capital's bloody, ignominious destruction, begins his indictment with: "Because of the many harlotries of the harlot." The "because" introduces the motivating element, both for the preceding verse and for the following three. Nineveh, Nahum asserts, is a harlot. The OT frequently applies this figure to Israel. In such association it denotes that nation's unfaithfulness to Yahweh, her idolatry and desertion of the true God, who is pictured as her Husband. By worshiping idols, Israel proved herself spiritually an adulteress. The point of view in this verse, however, is different. Nahum makes no mention of idolatry, and any spiritual affinity between God and Assyria is excluded. Rather does the prophet follow this line of thought: As a harlot dispenses her favors "for hire" (and that is the OT point of view, for instance, in Ezek. 16:31: "Thou . . . hast not been as an harlot, in that thou scornest hire"), so Nineveh, like a scheming prostitute, has cunningly sold her military aid to other countries, particularly to Judah, in the Syro-Ephraemitic war. As a lewd woman deceitfully displays her charms, uses enticements to deceive and ruin men, so Assyria has beguiled nations and lured them to their downfall. The idea of promiscuity and dishonesty may also be involved, as in Is. 23:17, where Tyre commits "fornication with all the kingdoms of the world upon the face of the earth," although there the emphasis is placed on Tyre's commercial activities. It may be that the showy, glamorous appearance of the harlot also symbolizes Nineveh's ostentatious display. Perhaps some emphasis is to be laid on the cruel city's end, which is to be that of an abandoned courtesan. Especially, however, does the prophet envision the ruin by which Assyria, harlotlike, has destroyed other realms, notably Ahaz' kingdom. Wherever the stress be laid, the picture is peculiarly appropriate for Nineveh because of its sensual Ishtar cult.

Lewd Nineveh is now described as "fair in grace," i. e., beauty, attraction (AV and RV, "well favored"), Prov. 11:16; 31:30. The city's magnificence, the splendor of its palaces and temples, its mighty armies, fabulous wealth, imposing art and architecture — all these are attractions which the brazen adulteress employs in luring victims to their destruction.

The prophet raises a further charge against the condemned capital. She is "the mistress of witchcrafts," that is, one who understands and employs the black arts. A similar combination of harlotry and sorcery is found in Jezebel, 2 Kings 9:22. Perhaps witchcraft is mentioned because of the philters, amulets, love potions, incantations, charms, spells, which are pictured as the harlot's stock in trade; or preferably because the Assyrians were utterly superstitious and wholly dedicated to sorcery. Archaeological investigation has proved how deservedly Nineveh could be called "mistress of witchcrafts." Thousands of tablets uncovered in the Mesopotamian valley show abysmal superstition. Hundreds of sorcery incantations have been brought to light. Astrology flourished widely as a means of foretelling the future. For the Assyrians the world was filled with omens to be found in moths, swallows, pigs, scorpions, wild oxen, sparrows, doves, cows, rats, crows, worms, dogs, hens, grasshoppers, lambs, sheep, foxes, fish, snakes, jackals. Amulets of stones, plants, bones, and insects were worn to ward off evil spirits. The formation of the clouds, the circumstances of rain and thunder, the course of birds in flight, the record of dreams, investigation of animal livers, and unusual circumstances at the birth of children or animals were considered particularly potent omens. Water, oil, and molten lead were poured and the resultant shapes interpreted. The signs of the zodiac were studied. Numbers, birds, and animals were classified as lucky or unlucky. Hideous demons ruled the fears and hopes of the Ninevites. They believed that human suffering, in whatever form it appeared, was caused by the activity of evil spirits, which took malicious initiative in plaguing their victims and which might be induced by sorcerers to assail any designated person. From the very beginning of life destructive beings menaced human happiness. *Labartu,* for example, a horrifying demon pictured as she suckles two swine, sought to destroy mothers at childbirth. *Ti'u* specialized in producing diseases, fevers, headaches. *Lilu* and *Lilitu* were malicious night spirits, male and female respectively. *Etimmu* returned from the dead to torture the living. *Namtar* was the pestilence demon, while *Akhkhazu,* the "seizer," was probably associated with jaundice. Large groups of demons, for example, *Utukku, Alu, Shedu, Gallu, Labasu, Rabisu,* and many others, were believed to practice systematic persecution of their victims. Nameless evil spirits found in living creatures, vegetation, and the elements were assiduously cultivated.

Nineveh is now indicted as the lewd witch "who selleth

nations through her harlotries." The usual explanation offered by those who retain the meaning "sell" is that the ruthless capital acquires these nations herself, i. e., robs them of their independence and brings them under her power (Deut. 32:30; Is. 50:1). Admittedly, however, the picture of Nineveh "selling the nations to herself" is unusual. Others have sought to give the verb the meaning involved in the English "to sell out," as Stnh., who suggests: "Perhaps the reference is to the way in which Assyria was ready to desert a smaller state in order to gain or retain friendly relations with a more powerful one." However, we know little in actual detail of such Assyrian policy. Still others accept a meaning which the similar verbal root has in Arabic, namely, "deceive," "cheat," "betray." It is said that "selling and cheating were somewhat closely related and may easily have been denoted by the same root." Actually, however, the verb has this force in no other passage. It is better, therefore, to retain the established sense "to sell" and to accept the statement literally, as declaring that the corrupt capital sold nations, so that their people individually became slaves to the Assyrians and others. Cuneiform records bear ample testimony to the enslavement of entire nations. Citizens of rebellious cities who were not impaled or blinded were often taken away as slaves.

In parallel indictment, the prophet continues, Nineveh sells "peoples through her witchcrafts." The picture changes somewhat and implies that by unholy means, dark, treacherous dealings, she relegates "peoples" (smaller nations or racial groups, Jer. 25:9; Ezek. 20:32; Amos 3:2) into slavery.

It should not escape attention that this representation of Nineveh pictures the capital in the full sway of her dominion. It is not a city robbed of influence, groggy after many attacks, tottering in its last stages of decrepit existence, but a world power disposing of other countries. This book thus cannot be dated after 626 or 621 B. C., when Assyria was in the weakened condition which foretold its end. The Nineveh of Nahum's day is not a senile state. Therefore only thoughtless repetition can insist, as is constantly reasserted, that while the upper time limit for the book must be the fall of Thebes, the lower limit must be the fall of Nineveh. The lower limit, viewed against the background of the entire prophecies, must be the years when Nineveh's power and might provoked the epithets which the prophet here hurls against it.

מֵרֹב — The *Mem* is causal, as in Is. 53:5; Ex. 15:23; Job 22:4. This מֵרֹב is not to be connected with the preceding verse as Ⓖ does, which gives this stuffed version: καὶ ἀσθενήσουσιν ἐν τοῖς σώμασιν αὐτῶν ἀπὸ πλήθους πορνείας, "and they shall be weak in their bodies because of the multitude of whoredoms." Hst. arbitrarily requests מְהִדְרְבוּ, "how numerous."

זְנוּנֵי — This is an abstract pl., indicating the series of individual acts, Ges., Gra., 124 *d*. It is dropped by K.-G. without explanation.

זוֹנָה — Du., with the critical approval of Hst., Sel., Stnh., Bev., and others, drops this as an erroneous repetition, to make the first part of the verse exhibit the same qînâ rhythm which the second contains. But Hebrew parallelism does not demand this.

טוֹבַת חֵן — This is the genitive of attribute, Ges., Gra., 128 *p*. Ⓖ, καλὴ καὶ ἐπίχαρις, "beautiful and pleasing." Ⓥ, "speciosae et gratae." חֵן is employed of beauty here as in Prov. 31:30; 11:16.

בַּעֲלַת כְּשָׁפִים — Cf. בַּעֲלַת אוֹב, 1 Sam. 28:7. Ⓖ, ἡγουμένη φαρμάκων, "the mistress of potions." Ⓥ, "habentis maleficia." K.-G. arbitrarily drops this designation.

הַמֹּכֶרֶת — Ⓢ, "who nourishes Babel." On the emphatic use of the article, see Ges., Gra., 126 *a*. Critics, dissatisfied with the plain form and the clear meaning, have offered הַמְשַׁכֶּרֶת.

"the one who makes drunken" (so Bu., followed by Mrt. and others), or הַכֹּמֶרֶת, "the one who ensnares" (so Hst., following K.-G. and Sel., who calls attention to מִכְמָר, "the net"), or הַמְכַתֶּרֶת, "the one who surrounds" (so alternatively Sel.). Htz., followed by v.Ho., Bev., and Jnk., assumes the meaning "one who deceives," on the basis of the Arabic root *makara,* with the same essential consonants. But as Dav.-Lan. observes, this Arabic verb is not transitive and requires a preposition. Ries., without explanation, brands this closing section of the verse a gloss.

> *v. 5 Behold, I am against thee — The oracle of Yahweh*
> *of Hosts.*
> *And I will uncover thy skirts upon thy face,*
> *And I will show nations thy nakedness*
> *And kingdoms thy shame.*

Having assumed the role of international harlot, Nineveh is to suffer a harlot's punishment. Her shameless actions will be matched by shameless exposure. This threat is introduced by the formal statement: "Behold, I am against thee — The oracle of Yahweh of Hosts," a literal restatement of the introduction to 2:14. The repetition not only implies the seriousness of the divine threat but also adds certainty to the fulfillment of its penalty. Since the Almighty has spoken twice, Nineveh is doubly doomed.

"I am against thee," Yahweh of Hosts thunders, re-affirming the inviolable principle that in the universal sway of His righteousness He can never countenance individual or national sins like those committed by Nineveh. God is against every land, no matter how wealthy, powerful, self-sufficient it may be, which disregards divine authority and tramples on human rights as the Assyrian metropolis has.

Two humiliating punishments, the consequences of the divine declaration "I am against thee," are decreed for the harlot city. The prophet announces, "I will uncover thy skirts upon thy face." The "skirts" are originally the borders, or the ends of long, flowing garments. In Ex. 28:33 f. this term is used for the "hem" of the high priest's robe. In Is. 6:1 it is reproduced as the "train" of God's garment. Uncovering the skirts really stands for uncovering what the skirts conceal. Apparently this exposure was part of the customary public disgrace decreed for harlots, and similar treatment is announced for Hosea's adulterous wife (Hos. 2:3), for unfaithful Israel (Jer. 13:26), for inconstant Jerusalem (Ezek. 16:37 ff.), for the people of Saphir in Micah 1:11. Certainly captives of war were made to endure the disgrace of nakedness. See Is. 47:2, 3 (of Babylon) and Is. 20: 2-4 (of Egypt and Ethiopia). Under either interpretation Nineveh is to suffer the identical shame which she had inflicted on others.

The extent of the uncovering has been debated because of the uncertainty attached to the phrase "upon thy face." One group of interpretations equates this with "before your face," "to your face," that is, the city of sin will witness the disgrace she is to suffer, but will be unable to prevent it. The difficulty with this rendition becomes apparent when we ask how the uncovering could take place, except to Nineveh's face. Besides, as the second portion of this verse shows, the revealing is to be made before "nations" and "kingdoms." Probably either the more drastic interpretation is to be preferred, which translates literally, "And I will uncover thy skirts upon (or over) thy face," so that Nineveh is completely uncovered and at the same time blindfolded; or the phrase is to be translated "in the front." This meaning is found in 1 Kings 6:3 ("before the temple of the house") "before the temple." Under either explanation the attention of those who gaze at the harlot city will be focused on this intimate exposure. Then that will be seen which is customarily concealed. According to Sel., the reference to the skirts shows that "harlots put on public exhibition covered their heads as mourners did, yet, unlike them, used their own filthy skirts." Neither Is. 47:3, Lam. 1:9, nor Hos. 2:12, which he cites, proves this statement.

Disgrace is added to indignity in the concluding words: "And I will show nations thy nakedness and kingdoms thy shame." Through God's retributive judgment the lands humiliated by the archharlot will behold her abject humiliation. She who disgraced others is now herself shamefully disgraced in their sight. Her fall is to be witnessed internationally — and gleefully. Evidence of the exultation which greeted Nineveh's end may be gleaned from Nabopolassar's account. Commenting on the empire's end, he writes: "As for the Assyrians, who since distant days had ruled over all the people, and with heavy yoke had brought misery to the people of the land, from the land of Akkad, I banish their feet and cast off their yoke."

נְאֻם יהוה צְבָאוֹת — Hst. drops this statement for metrical reasons, and G.A.Sm. is inclined to agree. Sel. keeps these words but says they are not to be counted metrically. Du., Stk., K.-G., and others remove צְבָאוֹת, claiming it is copied from 2:14. But if a word is to be removed because it occurs twice in six verses, much of the OT would have to be rewritten. For the repetition of יהוה צְבָאוֹת see, e. g., Amos 5:14, 15, 27; 6:8, 14.

וְגִלֵּיתִי — AV, "I will discover thy skirts." This "discover" is an archaic expression for removing a cover, here the skirt. Ⓢ, "I will throw back," is closer to the original. וְגִלֵּיתִי should be interpreted in the light of the synonymous חָשַׂף, "to peel off," "to remove," and thus "to uncover."

שׁוּלַיִךְ — This term originally denotes the hanging train or the edge of a garment, Is. 6:1; Lam. 1:9. Ⓖ, τὰ ὀπίσω σου, "your back parts"; Ⓥ, "pudenda tua."

עַל־פָּנַיִךְ — Du. boldly drops this phrase as borrowed from Jer. 13:26 and makes other changes to bring the line into conformity with the *qînā* measure, but Sel. insists that it must be retained for the same reason.

הַרְאֵיתִי — On the form, see Ges., Gra., 53 *p.*

מַעְרֵךְ — Ⓖ, τὴν αἰσχύνην σου, "your shame"; Ⓥ, "nuditatem tuam." The Hebrew word is derived from עָרָה, which, as its related forms in the Semitic languages show, denotes the condition of (or action resulting in) emptiness, nakedness. The absolute state מַעַר does not occur in the OT. The construct is found in 1 Kings 7:36, probably denoting "empty space."

> *v. 6 And I will cast abominations on thee, and I will make thee vile,*
> *And I will place thee as a gazingstock.*

The punishment of the arrogant harlot involves more than exposure and disgrace. The divine threat continues, "I will cast abominations on thee." Here, as frequently in prophetic writings, God ascribes to Himself action which He entrusts to others. Through His agents, her enemies, harlotrous Nineveh will be pelted with detestable things, "abominable filth" (AV and RV). The Hebrew term, often found as a designation of idols, here denotes that which is vile and repulsive. It has been conjectured that prostitutes were treated with such public derision. Whether or not this was customary, the sense of the verse is this: to express their hatred of the harlot city, her enemies will throw at her any loathsome object on which they can lay hand. A similar picture occurs in Mal. 2:3: "Behold, I will corrupt your seed and spread dung upon your faces, even the dung of your solemn feasts." See also 2 Kings 10:27.

In this way God threatens, "I will make thee vile." Struck by these nauseating objects, Nineveh, haughty, arrogant, now captive, has been vilified (the action is stronger than that indicated by the same verb in Deut. 32:15; Micah 7:6; Jer. 14:21; 16:18; it here means "to treat with vileness") before the world. She now experiences the fulfillment of the concluding threat, "I will place thee as a gazingstock," a warning example. Assyrian kings often paraded their captives. Sargon records that he exposed Mutallu, son of a rebel, to public gaze (*Annals,* 1. 210). Ashurbanipal recounts: "I put him [Daite] into a kennel with jackals and dogs. I tied him up and made him guard the gate in Nineveh" (Rassam Cylinder, col. VIII, 11 f.). The haughty city will suffer what she made others endure. Again he states: "I cut off the lips (and) took them [Elamites] to Assyria as a spectacle for the people of my land" (Rassam Cylinder, col. IV, 135 ff.). People will behold Nineveh, gaze on her as a spectacle of derision, and know that God's sovereign will has been executed in her destruction. It is a special mark of divine wrath that nations are not only despised but also in their downfall become memorials to the Almighty's anger and a gazingstock to their enemies. In Ezek. 28:17 Tyre and Sidon are threatened with the same punishment. In Obad. 12:13 Edom is rebuked for having "looked on" Israel's affliction.

This prediction was not without fulfillment. Even before the site of Nineveh was identified, people in the vicinity knew the ruins as the remains of a people whom Zeus himself had deprived of their senses. See Xenophon, *Anabasis,* III, 4, 10—12. Modern travelers have likewise commented on the dismal desolation which now reigns at Nineveh.

שִׁקֻּצִים — As the derivation from שָׁקַץ ("to make an object of disgust," "to despise") indicates, שִׁקּוּץ, the sing., denotes an object of loathing, anything filthy, abominable. The pl. is found predominantly in connection with idols but does not necessarily denote them. It is usually found with suffixes. For its occurrence see Deut. 29:16; 2 Kings 23:24; Is. 66:3; etc. The pl. may be intensive in the sense of "utter abomination." Ⓖ has βδελυγμόν, the sing., as does Ⓢ. Because of the prevailing association with idolatry, Kl. translates, "I will cast (thine) idols upon thee," that is, "I will bury thee under thine idols." For this meaning, however, we would expect a stronger verb and the pronominal suffix. Hap. unjustifiably drops this term as a gloss on the next word.

וְנִבַּלְתִּיךְ — Ⓖ offers κατὰ τὰς ἀκαθαρσίας σου, "on account of thine impurities." Codex ℵ Original has ἁμαρτίας, "sins." Ⓥ, "contumeliis te afficiam." Because Ⓖ and Ⓥ (partially) have a noun, Hap. reads נְבֵלָתַיִךְ, "thy carcasses." Du. wants נַבְלֻתֵךְ, "thy nakedness." Ries. asks for כְּנִבְלָתַיִךְ, "according to thy shameful acts." Hpt. Hst., and others omit this word as a gloss. But no uncertainties of the text exist to suggest or support any of these changes.

כְּרֹאִי — This is a pausal form for כְּרֹאִי. The כ is the *Kaph veritatis,* meaning (Ges., Gra., 118 *x*) "in every respect like." Without any cogent reason Stnh. and J.M.P.Sm. drop the כ as "dittography of the preceding *Kaph.*" The first *Kaph,* however, is a *littera finalis* and would hardly provoke dittography. The term is used first of all to designate the act of seeing, Gen. 16:13; then it serves as an equivalent of מַרְאֶה "appearance," 1 Sam. 16:12; Job 33:21. Here, however, it implies a "gazingstock," "a spectacle of warning." Ⓖ (similarly Ⓢ and Ⓥ) offers εἰς παράδειγμα, "precedent," "example."

> *v. 7   And it will come to pass that everyone who sees thee*
> *will flee from thee*
> *And will say: "Nineveh is laid waste.*
> *Who will mourn for her?"*
> *Whence can I seek comforters for thee?*

The picture of Nineveh, naked and besmirched, will be revolting in the extreme. Therefore the prophet, employing the dirge measure, predicts: "It will come to pass that everyone who sees thee will flee from thee." Those who chance to pass by will gaze for the moment and then hurry from the site of the devastated capital. The city, whose magnificence and wealth were unequaled, will become so loathsome in its ruins that people will hasten from it as a ghastly, pestilential horror. Ps. 31:11 presents a similar picture.

As they betake themselves away, these distracted travelers "will say, Nineveh is laid waste!" The total collapse of the swaggering city provokes an exclamation of astonishment and joy (3:19) on the part of all who know her fate. The well-nigh impossible has happened: "Nineveh is" — not merely defeated or captured, but "laid waste," with a shocking, shattering curse.

"Who will mourn for her?" each passer-by (or the prophet) asks, implying in rhetorical question that no one will bemoan the fate of the oppressive capital. She drops out of history, friendless and unwept, because her calculated cruelties had irreconcilably estranged her victims. Cf. Is. 51:19; Jer. 15:5.

Nahum, predicting the exultant refrain of those who have beheld Nineveh's collapse, resumes the record of his own feelings to emphasize the widespread hatred which marked the city's end. "Whence can I seek comforters for thee?" he says, apostrophizing the crime-laden city. As in the previous instance, we hear no answer to this question, for no one will show her pity. The rapacity and violence practiced by the tyrant mistress on the

Tigris have alienated everyone who could comfort her in this agony. Lam. 1:2, 9.

יָדוֹד, from נָדַד, with the usual assimilation of the נ. For this form see Ges., Gra., 67 cc. The tense would normally be a perfect consecutive after וְהָיָה; but Ges., Gra., 112 y, shows that frequently verbs in this position may take the impf. Ⓖ reads καταβήσεται, "will descend" (Codex A adds ἀπό σου, "from you"); Freer, ἀποπηδήσεται, "will leap away"; Σ, ἀναχωρήσει, "will draw back." Ⓥ, "resiliet."

מִמֵּךְ is elided by K.-G. as metrically superfluous.

וְאָמַר — The remainder of the verse introduced by this word is regarded as a gloss by Ries., who, however, gives no reason.

שָׁדְּדָה for the more normal שֻׁדְּדָה, Ges., Gra., 52 q. See Nah. 2:4; Is. 15:1. Ⓖ, δειλαία, "wretched." Ehr. asks for שְׁדֻדָה, "destroyed," used as a vocative.

נִינְוֵה is removed by Stk. as "metrically superfluous," also by Ehr.

יָנוּד — The basic meaning is "to move to and fro"; in a secondary sense, perhaps from the picture of shaking the head to and fro in a gesture of sorrow, it means "to show sympathy," Is. 51:19; Jer. 15:5; 48:17; Job 2:11; 16:4; 42:11.

לָהּ — Ⓥ, Ⓢ, Ⓣ, and some Ⓜ and Ⓖ MSS, followed by many critics, have the equivalent of the second person לָךְ. Perhaps this betrays the mistaken intention of securing agreement with the last word in the verse. Ries., without offering any reason, drops vv. 7 b and c.

מְנַחֲמִים — The versions frequently have the sing. Ⓖ, παράκλησιν, "comfort"; (ⒼA, παρακλήσεις); Ⓥ, "consolatorem," "comforter." Ⓢ reads similarly.

לָךְ — Ⓖ changes to the third person αὐτῇ, as though Ⓜ originally read לָהּ. Many modern interpreters make this alteration without MS authority and at the cost of reducing the dramatic force of the verse. Stnh. decrees: "The change of person is awkward: in both cases we must read either the third person or else the second." This demand for strict conformity is contradicted by Ges., Gra., 144 *p,* which observes: "In poetic (or prophetic) language there sometimes occurs . . . a more or less abrupt transition from one person to another. . . . From the third to the second pers., Deut. 32:15; Is. 5:8; Jer. 29:19; Job 16:7."

> *v. 8 Art thou better than No of Amon*
> *That {was} situated on the rivers?*
> *Water {was} round about her*
> *So that a sea {was} a rampart;*
> *Her wall {was} from the sea.*

In this and the following two verses the prophet taunts those who may have questioned his prediction of the Assyrian capital's inevitable end, by calling attention to the startling devastation which had recently swept over one of the most advantageously situated, best-fortified cities in the world of that day. By contrast he then implies that Nineveh's defense against the coming attack is far inferior, hence its capitulation the more certain.

Nahum begins this section with another question: "Art thou better than No of Amon?" The whole context emphasizes that he does not stress moral or political superiority but the advantages of strategic location. His question is rhetorical and implies a negative answer. No of Amon was Thebes, known to the Assyrians as *Ni'u* and to the Greeks as Διὸς πόλις, often with the addition "the great," the capital and metropolis of upper Egypt. Significantly, Thebes was called "the city" in Egyptian records. Situated 140 miles north of the first cataract at Syene (Assuan), it is represented today by the impressive ruins (temples, obelisks, sphinxes, palaces) of Karnak and Luxor, as by the destroyed residences at Kurna and Medinet Habu on the opposite, or western, side of the river. The city proper was originally built on the eastern bank of the Nile, but suburbs spread out on both shores. Its beginnings are lost in antiquity; but it rose to prominence as the capital of the eighteenth dynasty (about 2100 B. C.), when Aahmes I, founder of this dynasty, enlarged and embellished the city. Its splendor at that time and during the two succeeding dynasties is attested by the present-day remains. Its temples and palaces are said to have "found no equal in antiquity." They are called "the mightiest ruins of ancient civilization to be found anywhere in the world." Homer speaks of its wealth, its one hundred gates, its well-equipped cavalry. It was probably the first city of the Nile Valley — a leading center of Egyptian civilization. The comparison with Nineveh is, therefore, more striking. The Hebrew term *No*, with or without *Āmon* (Ezek. 20:14 ff.; Jer. 46:25), probably is a Hebraized form for the Egyptian "City of Amon." [1] He, god of Egypt at the time of the eighteenth dynasty, was the tutelary divinity of Thebes, the head of the pantheon in the territory influenced by that city, where he displaced the successor of Ra.

First No of Amon is described as a city "that was situated on the rivers," the branches of the Nile; for opposite the city the great stream, which at this point is about half a mile wide, is divided into four channels by three islands, especially at low water.

Again, the Egyptian metropolis had "water round about her." Some, supposing that this encircling water came from the annual inundation of the Nile, share the view of J.M.P.Sm.:

---

[1] No, the first part of the compound name, reproduced in Assyrian as *Ni'u*, may be derived from the older Egyptian *Nwt*, that is, "city," often denoting the capital. The second part, Amon (Assyrian *Amanu*), is Amon, head of the Theban pantheon. The AV "populous No" is based on a medieval interpretation of "Amon" as "multitude."

"When the Nile rises, it overflows the site of Thebes, the waters ascending several feet on the walls of the Temple at Karnak. At such times, the city might well have been described as protected by a sea, or surrounded by waters." It is not likely, however, that Thebes in all its glory was unprotected against flood; nor do we expect the prophet to generalize from an abnormal, seasonal appearance. Doubtless Nahum refers to the moats, canals, and channels about most of the city. These were helpful as diversion outlets at the time of the spring overflow, but they constituted a permanent protection at all times. Dav.-Lan. objects: "Thebes does not appear to have been surrounded by water"; but Nahum speaks generally, without implying that No of Amon was an island. Besides, present-day travelers see traces of many moats at the site of Thebes. The convenient higher critical verdict that these words are a gloss is thus disproved and the force of patronizing statements like this removed: "Allowance must be made for the fact that Nahum had almost certainly never seen Thebes and consequently was dependent for his information upon the reports of merchants and travelers. Under such conditions, a certain degree of exaggeration in the description is excusable and to be expected" (J.M.P.Sm.). Why is it almost certain that Nahum never saw Thebes and that his information had to be gleaned from merchants and travelers? Which of his statements is exaggerated? Yet Dr. similarly contends that Nahum was unaware of the city's topography, and Jnk. makes the utterly unjustified assertion: "In the description of the city it should be noted that Nahum hardly knew the place from personal observation and perhaps had no one at hand for information who had personally seen it. He knew that it lay on the Nile; and using his phantasy, freely he pictured her situation after the pattern of the Delta fortifications which were better known in Palestine than the cities of upper Egypt." It should be evident from Nahum's presentation, however, that he was well informed regarding the major factors in No-Amon's situation. His words contain nothing fantastic. Yet Spiegelberg *Aegyptische Randglossen zum alten Testament,* does not hesitate to declare: "One can scarcely imagine a more perverted picture of ancient Thebes than is here presented. Whoever familiarizes himself with the topography of Thebes as represented by the Karnak and Luxor of our own day must acknowledge that Nahum's description is in no way fitting. The famous capital lay on the Nile, like all great Egyptian towns, but it is simply unthinkable that it could have been strategically protected either by the river or by canals." Aside from the fact that the lower Egyptian Thebes which he would substitute was relatively insignificant and not the city to which Nahum refers, Spiegelberg's (and others') brash criticism of Nahum's statements is not borne out by an investigation of Thebes' location. The wide Nile, with its islands, the Karnak channel on the right bank and the Fadiliyah channel on the left, literally flanked portions of the city. If in addition the other channels, of which traces remain, are taken into account, No of Amon was unusually well defended by water.

So well was the Egyptian city protected "that a sea was a rampart." The phrase is often translated "whose strength was the sea," but that is not the prophet's point of view, nor does the Hebrew original offer any support for this rendition. If the text is interpreted as it stands, it means that the sea itself was a rampart in the city's defense. To understand the pointed picture involved, it must be emphasized that the word for "rampart" denotes the smaller, outer wall before the great city wall. At Thebes, Nahum declares, the first defense before the walls of the city was "the sea." By rather general consent it is agreed that "the sea" (*"yām"*) is an expansive term for the Nile itself. The river Nile to the present day in Egypt is called *al-bahr,* the sea. See also Is. 18:2; 19:5. Similarly the Euphrates is called the "sea" in Is. 27:1 and Jer. 51:36.

The outer line of defense, then, as the prophet describes No of Amon, was the Nile, the moats and the canals. "Her wall," the city's second protection, Nahum says, "was from the sea." It rose from the very edge of these waters. Hitherto overlooked in this connection is the fact that Amenhotep III built an artificial lake about a mile long and more than a thousand feet wide outside the city and that the large embankment erected to restrain the waters is still evident. This lake, perhaps also regarded as "the sea," would indeed be a formidable barrier against advancing enemies. The lake, with walls arising at its edge, may have been part of a fortification system, so that Nahum would be literally correct also in asserting that "her wall was from the sea."

The prophet has thus drawn a forceful parallel between the two cities. Nineveh, he implies, has boasted that it is more advantageously located even than No of Amon. Sennacherib, for example, exalts Nineveh in these words, which boastingly infer the city's unshakable and eternal firmness: "Nineveh, the noble metropolis, the city beloved of Ishtar, wherein are all the meeting-places of god and goddesses; the everlasting substructure, the eternal foundation; whose plan had been designed from of old, and whose structure had been made beautiful along with the firmament of heaven." [2] Yet, as a matter of fact, while the Egyptian metropolis was situated on the rivers, the Tigris at best touched Nineveh only at one point. Portions of No of Amon were almost surrounded by water, but the moats at Nineveh did not offer comparably expansive protection. No of Amon, with the Nile as a rampart, also had walls which started from the edge of the river, while Nineveh's outer walls had not been completed. Therefore Nahum's rhetorical question, "Art thou better [situated] than No of Amon?" and its implied negative answer led to the assumption that if the Egyptian city with its remarkable defenses fell, then Nineveh cannot expect to escape.

---

[2] British Museum tablet 103,000, col. V, 23—28, after Luckenbill, *The Annals of Sennacherib*.

תֵּיטְבִי — This form is anomalous. It has the first *Tsere* syllable of the *Hiph"il,* but is followed by the *Shewa* of the *Qal.* With Ges., Gra., 70 *e,* it is best parsed as a *Qal,* equivalent to תִּיטְבִי. This does not mean that the vocalization should be changed. Bev. misunderstands the force of the verb, insisting that it must be translated, "Shalt thou fare better?" Similarly Dav.-Lan. proposes, "Shall it go better with thee?" which, however, would require the addition of the personal pronoun. Ehr. changes this to "Wilt thou outlive [No-Amon]?" But No-Amon was destroyed long before this. Ries. proposes for this and the following word מִתְיַטְּבִים אֶנָּה, "they sing a dirge" — yet no explanation is offered.

נֹא אָמוֹן — This city, mentioned in four other OT passages, appears in this form only here. In Jer. 46:25 the word order is reversed, אָמוֹן מִנֹּא. Three times in Ezek. (30:14-16) it occurs simply as נֹא. The versions are peculiarly variant and contradictory. In the three Ezek. passages Ⓖ offers Διόσπολις, identifying the city as Diospolis Magna, Thebes, the capital of upper Egypt. Here in Nahum Ⓖ inflates its version to ἑτοιμάσαι μερίδα, ἁρμόσαι χορδήν, ἑτοιμάσαι μερίδα, Ἀμμών, "prepare a part, fit a cord, prepare a part, O Amon!" Many Greek variants occur, due to a misunderstanding of מִנֹּא. Lu. proposes, "No, du Künstlerin," derived from אָמוֹן, "artisan." The independent Greek versions, Aq., Σ, and Θ, are agreed in offering the equivalent of "Art thou better than Amon?" Ⓥ reads: "Numquid es melior Alexandria populorum?" Ⓢ asks: "Art thou better than Javan the Amonite?"

Despite all this, no doubt should remain concerning the integrity of Ⓜ, nor as to the location of No of Amon. Nevertheless Ries. drops אָמוֹן without explanation.

יְאֹרִים — Hpt. holds that this pl. is intensive. J.M.P.Sm. regards it as a pl. of majesty, while Stnh. decides that the pl. is "a characteristic designation of the Nile," a claim for which Is. 7:18, cited in substantiation, offers no support. These explanations of the pl. are unnecessary, if it is assumed, as above, that the actual plurality of river courses is described.

מַיִם סָבִיב לָהּ — This nominal sentence (Ges., Gra., 156 *a*) is attacked by Wllh., K.-G., and many others, who hold with Stnh.: "These words should probably be omitted as a gloss . . .; they come in somewhat disjointedly and interrupt the rhythmical flow of the v." However, this sentence must remain, for the prophet is determined to show No of Amon's vastly superior position. It is surrounded by water — an advantage of which Nineveh could not boast. Far from being disjointed, the statement adds a necessary factor in the prophet's presentation.

אֲשֶׁר — This is not to be dropped with Du. It is used here in the consecutive sense, as "so that," Gen. 13:16; Mal. 3:19. See Ges., Gra., 165 *b*.

חֵיל — Most critics follow Wllh. in affixing a suffix, reading חֵילָהּ "her wall," and translating, "whose wall was the sea." The picture is stronger, however, when Ⓜ is retained and translated, "so that a sea was a wall." The Ⓖ mistranslation ἀρχή, "beginning," is probably based on a wrong association with חָלַל, "to begin" *(Hiph"il)*.

מִיָּם — This is not to be changed into וּמַיִם (Ⓖ, καὶ ὕδωρ; similarly Ⓢ, Ⓥ, Lu., most critics). The preposition מִן is not used of material (Keil), but of origin or direction, "arising out of the sea."

> *v. 9* Ethiopia {was} her strength, and Egypt; and there
>   was no end {to it}.
>   Put and Libyans
>   Were among thy help.

No of Amon was not only impregnably situated, it was supported by notable military alliances and the almost limitless resources of confederated countries. "Ethiopia [was] her strength, and Egypt," Nahum recalls. "Ethiopia" is the comprehensive name for the territory and kingdom south of Syene (Assuan), embracing parts of the Sudan, Nubia, and Ethiopia proper, for many years called Abyssinia. It enjoyed independence since about 1000 B. C. The twenty-fifth, or Ethiopian, dynasty under Tandamani subdued all the Nile territory, and about 712 B. C. the conqueror, Pharaoh Sabako, established his capital at Napata in Upper Egypt. Thebes, as a center of the Ethiopian empire and its chief city, could depend on the strength of the armies mustered by the entire domain. This independent national existence of the Ethiopians helps account for Nahum's separate mention of Egypt in the restricted sense of the northern territory as distinguished from Ethiopia (Kush) in the south.[3] Not only was the power of Kush (Upper Egypt) available, but also the resources of North Egypt, subjugated by Kush, could be drafted for battle against No of Amon's enemy. The military supplies, the manpower, the native strength of the Nile country, north and south, were so vast that the prophet asserts, "There was no end to it." (Is. 2:7)

Besides Ethiopia and Egypt, two other countries are listed in the formidable array of allies who served No of Amon. "Put and Libyans were among thy help," the prophet declares, now addressing the Ethiopian capital. The exact location of *Put* (Gen. 10:6; 1 Chron. 1:8; Jer. 46:9; Ezek. 27:10; 30:5; 38:5) still remains problematical. It has been identified as Libya, on

[3] J.M.P.Sm., in objecting to this separate mention of Egypt, declares: "The inclusion of Egypt among the resources of Thebes, the capital of Egypt, seems gratuitous and the list seems designated to give the external helpers who co-operated with Egypt. . . . It seems safe to omit 'and Egypt' . . . (as well as 'and there was no end') as due to a glossator." But Thebes was not the capital of Egypt at this time, nor does the text offer the slightest indication that the prophet is desirous of listing only foreign help. If objection is taken to the separate mention of Ethiopia and Egypt, the cuneiform records themselves must be charged with inaccuracy, since Ashurbanipal, for instance, repeatedly mentions *Musur* (Egypt) and *Kûsi* (Ethiopia) together, as Nahum does here. See, for example, *Annals* (Rassam Cylinder), col. I, 53, 67, 78, 114; col. II, 28, 45.

the basis of the claim that Ⓖ reproduces this term with "Libya," that the Coptic name for the western territory in Lower Egypt is the consonantally related Phaiat, and that Josephus and Greek writers know a river Phut in Mauritania. None of these arguments is decisive, for Ⓖ often varies its translation, offering "Libyana" only in the poetic books. The Coptic is late, and Josephus' river need not specify territory. Besides, Nahum's mention of "Put and Libyans" involves a differentiation which appears to rule out every identification. Most probably Put is the Red Sea coast country as far south as the Somaliland. In favor of this we note the resemblance in name of the Biblical "Put" and the "Punt," the Egyptian designation for the East African country. This location seems to harmonize in a general way with other Scriptural references. In the Table of Nations (Gen. 10:6) Put is a Hamitic country, grouped, as here, with Ethiopia and Egypt. Put is likewise connected with Ethiopia in the other OT passages. See Jer. 46:9; Ezek. 30:5; 38:5.

The last of No-Amon's allies were the Lûbhîm (Dan. 11:43; 2 Chron. 12:3; 16:8), the Libyans (perhaps the same as the Lehābîm, Gen. 10:13; 1 Chron. 1:11), the inhabitants, generally, of the territory west of Egypt. The exact extent of their domain, as well as the early history of these people, who gave their name to this territory, is uncertain. All these mighty people in Upper and Lower Egypt, East and West Egypt, Nahum declares, suddenly addressing No-Amon, "were among thy help," that is, the impregnable capital could count them as allies ready to come to its aid. With coalition of these neighboring nations, Thebes indeed felt itself secure.

עָצְמָה is from עָצַם, "strength," as Deut. 8:17; Job 30:21; Is. 40:29; 47:9. The pronominal suffix of the third person sing. fem., to which the versions testify (Ⓖ, ἰσχὺς αὐτῆς, "her strength," and Ⓥ, "fortitudo eius") is co tained in the present Ⓜ reading, since the suffix הָ stands for the more usual הָ. This is explained in Ges., Gra., 91 e, which states that the suffix הָ‑ appears as הֶ‑ "repeatedly before *bᵉghadhkᵉphath* and other soft consonants." Therefore it is not necessary to follow Or., No., and many others, in changing the text to the more normal form. Nor is there any justification for Ehr.'s substitution of עֲצֻמָה, "numerous."

וְאֵין קֵצֶה — This qualifying clause (a favorite with Nahum; see 2:10; 3:3; also Is. 2:7) has been deleted as a gloss by Hpt., Stk., J.M.P.Sm., and others. The last named does not pause to offer an explanation for this decision. Ries. wants וְאוֹן in place of וְאֵין and קְצִינֵי for קֵצֶה to secure the reading: "Kush was her strength [and Egypt and On]; the princes of Put and the Lubim were her helpers." Yet, again without explanation, he denies the originality of the words in brackets.

מִצְרַיִם — Mrt. drops this, while J.M.P.Sm. and others, following Hpt., omit the next two words.

פוּט — (V), "Africa"; (G), τῆς φυγῆς, "of the flight." It has been conjectured that this rests on a misreading of פוּט as פוּץ, "to disperse." However, a confusion with פָּלַט, "to escape in flight," would be closer. Du. prefixes a connective *Waw* to פוּט; Mrt. a לְ, reading: "There is no end to Put"; and Hap. another לְ, changing the form to read לִפְלֵטָה, and dropping קֵצֶה. Thus he secures: "and there is no escape." These changes are entirely subjective and destitute of MS authority.

בְּעֶזְרָתֵךְ — (G), βοηθοὶ αὐτῆς (similarly (S)) brings the easier "her" and alters the noun to "helpers." This change of person (which significantly is not followed by (G)ᴬ) has been accepted by a preponderance of critics, who read בְּעֶזְרָתָהּ. It is unnecessary to alter the text, since this abrupt change of person is for emphasis. The prefixed בְּ may be the *Beth essentiae,* "in thy help," i. e., in the character and company of thy help, Ex. 18:4; Prov. 3:26 (see Ges., Gra., 119 *i*), or it may be simply local. It is unnecessary to draw the distinction suggested by J.M.P.Sm., who maintains that the abstract word for "help" is used here because it might "include all kinds of resources," while the concrete "helpers" would be limited. However, the term עֶזְרָה is by no means exclusively abstract; it has the concrete connotation in Is. 31:2; Ps. 27:9; 46:2.

> *v. 10 Even she went into exile in captivity.*
> *Even her babies were dashed to pieces at the head*
> *of all streets.*
> *And for her nobles they cast a lot,*
> *And all her mighty ones were bound in chains.*

The prophet now comes to the climax of his excursus on No-Amon. Despite the advantages of her natural location, the security of her walls, the strength of allied Ethiopia, Egypt, Put, and Libya, she came to an ignominious end.

A few details of her infamous finale are enumerated. Nahum begins, "Even she went into exile in captivity." The prophet does not pause to describe the attack strategy by which Thebes fell. He records only the final catastrophe: this opulent, well-fortified, widely allied city was overcome and her people sent captive into ignominious exile.[4]

We now have the original Assyrian records describing in detail the conquest of Thebes. After several delays, Ashurbanipal set out for Egypt on a punitive expedition. He swept over the delta cities, leaving a horrifying trail of fire, ruin, and death. In many cases those who refused to acknowledge his overlordship

[4] For many years the defeat of Thebes was labeled by some critics as Biblical fiction. Kuenen, Dutch contemporary of Robertson Smith and Julius Wellhausen, sought to discredit the truth of Nahum's account by asserting that no ancient historian mentions this conquest. He insisted that the unbroken continuity of Egyptian and Assyrian records neither left time for this destruction nor even made reference to it. As in many other instances, higher criticism spoke prematurely. Some of the most significant reversals of critical opinion necessitated by the archaeological advances are summarized by Walter A. Maier in "Archaeology, the Nemesis," *Concordia Theological Monthly* (1933), IV, 95 ff.

were flayed alive and their skins bleached on the city walls, while large numbers of others were impaled. At Memphis the deltaic overlords acknowledged his sovereignty, with the exception of perfidious Tanut-Amen. Driven relentlessly from one refuge to another, Tanut-Amen reached Thebes; yet instead of making a stand within its well-protected fortifications, the fear of Assyrian vengeance gripping his heart, he abandoned the city to its doom and fled. into the almost inaccessible hideouts of Ethiopia. Descending in swift marches, Ashurbanipal's armies soon gathered before Thebes. Resistance was futile, and the proud city, whose victorious armies had spread wide consternation, fell victim to the terror of the revenge-crazed Assyrians. Ashurbanipal's own account is concise. He says: "That city (Thebes) in its entirety, my hands conquered [with] the help of Ashur (and) Ishtar. . . . [Sil]ver, gold, precious stones, the goods of his [Tanut-Amen's] palace, all there was, brightly colo[red] (and) linen garments, great horses, [the people] men and women, two tall obelisks fashioned of glittering electrum, whose wei[ght] was 2500 talents . . . [I re]moved from the[ir] positions and to[ok] off to Assyria. Booty, heavy (and) [countless, I carried away] fr[om The]bes."[5] Convinced that he could not properly govern a city with the dimensions and traditions of Thebes from a capital as far removed as Nineveh, Ashurbanipal resorted to well-planned savagery. He made the razing of Thebes so complete and terrifying that the very recollection of his dealings with the perfidious city would help prevent further uprisings. His procedure, then, was that implied by Nahum. The city leveled with the ground, the people of No-Amon went into exile. They were not merely deported — they were made captive.

Not all the Theban population was led into exile. It frequently proved difficult to transport infants, sickly children,

[5] *Annals*, col. II, 28—37 (Edition B) in A. C. Piepkorn, *Historical Prism Inscriptions of Ashurbanipal*, 1933.

orphaned babies; and it was part of the Assyrian terror program to deal with such infants in the manner here described: "Even her babies were dashed to pieces." The usual purpose of this bestial practice, of course, was to exterminate the whole future population. Such unbelievable barbarity was not infrequent. It is mentioned, e. g., in Hos. 10:14; 13:16 (as punishment for Samaria); in Is. 13:16, 18 and Ps. 137:9 (Babylon); in 2 Kings 8:12 (Israel).

This shocking massacre of children occurred "at the head of all streets," probably the concourse of several thoroughfares, where the atrocity would be more spectacular and could be witnessed by larger groups. Perhaps people were wont to congregate there. See Is. 51:20; Lam. 2:19; 4:1.

Turning now from the helpless infants to the social antipole in No-Amon, the nobility, the prophet declares, "For her nobles they cast a lot." While the common people were taken captive en masse, the upper classes, valued more highly because of their position, education, and training, were awarded to individual conquerors by lot. This practice likewise was widespread throughout the Orient and is attested by Joel 3:3, indirectly by Obad. 11. The Assyrians themselves are on record as indulging in this practice of gambling with human lives.

Besides suffering the indignity of being awarded by lot, "all her mighty ones were bound in chains." The fettering of noble captives is widely attested. See Is. 45:15 ("men of stature" in Egypt, Ethiopia, and Sabea); Jer. 40:1, 4 (Jeremiah, of royal blood); Ps. 149:8 (the kings and nobles among the heathen); Judg. 16:21 (Samson); 2 Kings 25:7 (Zedekiah). The monumental representations by the Assyrians feature prisoners in bonds. Thus, the prophet recounts, did the apparently impregnable No of Amon disappear.

The commonly accepted time for this destruction of Thebes has been placed between the years 664 and 662 B. C. Assyrian chronology prefers the latter date and Egyptian the former. However, Prism F of Ashurbanipal's *Annals* seems to put the second Egyptian campaign in which Thebes was captured in the Resh-Sharruti, the beginning of Ashurbanipal's reign, 668—667 B. C.

The record of Thebes' devastation helps inferentially in dating these prophecies. Against earlier conjectures (made before the publication of Ashurbanipal's *Annals*) predicating an eighth-century date, the book must definitely be placed after the beginning of the second third of the seventh century. However, no justice is done the claims of the prophecies if a date shortly before 612 or 625 B. C. is hypothesized. Had a half century intervened between the destruction of Thebes and the prophet's reference to that event, his argument would have lost much of its force and vivid application. Besides (as even critics concede), the internal conditions of Assyria or Judah itself, as pictured here by Nahum and secular sources, were not those of the last quarter of the seventh century.

גַּם — Sel. reproduces this with "nevertheless" and finds this usage in Ps. 129:2; Job 18:5.

הִיא — Du. arbitrarily asks for הָיְתָה.

לַגֹּלָה — Ehr. objects that Hebrew does not say לַגֹּלָה but בַּגֹּלָה when used with הָיַד. Therefore he changes לַגֹּלָה to כֻּלָּה, "all of her." He also maintains that this justifies the presence of בַּשְּׁבִי, which would otherwise be lame and superfluous. However, it is possible to construe לַגֹּלָה with הִיא (not with יָהֵלַד) and to translate, "She was for exile" (הָיָה with לְ in the sense of "to become something," Gen. 2:7, 24; 17:4; 18:18; Ex. 4:4; Is. 1:22). Even if הִרְכָּה is construed with לַגֹּלָה, the translation "to go into exile" may be justified, though five other passages have בְּ. Nor is the use of גֹּלָה and שְׁבִי redundant, as Ehr. implies, for the two words are coupled in Ezra 2:1; Neh. 7:6. Ehr.'s substitution, כֻּלָּה, is a pure guess and suffers from the disadvantage of placing a third כֹּל into the verse.

הָלְכָה — Ⓖ, πορεύσεται, "will go." The perfect was likewise regarded as prophetic by Theodoret, Cyril, and others.

בְּשְׁבִי — Ⓖ, αἰχμάλωτος, "captured." Ⓢ omits this.

יְרֻטְּשׁוּ — Ⓖ, ἐδαφιοῦσιν, "they will dash to earth." Wllh., followed by many others, demands a perfect, רֻטְּשׁוּ, here and throughout the remainder of the verse. Nevertheless Ges., Gra., 107 *b,* shows that the imperfect may be employed in the sphere of past time to express action continued through a longer or shorter period of time, "very frequently alternating with the perfect." Perhaps the prophet visualizes the exile as a unified action, but the killing of the infants as a repeated, protracted procedure. For a similar occurrence of the imperfect after the perfect, see Ex. 15:12, נָטִיתָ יְמִינְךָ תִּבְלָעֵמוֹ אָרֶץ, "Thou stretchedst out [perfect] Thy right hand, the earth swallowed [imperfect] them." Here the imperfect "represents the Egyptians in a vivid, poetic description, as being swallowed up one after another." This usage indicates that actions which appear to have a single historical occurrence "are, as it were, broken up by the imperfect into their component parts" (Ges., Gra., loc. cit.). Even J.M.P.Sm. concedes that Wllh.'s "change is unnecessary; a vivid imperfect lends variety to the description."

כָּל־ — Sel. finds that this disturbs the meter. Following Ⓖ, he places it before וְכָּבְּדֵיהָ, "where it is metrically necessary," although it is found in its present position in all MSS.

וְעַל — Ⓖ adds πάντα. Du., K.-G., G.A.Sm., Stnh., Sel. accept this, "because this reading is favored by the rhythm" (Stnh.).

יַדּוּ — This is impersonal. See Ges., Gra., 146 *c,* for this construction and 69 *u* for the form. This is the regular perfect *Qal* of יָדַד. The same form occurs in Obad. 11 and Joel 4:3. Ges., Hwb., suggests that probably יַדּוּ should be read, from the related root יָדָה, "to throw."

וְכָל־גְּדוֹלֶיהָ — Mrt. and Hpt. omit this כָּל־ against MS and versional authority. Du. inserts an unproved גַּם before כָּל־ and is followed by Sel.

רֻתְּקוּ — This is the only occurrence of the verb רתק; however, the meaning "to put into bonds" is clear from the related Arabic and New Hebrew, as well as its derivative noun רַתּוֹק, "chain," 1 Kings 6:21; Is. 40:19.

בַּזִּקִים — The definite article, "bound in *the* chains," probably specifies the definite fetters which the prophet envisions, Ges., Gra., 126 *g*. This noun occurs otherwise only in Is. 45:14; Ps. 149:8; Job 36:8. The meaning "bonds" is established by the cognate Jewish-Aramaic זִקִין, "chains," with its denominative verb זקק, "to bind."

> v. 11   *Thou, too, wilt be drunken;*
>   *Thou wilt be hidden.*
>   *Thou, too, wilt seek a stronghold against enemies.*

Now the prophet applies the lesson which Assyria must learn from No of Amon's fate. If that city fell, despite its natural situation, fortification, and allies, so Nineveh without these advantages will assuredly be consigned to like destruction. The emphatic "Thou, too" shows the parallel destinies of both cities.

Nineveh's defeat is introduced with the dire forecast "Thou, too, wilt be drunken." The haughty capital, whose calculated cruelty for centuries enslaved her foes, will lose her composure when the enemy draws close for the capture. Bereft of her senses, too groggy to formulate intelligible counterplans, tottering in aimless circles, devoid of real power to resist, Nineveh, intoxicated, like devastated No-Amon, staggers before her fall. This figurative use of drunkenness, in the sense of "becoming stupefied," "confused," "losing one's senses," mental, spiritual inebriation, is frequent in the OT. See Jer. 25:27 (directed to Babylon): "Drink ye, and be ye drunken, and spue, and fall, and rise no more"; Lam. 4:21 (to Edom): "Thou shalt be drunken, and thou shalt make thyself naked"; Jer. 51:7: "The nations have drunken of her [Babylon's] wine; therefore the nations are mad." See also Is. 51: 17, 21 ff.; Hab. 2:15, 16; Obad. 16; Ezek. 23:33; Ps. 60:3; 75:8.

This figure representing Nineveh as drunken repeats the thought of 1:10 and may have been provoked by the widespread consumption of intoxicants among the Assyrians. Significantly Ashurbanipal is represented on a bas-relief with his queen, Ashursharrat, in a drinking scene. He reclines in an arbor beneath a vine heavy with huge clusters of grapes. His wife, Ashursharrat, sits on an imposing throne, while attendants with huge fans keep the air in circulation and banish flies.

Nineveh also received this warning: "Thou wilt be hidden." In the stupor of its sorrow it will no longer gleam in ostentatious pride; it will drop out of sight, completely reduced to obscurity, covered by its own ruins. No., following Keil, objects that drunkards do not hide themselves; but this objection is specious, for the hiding denotes a being hidden, i. e., beneath ruins. Obad. 16 shows how definitely prophecy has associated drunkenness with obscurity.

Thus, bereft of their senses, buried beneath the avalanche of sorrows, the Ninevites will look for help. Nahum continues, "Thou, too, wilt seek a stronghold against enemies." In its last days the city which once brought groveling kingdoms to its feet will seek desperately, as No of Amon must have done, for real fortresses from which to defend itself. The search will be in vain, for, as v. 12 implies, any stronghold in which the Assyrians may take their stand will soon collapse.

גַּם אַתְּ is found twice in this verse for periodic stress. It is used four times in vv. 10 and 11, with intentional repetition to show that even Nineveh will experience No of Amon's destiny.

תֵּשְׁכְּרִי — (S), "be unhappy." Du., followed by K.-G. and Sel., unnecessarily substitutes תִּשָּׁבְרִי, "Thou wilt be broken."

תְּהִי is used in preference to תֶּחֱזִי, which Hst. requires. J.M.P.Sm. calls this "an inexplicable jussive." However, Ges., Gra., 145 *p,* explains the form as an imperfect indicative. On the use of the verb with the participle to denote continued state or action, see Ges., Gra., 116 *r.*

נַעֲלָמָה is the *Niph"al* participle, "one who is hidden." However, Ⓖ, ὑπερεωραμένη, "despised"; Ⓥ, "et eris despecta"; similarly Ⓢ. The translation "hidden," though the obvious rendition of the Hebrew, has not found critical favor. Instead, (1) Dr., J.M.P.Sm., Bev., Dav.-Lan., Jnk., Sel., offer "to swoon," "to be unconscious." However, this gives the verb a meaning which it has in no other passage and cannot be justified by saying that the "Arabic has exactly the same idiom, using 'be covered' as equal to 'be powerless.'" It is precarious to transfer Arabic idioms to the Hebrew. Nor is Sm.'s final consideration decisive. He says: "The verb with a similar primary meaning is used in this way in Is. 51:20; Jonah 4:8; Amos 8:13; Ezek. 31:15." Wherever else any other verb may be found, the fact remains that the text of Nahum authorizes only עָלַם. (2) Hal. suggests, "Thou wilt hide thyself from fear," a meaning which cannot be demonstrated for the verb in this form. (3) Hap. and v.Ho. follow Ⓖ and Ⓥ in translating, "Thou wilt be despised." These versions should not be preferred to the Ⓜ, and here they present a decided anticlimax. (4) Htz. and No. offer, "Thou wilt be enshrouded in night." But the Hebrew offers no justification for this rendition. (5) Hst. translates, "Thou wilt be worried," תְּהִי עֲנֻמָה, but this is weak and rests on an emended reading. A review of all substitute renditions gives no reason for departing from the normal translation, "Thou wilt be hidden" (a meaning clearly substantiated by 1 Kings 10:3 and Eccl. 12:14), i. e., in the destruction of the city.

> *v. 12*   *All thy fortresses*
> *{Are} fig trees with first-ripe fruits.*
> *When they are shaken,*
> *They fall into {the} eater's mouth.*

When Nineveh seeks a defense against the invaders, the prophet reminds it, "All thy fortresses are fig trees." The pl., "fortresses," may refer both to the defenses of Nineveh itself and to the fortifications which guard the approaches to the city.[6] The point of comparison is introduced by the qualifying addition, "with first-ripe fruit."[7] Strictly interpreted, the "first-ripe" figs are the earliest yield of the tree, regardless of species (Ex. 23:16; Lev. 23:20, etc.). It is possible, however, that the figs mentioned are the first of the season. Such is the parallel usage in Num. 13:20, where the spies bring back the first-ripe grapes *(bikkûrîm)*, the earliest fruit. Nineveh's forts are thus symbolized not by the late figs, which ripen in August and September, but by the early figs, ready to be picked at the end of May and in June.

The point of comparison is not that of cowardice (Htz.), nor the high esteem which the Ninevites place on their fortresses (Stnh., who erroneously draws the inference from Jer. 24:2, where the early figs represent the better class of Judeans). The first-ripe fruits, highly prized (Is. 28:4), may imply the eagerly sought objective of the enemies who reach out avidly for Nineveh. The real point of the prophet's picture, however, is presented in his explanation, "When they are shaken, they fall into the eater's mouth." This stresses the ease and speed with which the Ninevite strongholds will fall. Those who gather the first-ripe figs need not laboriously climb high trees and then carefully

---

[6] Without justification Wllh. explains the "fortresses" as the defenses of the capital itself and excludes all fortifications outside the city. The position taken above holds that the development of Nahum's prediction is strengthened by the assumption that the fortifications include those outside the city.

[7] On the cultivation of the fig in Palestine see Gustaf Dalman, *Arbeit und Sitte in Palaestina*, I (1928), Part II, 378 f.

pick a few figs from each branch; when the trunk of the tree is merely shaken, the fruit falls, as it were, into the mouth of the eater, with a minimum of exertion. It is well known that fruit which matures quickly and ripens early in the season drops more easily than the later fruit, which develops slowly (Is. 28:4). If the prophet means the first of all figs produced by a young tree, the point of comparison would still be the ease with which they are removed, for such initial yields on small trees (the fully developed fig tree in Palestine ranges from sixteen to twenty feet high) are often subnormal. In the same easy way, at the final attack on Nineveh, the invaders, particularly in attacking the fortresses before the city, will not be forced to wage long, wearisome campaigns at the cost of much labor and blood. When the last assault begins, these defenses will fall quickly. See Rev. 6:13.

It may be objected that the capital did not collapse as easily as Nahum here predicts and that therefore the prophet's picture is overdrawn. The *Babylonian Chronicle* shows that all the hostile military operations covered the period from 614 to 612 B.C. However, it is not in accord with historical presentation to picture Nineveh itself as continually besieged for three entire years. Sporadic attacks were made on the city in 614 B.C., but the decisive campaign was waged in 612 B.C. The year 613 B.C. apparently left Nineveh itself altogether unassailed. Nor must it be overlooked, as the context shows, that the prophet here predicts only the fall of the Assyrian fortresses, particularly those outside the city proper. The *Babylonian Chronicle* specifically lists Tarbis, a district immediately north of Nineveh, as captured in 613 B.C.

Here, too, the avenging power of God is manifest. Repeatedly Assyrian kings boast that they captured enemy fortresses. Now their own strongholds are captured — and with comparatively little effort.

Hpt. changes the verse order here to make vv. 12 and 13 follow 15 a, while Stk. transfers v. 12 to follow v. 14a. Even J.M.P.Sm. concedes that these realignments offer no improvement. This is an understatement; for such radical, unauthenticated inversions forfeit the forceful development of the prophet's presentation.

כָּל־ — K.-G. arbitrarily drops this.

עִם — Critics change this to עַם (G.A.Sm., "troops") with various suffixes: עַמָּם, "their people" (Du., K.-G.); עַמֵּךְ, "thy people" (Sel.); עַמֵּךְ, "thy people" (Mrt., No., J.M.P.Sm.). Bev. explains this form as supplying the consonants "which doubtless fell out of Ⓜ by haplography" and reads, "Thy defenders are first-ripe figs." But even Stnh. objects to the emendation of עִם to עַם and asserts that (1) "people" does not form "a very exact parallel to 'fortresses'"; (2) v. 13 refers to Nineveh's defenders, "and therefore we should not expect that reference to be anticipated here"; (3) the reference to the first-ripe figs as falling into the eater's mouth is applicable to the fortresses, but not to the people. Despite this correct reasoning, Stnh. (as Hst. and others) proposes: "thy cities (עָרִיךְ) are first-ripe figs." This, however, is equally unsuitable to the picture and shifts the emphasis from Nineveh to other unidentified cities. Such emendations, entirely apart from their lack of proof, do not offer adequate parallelism or harmonious development. The translation of the textually uncontestable Ⓜ: "All thy fortresses are fig trees *with*" (עִם denoting accompaniment, as 1 Sam. 17:42) is not accepted by critics (1) because it yields too short a line (J.M.P.Sm.); and (2) because the verse "is lacking in parallelism" (ibid.), although the Hebrew offers graphic, synthetic parallelism and should be retained.

> *v. 13   Behold, thy people in thy midst {are} women!*
>   *For thine enemies the gates of thy land are*
>   *open wide;*
>   *Fire consumeth thy bars.*

Nineveh's outer fortresses fall, and the city itself gives way to the attacks because its defense is demoralized. Envisioning this collapse, the prophet cries, "Behold, thy people in thy midst are women." Although not necessarily restricted to the defenders (so G.A.Sm., Bev.), the term "thy people" doubtless includes the soldiers garrisoned within the walls to protect the city. (See Num. 20:20; 21:23, for "people" as "troops.") The Ninevites generally have become women. This picture is not unknown to other prophets. Is. 19:16 says that the Egyptians become "like unto women," and Jer. 50:37 and 51:30 assert that the Babylonians are "become as women." This is generally interpreted to mean that the city's defenders are destitute of all courage, unable or unwilling to acquit themselves as men.

Quite overlooked in this connection have been the traditions of the effeminate degeneracy in Assyria shortly before its fall. A picture of this survives in the *Deipnosophistae* of Athenaeus, which portrays Sardanapalus [Ashurbanipal] with painted, pumiced face, blackened eyebrows, dressed in a woman's garments and sitting in the midst of his concubines. Popular tradition often distorts abnormalities, but the true historical representation of Ashurbanipal as "a frightened degenerate" may well typify the perversions which provoke Nahum's prediction, "Thy people in thy midst are women."

J.M.P.Sm. attacks the veracity of Nahum's prediction concerning this effeminacy and objects: "As a matter of fact, the defence of Nineveh was prolonged and heroic." This statement is destitute of all historical support. No account of Nineveh's denouement records directly or inferentially any tribute to the heroism of its defenders. The city itself, it will be recalled, was besieged for almost three months, and the three decisive battles outside the city were fought in a single month; but no evidence of outstanding bravery has been preserved.

With the forts outside the city fallen, the morale broken, the prophet continues, "To thine enemies are the gates of thy land open wide." These gates are either the mountain-pass approaches to Nineveh (for the use of "land" in the sense of "territory," "domain," see 1 Sam. 9:4, 5) or any Assyrian fortifications in control of the roads leading to the city. These natural entrances or the fortifications have been captured so that the gates are wide open.

Finally, the prophet predicts, "Fire consumeth thy bars." The term translated with "bar" may denote a beam to join boards or a large piece of timber to restrict the entrance to a fort, Deut. 3:5; Judg. 16:3; 1 Sam. 23:7; Amos 1:5. Sometimes the "bar" was of iron (Is. 45:2), sometimes of bronze (1 Kings 14:13). The word is also used by metonymy for the door or gate itself (Jonah 2:7). In this context the bars are best explained either as part of the entrance fortifications just mentioned (see Deut. 3:5; Judg. 16:3; 1 Sam. 23:7; Amos 1:5) or figuratively as any defense obstruction. If the city gates and bars were destroyed by fire, the capital itself would be open to attack on all sides, and v. 14, which bids the inhabitants to prepare for a siege, would be out of place. Rather does Nahum here predict that the outlying fortresses and barriers will be captured and then destroyed by fire, the usual climax to Assyrian conquest and victory. Note the stereotyped formula in the records of Assyrian conquests, "I devastated, I destroyed, I burned in fire."

Bev. asserts: "Possibly 13a is only a gloss to explain the fig-tree walls," but he offers no explanation. K.-G. inverts the sequence of this verse and conjectures that a part of 13a has been dropped. Mrt. and J.M.P.Sm. similarly transpose the last two clauses; yet the verse as it stands gives good sense and development.

עִמֵּךְ — This is omitted by Mrt., J.M.P.Sm., and others, but without authority and advantage. The word is labeled a scribal correction of עַם (v. 12), which got into the wrong verse. However, עִמֵּךְ is essential and forceful. Bev.'s "the troops of thy garrison" is unjustified.

נָשִׁים — Most of the versions have the equivalent of "as women," which Ries. demands. A typical instance of dilettante criticism is furnished at this place by J.M.P.Sm., who, instead of translating, on the basis of Ⓜ, "Thy people in thy midst are women," offers, "Women are in the midst of thee." Sm. explains: "The sense is the same in both readings; but the order of words is easier in the emended text and the phrase 'in the midst of thee' in MT is somewhat superfluous." But the nondescript statement "Women are in the midst of thee" is not on a par with the vivid Ⓜ. Hpt. arbitrarily substitutes יְשִׁימוּ, "they will destroy." Against all evidence, but moved by the desire to supply a missing accent, Hst. inserts נֶחֱרָשִׁים, "weaklings," after נָשִׁים and translates, "Thy men are women. Weaklings dwell in thee." Sel. adds נִמְסִים, "cowards," offering, "Thy people are women, cowards in thy midst." These additions, arbitrary as their opposing forms prove them, are adopted with the contention that the meter requires an additional word.

לְאֹיְבַיִךְ is placed in advance for emphasis. This is dropped by K.-G. as metrically superfluous.

פָּתוֹחַ — Du. and others brand this as a corruption of the following נִפְתְּחוּ, but without justification. Ges., Gra., 113 c, furnishes the grammatical and syntactical corroboration for this frequent idiom. The reason for this proposed excision is essentially the same as that which has motivated the mutilation of most other verses in Nahum, the requirements of a purely hypothetical metrical system. Whereas a word is inserted after נָשִׁים, the word after פָּתוֹחַ is elided, because

(Stnh.) "the meter suggests a line of three beats rather than of four, as the present text appears to have."

נִפְתְּחוּ — It is contrary to the factors which date the Book of Nahum to assume with J.M.P.Sm. that possibly "Nahum was writing at a time when these strongholds had already fallen," or to agree with Wllh.: "Here we have preterites. 'The gates of the land,' the fortified entrances on the boundaries, are therefore already taken by force; only Nineveh itself must still fall." The critical tendency is thus to push the book down to the latest possible date and to ignore the fact that the verbs are prophetic perfects.

אָכְלָה אֵשׁ בְּרִיחָיִךְ — J.M.P.Sm. follows Mrt. in putting this statement with which Ⓜ closes into the middle of the verse. J.M.P.Sm. declares: "This clause more fittingly follows v. 13a than v. 13b, as in Ⓜ. It would be unnecessary to burn the bars after the gates were opened." Sel. has the same specious objection. This is supercritical. The prophet simply explains why the gates are wide open — fire has consumed them. Or he may imply that some gates have been forced, while others were destroyed by fire. The prompting influence behind these artificial alterations again is the desire to secure a metrical pattern. Sm. explains: "Moreover, the metre is much improved by this arrangement." Sel. (similarly Hst., K.-G.) adds that the elided words are metrically objectionable and superfluous. Stnh. asserts: "The line is almost certainly not original. It is rhythmically suspicious; and destroys the effect of the preceding lines. . . . Moreover v. 15 has 'the fire shall devour thee.'" He thus holds that one mention of the fire is sufficient. However, far from nullifying the dramatic effect of the preceding predictions, the reference to the fire adds to the presentation. The objection that fire is mentioned two verses later and therefore can hardly be genuine here is contradicted by other repetitions in the book which critics themselves accept. For example, in 2:12 they retain the picture of the lion, although the lion is again mentioned two verses later. They keep the reference to the chariot in 2:5, although it is found again in 3:2.

> *v. 14 Draw thyself water for a siege!*
> *Strengthen thy fortifications!*
> *Go into the soil! Knead the clay!*
> *Grasp a brick mold!*

The scene now shifts from the outlying fortresses to Nineveh itself, as the prophet ironically asks the defenders to make extensive siege preparations.

The series of five imperatives starts with the sarcastic "Draw thyself water for a siege." Perhaps the water found in the city itself was not drinkable because of the clay contents of the soil. Besides, the water supply within the city was inadequate. Sennacherib, grandfather of Ashurbanipal, records that before he enlarged and improved Nineveh, "its people did not have [lit., know] any water for watering, but turned their eyes heavenward for showers of rain." In one of his major enterprises Sennacherib built an imposing aqueduct system. As his own account reveals, he dug eighteen canals, all of which joined the Khosr, made the lower part of this river a canal, irrigated the territory around Nineveh, and built a new canal from Mount Tas.[8] This scarcity of potable water in Nineveh itself gives unusual force to the prophet's urging, "Draw thyself water for a siege." If the invaders followed the usual strategy of hostile forces in antiquity, one of their first actions would have been to cut off the water supply furnished by Sennacherib's dam and its reservoir. Nahum, fore-

[8] D. D. Luckenbill, *The Annals of Sennacherib* (1924), pp. 78 ff. An investigation of Nineveh's water sources is presented in *Sennacherib's Aqueduct at Jerwan,* by Thorkild Jacobsen and Seton Lloyd (1935), especially ch. V, "The Water Supplies of Nineveh," pp. 31 ff.

seeing that the water would be withheld from the city, and inferring a long, protracted siege, tauntingly directs the Ninevites to lay up stores for the beleaguered days. He does not here urge the people of Nineveh to fill the moats for better defense (J.M.P.Sm.). If that were his intention, he would have urged: "Draw water for the moats," or, "Fill the canals." The Hebrew word here employed for "to draw" is never used for such tactical operations but always denotes the drawing of water (usually from a well) to satisfy the thirst of men and animals. (See Gen. 24:11, 13, 19, 20, 43-45; Deut. 29:10; Joshua 9:21, 23, 27; 1 Sam. 7:6; 9:11; 2 Sam. 23:16; Is. 12:3; 1 Chron. 11:18; Ruth 2:9.) For the same reasons the alternate explanation by J.M.P.Sm. is to be rejected: "Nahum probably refers to the perfecting and protecting of this system" (Sennacherib's waterworks).

Besides securing a water supply, Nineveh must defend itself. The prophet appeals derisively, "Strengthen thy fortifications." The last term is apparently comprehensive, including walls, turrets, and all places of defense. Here, unlike the emphasis on outlying strongholds in v. 12, the text refers to the fortified positions in Nineveh itself, the gates and the other strategic localities within the city. These must now be strengthened to resist the brunt of repeated attacks. In 2 Kings 12:7 ff. the term here translated "strengthen" is employed for the reconstruction of the temple, and in Neh. 3:19 the same verb is used for the restoration of Jerusalem's walls. For similar occurrences in the sense of "repair," see 2 Kings 22:6; 2 Chron. 24:5, 12; 29:3; 34:8, 10.

A topographical survey of Nineveh's ruins has revealed "traces of the counterwall raised by their inhabitants in their last extremity on the line where ran the city defense before the rebuilding of Sennacherib." Thus we are led to conclude that the frenzied Ninevites did exactly what the prophet here ironically urges them to do.

Since additional supplies of brick were required for the repair or construction of the fortifications, the prophet cries out, "Go into the soil," the Assyrian clay, which advantageously lent itself for the manufacture of bricks. This required that the soil first of all be moistened with water and then kneaded to make the bricks of uniform consistency. After these preparations the Ninevites are told to "grasp a brick mold" (not, as AV and RV, "Make strong the brick kiln"). The kneaded clay was cut into the desired shapes and sizes by a mold which often contained specifications regarding the period of its use. This repeated urging is not accidental. Huge quantities of bricks were required for repair and construction. Actual investigations made *in situ* show that while the width of the walls of Nineveh was usually about fifty feet, this figure was more than doubled near the city gate.

מֵי מָצוֹר שַׁאֲבִי־לָךְ — Ⓥ, "aquam propter obsidionem," "water on account of [for] the siege." Lu., according to the sense: "Schöpfe dir Wasser, denn du wirst belagert werden."

חַזְּקִי here means "repair" or "strengthen." Ⓖ, κατακράτησον.

בֹּאִי בַטִּיט — Without any MS authority, Grz., followed by No., v.Ho., Stk., Hst., changes בֹּאִי to בּוּסִי, "tread the clay." This is not indicated by Zech. 10:5 ("tread down their enemies in the mire of the streets"), which has no connection with brickmaking. Besides, the originality of Ⓜ is supported by the parallel Assyrian, to which Hpt. calls attention, *tîta erêbu*.

רִמְסִי בַחֹמֶר — For a similar usage of the verb see Is. 41:25. Ⓖ erroneously translates: ἐν ἀχύροις, "in chaff." Ries. wants בְּחֵמָר, "in asphalt"; but this is no improvement.

הַחֲזִיקִי — While the *Hiph"il* of the verb חָזַק may have the same meaning as the *Qal*, here, in distinction from the חַזְּקִי near the beginning of the verse, it means "to take," "to grasp."

מַלְבֵּן — The versions are unable to reproduce this correctly. Ⓖ, ὑπὲρ πλίνθον, offering the vague "brick" and ignoring the prefixed *Mem* of instrumentality. Ⓣ suggests "thy building"; Ⓥ, "laterem," "side"; Ⓢ, "promise." AV and RV, also earlier commentators, translate "brickkiln," but this is incompatible with the verb. The term is found otherwise only in 2 Sam. 12:31 and in the *Qerē* of Jer. 43:9. The meaning here, as in 2 Sam. 12:31 (though apparently not in the Jer. passage), is "brick mold," as suggested by the AV margin, "lay hold of the brick mold." The word occurs in this sense in New Hebrew, Aramaic, and Syriac.

> *v. 15 Then fire will devour thee.*
> *A sword will cut thee off.*
> *It will devour thee as the young locust,*
> *{Though} thou multiply thyself as the young locust*
> *And increase thyself as the locust.*

When the efforts indicated in the previous verse prove futile, "then" full disaster will sweep over Nineveh. All attempts at defense and all plans for lifting the siege having failed, the prophet warns Nineveh, "fire will devour thee." Destruction by flame was the common end of many captured cities, but not of all. Tradition recounts that the capital was reduced to ashes in the holocaust originating from the funeral pyre of Sardanapalus. Excavators since the days of Layard and Rawlinson have "shown that fire was a great instrument in the destruction of the Nineveh palaces." Alabaster slabs burnt to pulverized lime, large quantities of charred wood and charcoal, statues broken by the heat, "all attest the veracity of prophecy."

While the city is being destroyed by flames, the prophet proclaims, "a sword will cut thee off." The sword, here designating any death-dealing instrument (2 Sam. 11:25 uses "sword" in connection with death caused by an arrow), and fire are often pictured together in overwhelming catastrophes (see Deut. 28:22;

Joshua 8:19 ff.; 11:11; Judg. 1:8; 18:27; 20:48; Ezek. 23:25; 1 Kings 9:16). The Assyrian metropolis will not only be captured and consigned to the flame; it will be completely destroyed, its inhabitants killed.

The certainty and the extent of the massacre are emphasized by the prophet's notice, "It will devour thee as the young locust." The meaning seems to be either that the sword will consume the Assyrians as the young locust consumes, i. e., completely, or preferably that the fire will destroy the Assyrians as it kills the locusts. The locust here mentioned is probably the *attelabus,* before the last or its fourth stage of development, when the wings are still enclosed in a sheath, making the locust jump rather than fly until this sheath is removed. The AV and RV "cankerworm," which eats into plants, is too general. The prophet uses the young locusts as a forceful symbol of an immense army on the march. The comparison is usually not fully understood by the Western mind, but this was a graphic picture for every Palestinian reader, on whom contact with advancing locust hordes left the impression of innumerable multitudes (see Ex. 10:4, 5; Judg. 6:5; 7:12; Is. 40:22; Ps. 105:34; Prov. 30:27; Jer. 46:23). The Assyrians likewise used the picture of grasshoppers for multitudes beyond counting.

Nineveh is positively doomed, even as Nahum, addressing her, says: "Though thou multiply thyself as the young locust and increase thyself as the locust." Having introduced the picture of the locust, the prophet continues it to emphasize a startling characteristic of this creature, its astonishing power of prolific reproduction. Those who have never seen a swarming, seething mass of locusts can hardly begin to understand their astounding increase. Now, Nahum says, of all cities Nineveh has most increased like the locust; but though the teeming metropolis boasts of its crowded population and its heavily massed defenses, it cannot escape. Stnh. asserts that "the reference is not, as is commonly thought, to the massing of defenders within Nineveh,

but to the presence of a large portion of her population throughout her dominions and elsewhere for trade (cf. v. 16) and other
purposes. Just as the prophet has ironically bidden Nineveh
prepare for siege only to meet disaster and be completely destroyed, so he ironically bids her in these verses to multiply
her traders and officials only to discover that their disappearance
will be as sudden and as complete as that of the locusts, seen
one day and gone the next. In other words, not only the capital
but the population that represents her in the land will cease
to exist." However, the prophet does not maintain that both the
entire capital and those who represent her beyond her bounds
will cease to be; for in 3:18 the people of Nineveh and of
Assyria exist, scattered upon the mountains. It is historically
demonstrable that while the capital city itself fell, the kingdom
of Assyria, although in a drastically reduced and precarious position, did not immediately cease to exist. — An altogether different
interpretation is suggested by Bev., who sees "Assyrian soldiers
fleeing from conquered cities come pouring into Nineveh. But
this increase will yet not avail to save the city." After the strong
language employed throughout the prophecy, depicting the various
stages of Nineveh's destruction, it comes as an anticlimax to
declare that men from the defeated forts are seeking refuge in
Nineveh. Besides, they would probably flee as far from the
doomed city as possible.

Wllh., without stating his reason, draws the first half of
this verse back to v. 14.

שָׁם — Most commentators reject the translation "then" in
favor of the usual "there," asserting that שָׁם is never employed
as an adverb of time. However, the temporal usage may be
indicated in such passages as Ps. 14:5; 36:13; 66:6, and
perhaps Job 23:7. The temporal interpretation is doubtless
the stronger here and is to be preferred to the explanation
which makes שָׁם demonstrative, as though the prophet were
pointing to a specific place and crying, "There!" The change

of שָׁם to נֻם (Hpt., K.-G., Sel., Bev., Ehr.) is unauthorized, as is Ries.'s alteration to שִׁמְעוּ, "listen!" and Ri.'s substitution of אֻלָם, "nevertheless."

תֹּאכְלֵךְ כַּיָּלֶק — This difficult passage has been translated in various ways. (1) "The sword will devour thee as (it devours) locusts" (Htz.). The obvious difficulty with this is that the sword does not consume locusts. (2) "The sword will devour thee, though thou be numerous like the locust" (Or., Dav.-Lan.). This is open to the additional objection that it does not reproduce the full text. Besides, the thought of large numbers is expressed in the following sentence. (3) "The sword will devour thee as the locust devours" (Knabenbauer and others). Yet the paralleling of destruction by the sword and by the locust is not obvious. (4) Adopting a suggested text emendation, No., Bev., and tentatively K.-G. propose "The battle-axe will destroy thee," drafting an Assyrian noun, *kallaptu,* as a substitute for the well-authenticated כַּיָּלֶק. This rests on too flimsy ground and adds nothing essential, since the sword just mentioned is a comprehensive term for various instruments of death. (5) Most critical interpreters (Wllh., Oo., G.A.Sm., and a dozen others) seek to obviate the difficulty by dropping כַּיָּלֶק. J.M.P.Sm. explains: "These words are best treated as a gloss or as due to dittography." But the Hebrew MSS and the versions oppose this. The occurrence of the second תֹּאכְלֵךְ is substantiated by a second καταφάγεται, "is eaten," in Ⓖ B, א Original, Marchalianus, and Freer. There is no reason for resorting to the extreme of excision simply because "the words are hard to understand in Ⓜ." Sel. concedes that the elision is not altogether satisfactory, for he feels that another statement must be added after this phrase is dropped, although he offers no definite substitution. (6) Other isolated changes in the text which have found no wider critical favor are: the omission of כַּיָּלֶק and the transposition of בְּאַרְבֶּה as its substitute;

the omission of כַּיֶּלֶק and the construction of חָרֶב as subject of תֹּאכְלֵךְ (Du.); the substitution of כָּלָה for כַּיֶּלֶק (Hal.). These are artificial and unnecessary. (7) The most acceptable rendition seems to be: "It [the fire] shall devour thee as it [the fire] devours the locust." Here neither "the sword" nor "the locust" is the subject, but "the fire." The fact that the verb תֹּאכְלֵךְ has been used at the beginning of this verse with fire speaks for its association here with the same verb. This interpretation has the advantage of helping to restrict the figure of the locust to the Assyrians in this and the next verses. Other interpreters are at pains to show why the locusts are used as an emblem of the attackers in this and the next verses, yet as a symbol of the Assyrians in v. 17. Under the present explanation each mention of the locust in 3:15-17 refers to the Ninevites. Finally, this translation best brings out the force of the following concessive clause and shows that the locust is here introduced as a representation of that which is innumerable, yet which will still be destroyed by fire.

הִתְכַּבֵּד — A few MSS of Kennicott have the fem. הִתְכַּבְּדִי also here. On this flimsy basis many critics (Wllh., No., Mrt., Oo., and others) demand this reading; but the preponderant MS authority is for the present Ⓜ. Despite critical objection to the two genders, as voiced, e. g., by Dav.-Lan., who says this "is scarcely possible in grammar," Ges., Gra., 110 *k*, authenticates the use of the two genders as a syntactical nicety. It states: "In Nahum 3:15 the interchange of masc. and fem. serves to express totality (the nation in all its aspects)." Among other changes offered by such as do not content themselves with Ⓜ are: (1) הִתְכַּבַּדְתְּ (Hap.); (2) הִתְרַבִּי (Hpt.); (3) the omission of the word as a gloss (Ru., Ries.). None of these is required by sense, syntax, MS reading, or the versions.

הִתְכַּבְּדִי — Syntactically unimpeachable and rhetorically forceful, this word likewise has been unnecessarily attacked, and the following changes have been proposed: (1) the omission of הִתְכַּבְּדִי and כָּאַרְבֶּה (No. and Hal.). This is based on Ⓖ reading, which does not reproduce either of these words. However, some Greek MSS do have the literal equivalent. (2) הִתְכַּבְּדוּ (Ru.); (3) הִתְרַבִּית (Hap.). All these alterations are unnecessary, as is the whole critical trend to change Ⓜ and to construe 15 b as two independent parallel sentences. Apparently the prophet's point of view is best served by treating the two imperatives of v. 15 b as concessives. See Ges., Gra., 110 a, and Is. 8:9, 10. Under this interpretation the sense of the much-discussed verse would be this: "Whatever preparation you make in storing water, repairing walls, increasing the brick supply, you are doomed. The sword will cut you off; fire will consume you, as it consumes the hordes of innumerable locusts, even though you enlarge your numbers in the defense of the city so that they resemble the endless swarms of grasshoppers."

כָּאַרְבֶּה — Du. makes this the first word in the next verse in spite of MS evidence to the contrary.

v. 16 Thou hast made thy merchants
More than the stars of the heaven,
{Yet} the young locust strippeth and flieth away.

In this extremity, with the city in ashes and the inhabitants either fallen by the sword or in flight, Nineveh's wealth and commerce will fall, just as its defenses have collapsed. The prophet introduces this warning with a statement of fact, "Thou hast made thy merchants more than the stars of the heaven." References to Babylonian commerce is found in the provisions of Hammurabi's Code, laws 48—52; 101—107; 113—126; 180, 181, and in the Assyrian Empire business doubtless assumed a wider scope.[9] Many of the traders, it is true, were Aramaeans, as a study of the later merchants' names reveals. Toward the end of the empire, Aramaic endorsements and dockets are frequently found on cuneiform business tablets. Olmstead, *History of Assyria,* p. 532, believes that the Assyrians despised trade, as industry, and that commerce was carried on largely through subject nations. He admits, however, that the Assyrian armies of conquest were soon followed by traders' caravans, that Assyrian patrols encouraged business. Dominant nations are trade nations. Assyria was midway between the Near and the Far East. The Tigris, although not navigable by large ships, was open to smaller craft, particularly rafts. Adad-nirari III (812—782 B. C.) reached the Mediterranean. He was followed by Shalmaneser IV (782—772 B. C.), who turned to the north and the east, opening roads leading to the Caspian district and Iran. Under Ashur-banipal, for the first time in 800 years, western Asia was dominated by a single political rule. With the vast territory of the empire under one central government, commerce could flourish throughout this area as never before.

Nahum thus declares that in her opulent growth Nineveh has multiplied her merchants more than the (visible) stars of the heaven, a frequent figure of the innumerable, Gen. 15:5; 22:17; 26:4; Ex. 32:13; Deut. 1:10; 10:22, etc. This is no idle exaggeration. For centuries the traders left Nineveh for all parts of the empire, and the riches of a booty-heavy people necessarily produced much internal commerce.

Despite the heavy revenue from these merchants, Nineveh,

9 Diodorus (II, 11) writes, under the impress of wide Assyrian commercial operations: "Semiramis built other cities on the Euphrates and the Tigris, where she placed emporia for those who convey their goods from Media and Paraetacene. Being mighty rivers and passing through a populous country, they yield many advantages to those employed in commerce; so that the places by the river are full of wealthy emporia."

now destroyed, is destitute, forsaken. The prophet continues, "The young locust strippeth and flieth away." The locusts are the Ninevites in general, as in the previous verse, the thought being that the wealth and foreign connections produced by Nineveh's commerce have not been able to restrain the flight of its people. The country has been stripped of its productivity. The locusts find nothing left for nourishment, and they swarm away. This stripping (not "spreading itself," or "spoiling," AV and RV) probably indicates the locust's emergence from the pupa stage when it casts off the membrane fettering its wings and is thus enabled to fly away quickly, without hindrance. The Ninevites, who up till this time have been contented to remain firmly established in the capital city, now suddenly receive wings. In their precipitous flight they throw off every impediment which would hinder them from reaching safety.

Nahum's prediction in principle resembles very strikingly Ezekiel's (ch. 27) judgment on Tyre, the city which is called "a merchant of the people for many isles." Despite Tyre's extended commerce, and its merchants pushing through to the ends of the earth, the divine judgment on this city reads: "Thy riches and thy fairs, thy merchandise, thy mariners and thy pilots, thy calkers, and the occupiers of thy merchandise, and all thy men of war that are in thee . . . shall fall into the midst of the seas in the day of thy ruin" (v. 27). Tyre with the multitude of its riches and merchandising (vv. 32 and 34) shall fall with all the people in its midst. In the same way, Assyria, its unnumbered traders, its uncomputed wealth, will be so completely devastated that people flee from its ruins. This prophecy was graphically fulfilled in the complete collapse of Assyrian trade after the fall of the capital and the flight of its inhabitants.

הִרְבֵּית — This is turned by Wllh., whom No., G.A.Sm., and others follow, into an imperative, הַרְבִּי, "increase." Attractive as this may be, it is unnecessary and lacks MS authority. The few copies listed by Kennicott as having הרביתי are not decisive.

רֹכְלַיִךְ — Ⓖ, τὰς ἐμπορίας σου, "your tradings." Ⓥ, "nego-tiationes tuas." The term is not to be translated "thy mer-cenaries" (Calvin and others) or changed to רִכְבֵּךְ, "thy chariotry" (Du.).

מְכוֹכְבֵי הַשָּׁמַיִם — Ⓖ, inexactly, ὡς τὰ ἄστρα, "like the stars." Du. altogether subjectively offers כְּנֹבֵי הַסָּמָר, "like the hair locust."

יֶלֶק — Grz. prefixes a superfluous כְּ. Ehr. arbitrarily says the second half of the verse is probably spurious.

פָּשַׁט — Ⓖ, ὥρμησε, "set out." Ⓥ, "expansus est." However, the verb has two meanings which may be related, "to plunder" and then "to strip," "to undress." Passages like 1 Sam. 31:8; 1 Chron. 10:8 show the coincidence of both meanings. Here the verb may well describe the shedding of the larval locust membrane. Keil objects that the verb means only "to plunder"; however, the sense of "to strip," "to remove," is found in Lev. 12:23; 1 Sam. 19:24; Is. 32:11; Ezek. 26:16; 44:19; Cant. 5:3.

וַיָּעֹף — V.Ho. changes this to a copulative imperfect וְיָעוּף, but without reason and reward.

The last three words of the verse have caused considerable difficulty. Among the more important renditions are the following: (1) "The young locust plunders [or strips] and flies away" (so Keil, J.M.P.Sm., and others, some of whom arbitrarily advance this phrase to v. 15). This translation creates problems, for it uses the locust symbolism of the enemies, whereas in previous and following lines this refers to the Assyrians. Besides, why should the enemies fly away? (2) "The locusts set themselves in motion and fly away" (so Hap.). But this is based on dubious usage and forms a somewhat nondescript version of an otherwise striking text.

Likewise to be rejected is the similar interpretation, "The locusts spread their wings and fly away." These colorless translations take recourse to the incorrect ⑤: βροῦχος ὥρμησε καὶ ἐξεπετάσθη, "the locust set out and flew away"; and ⑦: "bruchus expansus est et avolavit." (3) "The locusts deposit their larvae and fly away" (v.Ho.). But this takes the thought out of the symbol, for how would either the Assyrians or their enemies deposit their larvae? Nor is there any authorized occurrence of the verb in this meaning. (4) Stnh. declares: "The writer clearly intends to say that Nineveh, with her merchant and other folk that swarm in the land, will vanish away as completely as the young locust flies away. But as the text stands, we miss any explicit indication of what will be the fate awaiting Nineveh and her vast trading population. The following clause, 'the young locust . . . flieth away,' can scarcely be said to give this. It is introduced very abruptly, and to suppose that the prophet left it to be inferred that Nineveh's merchants would wholly disappear by simply stating that it was the custom of the young locust to cast its sheaths . . . and fly off is very unlikely. He would almost certainly have expressed himself more clearly, especially as this was the main point which he intended to enforce. It is not improbable that a clause has fallen out and that the verse should end with *Thou shalt vanish like the cankerworm, which strippeth and flieth away.'* " Under this treatment a false meaning is read into the verse and then rejected. The verse does not say that the merchants, together with the Ninevites, fly away. It simply declares that though Nineveh has innumerable traders — and by implication immeasurable wealth — when the city is destroyed, the people will flee from it for their lives, quickly as the thick swarms of young locusts whose wings are fully emerged. (5) Bev. follows AV, "The cankerworm spoileth and flieth away," and he places this translation at the end of v. 15. But such partition and realignment is unacceptable. Many critics, including Mrt., Hpt., Stk., and others, revert to the convenient procedure by declaring that v. 16b is "best handled as a marginal note either on v. 15 or on v. 17" (J.M.P.Sm.). The reasons are typically subjective: "The phrase anticipates the thought of v. 17, has no close connection with v. 16a, and is superfluous in the poetical structure." It will be shown that far from anticipating the thought of v. 17, v. 16 has its own independent point and, together with vv. 15 and 17, contains a remarkable prediction of the hopelessness of destroyed Nineveh. The connection with v. 16a, the quick flight despite Nineveh's riches, has been shown above, and the claim that v. 16b is metrically superfluous is utterly subjective. Sel. seeks to eliminate these words, maintaining that the locusts "do not slip out of the stars"! He reveals one of the motivating influences in his statement: "They [these words] are of no use metrically."

> v. 17 *Thy guards {are} as the locust,*
> *And thy scribes as a swarm of grasshoppers*
> *Which alight on the wall on a cold day.*
> *The sun riseth, and they flee,*
> *And their place is not known. Where are they?*

In v. 15 the prophet shows that military power will avail Nineveh nothing. In v. 16 he predicts that the riches accumulated through commerce will not prevent people from fleeing. Now, in v. 17, he declares that the city's numerous officialdom will hasten to leave the doomed metropolis in the lurch. Maintaining the previous picture, Nahum prophesies, "Thy guards are as the locust." The meaning of the Hebrew term here reproduced as "guards" is uncertain. If this translation be correct, this opening statement shows that even those who might be expected to resist until the last will fail in the final crisis.[10]

"Thy scribes [are] as a swarm of grasshoppers," the prophet continues. Again the exact meaning and the full scope of the Hebrew word here given as "scribe" is at present not ascertainable. It seems evident, however, that the term denotes far more than an ordinary copyist. See the wide use of "scribe" in Judg. 5:14; 2 Chron. 26:11; 2 Kings 25:19. Probably it refers to an Assyrian official whose responsibilities were somewhat similar to those often associated with "secretary." The graphic belittling of Nineveh's officialdom should be noticed. The politically important personages, depicted on cuneiform reliefs as only slightly smaller than the king, are called "grasshoppers" and "locusts" in ridicule of their false pride and their cowardly flight.

These military and civil officials resemble the swarm of locusts, Nahum says, "which alight on the wall on a cold day." The cold day is not the winter, when the locusts do not appear, nor the night, since the term "day" is never used with this latitude of meaning, but the colder weather, particularly toward evening. Then the locusts alight and camp (AV and RV) on the hedges, walls, and fences. There they remain, torpid and almost motionless until "the sun riseth." But when the day becomes warm, "they flee." [11]

Tradition has preserved testimony to the flight of the Assyrian nobility. Diodorus relates how the king sent his sons and daughters to Paphlagonia, and the *Babylonian Chronicle*

[10] V.Ho. concludes that the reference to the merchants in the preceding verse, as to the scribes in this verse, is derisive and illustrates how literature and commerce had taken the place of warfare in popular esteem. Yet even in the last days of dilettante Ashurbanipal, Nineveh's armies were recording a series of decisive victories. The disintegration of the Assyrian Empire is not to be traced to a gradual disparagement of military activity, as v.Ho. implies, but to a sudden disaster which wiped out Nineveh and soon after the Assyrian nation with startling speed and completeness.

[11] See W. M. Thomson, *The Land and the Book* (1910), pp. 409, 410, in substantiation of the interpretation just given.

tablet seems to infer that the Assyrian monarch himself escaped from Nineveh. Again the avengement motif, by which Yahweh repays Nineveh in kind, is implied in the reference to this ignominious flight on the part of the doomed city's nobles. Repeatedly the Sargonide kings boast in their annals that before their approach the enemy sought escape in flight; now the Assyrian leaders must flee for their lives, as they made others flee.

It is better to construe the beginning of v. 17 as an independent sentence than to make it dependent on an artificially injected preceding imperative in v. 16, as do Sel. and others, who secure the translation, "Increase thy sacred officials." Neither Ⓜ nor versions have an imperative in v. 16.

מִנְּזָרַיִךְ — The meaning of this word, which occurs only here, is uncertain and has been interpreted in various ways. The versions offer little help. Ⓖ has the inexplicable ἐξήλατο, "he leapt." Ⓢ drops the *Mem* and translates, "thy Nazarite." Best among the versions is Ⓥ, "custodes tui." The most probable of these various interpretations seems to be "guards." The occurrence of the Assyrian *mas(s)artu* (pl., *masarâti*) or *massaru* (pl., *massari*) would support this meaning here. They, not the crowned heads and high officials, were found in such large numbers that they could well be pictured by the innumerable locusts; and the prediction that the guards, who were to protect the city, would flee like locusts adds to the force of the prophet's picture.

טִפְסְרַיִךְ — This noun, which occurs in the OT only here and Jer. 51:27, is likewise difficult and has been reproduced in several ways. Before the rise of Assyriology it was conjecturally translated as "captains" (AV, Ew., Or.) or as "princes," "leaders" (Kimchi). With the unfolding of the cuneiform vocabulary it was seen that the Assyrian *tupšarru*, literally, "tablet writer," "scribe," has etymological associations with the Hebrew טִפְסָר. There is good reason, however, for assuming that the term denoted a class of officials whose office was far more than that of a copyist. In Jer. 51:27 the noun seems to denote a higher military dignitary than a scribe, just as the Hebrew סֹפֵר may be used to designate military officials, perhaps those who muster the armies and keep the military lists, 2 Chron. 26:11; 2 Kings 25:19; Is. 33:18; Jer. 52:25. Similarly טִפְסָר may denote a secretary, more in the modern sense, an official of various capacities, here in connection with the Assyrian army. The versions evidently misunderstood the term, since Ⓖ offers ὁ σύμμικτός σου, "thy companion"; Ⓢ, "those who strive for thee"; Ⓥ, "et parvuli tui," probably mistaking the first syllable for טַף, "child." — Hap. drops טִפְסְרַיִךְ, and Hpt. changes it to טִפְסָרַיִךְ.

כְּנוֹב גֹּבָי — Many (Wllh., who says that the *corrigendum* has erroneously remained besides the *correctum,* No., etc.) follow Ⓖ in omitting גוֹב and reading כְּנוֹבָי. Hpt., followed by Ries. and others, prefers to omit גֹּבָי. Despite Ⓖ, ὡς ἀκρίς, "like the locust," Ⓥ retains both words in "locustae locustarum" and shows the early occurrence of the double form. It is not constructive exegesis to ascribe unusual constructions to scribal errors and to brand the recurrence of similar terms as dittography. AV "swarms of grasshoppers" may be correct if the repetition of the identical term be regarded as a paraphrase for the superlative conception. The combined phrase may be intensive, stressing the characteristic of these grasshoppers, either their size or their number. גוֹב itself occurs only here, but its meaning is clear from the related גֹּבָי. On the repetition of an expression to indicate superfine quality, see Ges., Gra., 133 *l,* and 2 Kings 25:15: כָּסֶף כָּסֶף, וְזָהָב זָהָב, "superfine gold," "superfine silver."

הַחוֹנִים — Ⓖ, ἐπιβεβηκυῖα. Grz. and Du. read the sing. הַחוֹנָה.

בְּיוֹם קָרָה — Wllh. prefers to read "in the cold of the day," but the correctness of Ⓜ is sustained by the recurrence of the identical phrase in Prov. 25:20, translated as "in cold weather."

וְנוֹדַד occurs only here in *Po"al.* No., Hst., Sel., K.-G. (who regards the word as a gloss), and others secure the pl. וְנוֹדְדוּ, by drawing the *Waw,* of the following וְלֹא back to the verb. This change in number is unnecessary, however, because the subject is a collective. For metrical reasons, but without evidence, Stnh. suggests נוֹדֹד, the infinitive absolute, and adds נוֹדְדוּ, securing, "they flee quite away." Hpt. omits the verb.

נוֹדַע — Ⓖ, ἔγνω. Ehr. asks for יָדַע.

מְקוֹמוֹ — No., Hap., Hst., Sel., K.-G., Ehr., and others arbitrarily change to a pl. suffix form מְקוֹמָם to conform to their earlier changes of number.

אַיָּם — The difference in the number of the suffixes between this and מְקוֹמוֹ is difficult. Perhaps the one agrees grammatically with גּוֹב in the sing., and the other logically takes the pl. However, all difficulty may be avoided by taking אַיָּם independently and translating, "Their place is not known. Where are they?" On this use of אַי with the suffixes in direct questions, see Ges., Gra., 100 *o.* Many critics change אַיָּם to אַיִּד and transfer it to the beginning of v. 18. They claim support in ⒼA, οὐαὶ αὐτοῖς. However, the term is grammatically and syntactically correct; and J.M.P.Sm.'s charge that the word is "weak and tautological" is unjustified. The translation "Their place is not known. Where are they?" is strong, vivid, and far from tautological. Without this addition the reader might interpret "their place" as "the locale" where they were before the flight, instead of the place where they now are, after the flight. Hpt., Hap., and K.-G. omit אַיָּם. No., Stk., and Kent want אוֹי לָךְ; Grz. and Hal., אַיֵּהוּ. Ries. eliminates the last four fifths of this verse and changes even that which he leaves to read, "Thy mixed people flies away as locusts."

> *v. 18 Thy shepherds slumber, O king of Assyria;*
>   *Thy mighty ones rest {in death}.*
>   *Thy people are scattered on the mountains,*
>   *and there is no one to gather {them}.*

Approaching the close of his oracle, the prophet emphasizes in dirgelike measure not only the permanency of Nineveh's ruined state but also the impending dissolution of the entire empire. Its dispersed people will never be gathered again.

The address shifts suddenly and dramatically to the "king of Assyria," probably one of the last rulers in the realm. This mention of the monarch, after the long, preceding record of Nineveh's demolition, presupposes that although the capital is destroyed, the nation continues to exist, even if meager and shrunken in territory. This is historically accurate. While Nineveh's collapse might be expected to spell an immediate end for the entire kingdom, it did not. Instead, for a few years its rule was precariously maintained over a drastically restricted area with a new capital at Haran.

The Assyrian ruler, here pictured, perhaps, as contemplating the devastated empire, is told, "Thy shepherds slumber." "Shepherd," a figurative designation for rulers and leaders, is otherwise employed with this sense in Num. 27:17; Micah 5:5; Zech. 11:5, etc. It is also a familiar cuneiform term which Assyrian kings use of themselves. These shepherds, leaders, generals, officials, sleep, not in carnal security and slothfulness (so Wllh., Htz., v.Ho.), for, as Nahum foresees, the city has already fallen, and such reference to neglect of its defense would form an anticlimax, contradicting the book's purpose — to show that the city fell in punishment by divine wrath. The sleep is figurative of the lifelessness in the grave, similarly Ps. 76:6; Dan. 12:2; Job 3:13; 14:12; Jer. 51:39, 57. As the Assyrian ruler surveys the ranks of his "shepherds," he learns that his warriors, administrators, and counselors are silent in eternal sleep.

Identical in structure and meaning is the parallel clause, "thy mighty ones," the "nobles," the prominent Ninevites, *"rest"* (namely, in death).[12] The *Babylonian Chronicle,* in discussing the city's fall, specifically records, "A great havoc of the chief men was made," thus perpetuating on clay the fact which Nahum here foresees in prophecy.

Their leaders silent in death, the people are without guidance and direction. Consequently they are dispersed. The shepherds dead, the flock is scattered. Therefore the prophet exclaims, "Thy people [not only the soldiers, so J.M.P.Sm., but the populace in general] are scattered on the mountains." The mountains, often inaccessible for large armies, yet filled with concealed hiding places for refugees, are those in the vicinity of the metropolis. To the west of Nineveh lay the Sinjar Range; to the east, chains of smaller hills rising in almost parallel steps to Mount Zagros; closer to the northeast were the Gordaean Mountains, with the summits of Nishir. Directly to the north rose the heights of Adiabene, and still farther north, the eminences of Jebel Jūdī, the mountains of Arrapachitis, and the Taurus Range, these last three forming a triangle south of Lake Van. In these heights the Ninevites, once proudly united in the strength of their superiority, are to be dispersed, unguided flocks with dead shepherds.

This scattering is final, for the prophet warns, "There is no one to gather [them]." Nineveh is wiped out forever; and when the people of the Assyrian Empire are finally scattered, the complete end of that nation has come. A day of rebuilding and restitution will never dawn. How exactly was this prediction, spoken in the apex of Assyrian power, fulfilled! Not only the capital, but subsequently the whole empire collapses and passes

12 Sel., *Der alttestamentliche Prophetismus* (1912), p. 141, maintains that "the nobles," as "the shepherds," refers to the Assyrian gods, defeated by Yahweh in His triumph over Nineveh. But the terms are not so used otherwise, certainly not in Gen. 48:15, as Sel. holds.

out of existence almost overnight, its fugitive peoples never to be reunited.

נָמוּ — Ⓖ, ἐνύσταξαν, "they nodded," "they napped." Cheyne, without giving adequate reason, substitutes נָסוּ, "they fled."

רֹעֶיךָ — Ⓢ, probably mistaking this as a pl. of רֵעַ, offers "your friends," which is followed by Ri. Most modern critics change the suffix here (and the others throughout the verse) to the fem., maintaining that these words are addressed to Nineveh. It is difficult to understand how the pronominal suffixes in vv. 18 and 19 (seven in number), all masc., can fail to show the Ⓜ's intention to address the king of Assyria. The Hebrew original, without the seven gender changes in two verses, is vivid and powerful.

מֶלֶךְ אַשּׁוּר — Ⓢ has simply "kings," in opposition to the preceding "shepherds." The address to the king of Nineveh is generally regarded by critics as a gloss. Three reasons are advanced to justify its removal. (1) "It spoils the *kina* measure" (Stnh.); but this cannot stand, since it is a mere assumption to hold that these verses were originally written in *qînā* meter and that this rhythm cannot be interrupted by an address to the king. (2) The mention of the Assyrian monarch "introduces a new personality at the very end of the prophecy" (J.M.P.Sm.); yet this fact lends to the close of the book the force of a bold climax. (3) The words " 'thy shepherds' are much more naturally addressed to a city than to a king, who is himself the shepherd of his people" (J.M.P.Sm.). However, the Assyrian king did have "shepherds," his nobles, governors, high officials. Somewhat naive is Bev.'s conclusion: "Nahum is still addressing Nineveh, and *not* the Assyrian king, who according to sound documentary evidence had committed suicide." There is no "documentary evidence" to this effect. Ri. concedes: "It cannot be seen why here at the end the address to the king of Ashur is improper."

יִשְׁכְּנוּ — Ⓖ, ἐχοίμισε, "(the king of Assyria) *put* (thy nobles) to sleep." Ⓥ, "sepelientur." Many critics maintain that Ⓜ is corrupt and offer instead of יִשְׁכְּנוּ the unindicated יִשְׁנוּ, "they sleep" (so Wllh. and the majority of modern critics). However, Stnh., Hst., Sel., and others suggest שָׁכְבוּ, "they sleep"; (Jnk., יִשְׁכְּבוּ). Ⓜ is rejected under the claim that the conception of "dwelling," "resting," is inappropriate. However, the verb שָׁכַן (contrary to Stnh.) is used of the body's repose in the slumber of death. See Ps. 16:9; 94:17; Is. 26:19. Wllh.'s and Sel.'s objection that יִשְׁכְּנוּ — which is the imperfect, while נָמוּ is the perfect — must be elided in favor of another verb in the perfect is removed by a study of the tenses. נָמוּ is a prophetic perfect, and "not infrequently the imperfect changes with such perfects either in the parallel members or further on in the narrative," Ges., Gra., 106 *n.*

וְפֹשׁוּ — Ⓖ, ἀπῆρεν, "he took away"; Ⓥ, "latitavit." The root פוּשׁ occurs only here in the meaning "to be dispersed." The Syriac and Jewish-Aramaic cognates emphasize the remnant conception. Most critics follow Hpt. in changing וְפֹשׁוּ to וּפֹצוּ, "they are dispersed." Stk. wants the sing., נָפֵץ עַמֶּךָ.

עַל־הֶהָרִים — K.-G. brands this as a gloss that "disturbs the meter"; but in the light of parallel in 1 Kings 22:17 it is eminently in place.

Sel., grouping vv. 18 and 19 together, explains them as the liturgical response of the congregation to the preceding prophecies.

> v. 19 *There is no healing for thine injury.*
> *Thy wound {is} grievous.*
> *All who hear the message concerning thee will clap*
> *{their} hand over thee.*
> *For upon whom hath thine evil not passed over*
> *continually?*

In the final lines of his oracle the prophet precludes all hope for a restored Nineveh. The proud city will be destroyed irreparably, the Assyrian kingship is inescapably doomed. Therefore the dirge concludes with the warning addressed to the capital, "There is no healing for thine injury." The original for "injury" really means a "breaking," or "breach." It denotes the destruction of a wall, Is. 30:13; or of an earthen vessel, Is. 30:14; or of part of the body (the breaking of a limb, Lev. 21:19; 24:20); and from this it receives the meaning "injury," "wound," referring to the destruction of countries (Is. 30:26; Jer. 6:14; 8:21) or of individuals (Prov. 16:18; 17:19; 18:12). The damage sustained by the fall of the capital and the subsequent collapse of the empire can never be healed.

Similar in purpose is the parallel statement, "Thy wound is grievous." No light, passing sorrow is the blow which has struck Nineveh and its monarch prostrate. The Hebrew for "wound" denotes an injury received from a blow (1 Kings 22:35; 2 Kings 8:29), but it is employed figuratively in Jer. 10:19; 14:17; Micah 1:9, as here, of a national injury or destruction. The term translated "grievous" is used to describe a serious, sometimes fatal sickness or injury.[13] See Jer. 10:19; 30:12. This is more than poetic imagery. Nineveh — and later Assyria — were irreparably ruined. Many Oriental cities have risen again after destruction, but not Nineveh. As the *Babylonian Chronicle*

---

[13] This term, as usage shows, itself does not necessarily denote an incurable state. The context (see, for example, the parallelism with "incurable" in Jer. 30:12; Micah 1:9, and other passages) brings this emphasis. In Nahum the previous verses emphasize Nineveh's irremedial collapse.

records, "the city was a mound and a ruin." It has never been permanently rebuilt. It was so completely wrecked that for centuries even its location was unknown. Scientists, approaching Kouyunjik and Nebi Yunus, the mounds covering the capital's site, believed that these hills were natural eminences. For 300 years after its destruction Nineveh remained desolate. Traces of later Seleucid, Greek, Roman, and Sassanian settlements have been uncovered, but these apparently were sporadic and failed to attain permanency. Even the largest of these communities could not be called restitutions of Nineveh and were far from being restorations of the Assyrian Empire.

Tragic as this announcement is for Assyria, it is greeted with rejoicing by those who have groaned under its tyranny. "All who hear the message concerning thee" (AV, RV: "the bruit," the report of Nineveh's destruction) "will clap their hand over thee." This is a gesture of malevolent joy and exultation, which Zephaniah (2:13 ff.) re-echoes: "He will . . . destroy Assyria and will make Nineveh a desolation and dry like a wilderness. . . . This is the rejoicing city that dwelt carelessly, that said in her heart, I am, and there is none beside me. How is she become a desolation, a place for beasts to lie down in! Everyone that passeth by her shall hiss and wag his hand" (cf. Ps. 47:2; 98:8; Ezek. 25:6; Is. 55:12). The news of Nineveh's collapse calls forth wide, tumultuous rejoicing. As the prophet could discover no one to bemoan Nineveh or to comfort her (3:7), so he finds that all who hear of her end break forth in glee. Besides Judah, the many tyrannized nations on the roster of Assyria's victims wildly celebrate her demise.

To justify this terrifying punishment and to teach the moral lesson that Nineveh is punished for its sins of aggression, Nahum asks in the concluding clause, "For upon whom hath thine evil not passed over continually?" The prophet is concerned not only with Nineveh's oppression of his own country. He has an international outlook.[14] Because Nineveh has progressively subjugated vast areas and ruled ruthlessly over many peoples, the prophet's unanswered query implies: even in its dying gasp and ignominious burial, the bloody city will be the object of wide ridicule. And with this rhetorical question, pausing for no reply, the oracle predicting Nineveh's end draws to its dramatic close.

כֵּהָה is found only here in the sense of "healing." Most moderns regard the word as unsuitable, because they insist it means only "quenching," "dimness." Sel., however, concedes that "quenching" fits well here, and Ⓖ interpreted it as ἴασις, "healing." Ⓢ and Ⓣ associated it with "grief," while Ⓥ offers "obscura." Most of those who reject כֵּהָה agree with Hpt. in changing the word to גֵּהָה, "healing," found only in Prov. 17:22. Quite overlooked heretofore is the fact that כֵּהָה and גֵּהָה are essentially the same word with a slightly different pronunciation. The two forms illustrate the same interchange of consonants as between כֵּן and גֵּן; סָנִיר and רֵגֵל; רֵגֵל and רָכַל; סָכַר and רָכַל.

לְשִׁבְרֵךְ — K.-G., without reason, insists: "Here, too, the suffixes are to be changed to the feminine."

עָלֶיךָ — J.M.P.Sm. asserts: "This is unnecessary to the sense and constitutes a blemish upon the otherwise perfect elegiac rhythm. It is probably the work of a glossator." But "the otherwise perfect elegiac rhythm" is secured only after several elisions are made. See below. This word can be removed only at the cost of precision.

כִּי עָלֶיךָ לֹא עָבְרָה רָעָתְךָ תָּמִיד — Not even the final clause of the book has escaped the attacks of critical analysis. J.M.P.Sm. and others consider this whole interrogative sentence a gloss. He raises the charge that the sentence "fails to conform to

[14] A tabulation of the conquests by Assyrian kings embraces all the adjacent and much of the known distant country. No nation within reach of Nineveh had permanently peaceful relations with her.

the metre of this closing strophe." But another critic, Stnh., answers: "It conforms to the rhythm of the preceding lines and rounds off the verse well." Sm. further charges, "It weakens the prophet's climax"; but Bev., liberally inclined as he is, admits: "It brings out so well Nahum's great point, that Nineveh is dying for its sins." Finally Sm. objects that this concluding sentence "is an attempt to justify the universal joy of the previous statement, which needed no such prosaic apology in the days of Nahum. The oppression of Nineveh was notorious, to be taken for granted everywhere." However, Sel. declares that no material objection can be raised against this line. He feels that תָּמִיד forms a better conclusion to the book than כִּי. In addition, Sm.'s argument is weak in this respect: if the weakness of the wealthy city were self-understood, why does the prophet mention it in other passages which criticism has graciously permitted to stand?

תָּמִיד — ⑥, διὰ παντός, "forever." The question without answer forms a most effective close to the prophecies.

Wllh. concludes his notes on Nahum with an unfounded remark that questions the authenticity of the whole verse. He asks: "Was it all over with Ashur and Nineveh when this conclusion was written?" Why regard this prophecy as post-Nahumic, when others, even more precise, are conceded to be genuine? Besides, the whole tenor of the verse points to a future destruction of Nineveh.

Bibliography

Arnold, William Rosenzweig, "The Composition of Nahum 1—2:3," *Zeitschrift für die alttestamentliche Wissenschaft*, XXI (1901), 225 ff.

Bevenot, Hugh, *The Old Testament, Nahum and Habakkuk*, in the Westminster Version of the Sacred Scriptures, 1937.

Bickell, Gustav, "Nahum's Acrostic," *Zeitschrift der deutschen morgenländischen Gesellschaft*, XXXIV (1880).

——— "Carmina Veteris Testamenti Metrica," 1882, *Zeitschrift für katholische Theologie*, 1886.

——— "Das alphabetische Lied in Nahum 1:1—2:3," *Abhandlungen der kaiserlichen Akademie der Wissenschaft, Phil.-Hist. Klasse*, Wien, 1894. Abhandlung 5.

Budde, Karl Ferdinand Reinhard, The article "Nahum" in *Encyclopedia Biblica*, III, 1902. See Cheyne.

——— "Das hebräische Klagelied," *Zeitschrift für die alttestamentliche Wissenschaft*, 1882.

Buhl, Frants Peder William Meyer, "Alteration of Megomah," *Zeitschrift für die alttestamentliche Wissenschaft*, 1881.

Cadman, Samuel Parkes, *The Prophets of Israel*, 1933.

Calvin, John, *Commentaries on the Twelve Minor Prophets*, trans. Rev. John Owen, 1846—49.

Cheyne, Thomas Kelly, "Nahum 2:8," *Journal of Biblical Literature*, 1896.

Davidson, Andrew Bruce, *The Cambridge Bible for Schools*. Rev. ed., 1920, by H. C. O. Lanchester.

Delitzsch, Friedrich, *Die Lese- und Schreibfehler im Alten Testament*, 1920.

Driver, Samuel Rolles, *Introduction to the Literature of the OT*. Edinburgh, 1891; new ed., 1914.

——— *The Minor Prophets*, in *The Century Bible*, London, 1906.

Duhm, Bernhard, *Die Zwölf Propheten*, 1910.

Ehrlich, Arnold B., *Randglossen zur hebr. Bibel*, 1908—14, Vol. V.

―――― *Ezechiel u. die kleinen Propheten,* 1912.

Eissfeldt, Otto, *Einleitung in das Alte Testament,* 1934.

Ewald, Georg Heinrich August, *Commentary on the Prophets of the OT.* Vol. III: Nah., Hab., Zeph., Zech., Jer.; trans. J. Frederick Smith, 1878.

Gaster, Theo. H., "Two Notes on Nahum," *Journal of Biblical Literature,* LXIII, 51 f.

Gesenius, Wilhelm, *Hebrew Grammar,* edited and enlarged by the late E. Kautzsch. 2d English ed., revised in accordance with the 28th German ed., 1919, by A. E. Cowley.

―――― *Handwörterbuch über das AT.* 15th ed., 1910.

Graetz, H., *Emendationes in plerosque Sacrae Scripturae Veteris Testamenti libros,* 1893.

Greve, E. J., *Vaticinia Nahumi et Habacuci,* 1793.

Gunkel, Johann Friedrich Hermann, "Nahum 1," *Zeitschrift für die alttestamentliche Wissenschaft,* XIII (1893), 223 ff.

Halevy, J., "Le livre de Nahoum," *Revue Semitique,* XIII (1904).

Happel, Otto, *Das Buch des Propheten Nahum erklärt,* 1902.

―――― "Der Psalm des Nahum metrisch untersucht," *Theologische Quartalschrift,* LXXX (1900), Heft 2.

Haupt, Paul, "The Book of Nahum: A New Metrical Translation," *Journal of Biblical Literature,* XXIV (1907), Part I.

―――― "Eine alttestamentl. Festliturgie für den Nikanortag," *Zeitschrift der deutschen morgenländischen Gesellschaft,* LXI (1907), 275 ff.

―――― "Nah. 3:11," ibid., LXI, 289.

Henderson, E., *The Book of the Twelve Minor Prophets,* 1897.

Hengstenberg, Ernst Wilhelm, *Christologie des Alten Testaments,* 2d ed., 1854.

Hitzig, Ferdinand, *Die zwölf kleinen Propheten,* 1838. 4th ed., 1881.

Horst, Friedrich, *Handbuch zum AT,* Erste Reihe, *Die zwölf kleinen Propheten, Nahum bis Maleachi,* 1938.

Humbert, Paul, "Essai d'analyse de Nahoum 1:2―2:3," *Zeitschrift für die alttestamentliche Wissenschaft,* XLIV (1926), 266 ff.

―――― "Nahoum II, 9," *Revue des études juives,* 1927.

―――― "La vision de Nahoum, 2:4-11," *Archiv für Orientforschung,* V (1928), 14 ff.

―――― "Le probleme du livre de Nahoum," *Revue d'Histoire et de Philosophie religieuses,* XII (1932), 1 ff.

Junker, Hubert, *Die zwölf kleinen Propheten,* Band VIII, 3 Abteilung, II Hälfte of *Die heilige Schrift des A.T.,* 1938.

Kautzsch, E., and H. Guthe, *Die Heilige Schrift des Alten Testaments,* 4th ed., 1923. Hosea-Chronicles.

Keil, Johann Friedrich Karl, *Biblischer Kommentar über das Alte Testament: Die kleinen Propheten;* 3d ed., 1888.

Kennicott, B., *Vetus Testamentum Hebraicum cum variis lectionibus,* 1776 to 1780.

Kimchi, David, *Der Kommentar des David Kimchi zum Propheten Nahum,* herausgegeben von Walter Windfuhr, 1927.

Kirchengesangbuch für ev.-luth. Gemeinden. St. Louis: Concordia Publishing House. Various editions.

Kleinert, Hugo Wilhelm Paul, "Nahum und der Fall Ninivehs," *Schriften der Königsberger Gelehrtengesellschaft,* 1910.

—— *The Book of Nahum,* 1874; Germ., 1868; in *Langes Bibelwerk.*

Kleinman, V., *Assyrian Sculptures in the British Museum,* Plates CI—CII.

Kuenen, Abraham, *De Profeten en de Profetie onder Israel,* 1875. 2 vols.

Luther, Martin, *Sämmtliche Werke.* St. Louis ed.

Marti, Karl, *Dodekapropheton,* in *Kurzer Handkommentar zum Alten Testament,* 1903.

Newcome, W., *An Attempt Towards an Improved Version, Metrical Arrangement, and an Explanation of the Twelve Minor Prophets,* 1785.

Nowack, Wilhelm Gustav Hermann, *Die kleinen Propheten, übersetzt und erklärt,* in *Handkommentar zum Alten Testament.* 4th ed., Göttingen, 1922.

Oesterley, W. O., and Theodore H. Robinson, *An Introduction to the Books of OT,* 1934.

Oort, Henricus, *Textus Hebraici Emendationes,* 1900.

Orelli, Hans Conrad von, *Das Buch Ezekiel und die zwölf kleinen Propheten,* in *Kurzgefasster Kommentar zu den heiligen Schriften Alten u. Neuen Testaments,* 1888.

—— *The Twelve Minor Prophets,* 1893.

Richter, Georg, *Erläuterungen zu dunklen Stellen in den kleinen Propheten,* 1914.

Riessler, Paul, *Die kleinen Propheten,* 1911.

Ruben, Paul, *Critical Remarks upon Some Passages of the Old Testament,* 1896.

—— "Nah. 3:1; 3:16," *Jewish Quarterly Review,* XI.

Sellin, Ernst Friedrich Max, *Das Zwölfprophetenbuch,* 2d—3d ed. Band XII, in *Kommentar zum Alten Testament,* 1930.

—— *Einleitung in das Alte Testament,* 1935, 7th ed.

—— *Der alttestamentliche Prophetismus,* 1912.

Smith, George Adam, *The Book of the Twelve Prophets,* 2 vols. Rev. ed., 1929.

Smith, John Merlin Powis, *The International Critical Commentary. A Critical and Exegetical Commentary on Micah, Zephaniah, Nahum, Habakkuk, Obadiah, and Joel,* 1911.

—— *Prophecy and the Prophet in Ancient Israel,* 1923.

—— *The Prophets and Their Times,* 1925.

Staerk, Willy Otto Alexander, *Ausgewählte Poetische Texte,* etc. Heft II, 1908.

—— *Das assyrische Weltreich im Urteil der Propheten,* Göttingen, 1908.

Stonehouse, G. G. V., *The Books of the Prophets Zephaniah and Nahum,* in *Westminster Commentaries,* 1929.

Umbreit, J. W. C., *Praktischer Commentar über die Kleinen Propheten,* 1845.

Van Hoonacker, A., *Les douze petits prophetes,* 1908.

Wellhausen, Julius, *Die kleinen Propheten übersetzt und erklärt,* Vol. V, in *Skizzen u. Vorarbeiten,* 1892. 3d ed., 1898.

Index

DATE DUE

DATE	ISSUED TO